THE GOOD AMERICAN

"One of the best accounts examining American humanitarian pursuits over the past fifty years . . . With still greater challenges on the horizon, we will need to find and empower more people like Bob Gersony—both idealistic and pragmatic—who can help make the world a more secure place."

—*The Washington Post*

"As a government official, I twice had the good fortune to meet Robert Paul Gersony, whose adventurous and consequential life is the subject of a remarkable biography by Robert Kaplan. . . . [Gersony's] story is inspiring because it affirms the possibility that facts, objectively researched and dispassionately presented, can change policy for the better. . . . Often upon reading a Gersony memo, the scales would fall from the eyes of important decision makers and remedial action would follow. . . . Having seen firsthand how Mr. Gersony improved policy and saved lives, I am grateful that this book will make his example better known. May it become an inspiration for others."

—*The Wall Street Journal*

"Robert D. Kaplan's outstanding book makes a strong case for U.S. engagement based on human rights and helping refugees. . . . [Kaplan is] one of America's most thoughtful chroniclers of foreign affairs."   —*The Guardian*

"An unexpected and entirely winning biography of Gersony, who worked as a U.S. foreign policy consultant during the 'golden age' of American diplomacy . . . Kaplan's book follows Gersony all through the rolling ambit of his world travels, and thanks to Kaplan's own considerable narrative gifts, those journeys are as vivid and compelling as any travelogue. . . . Whether the setting is Mozambique, Chad, Somalia, Rwanda, Bosnia, El Salvador, or Nepal, Kaplan's writing is unfailingly vivid. . . . *The Good American* appears at a time when U.S. intelligence agencies are under unprecedented scrutiny, and this broader import of his subject is never far from Kaplan's mind. 'The Bob Gersonys . . . of this world are gone,' confesses an official from the United States Agency for International Development. 'We're outsourcing our assessments to consulting groups now. We assume because of Twitter that we know what's happening on the ground in distant places, even if we don't.' Even so, reading Kaplan's account of smart, quiet, unsung heroism, readers will come away hopeful. If Bob Gersony can spend a life going out and really listening to other people, so can we."   —*The Christian Science Monitor*

"Revealing . . . a pleasure of a read . . . It confirms the power of vision, rooted in a clear sense of right and wrong, and underlines the importance of the United States remaining engaged internationally. . . . Kaplan's long and detailed narrative will draw you in quickly and hold you." —*Oxford Business Review*

"Having been a fan of Kaplan's many writings, I consider this book his most important contribution—in part because it shows how American political and security interests can be reconciled with the advance of human rights and humanitarian values." —*Providence*

"This is a book to read—it'll make you better." —*St. Louis Business Journal*

"A life story that reads like an action thriller." —*Kirkus Reviews*

"Kaplan's immersive, ground-level view of practical foreign policy-making gives it substance. This incisive account pays tribute to the people who uphold America's ideals to the world." —*Publishers Weekly*

"An elegy for a time when humanitarian aid figured more prominently in U.S. foreign policy . . . Kaplan writes with earnest reverence for a longtime friend and wistful praise for the particular blend of realism and idealism that Gersony represented, which seems less valued in today's world." —*Booklist*

"This graceful study of a courageous and humble man reminds us that history can be made, and lives can be saved, by diplomats who know how to reconcile the good with the possible."

—TIMOTHY SNYDER, author of *The Road to Unfreedom* and *On Tyranny*

"This excellent and absorbing biography reads like an adventure novel. It offers hope that one person has made—and can make—a difference. It also demonstrates why such people are exceedingly rare. I blithely lived through every crisis described in this book. I now understand them, thanks to Kaplan's absorbing, detailed writing. I also understand how one man, and a few dedicated people touched by this man, helped keep those crises from being worse than they were. Lord, grant us many more such hidden victories and the skilled writers, like Kaplan, to bring them to light." —KARL MARLANTES, author of *Matterhorn*

"For anyone who has stopped believing that one person can make a difference, or that government service is still a noble calling, or that facts still matter, or that the American brand can still hold fast to practical idealism, this book is the antidote to those fears." —JIM MATTIS, general, U.S. Marines (ret.), and twenty-sixth secretary of defense, author of *Call Sign Chaos*

"In an era in which public service is often belittled and the State Department is being hollowed out, Robert D. Kaplan offers a powerful rejoinder. His evocative portrayal of a deeply committed humanitarian professional, Bob Gersony, reminds us that American diplomacy can be both smart and humane. The story of Gersony and his generation of practitioners is a timely argument for why humanitarian issues deserve renewed emphasis—and why it's so important to revive America's foreign policy institutions and invest in the dedicated people who animate them." —AMBASSADOR WILLIAM J. BURNS, president, Carnegie Endowment for International Peace, and former U.S. deputy secretary of state, author of *The Back Channel*

"Robert D. Kaplan, one of America's greatest travel writers and geographers, provides the perfect antidote to present-day malaise with *The Good American*, the thrilling and dramatic story of aid worker extraordinaire Bob Gersony. Gersony spent his life working all over the world on behalf of the American people, few of whom had ever heard his name. Kaplan brings this quiet and unknown hero to life. In so doing he reminds us of what America at its best can achieve. This book is unputdownable." —MAX BOOT, author of *The Road Not Taken: Edward Lansdale and the American Tragedy in Vietnam*

"Robert D. Kaplan has done it again. He has written another superb book, filled with massive reportage—this time about a really good and effective man. Bob Gersony, an astonishing unsung and heroic American analyst, worked for decades in the most dangerous and demanding places in the world. He is fortunate that his biographer is Robert D. Kaplan. No one else could understand the heroic nature of Gersony's work and write about it so enthrallingly." —WILLIAM SHAWCROSS, author of *The Quality of Mercy: Cambodia, Holocaust and Modern Conscience*

"In *The Good American*, the writer and strategist Robert D. Kaplan chronicles the life of Bob Gersony, whose work with refugees in war zones during four decades on behalf of the State Department is the stuff of legends. Kaplan's piercing analysis of a life devoted to truth and the common good reminds us that America must rebuild and renew the State Department so that future Gersonys can continue to protect and honor America in the world beyond our shores." —NICHOLAS BURNS, Harvard professor and former undersecretary of state for political affairs

"If you want to understand why diplomacy is important and why it has to be conducted from the ground up, this is the book to read." —ODD ARNE WESTAD, author of *The Cold War: A World History*

BY ROBERT D. KAPLAN

The Good American: The Epic Life of Bob Gersony, the U.S. Government's Greatest Humanitarian

The Return of Marco Polo's World: War, Strategy, and American Interests in the Twenty-First Century

Earning the Rockies: How Geography Shapes America's Role in the World

In Europe's Shadow: Two Cold Wars and a Thirty-Year Journey Through Romania and Beyond

Asia's Cauldron: The South China Sea and the End of a Stable Pacific

The Revenge of Geography: What the Map Tells Us About Coming Conflicts and the Battle Against Fate

Monsoon: The Indian Ocean and the Future of American Power

Hog Pilots, Blue Water Grunts: The American Military in the Air, at Sea, and on the Ground

Imperial Grunts: The American Military on the Ground

Mediterranean Winter: The Pleasures of History and Landscape in Tunisia, Sicily, Dalmatia, and the Peloponnese

Warrior Politics: Why Leadership Demands a Pagan Ethos

Eastward to Tartary: Travels in the Balkans, the Middle East, and the Caucasus

The Coming Anarchy: Shattering the Dreams of the Post Cold War

An Empire Wilderness: Travels into America's Future

The Ends of the Earth: From Togo to Turkmenistan, from Iran to Cambodia

The Arabists: The Romance of an American Elite

Balkan Ghosts: A Journey Through History

Soldiers of God: With Islamic Warriors in Afghanistan and Pakistan

Surrender or Starve: Travels in Ethiopia, Sudan, Somalia, and Eritrea

THE
GOOD
AMERICAN

THE EPIC LIFE OF
BOB GERSONY,
THE U.S. GOVERNMENT'S
GREATEST HUMANITARIAN

ROBERT D.
KAPLAN

Random House   New York

2022 Random House Trade Paperback Edition

Published in the United States by Random House, an imprint and division of
Penguin Random House LLC, New York.

RANDOM HOUSE and the HOUSE colophon are registered trademarks of Penguin
Random House LLC.

Originally published in hardcover in the United States by Random House, an
imprint and division of Penguin Random House LLC, in 2021.

LIBRARY OF CONGRESS CATALOGING-IN-PUBLICATION DATA
Names: Kaplan, Robert D., author.
Title: The good American / Robert D. Kaplan.
Description: New York: Random House, [2020]
Identifiers: LCCN 2020012098 (print) | LCCN 2020012099 (ebook) |
ISBN 9780525512318 (trade paperback) | ISBN 9780525512325 (ebook)
Subjects: LCSH: Gersony, Robert. | United States. Agency for International
Development—Officials and employees—Biography. | United States.
Department of State—Officials and employees—Biography. | Humanitarian
assistance, American. | Refuge (Humanitarian assistance)—United States. |
Philanthropists—United States—Biography.
Classification: LCC HC60 .K3435 2021 (print) | LCC HC60 (ebook) |
DDC 327.730092 [B]—dc23
LC record available at https://lccn.loc.gov/2020012098
LC ebook record available at https://lccn.loc.gov/2020012099

Printed in the United States of America on acid-free paper

randomhousebooks.com

1st Printing

To Henry Thayer

... pessimism ... can drive men on to do wonders.

V. S. Naipaul, *A Bend in the River*, 1979

Glory is now a discredited word, and it will be difficult to re-establish it. It has been spoilt by a too close association with military grandeur; it has been confused with fame and ambition. But true glory is a private and discreet virtue, and is only fully realized in solitariness.

Graham Greene (quoting Herbert Read), *Ways of Escape*, 1980

CONTENTS

THE WORLD IS WHAT IT IS

Mozambique
February 1988

She was a displaced farmer from Chemba, near to the border of Sofala and Tete provinces, in central Mozambique. Her village was at
the intersection of the great Zambezi River and one of its tributaries.
She spoke to him through a translator in Sena, a Bantu language of
the Mozambique, Malawi, and Zimbabwe border areas. He had
found her wearing a black kerchief and blue blouse. She appeared as
"quite self-possessed," crouching on the dirt floor of the hut, and
beckoning him to sit beside her on a chair. The government troops of
FRELIMO had fled her village, she explained to him, and RENAMO
soldiers closed in from several directions, forcing the villagers to the
bank of the Zambezi. FRELIMO, the Front for the Liberation of Mozambique, had come to power as an anti-Portuguese guerrilla group,
with some support from Cuba and the Soviet Union. But it couldn't
control the countryside where RENAMO, an indigenous African,
anti-communist insurgency supported by apartheid South Africa,
was on the rampage. RENAMO soldiers executed her niece, and soon
afterward her niece's nursing daughter died of hunger and exposure.
The woman told him she saw half a dozen bodies up close: of two
young boys and other women and children. There were more bodies
still, but she didn't have the courage to look at them. The woman and
her own seven-year-old daughter then began to run but were chased
into the big river by more RENAMO troops who had just arrived and
were shooting at them, spraying the water's surface with bullets. People drowned, trying to escape the barrage.

She told him that "she tried as best she could," but exhausted, made the split-second choice to save herself and in a panic let go of her daughter, "who was swept away by the current and drowned." She said that "God helped me to an island in the river," where people from Mutarara, on the far side of the river, came with boats to evacuate them. She remained in Mutarara as a displaced person for five months. But then RENAMO attacked it and she fled again, helped by the cover provided by the outnumbered FRELIMO troops. She then walked roughly twenty miles north to a refugee camp across the border in Malawi. She remained at Makokwe camp in southern Malawi for three months. But "there was no future there," she told him. So she crossed the border back into Mozambique, where she stayed in a transit camp by a railway yard in Moatize, which was mortared by RENAMO. Then she escaped to a displaced persons camp in Benga, in Changara district, west of Moatize. She had been in Benga four months when he interviewed her on Monday, February 29, 1988, the third person he had interviewed there, according to his diary.

He remembered each person he interviewed by a distinguishing characteristic that he marked down in his notes. That way he could remember them as individuals, and thus preserve their humanity. This interviewee was "the woman with the black kerchief."

"The various expressions on her face, and the way she pronounced the words, were powerful and full of emotion. The moment she told me of letting go of her seven-year-old daughter's hand in the great River, her hand slowly waved in the air, as if she were letting go again, and again."

He had no children of his own yet, though he was already forty-three. But he was torn apart by the image of the woman's decision between surviving herself and letting her own daughter drown. He never got used to the stories he heard.

She was the 143rd of 196 refugees and displaced persons of the Mozambique civil war he interviewed, traveling between camps that were separated by hundreds of miles in war zones in Malawi, Zimbabwe, Tanzania, and Mozambique itself. He was eating one meal a day, interviewing people like her during all the daylight hours, concentrating hard so as never to ask a leading question. He lived out of a tent with a sleeping bag and mosquito coil, writing in his lined notebook and typing by candlelight as there was no electricity, remembering each voice through his fingertips.

It was merely another day of work for him, just another assignment, like all the others in war and disaster areas of the developing world: assignments which continued—literally one after another—for four decades, on several continents. He was often lonely, depressed, but lived in fear of being promoted out of what he was doing. He was truly calm only while interviewing and taking notes. It was in such moments that he attained the quality of an ascetic, inhaling the evidence almost. For him, listening to these voices was like slow breathing. So he never stopped doing it.

The surroundings meant little to him. In his mind, the towering and interminable bush of Mozambique had been reduced to the lined pages of his notebooks, where his swift, graceful jottings became a sacred script: all he was able to remember were the stories that these refugees and displaced persons had told him.

He was not a journalist or a relief worker. He worked for the U.S. government in a very unusual capacity. He deliberately avoided publicity, and thus many of those who flock to war zones barely knew he existed. In any case, as someone who was at heart an introvert, he was easily ignored by them. They made legends out of other people, not out of him.

I first met him in a cheap hostel in Khartoum more than a third of a century ago as I write these words, and crossed paths with him over the decades in Somalia, Liberia, Ethiopia, the Sudan-Chad border, Nepal, and other places. He was everywhere the news was, and also where it wasn't. Yet in a certain sense he was invisible, and he was happy that way.

To the media and the human rights community, Robert "Bob" Gersony was often the forgotten man.

This is his story.

It is the story of a son of Jewish Holocaust refugees who dropped out of high school, was awarded a Bronze Star in Vietnam, and then spent forty years interviewing at great length over eight thousand refugees, displaced persons, and humanitarian workers in virtually every war and disaster zone on earth as a special contractor for the U.S. State Department, the U.S. Agency for International Development, and the United Nations. The results were legendary "Gersony reports," of which Mozambique was one. The story of "the woman with the black kerchief" made it all the way up to Secretary of State George Shultz and Maureen Reagan, whom Gersony briefed days after returning from the field.

It was a standard pattern for him: living in the bush for many weeks and then briefing high policymakers in person about his findings. They listened to him and often changed policy accordingly—making it smarter and more humane—because of the way that Gersony was able to ingeniously integrate a concern for human rights within the framework of national interest. For the two were inseparable in Gersony's mind: a mind that eschewed grand schemes and was always emphatically loyal to the minutiae of the local situation, in which each far-flung place was a product of its own unique geography and history. Gersony's life is about how the granularity of distant places defeats all theories. It is about how if foreign policy ignores the effect it has on individual human beings it descends into a realm of inhuman abstraction.

Indeed, this is the story of a man who epitomized the American Century more than anyone I know or was ever aware of. His story is that of the Cold War and the post Cold War, of America's vast moral responsibilities in this world and its total immersion in it, which grew out of both America's geopolitical necessities and its aspiration to be an exemplar of humanity. It is a story of fieldwork and reporting, of letting the facts emanate from the ground up—what in particular the State Department for so long was so great and indefatigable at, and which he so typified. And it is a story of the last golden age of American diplomacy, as he interacted with ambassadors, assistant secretaries of state, and others who were giants in their day: a day when the bureaucracy at all levels had sufficient money and rewarded talent.

This is as much a picaresque as a biography: a series of overseas assignments that make up an epic life.

This is also a memoir: of someone else's life rather than of my own, since he unburdened himself in hundreds of hours of interviews with me, revealing a worm's-eye view of almost half a century of American actions in the developing world: an alternative history almost. But it is a conventional memoir in the sense that he and I have lived parallel lives: not only working around the world in the same countries—countries often obscure to journalists at the time we were there—but working on our own, usually isolated from colleagues, so as not to have our analyses conditioned by the views of the crowd.

And yet his effect on American foreign policy in many dozens of assignments was always positive and often dramatically so; he was always helping various administrations avoid pitfalls and do the right thing. I can't say the same for myself. Though I am proud of my journalism, I am not proud of the effect it has had in some key instances.

But this is no mere recollection. My subject has kept meticulous daily diaries and personal organizers throughout his career. There are, too, his own published reports and secret cables. In fact, Bob Gersony is an obsessive-compulsive—a characteristic you wouldn't ordinarily associate with someone who has spent a lifetime in places marked by disease and disorder. Of course, his behavior may be a compensation for those very conditions.

Think of him as an emotionally tortured character straight out of a Saul Bellow novel, engrossed throughout his life in the brooding and dangerous tropical settings defined by Joseph Conrad.

It is hard to imagine a better-documented existence than his. I interviewed almost a hundred others who crossed his otherwise solitary path, and who actually do remember him. Speaking to them—selfless humanitarian aid workers and development specialists;

diplomats during the State Department's golden age—I realize that if there were any other life I would have wished to have had, it would be his: a frugal, monastic existence that has been both obscure and extraordinary.

For a meaningful life is about truth; not success.

MANY SMALL BEGINNINGS

CHAPTER 1

Vietnam
1966–1969

Discovering Bernard Fall

was called up but got a medical deferment. But I was sick of people in Manhattan going to school and graduate school and getting un-limited deferments. I had started making $20,000 a year as a com-modity trader—a lot of money then. Yet it was a game, not life. So I didn't wait to be called up. I joined. My country was at war. I felt called to do this. I put a brave face on it, but I was scared. What had I gotten myself into?"

Vietnam saved Bob Gersony's life.

It lifted him out of the darkness of his youth.

"For me, Vietnam was total immersion in America itself. At Fort Gordon, Georgia, during basic training, real red clay country, I met my first Americans. I met Catholics! I don't know that in New York I had spoken to a Catholic before! I lived with Blacks. I met hundreds and hundreds of different people in Georgia and Vietnam."

There was a staff sergeant (three stripes up, one down on his chevron), a lifer, the senior NCO (noncommissioned officer) in the barracks in Saigon. He was maybe six feet tall with a belly, blond hair, and blue eyes: eyes slightly too close together and sunk into his head more than most. His bed was the first one on the right as you entered the hooch, which Vietnamese women in black pajamas would sweep daily.

"He was a real atrocity. I was one of two Jewish guys in the hooch—single and double wooden bunks ringed by sandbags where there wasn't a whit of privacy. I remember a refrigerator at one end filled with cans of Pabst Blue Ribbon beer. The staff sergeant would occasionally get loaded and then the real bullying would begin. His abuse was constant. 'The Jews killed Christ. They control the banks. They run the newspapers. They're all rich.' He never stopped. That was all we heard. Nothing original or creative: just a meat-and-potatoes anti-Semite. Nobody said anything or complained about him. Those were tough months.

"The other Jewish guy in the hooch was among the few Jews I met in the U.S. Army in Vietnam. I met this nice gangly kid from Iowa, Gary Galpin, a nerd like me, and others who I stayed in touch with for a few years. Yes, I met my country, the bad and the good.

"In basic training I had stood out and was offered OCS [Officers' Candidate School]. But I was happy where I was. I got an award, 'outstanding trainee of the cycle.' Later I got a Bronze Star for service, not the much more important Bronze Star for valor. But it was good enough." The Bronze Star now hangs in his living room, around the neck of a large sculpture of a pet dog from his younger days. "Those were the only awards I ever got in my life."

"People in the Army called me 'Doc,' short for doctor. I don't know why. *Yeah,* leaving Manhattan was like coming out of a cocoon. But I was no hero." Gersony was a typist in the Casualty and Medical Evacuation Division in Saigon. When the Tet Offensive started, casualties went way up and there was an avalanche of reporting to do, since all the dead and wounded had to flow to the right places. He volunteered to stay for a few extra months and left Vietnam as a specialist 5 (the equivalent of a low-ranking sergeant). His overriding ambition was just to come back alive, even though he was almost never in danger. And that's been his overriding ambition for over four decades.

In the years since, whenever he came home from Colombia or Iraq or the Chinese–North Korean border, or wherever he was, he would kiss the floor of his house. He had been scared all his life. He always thought that he would never come home from his assignments. "I'm conservative, a pessimist, I always have to think of the worst in order to prevent it from happening." From time to time he goes to the Vietnam War Memorial here in Washington and sees names on the wall of people he knew—and was one of—who didn't make it home.

"You can't imagine what a failure I felt like, especially to my father. There was something wrong with me. It was nobody's fault. I was just fucked up."

Bob Gersony's voice is loud, commanding, declarative, yet on the verge of breaking down into tears of frustration and thus intimate, despite the harsh New York gutturals. He has a clipped white beard and sometimes likes to wear a hat reminiscent of the African bush, which considering what he has done in life is not at all affected. He always seems to be staring into the distance, as if recollecting something, while rolling his head in a way that indicates he has even more to say. He is intense and often appears overwhelmed, as if taking on the pain and suffering of the world. His "look," when he focuses on a voice he once heard in Mozambique, Chad, Somalia, Rwanda, Bosnia, El Salvador, Nepal, or wherever else he has been, to quote W. H. Auden, "contains the history of man."[1]

Whenever we meet for an interview outside his home, in whatever circumstances, he wears a jacket and tie, bending over at the waist rather than hunching his shoulders—as if bowing to you—in a stiff but formal greeting. He has a touch of the Old World about him, evoking a sense of reverence and authority. I can see why he was called "Doc."

Robert Paul Gersony was born in February 1945 in Manhattan, the son of refugees from Central and Eastern Europe, Grigori and Laura Gersony, who Americanized their names to George and Lola. They were modern Orthodox Jews, whose lives, particularly that of his father, revolved around the synagogue. His father, from Libau, a port city in Latvia, was sent by his family in 1935 to Amsterdam, to be an apprentice to a diamond merchant just as Hitler began to rev up his death machine. From there Gersony's father drifted to Belgium, France, Portugal, Mozambique (where he jumped ship in Lourenço

Marques from a boat going on to Shanghai), and finally came to America, where he arrived in New York from Lourenço Marques with the proverbial $50 in his pocket. He had made his way around Europe and Africa mainly as a grain trader and overseas salesman for the Jaffa Orange Syndicate in British Palestine.

"My father was smart and virtuous. He was a commodity trader all his life and his word was trusted. It's not like today in this digital world when every transaction requires documentation." In the spring of 1940, his father sensed that the Nazis would invade Belgium. The people he knew there said that he was crazy, since Belgium was a neutral country, even though Germany had invaded Belgium only twenty-six years before. But he offered to sell a large shipment of oranges at a much lower price if he were paid in cash immediately. He wired the money to Palestine and escaped to Marseille just as the Germans invaded Belgium and Holland. "In every place my father arrived he had to learn a new language and start a new life. Every time I've arrived in a new country over the past four decades I consciously tested myself against the world, the way my father did."

"Yes, Bobby's father, George, was quite resilient, but not unlike so many refugees at the time. He was a tall, heavyset, intimidating sort of man, but so clumsy—George Gersony couldn't even drive a car," recalls Ursula Strauss, the wife of George Gersony's business partner, and the only person alive who knew the family when "Bobby," as everyone called him then, was growing up. Ursula, in her early nineties, decidedly elegant despite her age, still talks with the British accent she learned at school in Great Britain as a refugee child from Hitler. "George spoke many languages well, but always with such a terrible accent," she says with a laugh. "George was all business, completely absorbed in his work. He couldn't make small talk, unless it was about the synagogue. He was just so intense, so impatient: a hard, formidable man, but with a heart of gold, and funny, in an ironic, world-weary, Jewish sort of way. When he screamed, which was often, nobody took him seriously."

Bobby was a terrible student. Even with studying he flunked exams. He had severe trouble recalling the meaning of text from memory, and so couldn't learn in the usual, regimented manner. Just as Bobby inherited his lifelong emotional intensity from his father, he also developed a lifelong hatred of the classroom and formalistic learning altogether: a signal reason why he would spend his life doing fieldwork. Fieldwork was less abstract and helped him overcome his learning disability.

Lola and George Gersony, Bob Gersony's parents.

Ursula Strauss remembers: "While George and Lola knew how to love, they simply did not know how to be parents. Lola was busy with bridge, music, tennis, but not so much with the children." Stepping into the Gersonys' home, with Lola's accent and Zsa Zsa Gabor manner, with all the lace tablecloths, was "like going back to Vienna," one of Bob Gersony's early girlfriends says: "His parents were so old-fashioned, they were like my grandparents. They certainly didn't know how to be *American* parents." George was a fairly old father, forty-one, at the time Bobby was born. He had no interest in Bobby's day at school, for example. "If you couldn't talk business with George, you practically couldn't talk with him," says Ursula Strauss.

"Bob's father had all of Bob's intensity and then some. George Gersony was just so large and imposing: he was absolutely penetrating. His presence filled the room. He was abrupt and full of energy, cutting you off in midspeech to get out of his chair and do something else. He was obviously a genius as well as a horrible parent," says another of Bob's former girlfriends.

"My father was tense. He made me and my sister tense. I got no advice from my father, nothing, even though my parents were constantly being called into school because of my low grades. The only thing I had to keep me company in my room was a typewriter. Throughout my life, I could only remember text through the physical act of typing."

In the United States, Gersony's father had become a broker for edible oils and industrial fats. Eventually, when Bobby was failing one test after another, George had enough money to transfer his son out of the public school system to the prestigious Peddie School in Hightstown, New Jersey, a boarding school near Princeton, a reserve for the WASP elite with its Victorian brick buildings and spacious, tree-lined lawns: the alma mater of such mid-twentieth-century establishment figures as Walter Annenberg and John J. McCloy. "It got me out of my home and away from my screaming father: you see, my father was brilliant, but stressed, nervous, afflicted, he actually broke chairs sometimes. Things would just set him off.

"There was an English teacher at Peddie, E. Graham Ward, a Harvard graduate, buttoned down, herringbone tweed, always looked at you sideways, then would break the smallest smile. He knew I was always in trouble, but he liked the way I wrote. At first I did well at Peddie. But then the same problems returned. I couldn't pass tests. I was 'invited not to come back the next year.' "

Following that, Ward, who went on to become a quite legendary teacher at Phillips Exeter Academy in Exeter, New Hampshire, and the Brooks School in North Andover, Massachusetts, wrote Gersony a letter, saying "You have real talent." Ward "thought I was someone when I thought I was no one."

Back in Manhattan in 1963, Gersony took a summer writing class, and that fall a friend of his father arranged for him to take courses at New York University. At the summer class he had submitted an essay about beatniks in Greenwich Village, in which he argued that they were living aimless lives, critical of society but not really contributing to society either. He was therefore confused about them and what exactly they thought they were doing. He got an A on the paper. So in the fall when his NYU professor asked his students to submit essay samples, Gersony had the idea to submit the same paper that had earned him an A. A few days later the NYU professor walked into the auditorium lecture hall and announced that he would read aloud samples of the best and worst papers he had seen. Gersony, sitting in the front row, was confident that his paper would be among the best—after all, he had already gotten an A on it. But it wasn't. Finally, the professor told the class about the very worst paper, and began to read passages aloud from what Gersony had written about the beatniks. The professor alternately smirked, sneered, and delivered the verbal equivalent of a literary hatchet job on Gersony. The paper was full of "pretentiousness," the professor concluded. "I flushed all over," Gersony recalls. "I became hot and fearful. I sat in absolute terror that he was going to make me stand up in front of this class of 150 students. I was so ashamed and traumatized that I still haven't gotten over it. I was too young to understand how one teacher could give an A and another an F to the same essay: how so much of criticism is subjective. I quit school immediately. I never took another class anywhere again. I never actually completed high school. I never had a graduation ceremony of any kind."

It was just so humiliating, especially since all the other Jewish children of his parents' friends in Manhattan were getting high grades and going off to elite universities.

"Bobby could have gone all wrong," Ursula Strauss, lifting her eyebrows, tells me in a very knowing manner. "But he didn't turn out wrong, did he? He turned out quite well. He has real social gifts, you know. He always had girlfriends, and every one of them was delightful and interesting. They all came to his wedding with their husbands and to his children's bar mitzvahs."

His father, at last realizing that his son simply couldn't manage school, hired him for a short time at his office. Leaving school would be the jump start he needed. Bobby and his father grew closer. After all, George—whose mind worked so fast that he would often skip whole portions of what he wanted to say—could now talk business with his son. The two would often go out to lunch in a basement Greek restaurant near his father's office, in the Standard Oil building in lower Manhattan, and would take walks on long summer nights. There was even a telex machine in their home that shook and clanged twenty-four hours a day, which constituted a running tutorial on the commodity business. Later on, in Vietnam and elsewhere, his father would write him letters on foolscap about the tallow and oil markets, about this tonnage he had sold, about that Egyptian tender, and so on. Nevertheless, "my father would never believe I could do anything right, after I did not go on in life to take over Gersony-Strauss Co."

The truth about George Gersony was that like other Jewish refugees, he kept a lot hidden. That was a reason why he was almost always all business. His sister, brother, and other members of his family and their friends were all murdered by the Nazis and their Latvian allies. When Bobby once asked him directly about all this one evening at home, his father, who was reading a book in bed, turned on his side and cried.

George Gersony was at this moment, among his many other ventures, selling tallow (beef fat used in the making of soap) to Pakistan under the U.S. government's PL 480 program, a form of foreign assistance that involved massive and complicated paperwork. It turned out that the young Gersony was very good and very fast at filling out forms. But then, the same weekend that President John F. Kennedy was assassinated in November 1963, there was the "Great Salad Oil Swindle" that almost crippled the New York Stock Exchange, and made Gersony's father go bankrupt. Essentially, a soybean oil trader had gotten $150 million in loans from Wall Street by using tanks filled with soybean oil that he had sold to commodity dealers, including Gersony's father, as collateral—except that the tanks were really filled with water, with soybean oil floating only at the top. They were practically worthless. "My father was ruined. He didn't want me in the office during this period and arranged for me to apprentice with another high-strung, tortured Jew, who dealt in, among other things, bird seed and animal by-products."

Gersony's new employer, Francis J. Koppstein, discovered that his protégé, in addition to being good at paperwork, had a quick talent for commodity trading. And so Gersony became a commodity trader like his father: an interlude in his life, but one that would have a profound influence on him, because of the commodity market's emphasis on statistics, the most basic economic trade-offs, and disciplined, ground-level practicality, all of which would prove tremendously valuable to Gersony later on.

Gersony was succeeding in life for the first time but completely unsatisfied. Manhattan suffocated him, especially after he had a chance to briefly visit the Midwest to inspect companies with which he and Koppstein did business. That was a trip he would never forget—opening a window on his country and the ground-level truths that the commodity trade offered him. In the middle of the freezing winter of 1964, he visited fifteen meatpacking plants in Green Bay, Wisconsin; St. Cloud, Minnesota; Dubuque, Iowa; Indianapolis, Indiana; and Chicago, Illinois, staying in the suburban homes of the plant managers, talking late into the night with them about *actuals* and *futures*. Could beef lips, normally used for rendering tallow and making dog food, also be useful for making other products for Koppstein's customers in France? And by the way, what about prospects for lard and pork livers? It was those sorts of questions that the nineteen-year-old high school dropout had to deal with constantly on this trip. The real revelation of this journey—and it truly was a journey of discovery—was the clean beauty of middle America and the "salt of the earth" types of people who populated it, and who showered him with friendliness and hospitality: so radically different from the world of Manhattan. Buried in a snowy winter whiteout, the towns of the northern Midwest dramatically widened his horizons.

Perhaps, deep down in his psyche, Gersony was a wanderer, like his father, always starting over, as his father had begun to do so successfully after the bankruptcy—rebuilding his business from scratch—often in a different part of the map. Gersony at this point in his young life simply wasn't grounded. School had proved impossible. And he wasn't quite ready to spend his life in the commodity trade. This is how Bob Gersony found his way to Vietnam: about the last place on earth at the time where one would have expected to find a young Jewish man, who had grown up in a Manhattan apartment filled with art and a grand piano, on West 77th Street facing the American Museum of Natural History—the same apartment where the opera star Renée Fleming would one day live.

In Saigon, the head of Gersony's casualty reporting unit was a Captain John Quandt, an officer with a sharp nose, black hair, and horn-rimmed glasses. His desk faced Gersony's, so there was no avoiding him, and the two frequently talked. Quandt valued him because Gersony was such a whiz at numbers, record keeping, and typing (over a hundred words per minute), all reasons for the Bronze Star he was later awarded.

"You should read Bernard Fall," Quandt casually told Gersony one day during a bull session about the depressing, gut-wrenching material that their office had to process 24/7. Quandt loaned Gersony one of Fall's books, which Gersony devoured and then returned. "While on R&R sometime later in Formosa, I picked up several knockoff edi-

Bob Gersony soon after he arrived in Vietnam.

Bernard Fall in Vietnam in 1967 shortly before his death in the field. His example motivated Bob Gersony's lifework of deep reporting.

tions of Bernard Fall and again devoured them. My months of reading and typing up casualty reports, plus what I learned from Bernard
Fall, revealed to me that Vietnam was not just beyond America's capability, it was beyond doing, period."

Bernard Fall was an Austrian-born, French-American war correspondent and historian, who had fought in the French Resistance
and later specialized in Indochina in the 1950s and 1960s. In 1961,
just as the Kennedy administration was escalating the war in Vietnam, Fall published *Street Without Joy: The French Debacle in Indochina*. In that book, which profoundly affected Gersony, Fall most
famously established his method of digging out ideas from firsthand
field experience, rather than from the comfort and safety of a library
or a government office in Washington. He was a from-the-ground-up
thinker rather than a from-the-top-down one. In 1967, the year before Gersony discovered his work, Bernard Fall was killed by a land
mine north of Hue.

Fall's message was that nations lose wars because of incomplete
ground-level intelligence of the most profound cultural variety, making them unable to grasp the mentality of the people they are trying
to help or change or conquer, a mentality accumulated from thousands of years of history in a specific landscape. The Americans
would lose in Vietnam just as the French had lost, Fall predicted,
because the Americans were given to abstractions that obscured the
cultural reality on the ground in Vietnam.

Street Without Joy depicts painful marches through roadless jun-
gles by French troops suffering with heavy packs on their backs, in
places where scrappy guerrilla fighters are needed rather than common infantrymen. He describes the light and mobile Viet Minh and
the plodding French, who needed proper roads and bridges to complete their laborious operations. In the course of a massively detailed,
tactical account of French military movements in Vietnam, Fall became the first writer to describe the new Cold War age of irregular
fighting, out of which modern counterinsurgency doctrine would
emanate. Fall writes about "the tiny human error" in a jungle en-

counter "which, even in the Atomic Age, still can shape human destiny."[2]

Fall's passages are filled with tragic human folly. There are the thirty French battalions demoralized by one Viet Minh regiment simply because of the impossible terrain, with its dense vegetation and labyrinthine villages whose populations were antagonistic to the French. The terrain itself kept the French from even knowing where they actually were. In Fall's account, the French commanders were only just beginning to realize that while the great set-piece victories of World War II were still fresh in everyone's minds, this new age of Cold War guerrilla fighting would be brutal to such a conventional mindset. Finally, there is *la rue sans joie,* "the street without joy," a string of heavily fortified villages stretching from Hue to Quang Tri, through dunes and salt marshes, which would prove agony for the French. With the nearest friendly village many miles away through dense forest, "this was not like Korea," and thus was a different war entirely. As Fall writes: "Night began to fall over the four thousand villages of the Red River delta, and the night belonged to the Viet Minh."[3]

"Fall made me really think for the first time in my life," Gersony says. Fall was the first author whose message Gersony could consciously remember the details of after reading. "Reading Bernard Fall began my journey towards an understanding of what America could do in the world and what it could not do, based not on some lofty ideal of history, but on knowledge and empathy of the human terrain itself, about places and people as they actually were.

"It is all about collecting information and insights from the field, so that we don't operate with one eye closed. It is about searching out that vital insight about a place that any journalist or relief worker has, but which wonks and highbrow policymakers often don't."

This all complemented Gersony's own experience at this point in his life. School and literature had so far been beyond him. Intellectually, he knew only the most basic, concrete aspects of existence: the commodity trade and the typing-up of casualty reports, memorizing each battlefield death or wound through the movements of his fingers. If the evidence did not exist right in front of him, it didn't exist, period. And following from that would come his belief in the essential wisdom of the common person, who also knew the world only from the grassroots level in the most immediate, concrete way. He simply trusted people at the bottom, like the plant managers in the Midwest—for whom economics were never abstract—and distrusted people at the top.

It was in this way that he would eventually discover the world of refugees and displaced persons. To him, refugees were people at the end of the chain of events that had begun with decisions made by those at the top and the beginning of the chain.

Gersony was to become the ultimate fieldworker: in continuous, tactile contact with the evidence. And he would let the evidence—rather than theories, of which he knew nothing—always drive his conclusions.

Today, Gersony's library in his home, surrounded by woods in Great Falls, Virginia, forty minutes from Washington, is a monument to that sensibility, elaborated on in the course of almost half a century. Amassed over a lifetime of travel, there are practically no books of political science with its grand and abstract theories, and almost nothing on *globalization* (another flimsy word). Rather, his shelves are packed and cluttered with works of local history, art, travel, and literature about specific parts of the world, since it is often in the guise of fiction where writers can more easily tell the truth. There is little here that is not the product of firsthand knowledge and encounters with terrain. Almost every geography is represented, from the Mosquitia on the Caribbean coast of Central America to the northern half of the Korean peninsula. Gersony seems to have a knack for quickly locating the best that literature has to offer on the area where he has to go next, so that Joan Didion's *Salvador* (1983) lies on the Latin America shelf above Noel Malcolm's *Kosovo: A Short History* (1998), where his books about the Balkans are. There are *The Lake Regions of Central Africa* by the explorer Sir Richard Francis Burton, published in 1860, and John L. Stephens's *Incidents of Travel in Central America, Chiapas and Yucatan,* published in 1841. I notice *The Bridge on the Drina* (1945) by Ivo Andric, the Yugoslav Nobel Prize laureate, and the British explorer Wilfred Thesiger's *The Marsh Arabs* (1964). The best of journalism is here, too, and not just Didion: such as Ryszard Kapuściński's *The Soccer War* (1990), essays about coups and upheavals in Latin America, Africa, and the Middle East; and Michael Ignatieff's *Blood and Belonging* (1994), about the still-resonant appeal of ethnicity and nationalism, despite the optimism of a supposedly unifying world that greeted the end of the Cold War. The entire globe is here in this library, but without exception it is built up from many geographic particulars. The shelves reveal a generalist, who has earned that old-fashioned title by burrowing deep into so many different regions.

Over the decades, with lots of work, he has learned to better remember what he has read, even without typing.

In his basement there are large and detailed maps of the regions where his research left the deepest impact on policymakers: Rwanda, the border areas of Mozambique, Uganda's Luwero Triangle, and so on. This emotionally wrought son of Jewish Holocaust refugees is a quintessential nineteenth-century man, someone for whom geography and culture are the beginning of all knowledge, one of the very few left in Washington or anywhere; an explorer dedicated to the often unpleasant and often wondrous granularity of places, who, nevertheless, doesn't quite fit the part.

It all started with Bernard Fall's ruminations about the ground-level reality of Indochina, which are right here on these shelves. It is in our libraries where Gersony and I meet each other, for I also throughout my career as an author and journalist have been obsessed with specific geographies and the cultures that emanate from them, and are specific to them, and are thus another reason for me to tell his story.

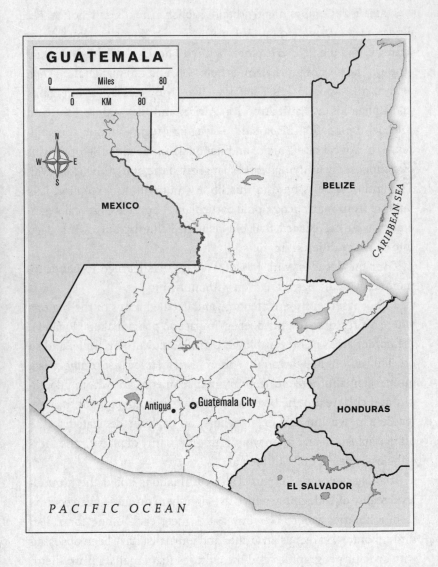

GUATEMALA

0 Miles 80
0 KM 80

N
W E
S

MEXICO

BELIZE

CARIBBEAN SEA

Antigua   Guatemala City

HONDURAS

EL SALVADOR

PACIFIC OCEAN

CHAPTER 2

Guatemala
1970–1977

The Gruesome Threesome

The writings of Bernard Fall had focused Gersony's mind on the problem of America in the Third World. But he was still young, in his midtwenties, aimless, and with few prospects. Gersony was offered two well-paying positions in the commodity trade in the Midwest, which he turned down. It was not a direction where he wanted to go. But in what direction he should go, he just didn't know.

His path to Guatemala began by accident, with little forethought, on the campus of Long Island University in Brooklyn, where a girlfriend was taking courses around the same time that he was released from the Army.

With her help, he sat in on classes about political transitions taught by Leon Sinder, the chairman of the sociology department and a cultural anthropologist, "a short Jewish guy with a big head of hair," born in Romania, who had flown over fifty combat missions in the Pacific in World War II. This was an era when college professors had military experience and had actually done something in their lives besides having gone to graduate school—and in subtle and indirect ways they brought these vital experiences into the classroom. Sinder, like Graham Ward, was another person who thought Gersony was someone, or might become someone, when he thought he was no one.

Sinder mentioned to Gersony that a colleague of his was going to lead a group of students on a field trip to Guatemala, and needed a

Bob Gersony in Guatemala in the 1970s.

driver and assistant to help him explore the terrain in advance. So at the end of 1969, Gersony went for ten days to the historic Guatemalan town of Antigua, as well as to some Mayan shrines and pyramids. Instantly, he became smitten with the people and the landscape, and while there met a "terribly overweight" Catholic priest from Oklahoma who invited him back. Gersony spent only a month in New York at the beginning of 1970 before he returned to Guatemala. Twenty-five years old with $3,000 in savings, he went to live at the Catholic mission in Antigua, paying $30 per month for room and board.

ANTIGUA, GUATEMALA, 1970. A rectilinear town of cobblestone streets and grand Spanish baroque architecture, ringed by three soaring volcanoes in a landscape of lonely, ocean-like vastness; with such fine all-year-round weather that it is justifiably called "the land of eternal spring." This old colonial capital teems with churches and monasteries, built hundreds of years ago, often in a state of majestic, charred, and rubble-strewn ruin on account of repeated earthquakes over the centuries. The stucco pilasters and pendentives are so intricate as to induce hallucination. There is an Angkor Wat quality to this place, with vines crawling over heaps of fallen masonry. The blazing, loose-fitting costumes or *trajes* of the indigenous Mayan inhabitants fill the landscape with color: twistingly woven ponchos, the design often specific to each village. The paganized Catholic processions with mahogany-borne floats appear refracted by incense from the swinging lamps.

There is smoke from the lamps, smoke from the volcanoes, smoke from burning wood scarring the white ceilings and porticoes, and dust rising from the porous soil, all intensifying the theatricality of the lush forested setting, in which a rugged geography and heavy rains, bringing floods, disease, and landslides, have for hundreds of years hindered development.

The entire visual drama of Spain's interaction with the New World is condensed here, a place that in the early nineteenth century was the political heart of Central America. Guatemala, geographically tucked away at the bottom of Mexico and utterly absent from world media consciousness, a place you would never think about, is also a place that deeply imprinted itself on Bob Gersony's memory. In a visual sense, it would be the only place ever to do so.

Though Vietnam put Bob Gersony on a certain path and gave him his worldview, Vietnam was also an ordeal of boredom and psychological survival, something he just had to get through. Guatemala, on the other hand, was sheer exploration and the most adventurous kind of personal fulfillment: something he had never before experienced in his life. This is why Guatemala made such an intense, lasting impression on him. After Antigua, and what happened there, he did not have to remember another landscape quite as vividly.

In Antigua, he was free at first to enjoy the place and absorb its landscape details, since he had as yet no firm plans there. For the rest of his life after Guatemala, everywhere he went he would have to hit the ground running, with enormous pressure on him and a job he had been assigned to do—usually a mystery he was ordered by superiors to solve. In such circumstances, for someone as compulsive as he became regarding work, the details of the landscape itself became more and more of a distraction, since he just couldn't wait to get to the embassy, and out into the field, to start gathering facts.

Gersony never really did develop an eye for landscape, despite the books he has accumulated over a lifetime. He barely remembers the details of the dozens of Third World capital cities from where he began his forays into the bush, despite the fact that he reads and collects the sorts of books he does out of a conscious dedication to *thinking locally;* to thinking about the factors peculiar to each country and its geography, rather than in terms of grand schemes and overarching ideas about the world. Bernard Fall taught him why this was important. But it was Guatemala where he first applied this lesson. *Respect the landscape, but the solution to each situation will lie elsewhere, in the world of men and women and their decisions.* Gersony, in sum, was never a fatalist, one who just gives up on a situation.

Guatemala was the beginning of a life dominated by many places that foreign policy elites ordinarily never think about, and of discovering the world, just as Bernard Fall did, from the ground up.

Guatemala actually constitutes one of the most famous geographies of the Cold War. Guatemala in 1954, along with Iran in 1953, were the two countries where the Eisenhower administration—specifically the two brothers, Secretary of State John Foster Dulles and CIA Director Allen Dulles—most famously toppled democratically elected governments seen to be hostile to American interests.[1] In Iran, the CIA, helped by the British Secret Service, deposed prime minister Mohammad Mosaddegh after he had nationalized the Anglo-Iranian Oil Company. A year later, the CIA deposed Guatemalan president Jacobo Árbenz Guzmán for expropriating land of the United Fruit Company and, more generally, for adopting a pro-Soviet foreign policy. Had Mosaddegh not been toppled and had his social reforms been allowed to take hold, the Iranian Revolution of 1978–79 that brought the radical ayatollahs to power might never have happened. In Guatemala, similarly, the 1954 coup ended years of mild social reforms, and ushered in decades of repressive military rule that spawned leftist rebellions, answered, in turn, by right-wing death squads.[2] Guerrilla warfare and assassinations became widespread. It was known as the Thirty Years' War. American policymakers didn't care. They were simply not going to tolerate the creation of a pro-Soviet regime of any kind so close to the United States. (This policy was redoubled after Fidel Castro came to power in Cuba in 1959.) Guatemala was an iconic demonstration of just how tragic the Cold War was for the developing world.

Starting with Vietnam, Gersony had begun experiencing not only the world, but specifically the Cold War itself, at ground level, from the Asian, African, and Latin American periphery where all the violence and casualties of that great global struggle occurred. Thus, as Gersony's professional life began to take shape, it is important at this juncture—at the very beginning of my story about him—to put the Cold War itself in historical context.

The United States and the Soviet Union were, in fact, engaged in a conflict over the very definition of European modernity. The two superpowers needed to change the world in order to prove the universal relevance of their ideologies, and Third World elites proved fertile ground for this competition, explains Yale historian Odd Arne Westad. The Cold War ethos "was at least as alluring and evocative as the imperialist ethos that it replaced," judging by the sense of duty and sacrifice of the advisers on both sides.[3] Gersony was to become one of them: a Cold Warrior even as he dealt almost exclusively with the victims, affecting in turn how he interacted with the State Department and other agencies. Indeed, the Cold War in Asia, Africa, and Latin America was more than simply a struggle for geopolitical positioning. It was also a test of the core ideas and values of both superpowers about the very path of historical change. What was at stake was nothing less than the question of whose side history was truly on.[4] In fact, the American and Soviet systems were both "imperial in all but name," observes Oxford historian John Darwin.[5] And in this neo-imperial struggle, it all came down to Vladimir Lenin versus Woodrow Wilson: that is, the Leninist model of seizing, holding, and extending state power that so attracted the new Third World elites, who were equally attracted by the Wilsonian model of self-determination and a rules-based international system of which they could be a part. The Leninist model really meant authoritarianism unbridled, whereas the Wilsonian model implied a world of democracies. (The competition between ruthless, top-down control as opposed to one of people determining their own fates is still with us.) It would become a struggle in which whole societies were devastated.[6] In short, for the Third World, there was no escape from the Cold War.

For it was a *cold war* in Europe only. In Asia, Africa, and Latin America it was hot, cinematic, and bloody. The aftershocks would continue beyond 1989. Bob Gersony would have a vivid front-row seat for key parts of it on several continents. And while each Cold War crisis had its own unique origins, Gersony would see them all through the filter of refugees and displaced persons.

Because the Cold War coincided with the collapse of European empires, between 1945 and 1970 (the first half of the Cold War) the number of independent states increased almost fourfold, creating many new battlegrounds. Indeed, twenty years after the atomic bomb fell on Hiroshima, no fewer than forty new states had been created.[7] It was a process that actually began in the midst of fighting Hitler, since World War II had exhausted and demoralized even the victor nations such as imperial Great Britain and France. Already, at the November 1943 conference in Tehran, where Allied leaders gathered to discuss World War II strategy, many critical matters were settled directly by Roosevelt and Stalin, with Churchill, the commander of the British Empire no less, only on the sidelines. And thus as the United States and the Soviet Union quickly rose to dominate the postwar world, there was a striking loss of prestige and influence among Europe's traditional imperial powers.

In Asia alone, as Westad notes, colonialism "seemed in free fall," as economic exhaustion in Europe—the upshot of a great depression followed by world war—met with rebellion in the tropics, with indigenous leaders like Nehru, Ho Chi Minh, and Sukarno suddenly emerging to eject British, French, and Dutch imperialists.[8] Making matters worse for these old empires was the new Soviet threat to Europe, which required Great Britain and France to reinforce their own defenses at home. One moral justification for European imperialism as it culminated in the early twentieth century was the promise of improving the lives of those under its rule, but that had become impossible for these economically wearied empires, beset with an overwhelming security challenge in Europe itself.

The United States and the Soviet Union filled the vacuum for the British and French in Africa and Asia. Though the initial American impulse was to look down on colonialism and celebrate the passing of empire, Washington's immediate fear was that the newly established states would be drawn into the embrace of the Soviet Union. And thus as anti-communism overtook anticolonialism, one imperial age was soon replaced by another, though it called itself by another name: the Cold War.

President John Kennedy was quite blunt about it, believing that the Cold War would be won or lost in the developing world. The establishment of the Peace Corps, with all of its idealistic aura, was part of his realpolitik strategy of heading off the expansion of Soviet influence. By the 1960s, as Europe itself settled into a generally immobilized conflict, violence in the developing world gave the Cold War truly global dimensions. The United States, having already used the CIA to topple regimes in Guatemala and Iran in the 1950s, now cheered on or supported rebellions and coups in Algeria, Ghana, and Indonesia, to say nothing of what it was attempting in Cuba and Vietnam. Meanwhile, Egypt, Guinea, Mali, India to some extent, and other postcolonial states all looked to the Soviet Union for support. Later Soviet allies would include Syria, Iraq, South Yemen, and Somalia, to name but a few. Then, in the 1970s, almost in unison, came the communist victory in Vietnam and the collapse of the decrepit Portuguese empire in Africa. The secession of Guinea-Bissau, Cape Verde, and the two sprawling colonies of southern Africa—Angola and Mozambique—were all the consequence of a bloodless coup against an out-of-gas reactionary regime in Lisbon. Angola and Mozambique would turn into panoramic wastelands of violent conflict as the United States and South Africa, employing their local proxies, fought the Soviet Union and Cuba, employing theirs. By the early 1980s, three decades after the coups in Guatemala and Iran, superpower conflict in the tropical periphery was at its peak.[9]

Through it all, the term "Third World" gradually came into vogue as a Cold War construction, after French journalists, beginning in the 1950s, began describing developing countries as *le tiers monde,* grouping together the "poor, nonwhite, and uncommitted" parts of the globe that lay apart from the first two worlds, those of the capitalist West (the first world) and the communist East (the second world).[10] The radical activist from Martinique, Frantz Fanon, would popularize the term in his pathbreaking manifesto, *The Wretched of the Earth*, published in 1961, which dealt specifically with the Algerian war. By then, the resistance movement against Great Power domination had already been formalized at the Bandung Conference in Indonesia in 1955, which drew the likes of Indonesia's Sukarno, India's Nehru, Egypt's Nasser, and Yugoslavia's Tito. The Non-Aligned Movement was declared for all the world to see in the Yugoslav capital of Belgrade in 1961, in a conference hosted by Tito.

Yet the Non-Aligned Movement was merely aspirational, and as time went on more and more of these new states found it necessary to side with either the United States or the Soviet Union in some way. And because the Cold War was so binary, any Third World regime could gain a superpower patron, no matter how lethal or foolish its domestic agenda.[11] For the Cold War was the organizing principle of the world in the second half of the twentieth century, igniting conflicts in Asia, Africa, and Latin America, or making them worse. It quickly became a backdrop to Bob Gersony's entire professional life.

But while elites in Washington believed they were bringing liberty to the world, that was mainly true in Europe, not in the vast Afro-Asian and Latin American periphery where Gersony labored. For in many of these countries American national interests—by supporting hated regimes—ran up against the very struggle for freedom and human rights. Thus, periodically, Gersony would find himself recommending against the very policy supported by the U.S. Embassy; or in support of the embassy but against ideological factions back in Washington.

His professional life would also continue beyond the Cold War, as he reported on conflicts and carnages that the Cold War had set in motion and were consequently aftershocks of it. More crucially, Gersony's life was a forerunner to today's concentration on the environment itself as a national security issue, as he was also dispatched to interview the victims of one natural and weather-related catastrophe after another. The Cold War, environmental catastrophes, genocide, and, most fundamentally, refugees all became part of his professional domain. And whereas foreign correspondents interviewed dozens, representing the State Department and other agencies he would often interview hundreds in each place: more than eight thousand refugees, displaced persons, and related others interviewed over a lifetime. Whereas an individual foreign correspondent might cover some or most conflicts and disasters, he would cover almost all of them.

Guatemala would be the first, in the course of his bottom-up experience of the Cold War and afterward from the battlefields of the developing world.

Of course, the Cold War, precisely because it was so archetypal, was a vast and crude generalization for the many dozens of crises going on around the globe that each had its own individual elements, themselves products of intricate little dramas with their own vivid realities for those in the field. It was as if the Cold War existed only on the surface, below which were depths and more depths of local minutiae. Gersony's life played out in the midst of these complex little pageants about which those in Washington usually knew next to nothing.

Thus, we return to Gersony first setting foot inside the forlorn Catholic mission in Antigua, Guatemala.

The Catholic mission where he stayed was, in part, a response to the growing power of Protestant evangelicals in Guatemala that were organized around the Wycliffe Bible society with its Summer Institute of Linguistics, which offered a better and more productive life in the present in return for conversion from Catholicism. Wycliffe's influence came from its translations of the New Testament published in each of Guatemala's twenty-two Mayan languages—the linguistic consequence of each indigenous community's isolation wrought by an impossible mountainous landscape. Indeed, beauty, poverty, and isolation were the upshots of Guatemala's lush, dizzying topography.

Add to this the numbing element of Indian stoicism, a product of millennia-old pagan traditions with Catholicism superimposed on them, together with the half-buried communal memory of the violence of the Spanish Conquest and the centuries of slavery that followed. Very few of the Indians spoke Spanish, the language of both the *ladinos* (those of mixed European and Indian blood) and the descendants of the Spanish conquerors themselves, who owned most of the plantations and other valuable land.[12] And because the Mayans knew only their native tongue, they had little access to education in a country where the whole school system was based on Spanish. The Indians, moreover, were relatively passive against the Grand Guignol of political intrigue and violence that continued to afflict this country, especially in the drawn-out wake of the 1954 CIA-inspired coup. Successive right-wing military governments ruled Guatemala while Gersony lived there. They would be followed by a truly brutal regime guilty of widespread murder against the Indians, after coming to power in a fraudulent election in 1978.

Gersony's first task after he arrived back in Antigua was to learn Spanish. But there were no Spanish schools. "One day I was in the central square by the cathedral, truly the most beautiful place I have ever seen, getting a shoeshine while communicating in basic Spanish with a garage worker, Luis Monzon, who told me he worked for the equivalent of fifty cents per week. I don't know, he just seemed sparky, ambitious. I said I would pay him a dollar a day to be my friend, and spend all his waking hours with me, teaching me Spanish." They traveled all over Antigua and its surroundings together. For Gersony, the great advantage of Luis was that he didn't know a word of English. For twelve hours daily, Gersony plodded through Spanish with him and with his Amsco workbook. It was altogether exhausting. Luis talked constantly. Gersony couldn't daydream for a minute. There was no escape; he had to learn.

Six weeks later he had advanced from the basic Spanish of guidebooks to a working knowledge of the language, which he would continue to build upon in coming years until he spoke Spanish fluently. Little by little, seeing Gersony with Luis, tourists and other gringos came over to him, asking where they could learn Spanish. It was an anomalous situation. The area's natural beauty and Antigua's historical monuments drew young visitors, hippie types and others, even as there was no place to study the official language. Gersony, with Luis's

Bob Gersony in Guatemala in the 1970s.

help, found families for the gringos to live with, ordered Amsco workbooks, and again with the help of Luis and others he met, set up Spanish classes offering individual instruction. The money Gersony made, which was very little, he gave to the Catholic mission where he was staying.

During this time, Gersony met an "extremely dark Mayan" named Aparicio Teleguario who spoke Kaqchiquel, one of the twenty-two indigenous languages. "Aparicio was eighteen and very personable, and wanted to write a history of his people in his own language. He was a brilliant local organizer. There was something alluring about him. He specifically had a plan for a radio program in Kaqchiquel. Sometime later he died of pneumonia after being misdiagnosed by a doctor, but he left me with an idea for the future. . . ." It was more than that: Gersony, with all the vitality and enthusiasm of someone young and on an adventure, became obsessed with doing something that would be true to Aparicio's memory. It was the beginning of Gersony's road to humanitarianism.

This was also the era of Catholic liberation theology in Latin America, in which priests and nuns, influenced by the poverty-stricken communities where they served, began in the 1950s to combine religion with a call for social and economic justice. It was a gospel of freedom from the tyranny of the Church's complicity with capitalism and despotic regimes.[13] Inevitably, liberation theology became an asset to Marxist opponents of the conservative oligarchical orders in Latin America that the United States, for reasons of Cold War geopolitics, was supporting. It led in some cases to radical reinterpretations of Church doctrine. In this way, Gersony, on one Saturday, the day before Easter, March 28, 1970, found himself invited to the wedding of a Catholic priest in the fog-wrapped village of Nahualá, surrounded by fantastic mountain formations, with the men in white, gray, and black kilts and the women in Spanish-imposed *trajes* of bold colors. Lay missionaries made up a half-pagan procession. It was beyond magical.

Here Gersony met an Englishman with a terribly glum expression because he had hoped to marry the bride himself. His name was Tony Jackson, the only person in his rather poor, working-class family to go to university. He had studied French and linguistics at Trinity College, Oxford. "Tony was absolutely charming and charismatic, a real inspiration, with his bowler hat, umbrella, and fine accent," not to mention his affinity for English Breakfast tea and the works of Lewis Carroll.

But Tony was even more than that. Completely unaffected and able to befriend anyone in an instant, Tony Jackson, with his rail-thin frame, moved his hand and body as he talked to you like an actor doing pantomime. Thus, the glum expression disappeared the moment he began talking with Gersony. In fact, Jackson, too, will never forget the moment of meeting Gersony. With a short black beard, black glasses, a mop of dark hair (just before he started losing it), and a fierce, unforgiving stare, Bob Gersony at twenty-five, however insecure he felt on the inside, could have been Che Guevara's aide-de-camp or a member of the Weather Underground. Gersony immediately poured out his grief to Tony about America's misadventure in Vietnam. They both agreed that the problem in Latin America was *land* and how unfairly distributed it was.

Tony Jackson, one of "the Gruesome Threesome," who helped Bob run the network of language schools in Guatemala in the 1970s.

Gersony had an idea. One day in Antigua a few months later, out in the rain, where Tony opened the umbrella to protect them both, Gersony offered to put Tony in charge of his small Spanish school, which had begun to grow with more and more students from the United States, Canada, France, and even a few from Japan. "Guatemala, Mayan Indians, the fabulous mountains and volcanoes, of course I will do it!" Jackson said, glad to be able to permanently escape from a job in Nicaragua—educating the elite for their Miami shopping sprees—that he hated. He gave Gersony $396 in savings for more chairs and workbooks, to add to those Gersony had bought himself with proceeds from buying and reselling native handbags to students. It was at this moment when the Spanish school had its true start.

It was the beginning of a lifelong collaboration. Though, according to a mutual friend, "Tony and Bob could not have been more different. Tony was charismatic and got along with everybody. Bob, on the other hand, was not particularly outgoing, despite possessing a strong wit." Jackson calls himself and Gersony the "odd couple," the British Oxford graduate and the American high school dropout, who disagreed on many aspects of politics, but who nevertheless would come to agree on the operational aspects of administering humanitarian assistance. For Gersony, Jackson would become his "lifelong ambassador to the left wing, and someone who would never complain about living conditions in the Third World, no matter how awful they were." At the time Gersony met him, however, Jackson was still a devout Catholic, and his left-wing politics would not flower until he returned to England and settled in Oxford.

On Christmas Day 1970, Jackson arrived back from Nicaragua for the last time to settle in Antigua, Guatemala.

"We rented classrooms for fifty-five students, who began to include NGOs," Gersony explains. These were aid workers in nongovernmental organizations, like the Peace Corps and the Canadian International Development Agency, who, while technically government employees, were lumped into the humanitarian aid category. "Everyone studied seven hours daily for five days per week. Tony was brilliant at inspiring students and inspiring teachers to teach. People would practically jump out of the window for Tony. That's how much he was loved. I was the bad guy in the act: the budget guy. The months went by and we grew to be 150 teachers and students." Gersony's policy with hiring teachers was not to care about credentials, but to look for good, animated talkers. "With that, we could teach them how to teach," he explains.

It never occurred to Gersony to apply for grants to run his school. All his instincts learned from his father and the commodity trade were about making the venture a self-sustaining business. Indeed, during his early days in Guatemala, he still didn't know what grants were.

Then Terrence Kaufman showed up in Antigua. He was in his midthirties, absolutely weird, endearing, with long red hair tied in a ponytail, a beard, and a ring in his ear long before its time. He looked like a pirate or a drummer for a heavy metal rock band—that is, he didn't present well. People tiptoed around him. Kaufman was a Mayan linguist with a PhD from the University of California at Berkeley, and already famous in his field for reconstructing proto-Mayan languages. After Gersony had the idea of having Peace Corps volunteers sent down to Antigua to teach descriptive linguistics and help Mayan speakers to compile dictionaries and grammars in their native tongues, Kaufman devoted several of his summers to helping implement it. The program empowered Mayans to be experts in their own languages and to build beyond the Protestant Bible translations.[14] It was during this period that Gersony kept thinking about the young Mayan Aparicio Teleguario who had died of pneumonia before he could start his radio program in Kaqchiquel. His and Kaufman's vision followed in the young Mayan's spirit.

The plan was launched. Gersony's school system, having grown out of a rudimentary operation nominally run by a group of tired Catholic priests, expanded further, with Peace Corps volunteers coming down to Antigua for two to three years each, under Kaufman's direction. It was 1972 now. Jo Froman, a very efficient and businesslike Peace Corps volunteer from Turon, Kansas, and a graduate of Beloit College in Wisconsin—a beautiful thin girl with blue eyes and long, light brown hair, according to Gersony's memory—was by this time helping Kaufman do a nationwide survey, using hundreds of informants, of all the indigenous languages in Guatemala, which numbered twenty-two, as they discovered.[15] "Jo Froman had the best technical ear for languages I ever encountered," Tony Jackson, himself a linguist, says. Froman just had this innate ability to immediately recognize long and short vowels and to imitate sounds and accents. Kaufman would go on to write the definitive book on classifying Mayan languages, published in Spanish. Froman would go on to get an MBA from Harvard.

"I had never heard of Bob Gersony until I was told I needed to see him in Antigua to arrange a Peace Corps–sponsored Kaqchiquel course," Froman recalls to me. "On the appointed day, I left at dawn for the long ride on a converted school bus with chickens, and arrived exhausted and out of sorts at midday. I was furious that no one knew

Jo Froman, a brilliant linguist and one of "the Gruesome Threesome," in Guatemala in the 1970s.

who I was and that there was no sign of Mr. Gersony. Hours later, a dilapidated Toyota Land Cruiser pulled up. Even before he shut the door, I laid into the person who answered to 'Bob Gersony,' berating him for his rudeness. He listened patiently to my rant, then said, 'So you're Froman, not the quixotic person I was expecting. I just came from the funeral of a close Mayan friend.'

"I was absolutely intrigued within ten seconds of meeting him. His very surprising use of the word 'quixotic' captured me. He exuded such warmth. Bob is bimodal, you either love him or detest him. Though, as I came to realize, communicating in Spanish took away some of the harsher aspects of his personality."

"It was alphabet politics," Gersony said about those long-ago days in Guatemala. "One letter for each sound, lots of arguments about how to spell each consonant, and whether or not to impose the Spanish writing system on dialects that had never or rarely been written down. Linguists are a bunch of prima donnas," owing to their wizard-like talent to master multiple languages and dialects in their written form, making linguists, after a fashion, the ultimate intimidating specialists in the liberal arts field.

Gersony's school kept growing and multiplied into a system with a board of directors, so that Antigua is to this day a center for the study of Spanish, indigenous languages, and local linguistics. Froman, Jackson (or "Jackers" as he was also sometimes called), and Gersony became known in the local NGO community by the not-altogether-flattering moniker of "the Gruesome Threesome," because of their dynamic, unorthodox, business-like, and unsentimental approach to Third World assistance. The very fact that these three extraordinarily different people had banded together was a tribute to Gersony's leadership qualities and judge of character, explains Reggie Norton, the Oxfam field director for Latin America, who first met Gersony in Guatemala. The three even had a mascot, Max the Wonder Dog, part German shepherd, part Belgian shepherd, and part wolf, who went off on his own all day long, visiting local schools and the market before returning home at dinner. "*Hola,* Max," the schoolchildren would say. (Froman would later take Max with her to Harvard, where he wandered around the classrooms there, too.) Gersony and Froman, working twelve hours a day, seven days a week together, became romantically involved for a time, and would remain friends for life, as would happen with his other girlfriends. As Gersony explains, "I'm not conventionally good-looking. I'm not an athlete. I don't have the gift of gab. But I'm a decent person and have led an interesting life. I never had a problem falling into mature relationships."

Froman explains: "As a humanitarian, genius, and mensch, Bob Gersony commands my admiration in a way few others do."

"Bob defied every label. He was an exotic cocktail of a man, with his sincerity, skepticism, courage, and humanity," says Ann Siegel, senior vice president of the American Museum of Natural History in New York and another former girlfriend, who keeps in touch with Bob and his family.

"I had often wondered what Bob would do with all his energy and ideas, after Guatemala had taught him to live dangerously," recalls British-born Alan Riding, a stringer for *The New York Times* based in Mexico City in the early 1970s, who would go on to a storied career as a staff foreign correspondent for the *Times* and author of the classic *Distant Neighbors: A Portrait of the Mexicans* (1985). "Bob and his *compañeros* Tony Jackson and Jo Froman always greeted me with lots of good gossip about Guatemala's fraught political situation whenever I would arrive there unannounced." As Riding explains, "It was a time of fierce repression by the military regime of General Carlos Manuel Arana Osorio, which included a state of siege, death squads, and a succession of murders of supposed leftist and even moderate opponents in [the modern-day capital of] Guatemala City." Riding himself was once dragged from his hotel during curfew by plainclothed goons who put him in jail until the U.S. Embassy won his release. "Fortunately, Bob's school in Antigua was not considered a nest of subversion."

Gersony, Jackson, and Froman were not oblivious to what was going on politically. After all, the house of the president of the much-hated United Fruit Company—a tool of U.S. influence—was practically down the street from them in Antigua. "But we stayed out of politics," Gersony says. (It was always "we" with Gersony.) "From the military point of view we were not left-wingers. We didn't tolerate drugs, we insisted on short hair for our students, so we took in no hippies. We were not agitators, but ingenues who were no threat to anyone. In fact, we were setting up a national resource that appealed to both the military and the Left, replacing an old-fashioned, missionary-inflicted model of language study with a homegrown, national approach. Tony went into the Ministry of Education every week to provide a progress report. The only group that didn't like us were the long-established Wycliffe evangelicals, who with their own linguistics institute saw us as competition."

By late 1975, still more or less broke and thirty years of age, Gersony realized it was time to leave Guatemala. He could easily "have gone wrong" there, as Ursula Strauss feared, drifting into an unstructured, somewhat aimless hippie lifestyle. After all, it was the place to do it, with such natural beauty and an abundance of drugs. But Gersony was never flaky. And he was never aimless, as his essay critiquing the beatniks, written when he was only eighteen, indicated. The fact that he now wanted to leave Guatemala also showed some degree of ambition.

Actually, Guatemala had given him the semblance of a college education. Though he was training hundreds of others, in effect he was the one being trained. He had learned Spanish fluently, and learned at an expert level the field of linguistics, without becoming a linguist himself. He had also learned to run a business, something that synchronized well with his talents for accounting, record keeping, and commodity trading. He learned, too, from Tony Jackson "how always to be nice to people, how not to be a prick." He had become well known to Oxfam, the Ford Foundation, the Peace Corps, and other NGOs. And in creating a self-sustaining operation, he had learned that "charity can be a business, that you don't have to be a naïve idealist to improve the situation of indigenous communities."

It was starting to become clear that Gersony fell into the category of the "twice exceptional," or 2e, that is, people who have had exceptional learning issues—those who while growing up could not cope in a traditional school environment—but who are also exceptionally gifted in other ways.

Two other events further matured and seasoned Gersony during this phase of his life. Early in his stay there, he read a book that he had brought along from his father's library: André Schwarz-Bart's 1959 classic, *The Last of the Just,* about the *Lamed-Vov,* the thirty-six "just" men of Jewish tradition, who according to legend appear in every generation. Their personal merit keeps the world from entire destruction. They accomplish this task by experiencing and internalizing all the pain of the world. The novel begins with a medieval pogrom and ends as one of the *Lamed-Vov* comforts inmates in their last moments in a Nazi death camp. The book covers eight centuries of Jewish persecution and suffering. "Rivers of blood have flowed, columns of smoke have obscured the sky, but surviving all these dooms, the tradition has remained inviolate down to our own time. For the *Lamed-Vov* are the hearts of the world multiplied," Schwarz-Bart writes.[16] Upon finishing the book's last page, Gersony determined to live up to the standard of the *Lamed-Vov.*

"The book underlined how I would define integrity. It reinforced how I wanted to act throughout my life. I told myself I would take chances, particularly bureaucratic chances as it would later turn out, by not adopting a policy of keeping my mouth shut together with a go-along/get-along evasion of responsibility. I'm a child of refugees, a member of a persecuted race who lost members of my own family.

I would not countenance mass murder in Uganda or Mozambique or other places, therefore. I believed very early in the responsibility to protect, without becoming ideological about it."

The Last of the Just also left a deep imprint on Gersony because of something that had happened when he was eleven years old. It was Yom Kippur and he and his father sat in special seats close to the *bima* in the packed Manhattan synagogue, since his father was a major donor. Everyone was quiet, waiting expectantly for the Kol Nidre service to begin. Then a man, inoffensive, invisible almost, walked into the back of the synagogue. He was dressed in his Sunday best, with a tie and vest under a suit. But it was all so threadbare, with holes and stains all over; as if picked up at a Goodwill store. He was clearly a poor man. Suddenly the rabbi's son-in-law spotted him and asked the man in a loud voice to leave, since the service was only for members of the synagogue—those who had purchased subscriptions. "But I only want to hear Kol Nidre. Then I will go," the poor man said. "I'm sorry, unless you have bought a ticket, you cannot stay," the rabbi's son-in-law replied with mock respect. "Can I give my seat to that man," Gersony whispered to his father. But his father hushed him up. "And that was it," Gersony said. "The man had to leave. He was a poor Jew. We should have honored him. Instead, we threw him out, and nobody—nobody spoke up. I was so close to standing up, but I didn't. At the time I felt that I had had it with Judaism. It formed the kernel of my resolution to always speak out no matter the job and policy consequences. Though I wouldn't actually fulfill that vow until I read *The Last of the Just*."

The other event in Guatemala happened on the morning of August 12, 1973. He was in a bedroom of an enormous old colonial house that he, Froman, and Jackson rented off the main square in Antigua. By this time his school business was set up, and they could afford the house. The phone rang. His number was 406, he remembers. There were only three-digit phone numbers in Guatemala in those days, owing to the paucity of phone lines. Jo Froman picked it up, and heard the terrible news. She will never forget the moment of telling it to Bob. When Bob eventually got to the phone, his father's voice informed him that his younger sister, Mimi (Cecilia Clare), had died of a heroin overdose. She was twenty-five. He got home that night via Miami and slipped into his old bedroom after midnight. His parents were sleeping and he decided not to wake them. But then the bathroom light went on. His mother and father were in the doorway crying. He started to cry. His father showed him how to arrange a burial. The funeral marked the first time that he gave a speech: about the need to reduce the profit motive from drugs by legalizing some of them, a position he still holds. "Mimi and I were both very smart people who failed early," he said.

Any death is sad. But the death of a young person, especially within the immediate family, is a weight that never gets easier to bear. As time went on in Guatemala, Gersony became even more organized, and more dynamic. As he turned thirty, it was hard to imagine someone with greater focus and clarity, even though he had no clearly discernible career path yet.

Then, in the middle of the night of February 4, 1976, the day after he, Froman, and Jackson left the country to meet with Ford Foundation officials in Mexico City—with Gersony not planning to return to Central America—the great Guatemalan earthquake struck, registering 7.5 on the Richter scale: 23,000 people died, trapped in their adobe houses; 76,000 were injured, and thousands more were left homeless. Cities all over the country suffered damage. The Gruesome Threesome immediately returned to Antigua.

Because of the landslides triggered by the quake, much of the country was now inaccessible. Late one night, after initial emergency operations, and after Oxfam's Reggie Norton had received approximately $1 million in donations, Gersony, Froman, and Jackers were in Reggie's house feverishly talking about what to do next with Fred Cuny, a soon-to-be-famous disaster relief specialist who would disappear under mysterious circumstances in Chechnya in 1995, and whose remains were never found. Suddenly Roland Bunch of the Oklahoma City–based World Neighbors charity walked into the room with an indigenous Mayan. Bunch was completely covered in adobe dust. He hadn't changed his clothes in a week and smelled awful. "Roland was a real sight, a showstopper," Gersony remembers. Bunch said he had walked into San Martin and some of the other, worst-affected areas and just started interviewing people, for seven days. "We need to respond to *what the people think*!" he exclaimed. "And what they think is, 'Stop sending food!'" Bunch observed that Guatemala had just experienced one of its biggest maize harvests. Thus, food donations were only making things worse. "The free maize being distributed all over the place has blown away the price," he said. This simple fact was a revelation to all of them, especially to Gersony, because, in the spirit of Bernard Fall, someone had emerged from the field with news that altered the analysis of elites in Guatemala City and foreign capitals. And he had done this by speaking with the affected people themselves. What Bunch had said also made intrinsic sense to Gersony, steeped as he was in the world of commodity trading.

But appeals had already gone out for food, medicine, clothes, and so on. Alan Riding, who arrived from Mexico City to report on the earthquake for *The New York Times,* remembers being "most surprised when Bob and Tony Jackson, who were already engaged in emergency assistance, awakened me to the fact that sending in food from the outside was, in fact, counterproductive: although villages were damaged, their land was not. Thus, food donations had the effect of pushing down the local price of basic agricultural commodities that the peasants relied on to make an income." In other words, as Riding explains, "so-called foreign generosity completely disrupted local markets. But it was Bob especially who made me think about development in fresh ways, and with such warmth, humor, and intelligence." Of course, Gersony had passed on to Riding what he had just learned from Roland Bunch, whose own wisdom had come from being in personal contact with the evidence at great risk and extreme discomfort, something that made a lifelong impact on Gersony.

Gersony now truly began to think for himself. The peasants did not want to rebuild their homes with clay tiles, which had killed them with their weight and also suffocated them. They wanted to rebuild with sheet iron—galvanized zinc or lamina, to use its other names. It was ugly, which horrified the expatriate aid community with its love of aesthetics, but much lighter and more efficient. Yet prices for lamina had quadrupled. Gersony had the idea to sell the peasants galvanized zinc at a much-reduced price, along with the pressure-treated wooden posts to hold the roofs up. On Reggie Norton's advice, Gersony went to a roofing factory in neighboring El Salvador with money from Oxfam and negotiated a deal. Here, again, his experience in contracting learned from the commodity trade came in especially handy. The man who had cornered the market on beef lips as a young commodity trader now did likewise with lamina. Within a week, the first trucks arrived, and zinc roofs were selling "like hot cakes" at half price or less to those whose homes had been destroyed. It was quite a sight to see the long lines of small Mayan peasants carrying the zinc-iron sheeting on their backs, held there by a strap tied around their foreheads.

"It concentrated the minds of the NGOs," Gersony recalls. "For me, the roofing program was an example of business-like accountability with record keeping, receipts, and so on. It reinforced the idea of not creating dependency. All we were doing was giving the poor population a break on the price. They had money from the good harvest, as long as outside donations did not further depress the price of food. The dignity element dominated. However, the NGO community," he goes on, "whenever a catastrophe strikes, often rush in and create dependency. When you give stuff away, local officials can decide who gets it, based on their connections. But if you merely sell supplies, self-selection kicks in. People who need it, get it. It's certainly not a perfect approach, but it does, to repeat, emphasize dignity over dependency. Many NGOs [though not Fred Cuny] were antagonistic because we were selling to people that they were portraying in their publicity campaigns as completely helpless."

Oxfam director Norton adds, reflecting back on decades in the humanitarian field: "The NGO world, when you break it down, is often about buying materials at the lowest prices you can find. It requires a first-rate business mind as much as anything else."

Bob Gersony with the humanitarian aid worker Fred Cuny in Guatemala in 1976.

By the spring of 1976, the roofing program had become self-sustainable, and Gersony was finally ready to leave Guatemala. Oxfam asked him to attend a conference at the presidential palace in Guatemala City that would bring together all the donor countries, in order to provide progress reports. He didn't want to go. Though still at the very beginning of his career, he already hated those events. But he went anyway and sat at the rear to listen. Suddenly a guy with a big, bushy mustache planted himself in the chair next to him and pumped his hand into Gersony's. "I'm Fred Schieck, deputy director of USAID [the United States Agency for International Development] in Guatemala. Come back to my office later and let's talk."

USAID, a bureaucracy that grew indirectly out of the Marshall Plan and was established during the Kennedy administration, was essentially the Third World development arm of the State Department, even though the two bureaucracies were distinct and periodically at odds: whereas the State Department was all about influence, USAID was all about getting its projects done, and the two goals did not match up all of the time. Nevertheless, because the United States and the Soviet Union competed for influence everywhere, and influence was often (but not always) obtained through foreign aid, USAID combined national interest with humanitarian interest. Unsurprisingly, the people who staffed its bureaucracy were among the most idealistic in the U.S. government.

"Fred Schieck was a fuzzy-friendly teddy-bear type, and he knew all about me," Gersony remembers. Indeed, Schieck, with his velvety soft voice and easygoing informality, was the kind of guy you imagine always dressed in various shades of brown. The two talked for several hours about the competing philosophies of development aid. Gersony held forth about how the self-selection of beneficiaries reduced middlemen and corruption. Schieck had a master's degree in business from Harvard. He was also a military gun buff who was grabbed by Gersony's idea that aid at its most efficient need not be paternalistic, or a handout. Schieck was actually part of a breed that would become quite familiar in the early and middle phases of Gersony's career: the moderate Republican humanitarian and realist-internationalist, whose spiritual godfather was Theodore Roosevelt. It is a type that barely exists anymore. He was proof that the face of the Cold War—for that was ultimately why Schieck was in Guatemala—could sometimes be quite benign. Schieck hired Gersony at $20,000 a year to help him manage USAID's local assistance programs: the beginning of a four-decade relationship with the U.S. government, though Gersony did not know it at the time.

"Bob was young, loud, dogged, a bit foul-mouthed, and yet articulate at the same time," Schieck recalls about their first meeting. "We at USAID in Guatemala knew what we didn't know, and therefore viewed Bob as someone who knew his way around the culture and highlands better than we did. The fact that Bob had built a language school system almost from scratch gave him instant credibility, even though his whole approach to aid was so unorthodox." Schieck was soon awestruck at the caravans of trucks and forklifts that brought the lamina up from the coast into the highlands, where crowds of peasants had collected to buy the roofing materials at bargain prices. "Bob Gersony," Schieck went on, "was from the start obsessed with accountability, so we hired accountants and auditors for the project, which Tony Jackson helped Bob run from the field."[17]

Congressional staffers and USAID officials got word of the operation and flew down from Washington to see it firsthand. "We worried about those people too poor to afford the cut-rate building materials, so Bob set up road improvement projects to pay salaries, enabling people to afford the lamina roofs and posts, like a New Dealesque infusion of cash. The Guatemalan countryside began to change from a panorama of picturesque clay-tiled roofs to one of glinting-in-sunlight lamina," Schieck remembers. "Still, the idea was hard to sell to other disaster zones since it went against the ideology of humanitarian assistance."

While the local aid community remained suspicious, the military and the oligarchs worried that empowering the peasants would allow them to rise up and challenge the ruling establishment. One day Gersony was called into the office of the minister of defense, Fernando Romeo Lucas Garcia, an intimidating man with a mournful and resolute expression and large mustache: a Latin American dictator-type straight from Central Casting. Sitting next to Lucas Garcia was an international aid official, a rival of both Gersony's and USAID's approach to rural development in Guatemala. In the presence of that official, the minister of defense, in full military regalia, told Gersony to stop doing his projects aimed at removing the rural population's dependency on the Guatemalan government and the international aid community. "Do you know what can happen to you? Things happen to people who don't pay attention to what we say," Lucas Garcia warned Gersony. Gersony told him he should speak to his superiors at USAID, and then quietly explained his theory of development to him. Leaving the office, the aid official gave Gersony "fatherly advice," to do what Lucas Garcia had said.

"I went to bed that night with convulsions, nausea. I was sick and trembling for two days. I was so terrified. I couldn't eat. All I did was drink liquids. It was the first of my physical emotional crises."

Schieck bought Gersony's safety by making a hefty donation to the local chapter of the Masons, to which many in the upper reaches of the Guatemalan government and military belonged. Lucas Garcia went on to be elected president of Guatemala in a fraudulent election in 1978 and was in power for four years, during which time he murdered and butchered many thousands of people in response to a rebel offensive, and later would stand accused of torture and genocide against the Mayan population. His counterinsurgency modus operandi included the burning of villages and the slaughter of farm animals. Lucas Garcia died in exile in Venezuela. Gersony's encounter with him was a forerunner to a career in which he would be periodically in danger; in which he never learned how not to be afraid.

Gersony had arrived in Guatemala with no Spanish and almost no money. He left as one of the most influential foreigners in the country, with fluency in the language. He still had no credentials, though, and never would. There would never be a title or a degree or an affiliation to his name. Thus, in the ordinary careerist sense, he had risen as far as he ever would. That would always be the essence of his insecurity, even as it was central to his sheer drive, creativity, and unorthodox thinking.

In her diary at the time, Jo Froman wrote presciently: "Gersony doesn't belong to me. He belongs to the world. If you could just have a part of him for a short period in your life, you were forever fortunate."

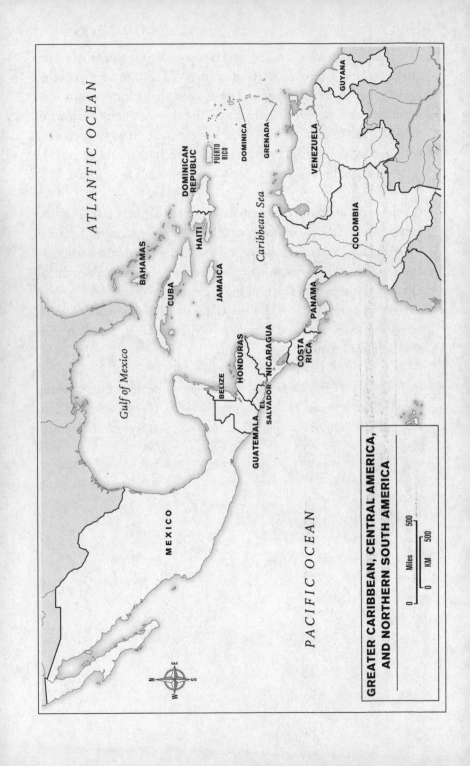

ATLANTIC OCEAN

Gulf of Mexico

MEXICO

BAHAMAS

CUBA

HAITI

JAMAICA

DOMINICAN
REPUBLIC

PUERTO
RICO

DOMINICA

GRENADA

Caribbean Sea

GUYANA

VENEZUELA

COLOMBIA

PANAMA

COSTA
RICA

NICARAGUA

HONDURAS

BELIZE

EL
SALVADOR

GUATEMALA

PACIFIC OCEAN

N
W   E
S

**GREATER CARIBBEAN, CENTRAL AMERICA,
AND NORTHERN SOUTH AMERICA**

0   Miles   500

0   KM   500

CHAPTER 3

Dominica, El Salvador, and South America 1979–1983

A Packed, Dirty Petri Dish of a Country

After a year of working for USAID, Gersony finally departed Guatemala. In his early thirties still, he was already a somewhat unusual type: a business-oriented math brain with a non-ideological conservative streak, in a liberal Third World development environment. USAID brought him to Washington to brief the House Appropriations Committee on his philosophical approach to development and what he had accomplished in Guatemala. Gersony told the congressmen that USAID should stay in the business of directly managing projects, rather than going full-bore into giving money to relief charities to do the actual work, since it would keep USAID, or AID as it was known in Washington shorthand, operational, dedicated to fieldwork, and prevent it from becoming a mere agency of bureaucrats unwilling to take risks and responsibility. He also told them about what he had learned from Roland Bunch: that you have to listen to people on the ground who are most affected and stay in direct contact with the evidence. And you had to see individual people in the Third World "as vigorous and commonsensical in their opinions."

A member of the Appropriations Subcommittee on Foreign Operations was Ed Koch, a Democrat from New York City, who was about to run for mayor there. Koch, a strong supporter of human rights within the context of fighting the Cold War, wanted especially to hear what Gersony had to say about foreign aid. Koch was one of those great practical progressives who linked anti-communism, human rights, and fighting poverty at home with a wheeler-dealer approach to politics. Gersony fervently pitched Koch on a private, business-like approach to foreign aid. He explained how he had learned that many deaths in the Guatemalan earthquake had been caused by heavy roofs falling on people, so he advocated selling them the lamina roofs at a reduced price, and investing the excess aid money in creating jobs and fixing roads and water systems.

"Don't give away anything," Gersony advised Koch, in an echo of Franklin D. Roosevelt. "Make people pay and provide work for them." Koch, himself a straight shooter, appreciated Gersony's directness and clarity of mind.

Koch then asked Gersony what he thought of U.S. government foreign aid in general.

"Too much of it is a waste of money, since it is not integrated with a plan for governance or business development," Gersony said.

Koch smiled.

"The whole meeting was a classic Bob Gersony performance," said Charles Flynn, a Koch aide. "Blunt, passionate, well-argued, and against the grain."

After Koch was elected New York City mayor in November 1977, he put Gersony in charge of his anti-poverty program under Commissioner Haskell G. Ward. The various fiefdoms that made up the City's anti-poverty program, especially the Community Development Agency, were rife with corruption. "I feel like I'm in a sewer," Koch would say, whenever he was briefed on the subject. Koch called those who ran the fiefdoms "poverty pimps." At one point, Gersony and other staffers were threatened at knifepoint by local Hispanic activists angry at the mayor's office. Gersony spoke to them in Spanish to calm the situation, asking their help for the translation of certain words, in order to show respect, a trick he had taught himself in Guatemala. As neurotic as he was, he was the opposite of a coward.

Koch came to realize that he couldn't take on the whole Byzantine power structure of the poverty program and so much else in the city's government. Gersony, personally offended by the corruption, however, would not compromise with, or on behalf of, the mayor. "Again, it was a matter of Bob's absolute integrity," explains Flynn, who had joined Koch's mayoral staff. So Koch offered Gersony the more prestigious job of chairman of the Board of Estimate. The Board of Estimate, a body later declared unconstitutional, was where New York City's opaque, convoluted politics began to resemble the shadowy and interlocking arrangements of the Islamic Republic of Iran. The board had to approve every city contract over a certain amount of money. The mayor, the City Council, the comptroller, and the borough presidents were all represented on it. Thus, it was a perfect venue for backroom deals and blackmail. "It would have meant a lot of personal confrontations, which I dislike," Gersony says. "For example, the Brooklyn borough president, Howard Golden, was the rudest person I ever met. I just didn't feel I had the juice for the job. You had to be a real tough prick to run the Board of Estimate." Gersony turned it down.

His brief career interlude in city government was over. He hadn't yet learned how to suffer politicians and their deal-making—how to observe and analyze, but not always to condemn—often a necessity for getting things done. "New York City was the one part of the Third World where Bob Gersony failed," observes Ann Siegel wryly. For years afterward, according to Flynn, Mayor Koch would ask wistfully about Gersony, and what he was up to.

But having realized his limitations through the experience in New York City government, Gersony next called Fred Schieck and Ed Coy, Schieck's boss in Guatemala, for another assignment in the Third World, where the challenges were in their own way less daunting. Coy was now head of USAID operations throughout the Western Hemisphere. In September 1979, he sent Gersony as his representative to the island of Dominica in the eastern Caribbean, where Hurricane David, a devastating Category 5 storm, had just left three-quarters of Dominica's population of 75,000 homeless.

DOMINICA, THE WINDWARD ISLANDS, THE LESSER ANTILLES, 1979. Mountainous, hot, steamy, with tear-dripping humidity: lush with banana and grapefruit, some dark sand and rocky beaches, but without the white sand that attracts tourists, making Dominica back in the late 1970s different from many other places in the Caribbean; an island of earthern roads and picturesque, faded clapboard houses and shanties. There were political slogans on many a wall: "PJ Big Thief—Alliance Is the Answer," a reference to former prime minister Patrick John. It was a place debilitated by smallness. The get-up-and-go crowd had already emigrated. Colonized by both the French and the British, English is spoken alongside Creole French and a bevy of hinterland dialects, themselves the product of isolation within separate highland valleys.

"A Caribbean hurricane makes sounds like out of a horror movie," recalled Sally Shelton-Colby, the U.S. ambassador to Barbados and the eastern Caribbean at the time Gersony was dispatched there, and someone with many years of living experience in the region. The thirty-five-year-old ambassador, who would later marry the CIA director William Colby, combined an elegant mien with a strong, albeit somewhat self-dramatizing character and sense of adventure. Sally was a staunch Democrat, appointed by President Jimmy Carter, but she was also a firm anti-communist, the moderate Democrat equivalent to Fred Schieck on the Republican side. Indeed, almost every boss Gersony would interact with over the coming decade until the collapse of the Berlin Wall would embody that sturdy, moderate national security consensus that no longer exists: the casualty of the end of the Cold War's unifying tendency and failed interventions in the Middle East.

As soon as the hurricane hit, Sally tried to get to Dominica from Barbados to make a damage assessment. An admiral at the U.S. Naval Station in Roosevelt Roads on Puerto Rico picked her up in his official plane and they flew to Melville Hall, the small airport on the northeastern coast of Dominica. Melville Hall functioned as the only entry point by air into the island, and the drive to the capital of Roseau, on Dominica's southwestern coast, was long, treacherous, and mountainous. The hurricane had made the road impassable; nor was there electricity or water now on the island. The leaves on every tree had been hauled off. "Well man, me house mash down," many a local said in sonorous Caribbean English. Sally located a missionary with a small plane willing to fly from Melville Hall to Roseau, since the U.S. military plane had to turn back. Without any lights as night fell, Sally arranged for the cabinet members of the island government to line up their official cars with their bright lights on by a sugarcane field outside the capital, in order for the pilot to land on a dirt strip. At Melville Hall, the missionary started the engine but it died. He tried a few more times until it kicked into gear. "The plane rose at the last minute before it hit a mountain. That's just what you go through," she sighs. The Foreign Service is like that, she seemed to say: crazy risks that become routine, which the public rarely appreciates or even knows about. And it is no less so in the Caribbean or Central America, whose very proximity to the United States obscures their often dangerous wild-and-woolly aspect.

Now the hard stuff began: dealing with the new, thirty-six-year-old prime minister, Oliver James Seraphin, known as "Perry." As Sally explains, "I was worried that the relief supplies we would be sending to Dominica would go to Perry's supporters," strengthening his grip on power. This mattered, since "Perry was a bit too close to the Marxist rulers of Grenada," an island to the south of Dominica in the eastern Caribbean.

"Perry was young, handsome, charismatic, and well aware of it," Gersony recalls. "Perry wanted to let the Cubans in and follow Grenada's Marxist template. But he had a problem. He needed the $5 million that the U.S. Congress had immediately appropriated for hurricane relief, a lot of money back then, especially for a small island. The hurricane was that crucial external event that could reshape regional politics. Everyone was aware that the right-wing Nicaraguan junta of [Anastasio] Somoza fell from power that year because of a train of events that began with his inadequate response to the earthquakes of 1972."

Gersony, who arrived on the island shortly after Sally had done her assessment, began to meet with Perry and explain the approach to aid that he had developed in Guatemala. In those days, it was not unusual to have a USAID contractor—someone not even a regular employee—negotiate with a prime minister of a small country. Contractors did not have the negative association that they developed in the course of the Afghanistan and Iraq wars, when the word became synonymous with "mercenaries."

"Perry always agreed to see me. He had a sidekick, an oddball evangelical hustler who clearly was angling for influence, and didn't like my idea of promoting local credit unions to control the $5 million in aid money. Perry wanted the $5 million for himself to give away, so he would get the political credit for it. But that's not how AID worked. We needed accountability.

"Dominica," Gersony goes on, "was like a small experiment in a crystal ball. It was perfect for using the money to pay the peasants to do road repairs, and then allow them to buy the roofs, nails, hurricane straps, and other materials at low prices with the money they earned. I told Perry the villagers would be proud to buy the relief materials, rather than get handouts. He, his evangelical buddy, and I began to have real screaming matches. But Sally held firm. The ambassador doesn't give an inch, I thought."

Bob Gersony in Dominica in 1979.

"I simply trusted Bob. He was thoroughly knowledgeable and professional," Sally says.

The State Department inspector general and the General Accounting Office would later certify that none of the $5 million eventually given to the credit unions was lost or misplaced. Says Gersony: "If you empower people, they won't be corrupt. Through relief assistance we created a constituency that would later throw out a pro-Cuban populist. Humanitarian aid can be an incredibly powerful tool when done right."

Indeed, Perry Seraphin's downfall soon after was tied to his disagreement with Gersony. At first the prime minister threatened to end the project. Then his supporters, along with an army unit he had mobilized, looted the large warehouse where much of the roofing and other relief supplies were thought to be stored, and distributed them freely about the island. The problem was that only defective, rusted supplies were kept in that particular warehouse, and so it became a public embarrassment for the prime minister. It was a factor in his losing the election the following year to Eugenia Charles.

Whereas Perry Seraphin was prime minister of Dominica for only a year, Eugenia Charles, sixty-one at the time of her election, would remain in office for fifteen years. A student at the University of Toronto and the London School of Economics, her politics were center-right. She was a tough, formidable, don't-mess-with-me woman, who became known as the "Iron Lady of the Caribbean," though one U.S. official remarked that British prime minister Margaret Thatcher was "like a kitten" compared to Eugenia Charles. More crucially, Charles would provide President Ronald Reagan with the regional diplomatic cover he required for the 1983 invasion of Grenada and toppling of the Marxist regime there, which, in the imperfect universe of foreign affairs, was easily done with few adverse side effects unlike earlier interventions in Iran and Guatemala.[1]

So ended the Soviet and Cuban threat to the eastern Caribbean. American forces captured and deported from Grenada hundreds of Cubans, Soviets, East Germans, Libyans, Bulgarians, and North Koreans.[2] "Now we simply neglect the region," Sally Shelton-Colby laments. "Face it, our aid in the region was all about the Cold War. And some of these small, poor, and troubled islands might in the future be ripe for takeover by international criminal organizations," as transfer points for narcotics and other contraband.

Gersony's firm stand on relief assistance being accountable and empowering had been a factor in the chain of events that led to the end of the communist power play in the eastern Caribbean. But in the midst of it all he had a breakdown. His first emotional-physical crisis had occurred after being threatened by Lucas Garcia in Guatemala. This time, going back and forth between Barbados and Dominica, and back and forth on the awful mountainous road between Melville Hall and the capital of Roseau—working grueling hours seven days a week, always obsessed with logistics and implementation, always fighting with Perry Seraphin—he collapsed unconscious at the USAID mission office in Bridgetown, Barbados. Four days later he was back at work. Tony Jackson, who had followed him from Guatemala to Dominica, backstopped for him in the interim.

The overseas operations director worldwide for Oxfam, Michael Harris, who had himself visited Dominica following the hurricane, agreed to send Jackson there after Jackson told him he would be working for Gersony. "If anyone can do something about Dominica it's Bob Gersony," Harris told Jackson. Such was the thirty-four-year-old Gersony's reputation by now. But Gersony himself did not internalize this. His two physical breakdowns would set a pattern of overwork tied to insecurity. He couldn't relax without feeling guilty. And because of a sensitive stomach he would almost never drink alcohol, robbing him of another form of quiet release.

A few months later, two scientists at the Bureau of Mines and the U.S. Geological Survey, Brian Brady and William Spence, predicted that the Lima, Peru, region would experience major earthquakes during the summer of 1981, on June 28, August 10, and September 16. Predictions that specific were highly unusual and sent the real estate market in the Peruvian capital into a tailspin. Moreover, a certain USAID adviser, influenced by the doomsday spiritualist Elizabeth

Clare Prophet, decided that someone had to journey to Lima to prepare for the seismic events. The predictions would later be repudiated, but in the meantime USAID had sent Gersony to Lima.[3]

Gersony was in a bind. He knew the mission was useless—preposterous. And the U.S. Embassy people with their cold stares let him know that, too, in no uncertain terms. Adding to his depression, it rained constantly. During the months he was there, he would never even get to visit the famed Inca citadel of Machu Picchu.

"Lima was a mess. Because of a failed land reform program, millions of people had migrated into the outskirts, building 'young slum' towns called *pueblos jovenes*. It was an overwhelming urban nightmare. So never mind the earthquake predictions, I decided I was going to surprise everyone with a report that could be useful for any natural emergency in the future."

With his fluent Spanish, Gersony interviewed municipal officials in the electricity, water, and sewage departments, as well as plant managers and people in the foreign NGO community. He learned that areas of the inner-city slums were owned by the Catholic Church and that people had been killed in the past there by broken power lines that sparked fires. Again, he worked seven days a week, received an education in urban planning, and tried to get the city to install seismic monitors to shut off electricity in the event of an earthquake. The written result after many weeks in Lima was eighteen small volumes, a sector-by-sector analysis, about what Lima had to do to withstand earthquakes and floods.

Gersony was still in the very early stages of building a caseload of experiences rather than credentials that he could put on paper for a job interview. He was just very good—and getting better—at figuring out the truth of a local situation quickly, and developing a plan, within the boundaries of resource and other constraints, that promised to improve the lives of ordinary people—yet was tied to U.S. national interest during a global ideological struggle where every country was in some small sense strategic. He was fated to be essentially a freelancer whose experiences lay wholly outside the classroom and government and academic bureaucracies. He was the opposite of a careerist.

And what united these early forays in the Western Hemisphere was the various lessons he learned about how to deal with people in power, in his own government and in others, while helping the powerless.

One assignment quickly followed another . . .

EL SALVADOR. Flat, minuscule, the smallest country in Central America, yet with the region's highest population density—and full of hardworking and competitive Ladinos. "They're a hot people," Gersony recalls, "sparky, business-oriented, not fatalistic like the Mayans in Guatemala or the laid-back campesinos in Honduras": harsh generalizations to be sure, which at first helped him orient himself geographically and culturally, before he began to be immersed in the world of individuals, from where his solutions would always emerge. This was a big, small country with suffocating, fish-tank air, whose vast landscape of war and atrocity in the 1980s made it appear overwhelming. Between September 1980 and September 1981, according to the U.S. Embassy in San Salvador, there were almost seven thousand political murders, with most assumed to be the work of government forces, often trained by the U.S. military. Famously, in December 1981, the remote hamlet of El Mozote was completely exterminated in a series of massacres. The men were all blindfolded and killed, the women raped before being burned and murdered. Nor were the children spared. A "thicket of automatic weapons" brandished by several different security forces greets the visitor at airport immigration, writes the novelist and journalist Joan Didion, who visited the country the same year Gersony was there. Leaving the airport she observed a panorama of "underfed cattle and mongrel dogs and armored vehicles . . . fitted with reinforced steel and bulletproof Plexiglas." And everywhere the "clicking of metal on metal" and walls atop walls with barbed wire.

"Didion's description of civil-war-torn El Salvador is exactly what it was like," Gersony says. Beneath the carapace of Cold War Right and Left, there were no issues at stake really—only ambitions. El Salvador was the ultimate frontier, with Spanish colonial life mainly located in Guatemala to the north and Colombia and Panama to the south. Even the great Mesoamerican cultures barely got this far in their expansions. "There is a sense in which the place remains marked by the meanness and discontinuity of all frontier history," writes Didion, "by a certain frontier proximity to the cultural zero."[4]

Gersony arrived in the capital of San Salvador in December 1981. San Salvador back then was vanilla, antiseptic, with modern residential areas and a sense of security that vanished the moment you left the city. It was very pleasant and walkable—unlike steeply hilled Tegucigalpa, the Honduran capital, or congested, smog-bound Guatemala City. You could actually stroll the streets of San Salvador at night in the midst of a dirty war.

At the time in the country, there were hundreds of thousands of displaced people out of a population of under five million. The lines of battle were basically these. The Farabundo Martí National Liberation Front, or FMLN, were left-wing guerrillas sponsored by the Sandinistas in Nicaragua and facilitated by the Cubans. "But the causes of dissatisfaction were rooted in the social and economic conditions," Gersony explains, "and not invented out of nothing by the Nicaraguans or the Cubans."

The large wealthy families owned all of the prime real estate on the Pacific coast, with order enforced by a right-wing military, a number of whose units had been trained at the School of the Americas at Fort Benning, Georgia. Traveling north from the coast toward Honduras, the land became poorer. The left-wing guerrillas were in the north, and so were the migrants who journeyed to the Pacific coast to work in the cotton and sugar fields, and on the cattle ranches of the wealthy estates along the Pacific seaboard. As a response to a growing, anti-government, pro-socialist movement, organized around the FMLN, the ruling establishment set up death squads, which notoriously "stamped a white hand, or *Mano Blanca*," on the bodies of its victims and on their houses, Gersony remembers. The Salvadoran death squads "were vicious, efficient killers," he says.

Gersony put up at the Sheraton. This was after two American advisers and the Salvadoran head of the land redistribution agency had been slain by national guardsmen in the hotel coffee shop the previous January. Prior to the Sheraton killings there had been two other infamous murders carried out by right-wing death squads. In March 1980, Oscar Romero, the Roman Catholic archbishop of San Salvador—an indefatigable advocate for the poor, associated with liberation theology—was assassinated with a single bullet as he said mass in a small chapel. A month earlier Archbishop Romero had written to President Jimmy Carter asking him to end U.S. support for the Salvadoran military. A United Nations truth commission would later find that the murder was planned by officers organized by Roberto ("Bobbie") d'Aubuisson, a former army major and national right-wing political leader. Romero's killing was a factor in the rapid escalation of the civil war.[5]

Months afterward, on the night of December 2, 1980, three American nuns and a lay worker were kidnapped, raped, and executed, their bodies discovered along an isolated road the next day by peasants. Again the murderers were Salvadoran national guardsmen.[6]

It was Gersony's job to do an assessment for USAID and the U.S. Office of Foreign Disaster Assistance about what could be done to alleviate conditions for the hundreds of thousands of displaced persons from the war, whose numbers kept growing. It was unsafe to drive around, and so the offices of the defense attaché and the MILGROUP (Military Group) within the U.S. Embassy arranged for Gersony and two others to travel by helicopter, interviewing inhabitants at displaced persons camps. Helicopter travel was not altogether safe, as bullets whizzed a few feet away at low altitudes. Still, Gersony was able to get around the country.

The MILGROUP was at the heart of U.S. military assistance to the Salvadoran government, which turned out to be a great success or abject failure depending upon how you looked at it: geopolitically or morally. Those focused exclusively on human rights such as the late *New York Times* columnist Anthony Lewis would point out that $1 billion of the $5 billion the United States spent in El Salvador in the 1980s was for military aid, during a time when the Salvadoran armed forces killed 40,000 civilians.[7] Yet the MILGROUP's fifty-five Army Special Forces trainers, or Green Berets, arguably accomplished more than did 550,000 American troops in Vietnam: instructing the Salvadoran military on how to slow down a communist-inspired insurgency, even as it transformed itself from a 12,000-man, ill-disciplined constabulary force to a more professional 60,000-man army. Whereas in 1980, there were 610 murders per month, by 1987 the number was down to 23.[8] It was messy, thankless, and morally tainted. As in the case of Guatemala, El Salvador was simply too close to the United States for Washington to countenance the establishment of a pro-communist regime there, so it held its nose at the horror. The United States had already gotten deeply involved fighting wars for decades in Vietnam and Laos for the same reason, even though they were on the other side of the globe. This was the abject cruelty of the Cold War, which started in Europe and ended there, but which was fought in the developing world.

However, perhaps the ultimate reason why El Salvador was not "lost" had to do with the collapse of the Berlin Wall in 1989, which for a time robbed the Latin American Left of momentum, and was consequently a psychological boost to the Salvadoran Right.

Meanwhile, Gersony was in the middle of it all, merely trying to help people. Yet because he worked out of the U.S. Embassy, he understood just how rotten the predicament American diplomats found themselves in was: another Cold War case of legitimate interests colliding head-on with legitimate humanitarian concerns.

"We discovered that as the war got worse, everyone was on the move to the next safest settlement, leapfrogging from farms to villages, to towns, to the departmental capitals which the army could protect. Rural areas were under the protection of the guerrillas. But with so many on the move," Gersony explains, "and squeezed into the camps, there was no thought about sewage, electricity, inoculations. There was no clean water, no place to crap. It was a packed, dirty, petri dish of a country. You couldn't grow subsistence food. The economic crisis had devalued wages. The camps were filled with young men just wandering around. It was a formula for crime, chaos, and continued guerrilla war."

What could he do?

"Dignity of work was always important to me," he says. "I had created thousands of jobs in linguistics and rebuilding in Guatemala, and perfected a system in Dominica. I had admired [Franklin] Roosevelt's WPA," the Works Progress Administration, which had employed unskilled laborers during the Great Depression. "But when I got to El Salvador it was all food handouts, with the army getting the first cut. So there was little cash employment. With no jobs, the towns were hotbeds of resentment, ready for even more violence. There is nothing more destabilizing and politically dangerous than people—otherwise used to work—doing nothing. They were easy to pull into right-wing death squads; or into left-wing guerrilla units."

Gersony saw the beautifully rounded stones in the rivers, and yet saw how people were walking in mud up to their ankles. The solution became clear: employ people to lay cobblestone streets, for one thing. "I always insisted on paying a practical wage; after all, farmers have to be able to pay people to harvest their fields. If you pay too much, the more likely that jobs will go to cronies—because unemployment is so rife in these countries, big shots always want their friends and friends' kids to get the good jobs. I did market surveys, with the idea that we should always want to be the employer of last resort. If nobody wanted to work for us, it meant that we were not needed in the first place."

He recommended a massive cash employment program for the displaced heads of households. "No more food handouts. They will build latrines, sewage canals, storm water drainage—and cobblestone streets. It was a lot cheaper than road paving." USAID put twenty thousand Salvadorans to work for several years, all because of Gersony's idea. The cobblestone streets are there to this day. Every payday, displaced people bought food from local vendors. As in Guatemala and Dominica, the economic theme was using markets as a tool to alleviate suffering. Again, the use of credit unions and cooperatives at the local level, through which the program ran, meant that there was little or no corruption. The credit unions had been established by the Catholic Church in the 1950s and the Peace Corps worked through them. They were rustic frontier banks that were trusted. "I'm an opportunistic parasite," Gersony explains. "I have never been interested in starting something new," but rather in working through existing organizations in the private sector that had a track record.

"The guerrillas didn't attack us because it would have imperiled twenty thousand jobs and turned the population against them," he says. USAID pumped $100 million into the program over five years. It became the go-to project for visiting congressional delegations from Washington to see.

It was at this point that Gersony came up against the U.S. ambassador to El Salvador, Deane Hinton. Hinton was an old-time, scars-on-his-back, don't-fuck-with-me ambassador. He was a diplomat who knew how to be very undiplomatic: a human force field that concentrated on the application of personal pressure. He once said that the novels of V. S. Naipaul and Joseph Conrad would have prepared him better than all the briefings he got in Washington for his first ambassadorial post in Zaire, where he would later lock horns with its dictator, Mobutu Sese Seko, and be declared persona non grata. Hinton spoke Spanish badly with a high Montana twang, but he spoke it. He would be the first of a series of formidable—in some cases larger than life—ambassadors and foreign service officers that Gersony would encounter in the course of his career: the kind of powerful thinkers and operators (as opposed to ideological crusaders) who were, nevertheless, all Cold Warriors of the moderate Left and the moderate Right, and who, once again, barely exist anymore in the State Department. These men were powers in their own right. For the most part they were generalist troubleshooters who belonged to an earlier age, rather than area specialists.

In a somewhat sympathetic portrait in her book *Salvador,* Joan Didion, writing for the left-wing *New York Review of Books,* described Hinton as a force of nature who simply never got discouraged.[9]

In El Salvador, Hinton truly had a lot to contend with. As he himself writes in his diplomatic memoir, "Every day brought appalling reports of bodies, often mutilated, found here and there. Some killings seemed to be attributable to the left, but far more looked like victims of right wing 'death squads.'" He goes on to write about how with all the murders, especially those of the nuns, El Salvador had "echoes of our debacle in Vietnam," with highly critical media reports discouraging the morale of foreign service officers. The embassy felt genuinely caught in the middle between trying to prevent a Leftist, pro-Cuban takeover on one hand and dealing with a critical international media on the other.[10] Though the media often did get things right. Hinton's cables had downplayed the massacres at El Mozote, which required journalists, notably the *New Yorker*'s Mark Danner, to later expose.

America's hopes were pinned on Napoleón "Napo" Duarte, a passionate Christian Democrat and engineering graduate from the University of Notre Dame in Indiana, who had been elected president in 1972. But before he could take office, the oligarchic families intervened and he was imprisoned and tortured. International pressure saved his life and he went into exile in Venezuela, from where he returned to join the Salvadoran junta in 1980. In the March 1982 election for the Constituent Assembly, Duarte's Christian Democrats had won more votes than other parties, but had little chance of governing. The five rightist parties said that they had enough votes to form a coalition and that the new president would therefore be the death squad leader Bobbie d'Aubuisson.[11]

So Hinton went to work behind the scenes, subverting the local democratic process in order to install a more civilized government. A loser needed to be installed as the winner for the sake of a Cold War contingency, which in this case was also the right thing to do. "Publicly," Hinton writes, "I stressed the need for national unity to confront the Marxists. Privately I worked to convince the security forces

that d'Aubuisson would be the kiss of death for their hopes of continued American equipment, money, and support." Senior officers, not
wanting to lose tens of millions of dollars in military assistance—and
who preferred to be harassed by the Pentagon and State Department
rather than to have to take orders from d'Aubuisson, a young
ex-major—pressured the politicians to relent. As Hinton later told
Joan Didion in reference to d'Aubuisson, "We stopped that one on
the one-yard line."[12]

Hinton's logic prevailed: the Salvadoran right wing had no place
else to go except to America for help, so pressuring them to appoint
a less toxic guy as president was always destined to succeed. El Salvador was not a world of black-and-white moral absolutes.

It was in the midst of all these events that Gersony walked into
Hinton's office. "The ambassador had a huge face with little bits of
hair on his head. He was urbane and polite, and then would start
cursing like a truck driver. Everyone was afraid of him. He had a way
of cutting immediately to the bone of any issue."

Hinton approved Gersony's jobs program in an instant (though
years later it would be corrupted and undermined by Duarte's people). "But I wanted to stop the food aid," Gersony goes on. "It wasn't
needed anymore, and the Salvadoran army was siphoning some of it
off anyway. I had sold the AID guys on how I saw the situation. But
Hinton looked me in the face and just said, 'Don't fuck with food
aid!' That's basically all he said. He knew that food aid was the third
rail of development politics back in Washington, and therefore you
should never cut it off." When the ambassador was younger and
posted in Chile, he had sent a cable recommending a cut in the
PL 480 U.S. government food program, administered there by Catholic Relief Services. He got an immediate, angry reply from Washington telling him no, so he had learned his lesson. "But I was a
sanctimonious zealot," Gersony says, "a horse's ass. I got carried away
with my own beautiful arguments [on account of starting to become a
good briefer]. I argued with him and he just ended the conversation,
and never wanted to hear from me or the AID people again on this
matter. He was right. Guns, bullets, supplies, land reform, all were

more important in the larger scheme of things, regarding the destiny of El Salvador, than my little program. Hinton had lost patience with me. But as the years go on, I respect his example more and more."

Hinton would next be appointed the U.S. ambassador to Pakistan, another high-stakes, highly complex, thankless assignment, where, in addition to overseeing the aid mission to Afghan refugees, he would support the introduction of shoulder-fired Stinger missiles to the Afghan mujahideen, turning the tide of the war against the Soviets.

Gersony had in fact developed into a good briefer: honing deliberately flat language that counterintuitively enhanced the drama of a situation, as well as depoliticizing it and achieving objectivity. "I tried to take all the edge and emotion out of my written reports, and replace tendentiousness with boring words." Partly through Hinton's example, and the way in which he had failed in briefing him, Gersony gradually learned how to anticipate the questions of policymakers who had to focus on the larger strategic picture beyond development and human rights.

In April 1982, Gersony, having just returned to Washington from El Salvador, delivered a series of briefings on displaced persons there. At the second briefing, in the conference room of the State Department's Office of Foreign Disaster Assistance, Gene Dewey came and listened.

Arthur E. (Gene) Dewey was the deputy assistant secretary of state for the Bureau of Refugee Programs, a post he would hold throughout much of the Reagan administration. Later he would become a United Nations assistant secretary general for refugees; and then, under President George W. Bush, assistant secretary of state for population, refugees, and migration. Dewey was another moderate Republican internationalist like Fred Schieck; an Army officer for twenty-five years with two combat aviation assignments in Vietnam and degrees from both West Point and Princeton. In fact, Dewey was a classic, operationally minded soldier-diplomat in the imperial mode: an avid hunter with a flat, middle-American accent that lent him credibility, a participant in national prayer breakfasts who took

Presbyterian Bible study seriously. Honest, avuncular authority and clarity of expression emanated from him.

Concerning Bob Gersony, there was just something about him—and something about his briefing—that Gene Dewey immediately grasped, and so he invited him back to his office for a chat. When Gersony told him that he had served in Vietnam, Dewey liked him even more.

Dewey explained his logic to me: "I had always been frustrated by the FSO [Foreign Service Officer] reporting system. As a White House Fellow in 1968, I was assigned to AID. It was during the Biafran War, and so I decided to go to Nigeria to see the situation for myself. It fit with my military background, even though the FSOs didn't like the idea of a White House Fellow poking around on their turf. A report came in from the war zone requesting two hundred trucks. I was suspicious. But the FSOs told me that you don't argue with a humanitarian request. I investigated on my own and, with the help of a Swiss diplomat, discovered that we didn't need two hundred trucks.

Assistant Secretary of State Arthur E. ("Gene") Dewey, Gersony's most important mentor, negotiating with the king of Bhutan the return of Bhutanese refugees in Nepal, Thimphu, Bhutan, 2004.

What we needed was maintenance for the trucks already in the field. Nothing I saw in the State Department ever since convinced me that I was wrong about FSO reporting issues. Then Gersony showed up and delivered his briefing on El Salvador.

"I had already heard good things about Gersony's work in Guatemala in the 1970s and so was curious to meet him," Dewey continues. "He shocked me with his emotional intensity despite the low-key language he used. He spoke with a pen tied around his neck on a leather strap, his trademark. His briefing technique was laborious, analytical, and grounded in specifics. It was all based on what ordinary people had told him. He clearly had situational awareness—what the Foreign Service has always desperately needed.

"At the time I had a problem getting food aid up the Nile into eastern Sudan. I knew that enormous private barges of beer were having no issue coming north up the river, quite economically. So why couldn't the World Food Programme do that, rather than trucking vast distances? I asked Gersony if he would be willing to go to eastern Sudan to investigate."

Gersony said sure, he would go. As a former commodity trader and the son of one, he found the problem interesting. He was also ambitious to expand his reach beyond Latin America—which he feared he would never escape from, especially after a consulting assignment in Nepal fell through.

Gersony was starting to see men like Deane Hinton, Gene Dewey, and Fred Schieck as role models. They were authentic heartland Americans, almost exotic in their way, at least for someone from New York with a Jewish background. Such men were idealists at the end of the day, but the kind without any illusions about how the world actually operated.

But Dewey never called back. "I simply got diverted on other issues at the time," he tells me nonchalantly thirty-six years later.

So Gersony went back to the Latin America circuit.

Every once in a while, the Humboldt Current, which flows northward a few hundred miles off the western coast of South America, goes up a degree or two, connected as it is to the El Niño phenomenon, and sets off epic floods in some places and droughts in others. John Sanbrailo, the head of USAID in Lima, said, "This is a disaster of major proportions, but no one outside of here knows about it."[13] While waiting for Gene Dewey to call back about going up the Nile, Gersony spent 1983 in Ecuador, Peru, and Colombia dealing with these climate-induced catastrophes.

He first went to Ecuador, which is really two countries. There is the capital of Quito, at 9,350 feet elevation in the Andean mountains, cool though close to the equator, beautiful with clay-tiled roofs and with its indigenous population. Then there is much larger Guayaquil to the southwest: a steamy, unpleasant, all-business port city—a muggy, dirtier Houston—with volatile politics and suffering from a huge urban migration. The lowest part of Guayaquil, bordering the sea, is prone to tides and consequent floods. It was home to several hundred thousand people living in flood-prone slum conditions and called by the evocative name El Guasmo.

The Ecuadorian government decided to help by building all-weather roads in a grid pattern, raised a few feet above ground level, throughout El Guasmo. But this merely trapped the water and created quadrants of floating garbage and human feces. Gersony went to inspect and, working with the local corps of engineers, got U.S. funding of several hundred thousand dollars to install drainage pipes. At this point people were literally living in feces, and the sight of Americans from USAID working with Ecuadorians to solve both an immediate and a long-term problem in the heart of the nation's biggest city had its impact. Again, it was the Cold War, and Ecuador, like Peru, was an American client state. By now, Gersony had become USAID's go-to guy for Latin American disaster relief.

While in Guayaquil, Gersony got a call from USAID to head south just over the border to northern Peru, where there was a flood in the region of Piura. But AID first wanted him to fly all the way down to Lima, where he had been before, so he could travel alongside Peruvian president Fernando Belaúnde to the afflicted area itself. Belaúnde was a long-standing and well-regarded, democratically elected leader, a moderate linchpin of American influence in South America. Outside of Perry Seraphin, the prime minister of a minuscule Caribbean island, Belaúnde would be the first foreign leader or high-ranking official of consequence that Gersony would brief in his budding career.

Rather than be impressed with himself, Gersony says: "My first reaction was, I hate this shit. They told me I would be the Peruvian president's adviser. But I knew nothing! Since neither of us had been to the flood region, neither of us would have any real information, and so I knew I would have nothing to brief him about during the trip back north from Lima. I'm terrible at small talk. I was now scheduled to get to Lima at midnight and had to be ready to leave the luxury hotel there at five A.M. the next day. Big shots just fuck up your schedule. As you would expect, I learned nothing from him. And I wasn't dressed right, one minute with a president, the next in the field," he said, still exasperated decades later.

After a brief tour of the flood area, the presidential airplane dropped Gersony off at an abandoned airstrip near Piura without a person in sight. Rather than surreal, it was in its own way a typical Third World experience. He waited in the rain, and waited some more, exhausted without having gotten much sleep the night before. Finally a car picked him up with a local official inside.

Piura was forty miles from the sea. The Pan-American Highway went through it. But like the other nearby roads, it was washed away. It was raining all the time, in a desert that could not absorb water. There were serious health problems, but no medicine. After he had been there several weeks the rain let up. Gersony sent a cable about the specific medical supplies that had to be flown in—generally basic stuff like aspirin, packed in thick, triple-sealed plastic, as he instructed. He authorized $100,000 to be spent to get a road open from the coast at Paita. He never did get the road open on a regular basis despite spending the money. "I learned from that experience to always listen to engineers on the scene. I was there on my own. I got this bug about opening the road. My isolation helped cause my faulty analysis. I was ashamed, sitting in my cheap hotel eating alone, with

bugs and locusts jumping into my soup, and the road still not open."
(As it would later turn out, however, the road project mostly succeeded.)

While he was out in northern Peru, in the spring of 1983, Gersony
was visited by an official from USAID's Office of Disaster Assistance,
Timothy Knight, a southerner and graduate of the University of
North Carolina at Chapel Hill. Knight would be struck dumb by Gersony's sheer energy, surviving in a land visited by all the plagues of
Egypt. This meant little to anyone at the time, but twelve years later
the Knight-Gersony connection would have momentous consequences for Bosnia in the wake of the Dayton Accords.

Gersony's cable about his whole experience in northern Peru
made its way all the way up the bureaucratic chain to M. Peter
McPherson, the administrator of USAID under President Reagan,
and a former Peace Corps volunteer himself.

At this time Congress was in one of its periodic struggles with
Syria over events in Lebanon and the Arab-Israeli dispute. Congress
had recently deobligated $90 million in USAID money for Syria.
Mainly as a result of Gersony's cable, McPherson got the money
transferred to El Niño reconstruction in Latin America. In Lima, Sanbrailo wanted the reconstruction money handled by a Washington
"Beltway Bandit" firm, the kind that feeds off government contracts.
Gersony argued against it. He had learned about Beltway Bandits in
Guatemala. They usually had high overheads while relying on just a
few people for help and information on the ground. Gersony convinced Sanbrailo to hire him instead, and he would recruit aid workers by taking out advertisements in *The Economist* and *The Wall Street
Journal*. They got hundreds of applicants and were thus able to find
the dozen highly qualified people that they needed.

Gersony, feeling himself on a treadmill doing small-time stuff,
unable to advance, headed next to Popayán, Colombia. This was the
summer of 1983 and the whitewashed colonial city in the southwest
of the country, established by conquistadors in the mid-sixteenth
century, had suffered a devastating earthquake some months earlier,
on March 31. The Canadian government had asked him to do an as-

sessment. It wanted to send a thousand prefabricated houses to Popayán, but at much higher cost than the original housing, from a company with connections to the Colombian authorities. Gersony saw that the idea was a "loser." Here, too, he drew on his Guatemala experience. The prefabs were so expensive and yet not sufficiently sturdy. In addition there were cultural issues to consider, given the architectural dignity of the historic city. So he recommended against the idea.

When Gersony returned from Popayán, Fred Schieck asked him to go to Bolivia. Schieck was concerned about how drought relief there was being handled. In the extreme highlands near the capital of La Paz, with its population clad in sombreros and colorful Indian ponchos, half the llama herd had died. Farmers and herders were suffering most, while the tin miners and others in local industry were not affected. The United States had sent 85,000 tons of food aid. But Schieck was worried. "He had an intuition," Gersony says.

The man in charge of the relief effort at the U.S. Embassy in La Paz was near retirement age. He was topped off, had not advanced in his career, and to Gersony appeared resentful. But there was an assistant program officer for USAID there, Bill Garvelink, who seemed sharp, sardonic, and politically savvy, and who had experience as a staffer for the House Foreign Affairs Committee. Garvelink had just joined the Foreign Service and this was his first overseas assignment. He would go on to direct major disaster and humanitarian assistance missions around the world, and become ambassador to the Democratic Republic of the Congo. On the Iraqi-Turkish border, in the aftermath of the First Gulf War, Garvelink lost an eye when his retina detached and he could not get help in time. In 1983, Gersony had such a good feeling about young Garvelink that he asked him to go along on the assessment tour of the Bolivian highlands. It would be one of the very few times Gersony traveled with anybody. Garvelink, in turn, credits his career success partly to what he learned by just watching Gersony operate.

The Bolivian Altiplano was high, flat desert, among the more desolate landscapes in the world, especially suitable for growing potatoes. The air was thin. There was mass suffering. El Niño, which had caused heavy rains and floods in Peru and Ecuador, had caused drought in this part of Bolivia. Gersony and Garvelink stayed in roadside pensions. These would rank as one-star hostels at best. There was often no heating, and Gersony and Garvelink had to use outhouses at night. Garvelink had never seen anyone like Gersony.

"Gersony was always leaning forward in the car's back seat, talking to the driver in his perfect, native Spanish. I've seen aid officials and ministers all over the world and they talk to each other and never to real people. Gersony would see a guy in a field with a cow, order the driver to stop, and go out to talk to the farmer. He had a manner, this way about him, of how to build rapport with people. 'How many animals do you have? Have you lost your crop?' He would talk for minutes on end with market women in crowded stalls. Most of all," Garvelink continues, "Gersony knew how to listen. He took his time with people. That was his real secret. He was always writing in notebooks, writing down everything, even people's messages he saw scrawled on the walls. He ended the day in midsentence and began the next morning in midsentence."

Garvelink and Gersony compiled mortality statistics on people and animals, tracked market prices of commodities, and followed the trail of relief supplies, especially food. Over a period of several weeks of research in the Altiplano they gradually discovered something appalling: that the only persons who could get food aid were those with government identification cards. But the farmers and herders affected by the drought didn't have them, while the tin miners and other people in the towns—who were not affected by the drought—did.

"Relief was not getting to the people who needed it," Garvelink states flatly. Gersony knew that the U.S. Embassy in La Paz was at fault. But rather than blame anybody, he recommended that the USAID office in the Bolivian capital create cash employment by building roads so the farmers and other victims could earn the money to buy food. And he thought that the project should involve local priests, who over his years in Latin America Gersony had learned to have a high respect for.

Meanwhile, USAID in Washington was having another debate about how to allocate the funds transferred from Syria to the South American countries hit by El Niño. Gersony recommended that most of the assistance go to Peru, where the damage was on a vaster scale than in Ecuador and Bolivia. This gave the embassy in La Paz another reason to distrust Gersony, who in the minds of the Bolivia-based Foreign Service officers was merely a troublesome contractor: one who had already found fault with their assistance program in the Altiplano.

But as soon as Gersony got back home to Washington from Bolivia, his mind still immersed in this bureaucratic infighting over assistance to Andean Latin America, the phone rang.

Gene Dewey was on the line. The significant part of Bob Gersony's life was finally about to begin.

BIG PLAYS

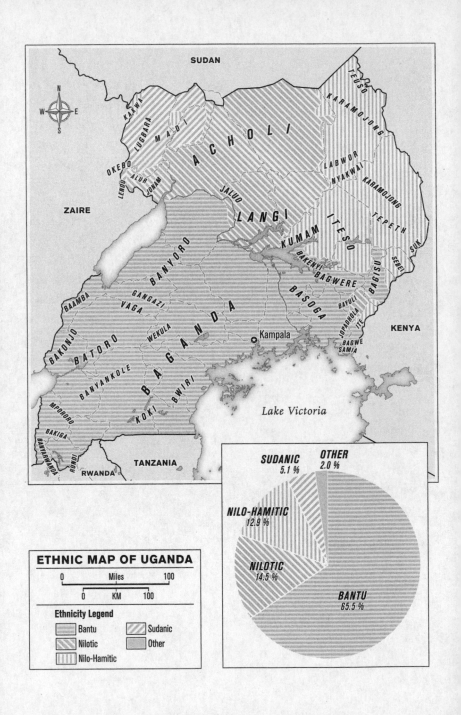

ETHNIC MAP OF UGANDA

Miles
0   100

KM
0   100

Ethnicity Legend

Bantu
Nilotic
Nilo-Hamitic
Sudanic
Other

SUDANIC
5.1 %

OTHER
2.0 %

NILO-HAMITIC
12.9 %

NILOTIC
14.5 %

BANTU
65.5 %

CHAPTER 4

Uganda, Luwero Triangle
1984

Hundreds of Stick People

C ome to the office. I have something for you," Gene Dewey said over the phone. "We have a gap in the embassy in Uganda. Would you like to be acting refugee coordinator there for six months?"

It was January 1984. Gersony was almost thirty-nine years old. "This was it," he thought. The door was finally open for him at the State Department. "My heart was pounding," he remembers. Moving from USAID to the Bureau of Refugee Programs meant moving inside a more politically prestigious realm—from a sister agency to Foggy Bottom itself. It also meant the chance to define himself beyond the Latin America circuit, where people spent their lives in obscurity. He wasn't becoming a careerist; he was just a bit bored, the way journalists become when they have covered the same story for too long. From Dewey's perspective—and that of the Foreign Service officers at the U.S. Embassy in the Ugandan capital of Kampala— Gersony was merely filling a routine assignment. There was no controversy, no drama.

Gersony's plane swept over Victoria Nyanza (Lake Victoria) into Entebbe airport on the northern shoreline of one of Africa's great lakes, the same airport where only seven and a half years earlier Israeli commandos had freed hostages from a plane hijacking in one of the most daring rescue raids in military history. The road from Entebbe, inland and north, to Kampala was lined with rustic snack bars and restaurants, and many auto and tire repair shops. Tire re-

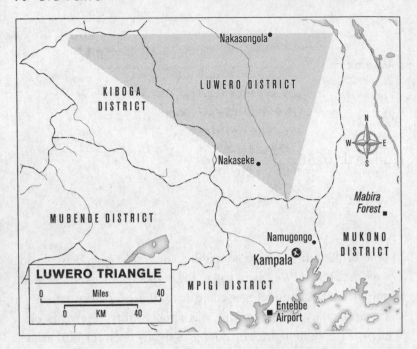

Nakasongola●

LUWERO DISTRICT

KIBOGA
DISTRICT

N
W ⊕ E
S

Nakaseke ●

Mabira
Forest ■

MUBENDE DISTRICT

Namugongo ●

MUKONO
DISTRICT

Kampala ✈

LUWERO TRIANGLE

0   Miles   40

0   KM   40

MPIGI DISTRICT

Entebbe ■
Airport

pair shops are ubiquitous throughout sub-Saharan Africa, like shoe
repair shops used to be in an earlier, industrial age America, an in-
dication of constructive frugality in the face of limited supplies and
the expense of always buying something new. There were also
mounds of garbage, shanties, and one-hut establishments that serviced truckers.

The residential areas of Kampala that he passed through were
leafy, vine-covered, manicured, with stately mansions featuring
wooden wraparound verandas. There was a quiet colonial ambience
to this garden city, with sidewalk restaurants open and crowds of
people drinking Tusker beer. Anglican and Roman Catholic cathedrals topped two hills. Police and soldiers were not much in evidence.
"No war, no problem," Gersony thought momentarily. The dramatically diaphanous sunlight was such a pleasure: "such a contrast to
grim and rainy Lima," he thought. This only contributed to his hopeful mood. He checked in at a modest, two-star hotel. In the weeks

and months ahead he would house-sit for various members of the embassy staff. It would take time, months, in fact, but Gersony would come to see Kampala to be as deceptive as San Salvador, in regard to what was happening in other areas of the country.

A self-starter, without the pedigree of having graduated from a good school and joining the Foreign Service almost as an entitlement, Gersony knew this posting was one of life's handful of pivotal opportunities that had to be utilized to the fullest. Anxious as he was to make a good impression, the U.S. Embassy became his life. He worked twelve-hour days, from eight A.M. to eight P.M. Whereas the British High Commission in this former colonial protectorate was a spacious, multistory palace with a large staff that consumed all of the oxygen in the diplomatic community, the U.S. Embassy was a simple, wooden barracks-style building, practically in the stables of the British High Commission, with only a few diplomats. Most of the offices faced a parking lot and a fence, on which ungainly Maribou storks would come to rest every late afternoon. But to Gersony it didn't matter, since for the first time in his career he had a big office with three desks and a safe.

The U.S. ambassador was Allen C. Davis, a courtly, smiling, unflappable Tennessean, who underneath his diffidence was absolutely passionate about human rights. In the Foreign Service of the 1980s still, you had to hide or at least moderate such emotion. Davis had joined the Navy from middle Tennessee in order to see the world, and had the steely nerves to land planes on aircraft carriers. He later graduated from Georgetown, and served in so many posts on different continents that his career constituted a world geography lesson.

The deputy chief of mission, or DCM (the number two person at the embassy), was John E. Bennett: balding and bullet-headed, somber, humorless, he measured every word he spoke, and often traveled around with a police radio scanner, an interest acquired from his father, who had mastered high-speed Morse code. Bennett, who had been a sergeant in U.S. Army Intelligence, was born in the far north of British Columbia, and had immigrated to the United States by way of Whitehorse in the Yukon territory to Nome, Alaska. The crisp exactitude of his voice, with the faint trace of a Canadian accent, spoke to his character. In fact, there was a stiff, formal sense of foreboding about Bennett. Yet he was one of the best, most thoughtful cable writers and editors in the business, and taught Gersony how to translate his talent for delivering good briefings to writing good cables.[1] He also taught Gersony about the Foreign Service culture in general. Bennett, like Ambassador Davis, was a quiet and committed humanitarian. As U.S. ambassador to Equatorial Guinea in the 1990s, he would often publicly rebuke by name the dictator Teodoro Obiang and all his associates for human rights abuses.[2]

Bennett and Davis both believed deeply in the Foreign Service as an institution, but they were willing to press at the edges to better defend American values. I encountered Bennett twice in my own reporting career: in Uganda not long after Gersony had left, and in Karachi, Pakistan, in 2000, where he was posted as U.S. consul general. On both occasions he delivered among the most tightly structured, detailed, and rigorous analytical seminars I ever got from an American diplomat. It is through such cables and briefings that the Foreign Service communicates internally. Bennett and Davis, spending their lives in tough postings as they did, registered in their very persons the understated greatness of the American Foreign Service during the Cold War decades, when reporting from the field and knowledge of culture and languages were the coins of the realm. Gersony was lucky indeed to have the opportunity to be mentored by them.

The USAID director was Irv Coker, tall and stately, superficially affable, who became one of the first African Americans to have risen so high in the organization. He inadvertently would change the course of Gersony's career.

Gersony found himself responsible for a country that, because of its weak borders and the tendency for war among its neighbors, was perennially plagued by refugees. On the map it was a rather small country, but with a vast terrain as far as refugees were concerned. And it was a highly complex country of many ethnic groups, as I will shortly explain—all with significant humanitarian implications, and poised on the brink of catastrophe.

Things did not begin well. Just after his arrival, still jet-lagged, Gersony was forced to put on his Brooks Brothers summer suit and go to a formal reception in the garden of the British High Commission. "I just hated those events," he says. "I was the perfect idiot. There was a man with an ill-fitting tweed jacket and rumpled manner resembling Elliott Gould. I called him by his first name in front of Davis and Bennett. He was the British high commissioner, Colin McLean, the most important foreigner in Uganda. I worried all that night that I had made a terrible first impression." As it turned out, neither Davis nor Bennett cared, especially after Gersony went to work in his usual obsessive way, starting with learning about the country's history and geography, which is where I came into the picture.

Uganda, which is the size of Great Britain, and whose arbitrary borders are the result of the 1884–1885 Berlin Conference of European powers, is, because of its numerous tribes, more like a loose association of many nations than like one. It is as culturally diverse as India, and was in the 1980s as politically fragmented as civil-war-torn Lebanon. "Tribalism isolates you and is part of your identity," Grace Ibingira, a former Ugandan cabinet minister and ambassador to the United Nations, told me in 1986 during my own visit to the country. Tribalism, as Ibingira and other Ugandans explained to me, is an amplified form of sectarian conflict, existing in places where people of different languages, traditions, features, and occupations live in physical, but not psychological, proximity. John Bennett, still the DCM in 1986, told me, "There are no horizontal linkages here—no unifying elements of history, ethnicity, or even religion. Nation-building can only start with particular groups and work upwards from the grassroots."[3]

Because civilization in Uganda was so far advanced prior to the arrival of the British, the colonial legacy was that much more controlling and therefore intense. In 1862, when John Hanning Speke became the first European to locate the source of the Nile at Ripon Falls on the northern shore of Lake Victoria (east of Entebbe), the area now known as Uganda already boasted several substantial Bantu kingdoms, each with its own army, law courts, administrative system, and unambiguous sense of identity. During the years of the protectorate, beginning in 1894, the British sharpened these divisions within the Bantu community by favoring the Baganda, whose kingdom was the most advanced, for posts in the colonial civil service. However, for the colonial army the British chose what in their minds were the tall, fine-featured Nilotic nomads from the north—Iteso, Langis, and Acholis—because they were considered by the British to be more warlike than the supposedly sedentary Bantus. Meanwhile, the activity of Catholic and Protestant missionaries from Europe led to religious cleavages accompanying the tribal ones. It was a shattered polity that emerged at independence in 1962, exactly a century after Speke's arrival.[4]

The Baganda soon deserted the coalition of Uganda's first prime minister, Apollo Milton Obote. Obote, a member of the Nilotic Langi tribe, was forced to rely more and more for support on his own kinsmen and the closely related Iteso and Acholis in the army. When his commander in chief, Idi Amin Dada, staged a coup in January 1971, one of Amin's first acts was to slaughter Langi, Iteso, and Acholi soldiers who had been loyal to Obote in their barracks. Bodies soon started floating down the Nile and turning up "by the hundreds" in the Mabira and Namanve forests.[5] Though a Nilotic northerner like Obote, Amin was a Muslim from the minor Kakwa tribe, which inhabits a sliver of territory on the other side of the Albert Nile bordering Zaire (Congo) and South Sudan, in the extreme northwest of Uganda. With a much narrower base of tribal support than his predecessor had, Amin turned out to be far more brutal in his tactics. Most of his soldiers were recruited from Sudan and Zaire, and the few indigenous Ugandan soldiers were Kakwas and others from the northwestern border region. For the Bantu especially, loyal to the memory of their great southern tribal kingdoms, and the most educated of

Uganda's peoples, it was as if their country had sustained another foreign invasion.

During his eight-year rule, from 1971 to 1979, until his clumsy attempt to annex part of Tanzania resulted in an invasion that deposed him, Idi Amin soaked this lush, sylvan country of 10 million with the blood of several hundred thousand people. Several hundred thousand more were made homeless. The suffering was widespread, but not completely indiscriminate. All Langis and Acholis were in danger. So was any Bantu with a house, car, or another possession that one of Amin's thugs might covet.

Amin expelled the South Asian business community in 1972 in humiliating fashion, decimating the nascent middle class and thus precipitating a steep economic decline from which Uganda had yet to recover by the time of Gersony's arrival. However, the basic machinery of state, including public services such as water and electricity, remained intact. To the outside world, Amin's physical bulk and buffoonery lent a bizarre, comic-book quality to his atrocities. The international press dubbed him Big Daddy, and in sub-Saharan Africa for a time he became "a sort of perverse folk hero," wrote the *Los Angeles Times* correspondent David Lamb.[6] Amin promoted himself to field marshal and was called Lord of All the Beasts of the Earth. (The Israelis humiliated him with their hostage rescue operation at Entebbe, carried out right under his nose, after he had colluded with Palestinian and Baader-Meinhof Gang hijackers.) Though, as Gersony's work would reveal to the outside world, even worse was to come after Amin, though there would no longer be a colorful madman to draw the world's attention to the slaughter.

Two ineffectual Ugandan exiles handpicked by the Tanzanian government, Yusufu Lule and Godfrey Binaisa, followed Amin in quick succession. Next came a military commission headed by Paulo Muwanga, a loyalist of former prime minister Milton Obote. Muwanga, by all accounts, rigged the December 1980 election that returned Obote to power. Bennett described Obote to me as "an amoral tactician without a strategy." From the moment of his return from exile, Obote played tribal politics to the fullest in order to hang on to power, but he never really got control of the army, which was disintegrating into a rampaging mob. The army reverted to the old British pattern of Iteso, Langis, and Acholis, which Obote had relied on at the end of his first, ill-fated attempt at governing Uganda. Amin's Kakwa soldiers deserted over the border to Sudan and Zaire, making cross-border forays against Obote's army in the West Nile region of Uganda's northwest. In mid-1981 came Ugandan army reprisals against the civilians of West Nile, including a June massacre of sixty people, among them women and children, at the Verona Fathers' Ombachi mission, sparking an exodus of 100,000 Kakwa, Madi, and Nubi tribesmen into Sudan and Zaire.

But the real challenge to Obote's rule would come not from the far-flung border region of West Nile, but from the traditional Baganda homeland just to the north of Kampala, in an area called the Luwero Triangle, a highly populated area more or less defined by two main roads: one leading straight north from Kampala and the other leading northwest out of the capital, forming two sides of a rough triangle between them. Here Yoweri Museveni, one of the losers in the disputed 1980 election that brought Obote back to power, set up the National Resistance Army, or NRA. Museveni was a radically different kind of Ugandan leader. Unlike Idi Amin and Milton Obote, he was a southern Bantu-speaker, of the Banyankole tribe. Whereas Amin was uneducated and Obote never finished college, Museveni had a degree from University College in Dar es Salaam, the Tanzanian capital, and had taught economics. Also, having led a guerrilla struggle against Amin in the 1970s, Museveni had political and military experience that the former transition leaders, Lule and Binaisa—both highly educated men—had not had. But what really distinguished Museveni from almost every other political personality in postcolonial Uganda's history was ideology—the fact that he had one. He spoke persistently and with conviction about democratic rights, the dignity of women, and the triumph of nationalism over tribalism. Consequently, he created an authentic *movement*.

Peasants soon began switching their allegiance to the NRA located inside the Luwero Triangle, as they fled government troops.

This was the situation at the beginning of 1984, when Gersony got down to business at his desk in the U.S. Embassy as the acting refugee coordinator. Whereas the military situation in the Luwero Triangle was producing internally displaced persons, the purview of USAID and Irv Coker, Gersony's marching orders were to pay attention to Uganda's outlying regions, where movements across international borders had produced refugees. Though travel was not required of his job, he immediately decided to make an extended, three-pronged tour of the country's borders. "Nobody sent me out [of Kampala]. I sent myself out." He got nothing but encouragement from Ambassador Davis and John Bennett.

Gersony secured a four-wheel-drive vehicle with air conditioning and every spare part imaginable. Gersony, early on in his African forays, would always insist on three spare tires, chains or winches, a toolkit, and so forth. The driver, Joseph, wore a white shirt and tie, a bit out of place given where they were headed. Joseph would be the first of many embassy drivers—Foreign Service Nationals—that Gersony would work with in the course of his career: all, without exception, were highly skilled, dedicated, and utterly essential to Gersony's work, and most were quite brave.

The two traveled first to the Mbarara region of southwestern Uganda, near the borders of Rwanda and Tanzania. The area had been in turmoil since the autumn of 1982. Obote's minister of state for security, Chris Rwakasisi, himself from Mbarara, had wanted the Banyarwanda to get the hell out of Uganda. The Banyarwanda were Rwandans from over the border who had settled in Uganda twenty years earlier because of tribal disturbances in their own country. These refugees were mainly though not exclusively Tutsis, with a reputation for being a smart and dynamic commercial people, who took up territory with their cattle. Hatred of them was widespread. While Gersony was preparing for the trip in Kampala, one Ugandan told him: "I long for the day when there are no more straight-noses" in Uganda, a reference to the Rwandan refugees.[7] Moreover, the Tutsi Banyarwanda were cousins of the Banyankole, rebel leader Yoweri Museveni's people—another reason why Rwakasisi wanted to get rid of them.

About fifteen months before Gersony arrived, Rwakasisi had organized a "chasing" of the Banyarwanda. It was a low-calorie version of Kristallnacht, in which troops and local sympathizers beat up and terrorized the Banyarwanda and chased them back over the border and into two refugee camps, Oruchinga and Nakivale, just north of the Rwandan and Tanzanian frontiers. But the Tutsi Banyarwanda had started filtering back from Rwanda and in December 1983, a few weeks before Gersony got there, Rwakasisi repeated the process all over again.

Gersony interviewed the refugees and NGO workers in both refugee camps, and in the towns. The atmosphere in this red laterite landscape was hot, dusty, and tense, but stable for the moment. People, especially those working for the foreign NGOs in the area, seemed especially pleased that someone from the U.S. Embassy had actually driven this far out and had the time to listen to them. Gersony was all eyes and ears. He knew what he didn't know, meaning that while his fluency in Spanish and years spent living in Latin America had made him a regional specialist, he knew little about Africa and used this and future trips as an excuse to build up knowledge. "These people were poorer and had a lower educational level than in Latin America, but they were lovely, nevertheless, and I was glad to be there." In Africa he began the lifelong habit of eating once a day, often alone in a cheap hotel room, a pattern he had picked up on his own, since the fewer people who saw him in public—and poking around—the less suspicion he would draw. Also, as I've said, he had a sensitive stomach. In this and other ways, he was not a natural traveler or explorer (quite the opposite, in fact), and so the less he ate, the less likely he was to become sick. A favorite snack became the small, delicious guinea bananas prevalent throughout much of sub-Saharan Africa.

The trip had its tense moments: at some of the dozens of road-blocks, late at night, he was forced to dismount at gunpoint from the car. Then there was the swarm of angry bees that chased him out of the bathroom of one seedy hotel.

He next went to the far-off West Nile region, Idi Amin's home turf, site of the Ombachi massacre, and drove along the borders with Zaire and Sudan at Uganda's extreme northwestern point, interviewing NGO staffers and Ugandan refugees who had returned from those countries. Again, it was dry, hot, and on edge, yet momentarily stable. Finally, he drove to the far-off northeast, by the border with Kenya. Here lived the Karamojong, cattle keepers and rustlers, who lived off the meat and milk of the cattle. It was said that they could ride under the belly of their beasts across the border where they stole from other herds, and were a constant source of tension between Uganda and Kenya. When Amin was toppled, his loyalists abandoned stores of weapons in the area, and the Karamojong thus acquired AK-47s, adding a sinister nature to their cross-border cattle raids. "I hated it there—*oh*, was it hot and remote!" Gersony whines, as if still there. "AID wanted the Karamojong to settle in farming communities—dumb idea, given their culture."

He was learning, and as a consequence sending cables, even though nothing much was going on at the time in these border regions. But he was quickly making an enemy of the feared Chris Rwakasisi, the minister of state for security, who hated some of the very groups Gersony was reporting on. Says Robert Houdek, at the time the political counselor at the U.S. Embassy in Nairobi, Kenya, who was starting to see copies of Gersony's cables: "I was so impressed with what Gersony had to say, and how well documented it was. But I was so afraid for him. Rwakasisi wanted him dead by now."

Gersony next decided to write what would become a bound, massively detailed sixty-seven-page report—like he had done in Lima—about everyone he met and interviewed during his forays, in order to leave a record behind for his successor, "so he or she wouldn't have to reinvent the wheel." The report included maps, tables, chronologies, and contact lists. After all, because of his six-month assignment, he knew he was only going to be in Kampala till midsummer, and no refugee coordinator at the U.S. Embassy had ever written such a thing before. Bennett, who was also anal and well organized, absolutely loved it.

Because May 31 was the deadline for submitting country human rights reports to Congress, Gersony wrote night and day, and sent off to Washington a half-inch-thick dossier about his Uganda travels only four months after he had arrived in country.

Now, after writing up three field trips, he felt he could relax and coast a bit—not that he knew how to relax. Nevertheless, he felt he had made his impression on his superiors.

But something intervened.

While Gersony had been rushing to complete his refugee reports, Obote killed about a hundred Christian pilgrims at the Martyrs Shrine in Namugongo, only ten miles north of Kampala, because he thought a priest had been collaborating with Museveni's National Resistance Army. The massacre got Ambassador Davis's attention.

Davis had recently been to Nakasongola, at the northeastern extremity of the Luwero Triangle, where he visited a displaced persons camp with three thousand people. But when Davis returned to the site several weeks later, there was not a soul left in the camp. What had happened to these people? he wondered. The ambassador suspected something bad, especially as the North Koreans were known to be advising Obote's troops on how to eliminate the peasants backing Museveni. Davis went to see Obote and Rwakasisi. They assured him that these people "all went home." Davis didn't believe that people would just go back to their villages in the midst of the war. Davis wanted an accounting, since the United States was providing Obote's government with aid. The ambassador made himself a pain in the neck to Obote. He refused to stop badgering the Ugandan leader about what had happened to the displaced persons in Nakasongola. Both Davis and Bennett saw Obote as someone who was very smart, but also under a great deal of pressure, because he was so in over his head with criminal types like Rwakasisi. Between Rwakasisi's own bloodthirstiness, the massacre at Namugongo, and the disappearance of thousands at Nakasongola, Davis knew he was in the midst of something awful.

Davis needed a thorough report about what was happening in the Luwero Triangle. But Irv Coker, the USAID director, whose job it technically was to handle internally displaced persons, was unavailable. So Davis went to Gersony and said, "You're just going to have to do it, and add it to the refugee report you did." Bennett interjected, "Sorry, Bob, that you got stuck with this."

On the advice of Bennett, Gersony went to see the Swiss troubleshooter in Uganda at the time, Pierre Gassmann, the local head of the ICRC, the International Committee of the Red Cross. Somewhat short and stocky and perfectly fluent in French, German, and English, like so many Swiss, Gassmann provided Gersony with the lay of the land. Gassmann was also passionate about human rights, but from a business and private-sector perspective. He and Gersony liked each other right away. Gassmann was practically the same age as Gersony, and had gotten his start in the ICRC in the Biafran war in the late 1960s and the Angolan war in the mid-1970s. Pierre smoked, was sophisticated in a very European way, yet was taken with this humble Jewish sufferer who was obsessed with human rights, and always wanted details and—later on in Uganda—numbers, and more numbers.

They became close friends, meeting every Sunday at the American Club in Kampala with its comforting extraterritoriality, where beside the swimming pool and tennis courts, over hamburgers, French fries, and Coca-Colas, Gassmann gave Gersony a long-running tutorial about Uganda and the rest of sub-Saharan Africa. One of the missions of the ICRC is tracing, and years later, after Gassmann became famous within the humanitarian community for his service in trouble spots like American-occupied Iraq,[8] he got the ICRC to trace the fate of Gersony's family in Nazi-occupied Latvia. Gassmann would fly to New York from Geneva to attend the funeral of Gersony's father in 1996. Today Gassmann and Gersony get together annually in New York to attend the Metropolitan Opera and

Bob Gersony with Pierre Gassmann, the Swiss relief expert, in the mid-1980s.

dine at the Russian Tea Room. Gassmann explains his lifelong friendship with Gersony this way:

"In the early years, I entertained the notion that Bob might be a kind of CIA guy. After all, he was always popping up in war zones with a slightly different affiliation, USAID, State Department, UNHCR [United Nations High Commissioner for Refugees], and the like. But as each assignment was completely humanitarian, and Bob remained so humble, he became a *real* person to me. I don't have many close friends. But Bob is just different."

Gassmann told Gersony that Obote was "tightening the screws" on the Luwero Triangle, especially at the choke point of Bombo Barracks, the only vehicular entrance to the area at its southern corner, fifteen miles north of Kampala, in order to extinguish popular support for Museveni's rebellion. There, an extensive torture facility had been set up, where soldiers applied hot plastic to the skin of the victims. There were documented stories of molten tire rubber dripped onto a victim's face from a burning tire suspended above, administered by East German– and North Korean–trained military police. In addition to the masses of skulls later found throughout the Luwero region, skeletons would be discovered of small children with their hands tied behind their backs.[9]

Ambassador Davis sent Gersony to see the papal pro-nuncio in Uganda, Karl-Josef Rauber. Rauber, from Nuremberg, Germany—who would go on to become a cardinal—was a modest, decent man with a soft, whispering voice. "We hear confessions," he told Gersony inside the Spanish-style nunciature in Kampala, with its painted tiles, paintings, and ornate desks. "So we know that a lot of bad things are going on. You've got to look at the situation, and if you need our help, come back to me." Obote's supporters were generally Anglicans from the northern tribes while the victims were the southern tribal Catholics, making Rauber especially concerned. Gersony knew that there were approximately 160,000 internal refugees or "displaced persons" in the Luwero Triangle who could be reached by aid workers. Those who could not be reached numbered 300,000. This was out of a total population in Luwero of three-quarters of a million. But though he nosed around in the diplomatic community, he had no way of getting inside the no-go zones. And he had never written a long report without visiting the affected area.

Then one day Bill Kirkham bounded into Davis's office, to check on what the Americans were up to. Kirkham, even by the standards of the mid-1980s, was a throwback, and a deep one at that: a white former British colonial officer, a big bear of a man, maybe six feet two inches tall, built like a marine with a loud voice, with an army visor cap over his short black hair, silver crowns pinned to his khaki uniform, khaki shorts, and high woolen socks, and with an erect military manner and brandishing a swagger stick. Kirkham, sixty-one, was a drinking buddy of Milton Obote and Chris Rwakasisi: he had been a deputy commissioner of prisons during the colonial era, and was now Obote's chief relief administrator. Kirkham vaguely reminded one of the infamous Bob Astles, or "Major Bob" as his friend Idi Amin used to call him. Astles, another former British colonial officer and veteran of the Indian Army, who became one of the most hated men in postcolonial Africa for advising Obote and then Amin—and financially prospering from the latter's misrule—was alleged to have been complicit with Amin's barbarous crimes. These were white men of empire who had gone native in the most extreme and most perverse way. Though Bill Kirkham would turn out somewhat different than Bob Astles.

"Kirkham is the key to everything going on in the Luwero Triangle," Gassmann had told Gersony. "Kirkham was a bit naïve," Gassmann now remembers, "but determined to make something out of the figurehead appointment that Obote had given him."

Davis formally introduced Kirkham to Gersony. Nothing much transpired. But on Kirkham's next visit, Kirkham suddenly asked, "Bob, how would you like to go along with me inside the Luwero Triangle?"

Gersony was dumbfounded and terrified at the same time. He had desperately wanted to visit the Luwero Triangle, but now that the opportunity had presented itself he was worried. He wondered about Kirkham's motive, since Kirkham had to know that as an embassy officer, he would have to cable back to Washington what he saw. Maybe Kirkham wanted the facts reported to the outside world. Maybe Kirkham thought that his friend Obote, famously immersed in alcohol, didn't himself know what was going on and was being manipulated by the Ugandan army. Gersony wasn't sure, and never would be. Neither would Pierre Gassmann, who also could not completely figure out Bill Kirkham. But the fact that Gersony was willing to go with Kirkham into the Luwero Triangle deeply impressed Gassmann. It was at this point that Gassmann began looking at Gersony as someone way out of the ordinary for a low-level American official.

The choke point and torture facility of Bombo Barracks was officially closed to foreigners and NGOs. No food or medical care was allowed into the Luwero Triangle. Kirkham drove up to the gate in his shiny beige four-wheel-drive Land Rover bearing a Ugandan presidential license plate, dressed in full military regalia. Gersony's stomach was in his mouth. Rough, disheveled soldiers surrounded the car, poking their rifle butts at it. They kept shouting. Kirkham sprung from the car, strutted forward with his swagger stick, full of braggadocio, like a character out of "Gunga Din."

"Do you know who I am?" Kirkham screamed at the soldiers. "Do you see this presidential license plate?" banging his swagger stick on it. The dressing-down continued. The soldiery was more like a mean, swaying, and explosive mob around the car. There was the smell of dust filtered by a blazing vertical sun. Gersony thought he had reached his end. The soldiers finally let the pair go through and on their way. Gersony's fear only intensified. The deeper you got into these places, the harder it was to get out, as if doors were closing behind you the further you went.

They drove on all day. Lone houses and little towns with shops began to appear. Everything was completely abandoned. *Nobody! Not a soul! In the middle of the day! Only stray dogs, many of them.* Two years later, on my own drive inside the Luwero Triangle, I saw a scrawled sign on a wall of a deserted hotel in the town of Nakeseke, where soldiers had been quartered: "A good Muganda is a dead one. Shoot to kill Muganda, signed the Soroti boys." (A Muganda is a single member of the Baganda group. Soroti is an area in the north inhabited by the Iteso, who helped form the backbone of Obote's army.[10]) After a while, Kirkham decided to leave the main road and go left off the tarmac. Another choke point with soldiers, another dressing-down by Kirkham, and then they continued on the bumpy dirt path. "What have I gotten myself into?" Gersony thought. More doors seemed to slam shut.

Suddenly they came upon a clearing, about the size of a soccer field, surrounded by thick vegetation, without any trees cut down or other signs that it had been prepared for something in advance.

They got out of the car.

"Laid out on the ground, in neat rows, were literally hundreds of stick people: emaciated, dying, their skeletons protruding through their skin almost, civilians of all ages and sexes, guarded by rough soldiers, angry and yelling at them," Gersony recalls.

"I began writing a cable in my head. I realized that my life might depend on me showing no emotion now." He did not dare to take notes, though he desperately wanted to. Looking around, his mind paralyzed for the moment, his next thought was "This is probably what happened to the three thousand displaced persons at Nakason-gola that Ambassador Davis couldn't get out of his mind."

Kirkham barked at the soldiers: "What's going on?"

"No food, no water, no medical care, nothing is allowed for these people," one soldier answered.

Kirkham and Gersony noticed two young girls, one with a leg severed above the knee and the other girl with a leg severed above the ankle.

"What happened?" Kirkham asked them. In a country of so many tribes with different tongues, many people spoke English. The girls explained that they had been gang-raped by soldiers, who afterward cut their legs off.

"How many other places are there like this?" Kirkham continued to bark at the soldiers.

They gave him a list. Kirkham's motive seemed more mysterious than ever.

Gersony: "At that moment I realized I was at a turning point in my life. I was seeing a concentration camp in this day and age, though one without barracks and barbwire. I understood, in a way I never could before, what had happened to my relatives."

Yet it was starting to get dark. Near the equator, night falls fast, since the sun does not spill across the curvature of the earth as it does the closer you get to the polar regions, causing dusk and dawn to linger. Gersony was scared. He knew he had momentous news. He just wanted to leave this place and get back to Kampala.

Suddenly Kirkham barked again to the soldiers: "We're evacuating these girls."

"Nobody leaves," a soldier responded.

A long argument ensued. "I would not have done that. I would have been a coward. I don't have that kind of courage," Gersony says. "I never saw an act of courage like Bill Kirkham arguing with those soldiers while night began to fall. I felt ashamed."

Kirkham put the two girls in the back of the Land Rover and they drove off.

They made it back to the tarmac. The sky was now yellow and blood red. A fifty-man Ugandan army unit was mustering out by the road.

"Attention. About face . . ."

Kirkham bounded out of the Land Rover, walked off the road, deeper into the base, leaving Gersony and the girls in the car. Gersony asked one of the officers, "What are your orders?"

"We are going to a village. Not a dog is to be left alive there."

"Carry on," Kirkham responded when he got back, stone-faced.

Gersony had real trouble interpreting Kirkham at this point. Was Kirkham acting the part of the Obote loyalist, while at the same time exposing to a U.S. Embassy official what was really happening in Uganda?

Later they found a shed held together by wooden sticks under a cloth, where someone sold them some guinea bananas, which they gave to the girls.

It was long past dark when they arrived back at Bombo Barracks with the girls. Again, the Land Rover was surrounded by soldiers. More shouting. Another dressing-down. Gersony couldn't swallow. Finally, they were allowed through, and soon were driving past the northern suburbs of Kampala. The adrenaline drained out of him, Gersony found himself suddenly overwhelmed with fatigue. After taking the girls to the hospital, Kirkham dropped Gersony off.

The next morning, Gersony met with Davis and Bennett and told them what had happened. Davis was alarmed, yet satisfied at the same time. "Bob, work with John to write a cable to the assistant secretary [of African affairs at the State Department]," Davis said. Bennett wrote the lead summary and streamlined phrases, but did not change a word of substance regarding what Gersony had written.

"Bob was a natural," Bennett remembers, "who could work the field and then put it all down for people in Washington. And he could type faster than any person I have ever encountered save Mrs. Kleka who taught me typing at the U.S. Army Intelligence School in the 1960s." Indeed, Gersony could move the keys so fast that he frequently beat the IBM golf ball. Davis signed off on Gersony's cable (which the CIA station chief had helped corroborate with his own sources). Like all State Department cables, it was officially sent to the secretary of state, but with "tags" indicating that it was really meant for African affairs, USAID, and the refugee and human rights bureaus, where the various assistant secretaries of state and deputy assistant secretaries of state would see it. State Department cables have four categories of importance: "routine," "priority," "immediate," and "flash," in order of ascending urgency. Flash meant a war or some such thing had broken out and those cables were rare. This cable was marked "immediate."

But days and more days went by and there was no response. Gersony was surprised. He had much to learn about how Washington and the State Department operated.

Meanwhile, Davis called one of his periodic meetings of the diplomatic and donor community, where he once again raised the issue regarding the mysterious fate of the three thousand people at Nakasongola, and the suspected atrocities in the Luwero Triangle. Neither he, nor Bennett, nor Gersony dared mention Gersony's trip and what he had seen, for fear of getting Bill Kirkham in trouble. In fact, Bill Kirkham's motives for taking Gersony with him on the trip became ever more of a mystery to them. The British high commissioner, Colin McLean, the Elliott Gould look-alike whom Gersony had mistakenly called by his first name at the garden party upon first arriving in Kampala, was in high dudgeon at the meeting, vigorously pointing out that there was no independent corroboration of anything amiss happening in the Luwero region. So the meeting ended inconclusively, with the Americans stuck because they were afraid to reveal everything that they knew. Many people in the diplomatic community were by now fed up with the British High Commission. McLean himself had been a district officer in Kenya during the colonial era, and in Uganda he was merely defending an African state that had once been Britain's own possession. *So the natives are restless, we've seen it all before* appeared to be his attitude.[11] "McLean was a nose-in-the-air type," Pierre Gassmann recalls. "He was always saying, 'In Uganda there is no alternative to Mr. Obote.'"

It was hard to act without Great Britain's approval in a place that had been part of the empire, of which there was still a mystique in 1984. There was an indefinable sense of deference still.

Now Gersony had to fly back to Washington for a scheduled consultation with Gene Dewey at the State Department's refugee bureau, at the halfway point in his six-month assignment.

Walking into Dewey's office, he explained that while the victims in the Luwero Triangle were displaced persons within Uganda—and not refugees from across an international border, which he had intended to focus on—he just felt he had to write the cable. Dewey had in fact liked the cable, told him to concentrate on the Luwero Triangle, and added that Gersony had his "complete executive support." Dewey told him to first brief State's Africa bureau.

The office director for East Africa, Richard Bogosian, was a Foreign Service lifer: heavyset, buttoned down, with tortoiseshell glasses. He seemed to like Gersony, but was worried about him: "Your cable gave me nightmares. But I need more information." He advised Gersony to write several more cables, about who the "bad guys" were, their biographies, who exactly was ordering the killing, and so on. Gersony was perplexed, still new to the State Department, and thus unsure whether Bogosian was simply being thorough or was stringing him along. Gersony was thinking constantly about the fact that the ICRC and the entire NGO and diplomatic communities were being for the most part excluded from even setting foot inside the Luwero Triangle.

Gersony next saw Ambassador James Bishop, a rail of a man with a goatee, who was a deputy assistant secretary of state for African affairs. It so happened that Uganda's Anglican archbishop, Yona Okoth, a northerner and friend of Obote, was coming to Washington and was scheduled to meet with Vice President George H. W. Bush. "Let's make a talking point for the vice president to raise in the meeting," Bishop offered. "The vice president will say, if the human rights violations in the Luwero Triangle do not stop, the United States reserved the right to do something." The meeting between Bush and Archbishop Okoth occurred on June 27, 1984. Bush told the archbishop that the "human rights situation in your country (army massacres, government failure to cooperate well in refugee relief/food distribution) is of great concern, as we've told your government."[12] Still, nothing happened. Nevertheless, Bishop would henceforth follow Gersony's career path through one African crisis after another. He recollects, "Gersony always did his homework in the most laborious manner, often taking his sponsors outside their comfort zone with unwelcome information."

Before flying back to Kampala, Roger Winter, an eminence grise in the Washington human rights field and an evangelical Christian who went to the same church as Gene Dewey, arranged for Gersony to brief the entire Washington NGO community. But still, nothing was generated. This was long before the days of blogs and social media when such a briefing could go viral. If the major newspapers and magazines were not aware of the story, it remained hidden.

Back in Kampala, Gersony went to work on the cables for Bogosian. The U.S. Embassy had no detailed biographies of the "bad guys" in Obote's circle. So Gersony went to Peter Penfold, the deputy British high commissioner. It turned out that the British had exhaustive biographies that they shared with Gersony. Gersony's cable, containing all manner of personal and salacious details of Obote's inner circle, had a blockbuster effect within the refugee and Africa bureaus, though it was essentially lifted from what the British already had for a long time in their files.

Also, soon after returning from Washington, at one of their Sunday lunches of hamburgers and French fries at the American Club in Kampala, Gersony asked Pierre Gassmann, the ICRC representative, how many people he thought had been killed in the Luwero Triangle. Gassmann ordered a survey of health experts, demographers, and

epidemiologists in Kampala and Geneva to extrapolate the population loss. He came up with a figure of 88,000 missing persons.

Gersony mused, only half-serious, "You need 100,000 to make it
into the PDB," the President's Daily Briefing prepared for President
Reagan each morning by the CIA. Gassmann said he would look
again into the matter and came up with "100,000 as an order of magnitude." Gersony dutifully reported this to Washington.[13]

Weeks went by uneventfully. One evening, after another late
night at the U.S. Embassy, Gersony drove back in his sedan to the
house where he was staying. As he left the parking lot, which was
adjacent to that of the British High Commission, another car flashed
on its headlights, gunned its engines, and began following close behind him. He could make out two African men in the other car. They
followed him into the business district. Gersony felt nervous. He
knew he possessed "guilty knowledge." He entered a roundabout and
circled the full 360 degrees twice. The other car followed him around
both times. It was a hot night with no breeze and he was sweating
profusely. Lots of people were at a popular outdoor café drinking
beer. He thought of parking by the café but lost his composure. He
had a clunky transmitter in his car, thanks to the advice of John Bennett. He radioed him what was happening. "Drive to my house immediately!" Bennett screamed back through the static. Gersony drove
to Bennett's house, shaking. The car behind him dropped off. Was he
merely being paranoid, or was it a deliberate attempt to scare him, or
monitor him?

Soon the time came for Gersony's last meeting of the diplomatic
community, before his assignment in Kampala was completed. Ambassador Davis asked him to sum up for the group "where we stand
on Luwero." Gersony mentioned the "order of magnitude of 100,000
missing people" that he had cabled to Washington, and said: "Government troops are going around on search and destroy missions
killing all the people they can find."

British High Commissioner McLean repeated that there was no
independent corroboration. Deputy High Commissioner Penfold
was more nuanced, but still backed up his boss. Again the Ameri-

cans remained silent, still afraid of compromising Bill Kirkham. As Gene Dewey would later tell me, the British were, in fact, aware of the "grave violations of international humanitarian law," but "desisted" in ever joining the United States in exposing or condemning the Obote regime, which the Foreign Office had to protect. Again, this was a time, less than a quarter century after the British Empire had ended in Uganda, when Great Britain still mattered in Africa. There remained a certain aura about it, especially in the Thatcher years. Moreover, because Uganda was landlocked, it was not particularly strategic and thus Western allies like the British and Americans could afford to disagree about it.

The Italian ambassador spoke next, mentioning the telecommunications project his government was negotiating with Obote. The European Commission representative said he had no instructions from Brussels to act. Papal pro-nuncio Rauber, sitting as usual in the humble, hard-back chair rather than on one of the couches, said, "These are our brothers being killed in the Luwero Triangle. We must do something." The German ambassador congratulated Ambassador Davis for his persistence and said, "With our history, we cannot afford to close our eyes." Ambassador Davis, on behalf of everybody, then thanked Gersony for his work. British High Commissioner McLean with great politeness thanked Gersony, too.

"Davis and Bennett never flinched. They never took a word out of my cables," Gersony says.

Fourteen years later, upon his retirement, interviewed for his oral history, Ambassador Allen Davis said this for the official record:

"Obote very often saw the world through a drunken haze, he would absolutely become vehement and say [to me], 'There is nothing bad going on. There are people trying to bring down our government and who do not wish this country well. What you are saying is false.' But there was a young man sent in by the Department of State named Bob. He was a specialist on refugees and displaced people. He was the instrument by which we finally got what we thought were hard facts. And they were almost too difficult for us to accept—the numbers of people dying and wandering around. It was absolutely scandalous."[14]

Nevertheless, Gersony left Kampala as thousands and thousands of people were being killed, and nothing was being done.

On Gersony's way back to Washington, Gene Dewey had sent him to Geneva, Switzerland, to visit with the U.S. refugee programs office there.

Nothing would come of his meetings in Geneva, though, which included an expensive dinner in a private dining room of the Perle du Lac on the shores of Lake Leman with U.N. officials. It was the kind of social event Gersony hated.

Gersony was perplexed. He was both intimidated by these international bureaucrats and upset with them at the same time. They had all the credentials and social graces that he didn't have, and worked in a glittering environment that he could only envy. But what exactly did they do? It was sort of a mystery to him.

Gersony left Geneva and the alluring world of the international human rights elite with absolutely nothing accomplished.

He spent several days in his one-bedroom apartment off Central Park West in Manhattan, decorated with his Guatemalan cloths and bric-a-brac, rent controlled at the time, banging out a final cable that summarized all he knew about Uganda and the Luwero Triangle on a red IBM Selectric typewriter (with automatic white-out), highlighting the punch lines in pink. His girlfriend Ann Siegel was with him. "To watch him type for hours on end at such high speed was something incredible. It is an image I will never forget, as if he were physically acting out his frustrations," Ann says.

Gersony actually did not talk much about Uganda to Ann while in New York. Most of what she knew about Uganda she had learned from his letters in the field, which he would write in the lonely nights after long days at the embassy in Kampala, explaining to her in typed print about the Banyankole, the Banyarwanda, the Luwero Triangle, and so on, letters that could take weeks to arrive, with hers crossing his in the mail. "It was the 1980s, but before email it was like the nineteenth century," she says.

Gersony returned to Washington.

Dewey told him to brief everybody in the State Department he could find. This would turn out to be a key moment in a process in which the refugee bureau was elbowing its way into actual policy operations, which were normally reserved for the geographic, "line" bureaus like African affairs, Asian affairs, and so on. Gersony delivered about a dozen briefings: he got a lot of love and sympathy, but no action. What really frustrated him was that a representative from the human rights bureau never seemed to be present.

He was at another turning point. Only by disclosure to the media could he see a way to move the issue of systematic mass murder and torture at Bombo Barracks and the rest of the Luwero Triangle. Yet he was afraid of losing his job and his security clearance. He was a contractor who had been working laboriously over a decade to build a reputation and credibility. And if he leaked, Davis and Bennett would take all of the heat. All the credibility and trust he had built up with them would be lost. What he didn't know at the time was that Bennett never minded "soft leaks," so long as "they were accurate."

Gersony had a friend, Frank Method, ten years older than himself, from Wisconsin: a giant of a guy, with a black beard and decidedly left-wing views. He was a fervent Catholic, and had worked his way up from humble beginnings to be an education adviser for the Ford Foundation. Method was a rough, tough cream puff of a man. "I don't know what to do," Gersony told him.

"I'm going to help you," Method responded.

Method's friend and neighbor in the Washington, D.C., area of Mount Pleasant was Patrick Tyler, a *Washington Post* reporter who would later rise to become the chief correspondent of *The New York Times*. Method talked to Tyler, who told him that Gersony should expect a call from his *Washington Post* colleague Caryle Murphy.

Gersony was staying at the Howard Johnson Motor Lodge on Virginia Avenue across from the Watergate complex, where some of the famous burglars had kept watch, and which offered him cheap rates. (It is now a George Washington University dormitory.) One afternoon he sat in a restaurant booth there for two hours talking with Caryle Murphy. It was a typical situation. The reporter was enthusiastic for the information, the informant was terrified and measuring each word he uttered, unsure if he was throwing his life away every extra minute he spent with the reporter. Murphy, several decades later, doesn't remember many of the details of the meeting, except Gersony's "passion for the issue, and his kindness."

For that night and the one following, Gersony's bedsheets were soaked with sweat. He was shaking and his thoughts raced with anxiety. He rose from his bed in the Howard Johnson on August 3, 1984, with bags under his eyes, on the morning of his very last State Department briefing.

"Is there anyone here from the human rights bureau?" he asked before beginning his brief. He was angry that no one from the bureau had ever come. No one sitting at the main table in the room answered his question. Then a somewhat short, intense guy with a fierce expression and black hair in one of the chairs crammed against the wall raised his hand. "I'm Elliott Abrams, assistant secretary of state for human rights and humanitarian affairs. You have my bureau's attention."

So Gersony unloaded about West Nile, Mbarara, Karamoja, and finally the Luwero Triangle, aided by the maps that he always brought along with him: it was a briefing that Gersony had given innumerable times by now, and thus he delivered it without notes, having leeched out of it any emotion or trigger words. It was that much more powerful to merely describe the small concentration camp he and Bill Kirkham had come upon rather than to condemn it. Let the policymakers condemn it. He was like a reporter who merely described what he saw, since, to quote Graham Greene, "even an opinion is a kind of action."[15]

After he finished there was silence. Then Mark Edelman, the acting deputy administrator of USAID, a Reagan political appointee, said: "I don't see how we can have an assistance program in a country slaughtering its own people. Close the mission"—even though Obote was officially an ally.

A former embassy staffer in Uganda said: "Don't cut aid off to the whole country. Just cut it off in the Luwero Triangle."

An embarrassed silence. The whole point was that the NGO community was to a great extent already barred from the Luwero Triangle.

Edelman replied: "The issue is, we can't support a regime that murders its own people like this."

Then Elliott Abrams spoke: "Of course, Mark is right. Otherwise our human rights policy is meaningless."

When the meeting ended, Abrams went up to Gersony to compliment him on his briefing. Abrams vividly recalls the moment decades later:

"It was the first time I ever heard or saw Bob Gersony. I remember thinking: this is *new*. This is not an AID brief. It is not an embassy brief. This is different. It's firsthand. It is rare, shocking. You know, you're an assistant secretary of state. You get daily reports from the embassies, from AID, from the CIA, from the National Security Council staff. But none of them can often tell you what is really going on in a country, at ground level, to ordinary people. No one can explain what the hell is happening, what does it mean. That was the amazing thing about this briefing, and about all of Gersony's work for many years to come. He could always tell you what none of the agencies could. Bob would go on in his career to gain an extraordinary amount of access to high officials, even though he was always a mere contractor—for an offline bureau no less! Because what he had to tell people really was *new*."

Shortly after Abrams returned to his office, the phone rang on his desk. It was the *Washington Post* reporter Caryle Murphy, who asked him to comment on disturbing reports about the Luwero Triangle. Abrams opened up to her on the record with what he had learned from Gersony's brief.

That Sunday morning, August 5, 1984, back in Manhattan, Gersony got a call from a friend in Washington, who told him frantically to buy the big weekend edition of *The Washington Post*. There was a hole-in-the-wall newstand on Columbus Avenue, which later became part of a pizza joint. Gersony saw that it carried two copies of the Sunday *Washington Post*. Gersony bought one of them and in the middle of the street began reading. Murphy's piece was on the front page, under the fold. The headline read "New Ugandan Crackdown Said to Kill Thousands."

The article began:

> The Ugandan Army has killed or intentionally starved to death thousands of civilians in the past few months as part of what appears to be an officially sanctioned get-tough policy . . .
>
> The deaths, mostly of women and children . . . are part of a campaign in the African country that Ugandans and foreign observers say is worse than the atrocity-ridden eight-year rule of president Idi Amin.
>
> Elliott Abrams, assistant secretary of state . . . called the situation 'horrendous' . . . He said in a telephone interview Friday that he plans to talk about it in detail at a congressional hearing this week.

Murphy went on to write that "between 100,000 and 200,000 Ugandans have been killed in the past three years in one area of the country known as the Luwero Triangle." She quoted Roger Winter, director of the U.S. Committee for Refugees, whom Gersony had briefed at length, as saying that while Milton Obote lacked "the buffoonery and notoriety" of Idi Amin, " 'the number of people affected by these crazy, irrational killings are [*sic*] larger.' "[16]

Gersony read the article, still standing in the street, both exhilarated and terrified, though he became calmer as he finished reading, because his own name had not been mentioned. Abrams had taken the issue on as his own and accepted full public responsibility. In the apartment he showed it to Ann, who caught his excitement. But then his anxious mind again began racing. "I may have to pursue a new line of work if they trace it all back to my interview with Caryle Murphy. . . ." Once more, he didn't sleep that night.

Back at the State Department that Monday morning, though the Africa bureau was quite upset, Dewey was pleased and Abrams had no problem with the article. "Gersony, you mousetrapped me," Abrams said good-naturedly. Abrams believed that Gersony had arranged for the *Washington Post* reporter to call him after the briefing, even though Gersony hadn't even known Abrams's name until Abrams had announced himself there.

Days later NGOs like the ICRC and Save the Children were allowed greater access to the Luwero Triangle, and the killing slowed dramatically. Other media reports began to appear. Abrams gave an interview to the BBC, which, because of its Africa Service, broadcast all over the continent and naturally had a greater impact in Kampala than the *Washington Post* article. "I played this bizarre, outsized role on the issue largely thanks to Bob," Abrams recalls. A *New York Times* editorial said, "Five years after its liberation from the butchery of Idi Amin, Uganda is again a killing ground. In recent months more than 100,000 people have been massacred or starved, according to reports the State Department finds credible."[17] In another *New York Times* piece, correspondent Clifford May quoted a Ugandan opposition leader as saying that, whereas Amin "would pick and choose his targets," Obote killed "at random."[18]

The Africa bureau was somewhat upset with the human rights bureau because of the damage that the disclosures about the Luwero Triangle had on American-Ugandan bilateral relations. Secretary of State George Shultz called Abrams and Assistant Secretary of State for Africa Chester Crocker into his office in mid-August. To some extent, it was a typical case of national interests versus humanitarian values. But the Africa bureau's viewpoint was less cynical than it may appear: after the horrors of the Amin years, the bureau had been trying to strengthen Obote as a vehicle for normalization. And since Obote's crimes had only recently been exposed, the bureau had insufficient time to fully rethink its approach. After hearing Crocker out, Shultz turned to Abrams, who merely said that nobody was disputing the facts of the case, as more and more corroboration for Gersony's reporting had been coming in.[19] Shultz reportedly said he was going to side with Abrams on this issue. "It's the kind of people we Americans are."

Crocker was annoyed with his own staff for being behind the curve on the whole Luwero Triangle human rights issue. A line bureau assistant secretary like himself depends on his information from his deputy assistant secretaries and his geographic region directors. Crocker now reflects: "I said to them, 'Why am I reading about this ex post facto in *The Washington Post*? Do I have to ask you for news when it is bad? Or can you volunteer it?' I was unhappy about not being ahead of the story."

In early September, Crocker made a visit to Uganda to repair relations and to talk about wider African issues. He and Obote walked hand in hand, African style, through the presidential gardens in Kampala. Obote had Scotch whiskey on his breath, Crocker remembers. Crocker never backed off the State Department's now-official assessment of what had happened in the Luwero Triangle, which was mainly based on Gersony's cables. But the avalanche of exposés that had started with Caryle Murphy's *Washington Post* article had wounded Obote politically around the world, and helped provide the momentum for the coup d'état that ousted him in July 1985. The ethnic-Acholi general Tito Okello ruled for six months until he, in turn, was replaced by Yoweri Museveni and his National Resistance Army.

In the end, it was Obote's utter reliance on tribalism that undid him. Lacking any program or ideology, he ruled through a tense alliance of Iteso, Acholis, and his own Langis within the army. Okello's coup, meanwhile, had brought Ugandan tribalism to its logical extreme, with one tribe, the Acholis, now attempting to dominate the other thirty-nine. Anarchy prevailed in the capital as large numbers of non-Acholi troops deserted to Museveni's NRA.

Museveni's capture of Kampala on January 25, 1986, was the culmination of a protracted and disciplined military campaign that in terms of strategy came closer to the Maoist blueprint than any previous African guerrilla struggle. Analysts in Kampala told me when I was there a few months after Museveni's takeover that the NRA could have occupied the capital earlier, but Museveni kept postponing the invasion until support for him was so overwhelming that his rule became inevitable. This time there was no looting or misconduct in the capital, or even in the conquered Acholi areas of the north. Museveni would still be in power a third of a century later, ruling at first as an enlightened autocrat and later on as a less enlightened one. Tribalism in Uganda could not be denied, but neither did it have to constitute a fate.

The United States had a new ambassador in Kampala by the time Museveni came to power, Robert Houdek, who had become a fan of Gersony's cables while at the embassy in Nairobi. Houdek arrived in Kampala soon after Allen Davis had finished his tour, and when the Ugandan capital was in chaos, with Okello's troops deserting and Museveni's about to move into the city. John Bennett was still there as DCM, though, and was able to use his police "lunch-box-size" radio and scanner to pinpoint the movement of Museveni's advancing army.

As soon as Museveni arrived in Kampala, he summoned Houdek, British High Commissioner McLean, and a few other diplomats to meet with him while his NRA was restoring calm to the city. The meeting took place under a tree outside the Lukiko, the old Buganda parliament building. One of Museveni's *kadogos*—orphans of war who made up a part of his army—brought Fanta and other soft drinks on a tray. Houdek vividly remembers that when the boy opened one of the bottles, the contents sprayed all over him. They all laughed, and then Museveni addressed Houdek in a deep voice: "I want to thank your president, and especially your Mr. Elliott [Abrams], for putting the spotlight on what was happening in the Luwero Triangle."

Museveni next turned to the British high commissioner, saying: "And you, sir, were never even in the game."

A few days later, McLean was asked to leave Uganda.

Museveni took Houdek to Luwero. They saw a small compound surrounded by elephant grass, where vehicles had not been for a few months. In one room, on the wall, someone had written in blood with his fingertip: "God Save Me." Out back were an assemblage of skeletons still with some skin on them, like dried leather. The hands were tied together with wire and the skulls had been crushed by tire irons, which were still lying nearby.

Museveni would become a platform for America to project power in the region, signaling the final eclipse of British influence in East Africa. "And we had been in such awe of the High Commission," Gersony recalls. As in Dominica, which saw the rise of Eugenia Charles, partly because of Gersony's actions, Uganda also proved that an aggressive human rights policy could be a complement, rather than an impediment, to U.S. strategic goals. (Of course, Museveni over the decades would prove to be no angel. Just witness his nurturing of the career of Paul Kagame, the Rwandan president—a man with Hutu blood on his hands, in spite of being an efficient technocrat.[20] Nevertheless, we can still say that Museveni has proven to be a vast improvement over Amin and Obote.)

Dewey says Gersony's work in Uganda was a "tour de force" that "spoke truth to power, whatever the consequences." It was "Bob's first big play." There would be others, much bigger ones, years down the road, also in Africa.

But what about Bill Kirkham?

His exact motives will forever remain a mystery. One may speculate that he had gotten tired of Obote's alcoholic benders and the descent of the national army into a rampaging mob. So he had gone to the British High Commission with his complaints but had gotten little sympathy. Then he heard through his friend Pierre Gassmann about this younger guy at the American embassy who was on top of these matters, and thus decided to take Gersony inside the Luwero Triangle with him.

William Ernest Evans Kirkham was later awarded the CBE and MBE, Commander of the Order of the British Empire and Member of the Order of the British Empire. He retired to Cape Town, South

Africa, where he would die peacefully at ninety-one, surrounded by children, grandchildren, and great-grandchildren.

What did Gersony learn during this first Uganda episode of his life?

He learned that the business of the State Department is writing cables. Indeed, State was organized around the need to report from foreign countries. In this way, the Foreign Service worked in parallel with the great print-and-typewriter-age newspapers of the day. To be "productive" in the Foreign Service was a term of art: it meant specifically to be a good and prolific cable writer. And John Bennett had taught Gersony all he needed to know about this.

But Gersony also learned that the bureaucracy rarely moves on the basis of one cable, no matter how dramatic. George Kennan's "long telegram" written from Moscow in 1946 remains an exception that proves the rule. You had to mount a bureaucratic campaign to sell your cable, and sell it, and sell it again until a spark caught fire. That, in turn, meant finding allies and neutralizing opponents: Don't excite your bureaucratic enemies, leave them be and try to work around them. Only if there is no other choice should you confront them. And the best weapon for such a confrontation is an unassailable methodology.

Gersony knew now that he needed a better, more scientific way of collecting information, and of translating his experiences into reports that others would not—and could not—doubt or question. Here is where his accountant-slash-bookkeeper-slash-commodity-trader mind would lead him toward an interview and reporting process that, more than anything he had done up until this point, would come to define his life, and alter his personality even.

The learning curve would be gradual. It would begin in his next assignment in Thailand, ripen in Sudan and Chad, and reach maturity and culmination in Mozambique, henceforth becoming his signature specialty throughout the rest of his career. But it was Uganda that had given him the germ of an idea.

CHAPTER 5

South China Sea
1984–1985

"Write It All Up. I Want Cables!"

Gersony finished the Uganda business insecure because he had become attached to controversy inside the Africa bureau, and thus wasn't sure if he would be allowed to work on the continent again. With the embers of Uganda still hot, Gene Dewey called him into his office and said, "I'm sending you to Bangkok."

Dewey wanted a blueprint about how to stop the piracy against Vietnamese boat people in the greater South China Sea, particularly in the Gulf of Thailand. UNHCR and the rest of the aid community were working the problem, but not coming up with answers. People were still desperately fleeing from Vietnam by boat, a decade after the communist takeover of the South and the consequent reunification of the country. The refugees used little fishing schooners designed only to hug the coast, but were desperately sailing them onto the high seas toward international shipping lanes, with all of their life savings with them. Pirates, often Thai fishermen, were robbing the refugees of their small amounts of gold, jewelry, and cash, and abducting the young women to gang-rape and subsequently throw overboard. Then, they rammed the rickety schooners to pieces and the occupants mostly drowned. Sometimes the boats broke up by themselves, and most of the occupants would be lost, unless they could grab on to a log and drift in some incredible way to safety. According to UNHCR, as many as 400,000 would die at sea before the crisis was alleviated.

Thailand, overwhelmed for years with refugees from both Viet-

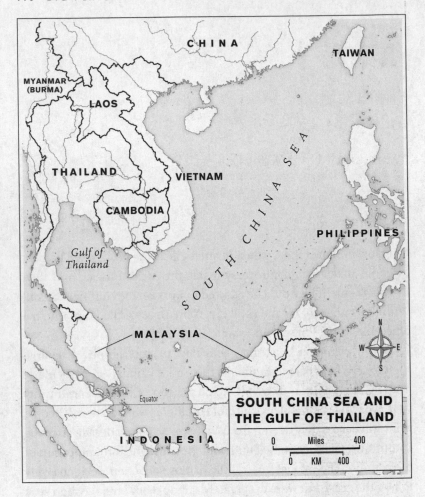

SOUTH CHINA SEA AND THE GULF OF THAILAND

nam and Khmer Rouge–controlled Kampuchea (Cambodia), was trying to discourage the boat people from coming there in the first place. In a policy of "humane deterrence," the Thai authorities insisted on detaining the seaborne refugees for a year in crowded camps to discourage more of them from coming. The international relief community in Geneva was abuzz with meetings that yielded nothing. Stephen Solarz, a Democratic congressman from New York, got the United States to appropriate $5 million to buy the Thai navy one coast guard cutter a year to find pirates. By the time Gersony met with Dewey, there were two Thai cutters operating in the South China Sea. The greater South China Sea, including the Gulf of Thailand, is 1.35 million square miles, fourteen times the size of all of the Great Lakes combined. "What are two cutters going to do? Are we out of our minds?" Gersony thought.

BANGKOK. Inert traffic under a thick and soupy gray sky. Motorcyclists and rickshaw drivers zipping between gridlocked traffic lanes. The city was a sprawling construction site with tinted-glass skyscrapers going up everywhere. Massive crowds swarming beside lines of street vendors; makeshift sidewalk eateries with their pungent odors beside antiseptic luxury establishments. The city was overpowering yet efficient, noisy but exceedingly polite. The Thais have a high social IQ, Gersony quickly figured out. They know how to please, whether they mean it or not. Everything is etiquette and custom. All the spicy smells were different from those of either Africa or Latin America. Gersony registered these sensations but wasn't particularly interested. His instinct was always the same: the truth and the answers were to be found in the field, beyond the capital city. So the quicker he could get out of Bangkok the better.

"I didn't go on any tours. I wasn't interested in temples or canals. I avoided dinners with people. I never see anything anywhere. I'm a workaholic." Whereas the State Department paid for five workdays a week, he worked seven and by now was negotiating for such. "He was one contractor who cost us a lot of money and this infuriated the green-eyeshade types in the office," Dewey remembers.

Gersony was a workaholic only because he was insecure. "I was nervous. Up until I was eighteen, my background in failure was quite extensive. I had no idea how to deal with the piracy problem. I could see no way out of it. Yet I was there not to report, but to solve. Solarz and the NGOs were all on Dewey's back. Who was I to come up with the answer?"

Of course, Dewey was already thinking of Gersony as an outside-the-box thinker, so he began to give him impossible assignments.

But before Gersony could get out of the capital and visit the refugee camps, he had to arrange permits and logistics for himself. So he was stuck in Bangkok for two weeks in the late summer of 1984. The first person he met was the refugee coordinator at the U.S. Embassy, Bill Stubbs. Stubbs, tall with a bushy brown mustache, was deceptively easygoing, appearing to give you all the time in the world, even as he had half a dozen people in his waiting room. After all, he had Cambodian refugees, Laotian refugees, and Vietnamese refugees, including boat people, all wallowing in massive internment camps in Thailand. Thailand at this moment in history, in the aftermath of the Vietnam War, the Khmer Rouge rampage in Cambodia, and the Vietnamese invasion of Cambodia, was hosting one of the world's largest refugee populations.

Stubbs took Gersony to see the Thai National Security Council director, Squadron Leader Prasong Soonsiri. Prasong was welcoming and hospitable, wearing a permanent, unreadable smile. He, too, was balancing this three-ring refugee circus against military, security, and domestic policy concerns, and was clearly under much pressure. Beyond gaining an appreciation for Thai sensitivities, after this meeting (and others) Gersony believed he still had no idea how to solve the problem, and never would. The members of the NGO community he met with in Bangkok were thankful for the new energy he was apparently bringing to the issue, but they had no substantial advice for him.

Finally Gersony flew from Bangkok to Songkhla, at the southern tip of Thailand, near the border with Malaysia, where he experienced a large and fenced-in refugee camp for the first time in his life. It shook him. At the moment, Gersony was in the company of his new host, the U.S. consul general in Songkhla, Franklin Pierce ("Pancho") Huddle, Jr., a constantly talking, whirling dervish of a man who was a linguist, National Geographic photographer, pianist, and windsurfer. ("Pancho" was the nickname for Franklin in Mexico, where his mother's family had lived for a time.) But Pancho also contained his fair share of cynicism. For Gersony was merely the most recent in a long line of consultants and NGOs who had come to Songkhla to work on the piracy issue.

For Gersony, emerging from his aesthetic seaside hotel, the Samila Beach, and the pleasant if nondescript U.S. Consulate—with the nearby blue water and lush vegetation making for a tourist paradise—the refugee camp was certainly a contrast: just dust, clay, and barbwire; nothing green, nothing growing. People were densely packed in prefabricated dwellings. It was an ugly place. "And what had the whole international community done for these people beyond demarches to Squadron Leader Prasong?" Gersony thought. Whenever someone said *Give the Thais another coast guard cutter,* Gersony crashed his hands against his head.

The first thing that came into his mind was that the occupants of this camp were survivors. So how did they survive? They had grabbed on to some flotsam and had then been picked up by Thai fishermen. As he would find out, rescues exceeded attacks. More Thai fishermen were rescuing these people than were stealing, raping, and killing them. This was something you rarely heard about in Bangkok, he thought.

He decided then and there that he wanted to speak to the refugees. He had done a bit of this in Guatemala and El Salvador. In setting up his language schools in Antigua he had learned that speaking to people one-on-one, isolated from everyone else except for perhaps a translator, was the most intense, coherent form of interpersonal communication. "I hate all types of meetings," he explains. "You don't get the truth in meetings like you do one-on-one. You never learn substance in a group since everyone is interrupting and performing for each other. People will not unburden themselves in front of others like they will before one neutral stranger." In other words, he had learned on his own what every good journalist instinctively knows. And because Washington runs on public events and meetings, he was coming to hate the entire Washington approach to learning about the world.

Gersony was at a turning point, though he didn't know it. He didn't yet know that what would come to define him over the next decade would be his desire not to talk (which would have made him more at home in Washington), but to listen.

So he interviewed more than twenty Vietnamese refugees one-on-one with a translator—though there was one woman who insisted on being present with her daughter, so it was a one-on-two interview. This woman and her two daughters were captured and gang-raped by pirates (Thai fishermen) for two weeks before being thrown into the sea, where they were able to grab on to logs and eventually be rescued by other Thai fishermen, some of whom sailed to Songkhla and others to Pulau Bidong on the other side of the border in Malaysia, where the woman's second daughter now was. Neither government would allow family reunification.

Gersony spent ten days at the refugee camp listening to such stories. He picked up some interesting details. The number of rescues was limited because survivors had to be fed and the fishermen, as well as incurring an extra expense, did not want to get diverted from their work. All the Thai fishing boats had identification numbers on their bows, which the refugees remembered. Yet there were rarely any arrests or prosecutions. Moreover, there were two kinds of pirates: a full-time, hard-core element and others who occasionally attacked Vietnamese boats that they just happened to come across.

The consul general, Pancho Huddle, was both impressed and mystified by Gersony. No previous consultant had hung around the camp this long, his head bent over, always writing in his notebook. But a notion was beginning to form in Gersony's mind. It occurred to him that the answer to the problem was not at sea, to be solved by the cutters, *but on land*—on the docks in places like Songkhla where the boats arrived and departed, and where the fishermen-turned-pirates congregated in bars and bragged about their exploits. That's where the intelligence was. He did not achieve this realization by sitting at a café table with a drink in hand and staring at the docks, the way it would happen in the movies. He actually didn't know when he got the idea. It was probably while furiously writing in his notebook while interviewing refugees. Gersony's mind was not particularly visual. His was more the mind of an abstract thinker—again, that of a commodity trader. His mind was at its most creative while he was writing down what people told him.

Gersony also knew that Refugee Programs was not a line bureau like the Asia or Africa or Latin America bureaus, that is, it was not operational: it was outside the chain of command and the policy decision-making hierarchy. So he couldn't do anything without the approval of the U.S. ambassador and the deputy chief of mission (DCM) at the embassy in Bangkok. Thailand at the time constituted the third-largest U.S. embassy in the world. Not only was Thailand the nerve center of refugee traffic, but it was a regional power in its own right, and a critical node to American influence in Southeast Asia during the Cold War and afterward. The embassy wasn't a building but a series of buildings with annexes. Thus, the ambassador and his DCM were not ordinary diplomats. They must be formidable characters, Gersony assumed, as well as the keys to unlocking the substantial influence of the State Department's Asia bureau.

So first he had to talk to Bill Stubbs, the refugee coordinator. He did not want to go to the ambassador and the DCM without a fully fleshed-out plan.

Gersony met with Stubbs. It turned out that the latter had a friend who was the head of the U.S. Drug Enforcement Administration (DEA) in Thailand. The DEA official who met with Gersony, courtesy of Stubbs, told him that he got information on drug shipments by paying informants at the docks.

"Can you recommend someone good?" Gersony asked.

"Matter of fact, I can. His name is Harold 'Tex' Lierly. Peace Corps veteran, speaks Thai, married to a woman who speaks basic Thai, and he now works for the DEA."

Gersony liked the combination. Peace Corps and DEA meant that Tex Lierly was both a humanitarian and a rugged law-enforcement type. Plus, he knew the local language and had gone native somewhat. All good things. Gersony next made a big ask of Bill Stubbs. Could he now have a full two hours of the busy refugee coordinator's time?

The plan that Gersony presented to Stubbs had four parts. Very briefly, this is what it entailed.

Part 1. Forget the coast guard cutters. "We're done patrolling the greater South China Sea. It has gotten us nowhere. It's the equivalent of claiming that we've done something, while in fact we've done nothing. It's the bureaucracy's way of just getting through the day."

Part 2. "We need *land* intelligence, informants and witnesses on the docks. We should forget about the part-time pirates of convenience. We will concentrate all of our efforts on the hard-core element, the ones who after their voyages get drunk and brag at the dockside bars. Survivors will need to be debriefed in the camps. The Thai Marine Police will need encouragement and assistance in this regard. A few prosecutions will change the whole atmosphere of the fishermen community. Tex Lierly or someone like him from the DEA running the whole operation from above will constitute the dynamic change factor. Call it external intervention."

Part 3. Start giving the Thais credit for all the rescues that their fishermen have done. "We're finished beating up on the Thais. By changing the public atmosphere, we'll get mission buy-in from the host country authorities." Show Squadron Leader Prasong some respect. Do something other than complain to him. Give him a two-for-one option. Tell him the United States will take in a certain amount of refugees: "I don't know, say 25,000. But for every refugee that Thai fishermen rescue we will allow into the United States an additional two refugees from Songkhla or the other camps." Yes, the Thais will play with the numbers. "So we'll give green cards to a few hundred more refugees. Big deal. We'll be helping to take the problem off the Thais' hands. It will change the atmosphere of the bilateral relationship and help the embassy's position here."

Part 4. Family reunifications within the refugee camp network in Thailand and Malaysia. "This is a no-brainer."

Stubbs liked the plan. He was tired of being the bad guy with Squadron Leader Prasong. He got Gersony in to brief the deputy chief of mission, whom Gersony had been avoiding. But finally he was ready. "This plan will sing," Gersony thought.

He was scheduled for forty-five minutes with the DCM. The meeting lasted twice as long.

"Come right in! I hear you're doing great work!" exclaimed the DCM, putting Gersony instantly at ease.

The DCM was rather tall, with a barrel chest and a large head. The office was big, airy, and full of neat stacks of paperwork. It communicated that nothing gets lost here. Nothing goes unread. There was a long couch and two easy chairs. Gersony had just met another legend in the Foreign Service, Charles W. Freeman, Jr., who insisted that everybody call him Chas.

Chas Freeman was a down-to-earth operator who made up his mind fast. He was also among the most brilliant diplomats ever to represent the United States, the one who in 1979 effectively created the refugee bureau within the State Department. His oral history reads like an intellectual feast, where he talks about, among so much else, the ascendancy and decline of the A.D. sixth century Byzantine general Belisarius and the nuances of the Saudi personality. (He later became ambassador to Saudi Arabia and his diplomatic cables would be considered the most insightful of the First Gulf War.) Chas's family tree in the United States goes back to both the Plymouth and Massachusetts Bay colonies in 1621. He was born in 1943 and grew up in the Bahamas. He took a double course load at Yale, where he read voluminously Russian, Spanish, and French history. He soon spoke

Charles ("Chas") Freeman (right), U.S. ambassador to Saudi Arabia, with Secretary of State James Baker III during the Gulf War crisis in 1991. Freeman provided critical help to Gersony in Thailand and Mozambique in the 1980s.

fluent Mandarin and Taiwanese, and translated for President Richard Nixon on his 1972 trip to China, as well as writing much of Nixon's and Henry Kissinger's China briefing books.

Someone like this doesn't lack confidence, and that's why he made up his mind so fast. After hearing about Gersony's plan from Stubbs earlier, he had made up his mind about Gersony before the contractor even walked into his office. In his oral history, Chas says about Gersony: "He's just a very indefatigable, wise investigator, who has a habit of getting to the root of problems and dissecting them in a way that facilitates designing a solution."[1]

Gersony hashed out the plan with Chas, including all the pros and cons, and told him about the refugees he had interviewed. The main worry Gersony had was that allowing the female survivors to testify against the perpetrators might raise the chances that the pirates would henceforth kill the girls rather than throwing them into the sea alive, where they might have a chance to survive. Gersony would later learn that this was a common generic worry of law enforcement;

yet, if you permitted crimes to continue merely out of fear of making the situation worse for some, you could never help the many more who were affected. The civilized world cannot afford to be paralyzed thus.

"Write it all up. I want cables!" Chas said. Chas thought at the time that at least here was one plan dealing with the piracy issues that would improve, rather than worsen, relations with the Thais, who had a tendency to take all confrontations personally. "Most consultants foul the nest; Gersony always left it in a better place," Chas Freeman explains. As it would turn out, Chas and Stubbs barely changed a word. It was then that Gersony knew he had the embassy behind him, and he once again thanked the gods for the mentorship of John Bennett in Uganda.

"See the ambassador," Chas said.

The DCM would certainly brief the ambassador of the plan ahead of Gersony's visit with him. It was to be little more than a courtesy call. However, the DCM knew that if Gersony could return to Washington able to say that he had met with the ambassador, it would improve the chances that the State Department and its Asia bureau would approve his plan.

Before his late morning meeting with the ambassador, Gersony had to take an antibiotic for the bronchitis he had caught from the refugees in southern Thailand. The instructions on the vial said only to ingest with food, otherwise nausea could develop. In his usual obsessive way, he took the pill before the meeting, assuming it would only be a courtesy call of a few minutes and then he could have lunch in the embassy cafeteria. It turned out the ambassador was late. When he finally greeted Gersony, Gersony was struck by the ambassador's dignified, gracious, and aristocratic bearing. "The ultimate WASP," Gersony thought. "I just wanted you to know that you've done a great job," the ambassador said in a crisp, lofty manner, intensifying Gersony's first impression. Gersony also espied all the beautiful oriental objects in the spacious office.

The ambassador, John Gunther Dean, was born a Jew in the German city of Breslau in Silesia in 1926, to a family that legally changed its name from Dienstfertig upon arrival in America. Educated at Harvard and the Sorbonne, he was fluent in English, French, German, and Danish. Dean would serve with distinction as an American diplomat throughout Asia and Africa. He opened the post in Togo, played a role in the Vietnam negotiations, and was the ambassador in Cambodia who was evacuated five days before the Khmer Rouge takeover; he was due to be ambassador to India after completing his Thai assignment. He was also the U.S. ambassador to Lebanon from 1978 to 1981, during the Israeli invasion. Smiling broadly, Chas Freeman says about this old-school ambassador, "John Gunther Dean was more than a dinosaur, he was a tyrannosaurus rex."

Dean had no doubts about Gersony, and with the pleasantries over, he asked Gersony where else he had worked. This would not be a five-minute courtesy call. When Gersony mentioned El Salvador, the ambassador asked, "How was my good friend Deane Hinton doing there?" It was at the moment when Gersony began to bring the Salvadoran death squad leader Bobbie d'Aubuisson into the conversation that he turned sweaty and pale, suddenly overtaken by nausea. Dean smiled, saw the problem, and pointed to the ambassador's private bathroom. Gersony returned after a few minutes and resumed the conversation. He had Dean's support for his anti-piracy plan.

His preliminary work done in Thailand, soon Gersony was back in Washington, where he briefed Dewey.

"See Wolfowitz. Give him the whole brief," Dewey said.

Paul Wolfowitz was then the assistant secretary of state for East Asian and Pacific affairs. He ran Asia for the State Department, in other words. He played a role in ousting Filipino dictator Ferdinand Marcos from power and would later become the U.S. ambassador to largely Muslim Indonesia, compiling an impressive career as an Asia hand, where he learned that societies like the Philippines and Indonesia, contrary to the predictions of realists and pessimists, could indeed evolve into functioning democracies. When he transferred that logic to Iraq, this belief would become his undoing. To Gersony at the beginning of 1985, Wolfowitz was practically an Elliott Abrams look-alike: another neoconservative Reagan political appointee, young, dark-haired, intense, highly intelligent, yet a bit more somber than Abrams, if still friendly. The appointment was originally scheduled for half an hour but Dewey got it extended to ninety minutes. Gersony needed the extra time.

"I'm not an executive summary kind of guy. I want my clients to know all the facts. Executive summaries are the bane of Washington," says Gersony. "They simplify a world that is in fact complex."

Wolfowitz was enthusiastic about everything Gersony told him. He was deeply engaged and kept asking questions throughout. What could go wrong? Gersony asked himself. He now had John Gunther Dean and Chas Freeman of the Foreign Service aristocracy and Paul Wolfowitz of the Reaganite neoconservative wing all on the same page. This was the Cold War when such divisions were muted compared to what would come afterward; it was a time when neoconservatives still had credibility. Gersony would soon get Elliott Abrams's support for the anti-piracy plan, too. "Bob was the first one who could explain to me what the term 'Thai piracy' meant in practice—what actually happened out at sea. Plus, he had a theory of the case, of what to do about it," explains Abrams.

But when Gersony brought up, in Wolfowitz's office, the two-for-one option in part 3 of his plan, which called for the United States to provide visas to two more boat people for every refugee that the Thais rescued, the Thai desk officer and the other Foreign Service officers in the room started coughing and turning cold.

"We can't really do that, Mr. Secretary."

"Why?" Wolfowitz asked.

"We'll explain later," they said, giving Gersony distant stares. Gersony was offended. He may not have been part of the Foreign Service brotherhood, but he did have top secret clearance. He could be trusted. But he did not complain. He could only propose a plan, but whether it was accepted in full as policy was another matter. He had had his fair hearing.

Dewey told Gersony to go ahead on part 2 of his plan: the dockside intelligence operation. Gersony was nervous. He had sold Tex

Lierly to everyone without so much as talking to him, or knowing where he was presently based. He located the DEA agent in Arizona near the Mexican border. Tex was pleasant enough and enthusiastic over the phone, but there was a problem. He was a GS-13, General Service-13, in the government bureaucracy rankings. If he took Gersony's assignment in Thailand, as prestigious as working for the State Department overseas would be, and as personally rewarding as it would be for him, he would be giving up his chance to be promoted to a GS-14. The difference in salary and benefits between the two rankings was very significant. Not to be promoted would undermine some of Tex's retirement plans.

Gersony discussed the problem with a friend at the refugee bureau, Alan Van Egmond, who said he could arrange a meeting between Gersony and DEA administrator Jack Lawn. The three of them met for lunch in Lawn's private dining room at the DEA. To Gersony such Washington connections were all miraculous. He never got used to it, or rather never took them for granted. Lawn, who was new in his job, heard Gersony out and said matter-of-factly that he would fix it. A few days later Tex Lierly was promoted to GS-14 and soon afterward stopped off in Washington before heading with his family to Thailand.

Tex came as advertised. He wore cowboy boots, had an easygoing manner, and was muscular in the way of a cop or a marine. "Made for the movies," Gersony thought. In his early forties, Tex Lierly was born in Morillton, Arkansas, but went to school at Texas A&M. Before going off to Peace Corps training in Hawaii, he bought himself a cowboy hat with boots to match. When his new Peace Corps friends met him all decked out, they christened him with the nickname. Tex was equally impressed with Gersony. "I could relate my Peace Corps experience and love of Thailand to him. He totally got it. Gersony was just full of so much enthusiasm. He was unique among government officials I met."

The impact of Gersony's plan was that no more coast guard cutters would be bought and family reunifications would happen immediately. The two-for-one visa option never did make it through the

State Department bureaucracy. But Tex's land-oriented intelligence operation, which he and Pancho Huddle worked out the details of, together with the Thai Marine Police, manifested dramatic results.

"What we did was low cost and down to earth," Tex recalls. "All our sources turned out to be land-based," just as Gersony suspected. Tex and Pancho Huddle marketed it as a Thai program, which further encouraged the Marine Police. "Tex worked patiently with the Thai Marines," Pancho remembers. "He had good people skills and was an exemplary guy."

They began by identifying the fleets of five to ten boats each of which regularly fished the territories where most of the attacks took place. They paid informants who were present at the docks and in the bars. At first they went after anyone they were suspicious of, but soon they were able to narrow the search down to the kingpins, usually the boat captains. The most effective sources were crew members of the pirate ships themselves, who were willing to accept payments for providing eyewitness information. This planted seeds of doubt in the minds of the ship captains, fearful that any member of their crews would rat on them if they attacked Vietnamese refugee schooners. With that the whole psychological climate changed.

For good measure, Tex, Pancho, and the Thai authorities ran a psy-ops, or psychological operations program. They developed a puppet show that made the rounds of the southern Thai villages where the fishermen generally came from. The show had the following themes: the basic immorality of piracy, and the facts that it was against the Buddhist religion and that piracy reflected badly on the Thais and Thailand as a nation.

By 1986 the number of those arrested reached fifty, as many as the four previous years put together. One convicted pirate received a death sentence by hanging, though it wasn't carried out.[2] By then the number of boats reporting attacks had dropped to 24 percent of the number of 1985, and in 1987 it had dropped to 7 percent. After a few years, the attacks virtually ceased.

Tex Lierly spent two and a half years in Bangkok and Songkhla working with the Thai Marine Police. They would be some of the best years of his family's life. His children learned to speak Thai and attended the international school in the capital. "Working on anti-piracy was like being back in the Peace Corps in the 1960s. I felt that I was doing good. I'm a romantic, I guess," he says. He is now retired from the DEA and living in Alamosa, Colorado, the front range of the Rocky Mountains.

CHAPTER 6

Sudan and Chad
1985

"Goran . . . Goran . . . Goran"

With the Luwero Triangle and South China Sea piracy under his belt, Bob Gersony was batting two for two with Gene Dewey at the State Department's Bureau of Refugee Programs, not to mention his previous successes in Latin America. Yet he would now have to prove himself again, since Dewey had another assignment for him. As a self-employed contractor, Gersony was only as good as his last performance.

Gersony would have to temporarily fill the slot of the refugee programs officer at the U.S. Embassy in Khartoum, Sudan. This was not a normal assignment like the one in Kampala, Uganda. In Khartoum, the previous refugee officer literally had to flee the country before finishing his tour. The circumstances are worth a long diversion from my narrative.

KHARTOUM, SUDAN. Dusty, sun-scorched, cratered, and disease-ridden at the confluence of the Blue and White Niles, a pattern of rectangles etched in sandpaper with a smell reminiscent of burning newsprint in the air: in the mid-1980s, this was an oversized village of people with dark complexions under flowing white robes. In the streets they moved like swans almost. Here Jerry Weaver, the U.S. Embassy's refugee coordinator before Gersony came in, filled out the missing parts of his personality. "I'm really a misfit who found my niche in a wide-open desert space among the Arabs," he told me

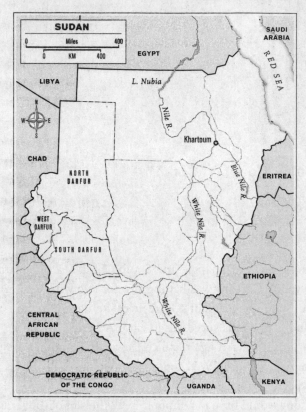

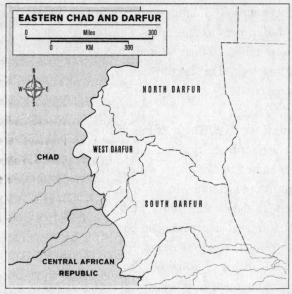

some years afterward at his farm in Newark, Ohio, where I stayed with him for several days in 1992.[1]

Weaver, born in 1939 into a working-class family, joined the Foreign Service when he was already forty and got posted to Khartoum. He was direct, rough-hewn, and lacking in the sophisticated graces on which the Foreign Service prides itself. Like Gersony, but for very different reasons, he was uncomfortable at diplomatic receptions. But put him in with a group of truck drivers, peasants, sleazy wheeler-dealers, or just about anyone other than upper-middle-class Westerners, and Jerry Weaver—a big, brawling former high school football player—showed unmatched social gifts. He never formally studied Arabic, but he picked it up, nevertheless. However imperfect his Arabic was, aided by his unaffected, outgoing personality, he could, to a significant extent, communicate. Weaver's social web in Khartoum soon began to include Greek ivory traders, Pakistani oil merchants, and all forms of smugglers: of people, as well as of goods. Weaver would begin to talk about how to fix rifle barrels or how to reload magnum shot in a spent cartridge shell, or what kind of fertilizer to use, and the Arabs would just sit there and listen.

Weaver had been at the Khartoum embassy for some time when a new ambassador arrived, Hume Horan, perhaps the greatest Arabic linguist in the State Department's history, who had spent his professional life serving in one Arab country after another. He was another Chas Freeman, the kind of intellect that has largely gone extinct in the electronic age. Horan, who was born in 1934 and died in 2004, and whom I knew well, was so cerebral that his eyes flickered about and drank light, focusing on some blank sheet of inner space, the kind a physicist might look at. It is as though he were disembodied: "a distilled brain in a jar," says Gersony about him. Hume Horan was also the polar opposite of Jerry Weaver. Whereas Weaver was a product of a forgotten, poor white working-class America, Horan, who looked like an airline pilot with a beautiful wife and children, was a product of boarding schools, Harvard, and the State Department's Arabist elite.

One day in the summer of 1984, a relief worker, a Swedish evangelical Christian, burst into Weaver's office at the U.S. Embassy and

Jerry Weaver, the State Department refugee coordinator in Sudan in 1984 who helped rescue the Jews of Ethiopia, with a lion he had just hunted. A colleague said Weaver was living in the wrong century.

began to cry. "They're dying: it's terrible; you've got to do something about Um Raquba." Um Raquba, which meant "mother of shelter" in Sudanese Arabic, was where thousands of Ethiopian Jews, known as Falashas, were being interned. They were part of the exodus of hundreds of thousands of people from famine-racked Ethiopia, now living in refugee camps in eastern Sudan. When Weaver visited Um Raquba, about eight Falashas a day were dying of starvation. Weaver had seen "shit holes" all over Sudan, but Um Raquba was the worst: a squishy sea of mud with thousands crammed into grass huts. There was little food or water and few blankets.

Weaver went to Horan, who slyly, nonchalantly told him to cable the State Department about "everything you've seen and heard." Horan knew this would be a sensitive issue in Washington on account of the Jewish lobby, and was careful not to ignore it, or even downgrade it. This cable would start a process whereby Weaver would gradually emerge as a go-between. He was the hub of a network that

included Sudanese officials and intelligence agents and Israeli officials and intelligence agents, all talking to each other—never directly—
but only through Jerry Weaver, who had designed a rescue plan for the
Falashas practically on his own, with Hume Horan's quiet, unflinch-
ing support.

At first, the Israelis wanted to stage a rescue: to get fellow Jews
who were starving out of the clutches of an Arab country. But at a
meeting in Geneva, Weaver bluntly told them, "If you try it, the Sudanese are just going to shoot you down. My friends in Sudan state security told me so. . . . There's only one way to do this thing. You've
got to move these people from Um Raquba to Gedaref and from Gedaref to Khartoum airport . . . with the full cooperation of Sudanese
security. You need a few vehicles, planes, and state security escorts."

"Would the Sudanese agree to this?" one Israeli asked.

"I'll ask 'em," Weaver shot back.

The area of eastern Sudan under discussion was one Weaver knew
well. It was where he often went hunting for gazelles.

Weaver's mind soon began working in overdrive. *There were so
many things to think about. Blankets were needed for waiting in the cold,
food in case the planes were late, potable water at the transfer points, a
sideband 500-mile radio operating on its own frequency, at least 50 metric
tons of fuel for the buses, lubricants, auto mechanics, and a garage for the
buses, the buses themselves, the drivers, Nissan patrol vehicles, etc., and
none of this could be bought on the open market in Khartoum, or else everyone would find out what was going on.*

Soon afterward, Georges Gutelman, a Belgian Orthodox Jew, would
arrive in Khartoum. He was stocky with dark hair and spoke a number
of languages, including Arabic. He ran a charter plane company and,
as he told Weaver and Horan, had a lot of experience in the "extraction"
business. The Sudanese weren't sure who he was, even as he bribed
people in the control tower. "And when the whole operation blew up in
a publicity storm, he was gone without a trace," Weaver told me.

Operation Moses, as it came to be known in history, began a few
days before Thanksgiving. Weaver, in a field jacket, carrying a long
cane, and armed with a Walther pistol, oversaw the vehicles and trans-

fers at Khartoum airport. From November 21, 1984, until January 5, 1985, Gutelman's airline flew thirty-five nighttime flights from Khartoum to Tel Aviv by way of Brussels. The morning after each flight Weaver notified Horan in his office and then cabled Washington.

Horan told Weaver that he would like to see the operation in progress.

"Yeah, no problem, Mr. Ambassador. Come on over to my place around 1:30 A.M. and we'll go to the airport together."

At Weaver's house Horan's eyes took in all the guns, scopes, magnum shot, mec reloaders, and other paraphernalia of Weaver's strange life. Horan knew that Weaver was "somewhat of a wild man," but he hadn't expected such a "pirate's den." Years later, Horan explained to me his tolerance of Weaver this way:

"I knew Weaver had his problems. He was living in the wrong century, a gun-in-pants-type fellow. His personal life was messy, sure. Stories went around the embassy about his local bimbos, and whatever else he did at night. But if I had transferred responsibility for the operation to your conventional, cover-your-ass FSO—the kind who dots his *i*'s and fills in his travel vouchers the first morning back from a trip—the Falashas would never have left Sudan. But Weaver had enough swash and buckle in him to break through any barrier." Weaver, during the months of planning and executing the operation, coordinating between Israelis and Arabs who never spoke to each other, was like a man juggling bombs with fuses lit, ready to go off.

Indeed, Horan added that Weaver had needed to handle large amounts of cash from the Israeli Mossad for payoffs and equipment purchases involving Sudanese Arabs during the operation, "and he did it without any of the money sticking to his fingers."

From Weaver's house the two of them drove to the airport. The ambassador lingered inside the car, watching through the window as four buses pulled up in the night to planeside and a dark, moving sea of humanity, straight out of a biblical time warp, began climbing up the ramp. Horan got out and made the rounds of Sudanese security officers, showing the flag as it were. Then he entered the plane, eyeing three Israeli doctors and nurses going up and down the aisle, ministering to people who had never seen a plane before. "They were all so silent. They had no suitcases, just the clothes on their backs. We went on for weeks, just pumping them out of Sudan," Horan said.

Weaver recalled that "the ambassador's eyes were lit up in shock and amazement, as if the whole thing was a revelation to him." Horan would tell me, "I felt that at that moment we were really behaving like Americans should: that this was what the Foreign Service was all about."

By the time Operation Moses was completed, some 10,000 Ethiopian Jews had been flown from an Arab League country to Israel.

Media leaks about the event in early 1985 led to Weaver's life being threatened. He had to leave in a hurry, with no time to pack more than an overnight bag. Embassy security officers had to collect his personal effects. And that turned out to be Weaver's undoing. The American security types didn't like the dirty dishes and the rest of the mess in the house, or the crossed spears or ivory tusks, or the skin of a lion that Weaver had killed covering his bed, either. FSOs, as a rule, collect exotic bric-a-brac, but this was simply too much. They took the place apart. First they found the marijuana, and then the guns, and then the gold bullion, which Weaver had kept in his house safe as a small investment. An inch-thick security file about Weaver was slammed on a desk in Washington. In 1987, consigned to a desk job in an annex of the State Department that offered no possibilities of promotion, Weaver resigned from the Foreign Service. They don't fire you in bureaucracies, they let you rot. He died in Ohio completely forgotten in 2016.[2]

"Jerry Weaver was the ultimate cowboy for good," says Gene Dewey, who managed him from Washington. "I remember when we were in Europe together for a meeting about the Falasha rescue plan, Jerry asked me to take back to the States for him a custom-made Austrian rifle with a Leica scope," Dewey laughs. Truly, Weaver was larger than life. He was a kind of Oskar Schindler in the desert.

Dewey told Gersony that his job in Khartoum would be to help repair the diplomatic fallout that Operation Moses and Jerry Weaver had left behind, owing to the public embarrassment suffered by the Sudanese Arab regime, and get the refugee office in the U.S. Embassy working smoothly again. After all, Sudan was a way station in the midst of regional chaos that went far beyond the Falashas. There were almost three-quarters of a million famine-stricken Eritreans and Tigreans trekking from Marxist, Amhara-dominated Ethiopia into eastern Sudan. (This necessitated a cross-border feeding program, which got food aid inside Ethiopia from Sudan to stem the flow of refugees.) Moreover, there were more than 100,000 refugees trekking from eastern Chad into western Sudan. Indeed, famine and disorder were affecting nearly one-fifth of Sudan's population of 22 million. There were also West Nile refugees from Obote's ethnic killing machine who had fled Uganda and crossed into southern Sudan. Finally, there was an ongoing war between the Arab Muslim north of Sudan and the African animist and Christian south of Sudan.

Sudan was partly why, back in the day, the 1980s were considered the decade of refugees. Though few remember that now.

Given the sprawling complexity of Gersony's new assignment, Dewey decided to travel with Gersony to Khartoum, in order to introduce him around the embassy and the NGO community.

They arrived in Khartoum from London at three in the morning. The airport was utter anarchy. It was actually the first time in his career that Gersony was stricken by acute culture shock. It had never happened to him anywhere in Latin America, or in Bangkok, and not even in Kampala. The arrivals building at Khartoum airport was like a series of dark, gangrenous prison cells suffocating in an intense heat that grabbed your lungs in a vise, with broken lightbulbs and banana peels on the floor. Everyone was yelling and pulling at you. Dewey was unfazed. On the other side of this hell there was a car waiting to take them to the Hilton hotel.

It was about 4:30 A.M. now. Dewey announced that they would meet for an early breakfast at six. He was relentless, and his military background really showed. Gersony, in jet-lagged agony, only wanted to sleep. An hour later, he struggled to the balcony of his room and saw the Nile flowing by. "I'm at the Nile!" he said to himself. "Why complain!" It was a life-affirming moment. Suddenly he realized that his life had not been a failure after all.

That same morning Dewey and Gersony made the rounds. They saw Nicholas Morris of UNHCR, who had not been particularly cooperative about helping the Falashas. Dewey had been pressuring Morris from Washington to be more energetic in general about helping Ethiopian refugees overall. Dewey had earlier sicced Fred Cuny on Morris. Cuny was an aggressive, somewhat tactless, and absolutely dynamic disaster relief consultant who sometimes worked for Dewey as a private contractor, and who knew how to get people and organizations cracking with his sharp elbows and confrontational style. It was a testy meeting. Dewey almost lost his temper with Morris. "But Dewey will leave in a few days and then I will have to get along with this guy," Gersony thought mournfully.

At the U.S. Embassy they met Ambassador Hume Horan and Deputy Chief of Mission David Shinn. The ambassador was, well, a presence in his own right. Shinn, with a fair complexion and black glasses, impressed Gersony as combining serious academic and historical knowledge, and yet he seemed quieter than John Bennett even, almost hermetic. "They're both really smart. I can work with these guys," Gersony thought. Whereas Weaver, because of the sensitivity surrounding Operation Moses, had worked directly for Horan, Gersony would report to Shinn.

Gersony, by this point in the day, having not slept the night before, was overwhelmed by the scope of his assignment. Sudan was truly an immensity of crises with millions of people at risk around its borderlands, he thought, less a country than a blank space surrounded by countries that were collapsing in their own right.

Khartoum had so little control over its hinterlands that a Libyan army convoy, bringing guns, grain, and dried-milk powder from the Mediterranean port of Benghazi 1,400 miles away, would reach the western Sudanese town of El Fasher before convoys from Sudan's own capital city were able to. "No umbilical cord links us with the central government," the commissioner of Northern Darfur, Abdul Hafiz, told me when I visited the far-flung famine-stricken province in 1985 as a journalist, during the same time Gersony was the embassy's acting refugee coordinator. Hafiz said his only way of communicating with Khartoum was by radio from El Geneina, near the Chadian border. It was no surprise that the goods on sale under the wattle stalls in El Geneina's market came by way of Libya and West Africa, rather than via Port Sudan by the Red Sea. There was nothing harder than moving goods from one part of Sudan to another.

Khartoum, in short, functioned more like a large trading post than a real political capital governing a real country. Yet U.S. assistance to Sudan exceeded $450 million at the time. This included over $200 million for emergency famine relief and $45 million in military aid. On the African continent only Egypt was receiving more American taxpayers' dollars. Not only altruism was involved. Sudan controls the headwaters of the Nile—the lifeblood of Egypt. Egypt's survival as a pro-American power in the Middle East was largely dependent on Sudan remaining submissive, and this submissiveness could not be taken for granted. The damage that Libyan leader Muammar Gaddafi could do from a foothold in Sudan, slashing at Egypt's jugular, the Nile, would be far greater than anything he could do by overrunning Chad or Tunisia even.

More than Egypt would be threatened by a Khartoum regime hostile to the West. Sudan reaches into the heart of sub-Saharan Africa. It had a long border with Marxist Ethiopia (practically a Soviet satellite at the time) and a coastline on the Red Sea. Were Sudan to be lost, it would join Ethiopia and Libya in an arc of Soviet influence stretching from the Strait of Bab el Mandeb at the mouth of the Red Sea to the heart of the Mediterranean. This, in turn, would have brought increased pressure on the pro-American governments in Kenya and Somalia, where the United States had the use of important naval facilities.

In short, Sudan was yet another example of where strategy and altruism were inextricable.

The Cold War, once again, provided a useful framework for Gersony's humanity. Indeed, this combination of national interest and humanitarianism came together most effortlessly in the person of the West Point graduate Gene Dewey, a gun-owning National Prayer Breakfast Republican of the moderate sort. In Dewey's mind, the dichotomy of fighting the Soviets and doing good for your fellow man was not a dichotomy at all, it was all part of a cohesive worldview: since Soviet Communism represented both a strategic threat and a moral one, it necessitated a policy of realist internationalism. It was a time, unlike now, when you could be a realist without being an isolationist who simply gives up on the world, and when fighting for human rights served a strategic purpose, since human rights played a part in weaning dozens of countries away from the Soviets. That's why the Cold War will always remain special to me, as someone who reported on it not only in the Third World, but in Eastern Europe, too. Of course, there were also arguments about why the United States was supporting Third World dictatorships, especially in Latin America. But they were muted compared to the philosophical battles between realists and idealists that would rage soon after the Berlin Wall fell, when there was no security threat to concentrate the minds of the Washington and New York elites. During the Cold War, it was easier for someone like Bob Gersony, who harbored a conservative streak of national self-interest, to also be a humanitarian.

When Dewey left Khartoum, Gersony had to leave the Hilton.

But where was he to stay?

That choice was easy, even if it raised a few eyebrows among the straitlaced Foreign Service officers at the embassy. Gersony chose the Acropole Hotel, a spotlessly clean, brilliantly managed intelligence-gathering factory all its own, costing $20 per night including breakfast and dinner. Here was where all the NGO workers and almost all the journalists stayed. People would knock on your door at ten at night there, having just returned from some refugee camp in eastern or western Sudan, or from the war zone of southern Sudan, and literally pour their hearts out to you. At the Acropole, you didn't have to work hard to be informed about what was going on in the country. You simply announced your arrival and what room amid the cavernous hallways you were staying in.

The hallways frequently opened out into common areas with ceiling fans whooshing, where I fondly recall some of the greatest bull sessions I ever heard in my lifetime.

The Acropole was a monument to the inventive cunning and shrewdness of the Greek trading community in Africa. You stayed at the Acropole partly to avail yourself of the hotel's Greek managers, who dealt with Sudanese officialdom better than any Western embassy staff could. My visas were never arranged at the Sudanese embassy in Athens, Greece, where I was living in the 1980s, but by the managers of the Acropole, who had them waiting for me at the Khartoum airport. It may be an irony that while hundreds of millions of dollars of emergency assistance poured into Sudan during the great famines of the decade, what in the end really held the relief effort together were the Acropole managers: a trio of Greek brothers from the island of Kefalonia in the Ionian Sea, whose father had come to Khartoum in the wake of British rule. George, Athanasios, and Gerassimos Pagoulatos and their wives ran a fifty-room hotel, arranged not only visas but visa extensions and internal travel permits, helped clear consignments through customs at Port Sudan, dispatched hand-carried documents throughout Europe, and otherwise ran errands for the relief effort all "with the courtesy and aplomb" of captains "of a luxury liner," observed the European-American journalist Edward Girardet.[3]

Emergency Palace was the sobriquet given to the Acropole, which was also compared to Rick's American Cafe in the movie *Casablanca*. The only thing the Acropole lacked was liquor, a sacrifice necessitated by Islamic law. Nevertheless, the conversations that took place over the curried rice, Nile perch, and freshly squeezed lemon juice prepared by "Mummie," the matriarch of the Pagoulatos clan, had a delirious, intoxicated quality: the effect of the heat, no doubt.[4]

The Acropole was perfect for Gersony, who ate only one meal a day and did not drink alcohol or caffeine. Dinners were always at a set time, where he would always do what he was still only starting to do best—what would eventually define his life, in fact: talk very little and just listen. "I'm a listener," he says. Just as he had listened one-on-

one to the Vietnamese refugees in Thailand, at the Acropole he tried hard to listen to the conversations at the other tables. A pattern set in for him. He would travel vast distances in the wet season, battle floods and rains and cholera outbreaks, and come back to the Acropole, where everyone would give him their own stories of their own adventures. "But I tried not to trade. I don't trade. I'm a receptacle of information. Remember, I was working for the U.S. government. I had to be careful. And so throughout my career I have usually avoided journalists."

"Robert was a bit of an enigma to us in Khartoum," says Graham Miller, an Australian relief worker who also stayed at the Acropole. Miller is a tall, bearded, and bluff geologist with an outgoing, magnetic charm. As someone who had succeeded in business, he was now applying his management skills to humanitarian work. He would disappear for months inside the drought-affected, ethnic-Tigrean areas of Ethiopia, where he would undertake surveys and establish water wells. Upon returning to Khartoum, he would always have dinner with Gersony to relate his experiences, and Gersony, as usual, would listen and try to say as little as possible. This is why some people who were unsophisticated about the workings of the U.S. government bureaucracy assumed Gersony worked for the CIA. His quietness and awkwardness, his dislike of meetings and events—including bull sessions and diplomatic receptions—often lent an air of mystery to him. Miller, who got to know "Robert," as he called him, well, correctly understood that Gersony worked for some branch of the State Department.

It was Graham Miller who introduced Bob Gersony and me to each other in April 1985 at the Acropole, two days before the coup that toppled President Jaafar Nimeiri, which I had told Gersony at our first meeting might be coming. We were in the steamy, sweaty dining area of the Acropole, a hothouse of smells and feverish chatter among journalists and relief workers trading stories. Gersony and I saw each other as if across a great chasm of other bodies, and we began talking. The connection was instantaneous. When I returned to Khartoum that summer, both Miller and Gersony would help me on my first article for *The Atlantic*—about Sudan. And Gersony would inspire me to go to Uganda that year for my second.[5] I detected a depth, soberness, and self-awareness in Gersony that instantly appealed to me. He was strikingly different from all the journalists and relief workers, who were naturally more voluble social sorts. Gersony struck me as a very warm and emotional person, but decidedly not smooth in talk and manner. He seemed intensely cerebral, discreet, secretive almost, but not in a rude way. I liked that.

While people may have had their doubts or suspicions about Gersony, the etiquette of the Acropole was that everybody supported each other, the professional jealousies and competition notwithstanding. "Once I had a high fever and stayed in my room for a few days," Gersony recalls, "and Barbara Hendrie," a relief worker whose sheer friendliness made her the reigning spirit of the Acropole, "constantly brought fruit juice to me."[6]

One night around ten P.M., a medical doctor from Connecticut knocked on Gersony's door. The doctor had been working with the Tigre People's Liberation Front (TPLF) inside Ethiopia and had walked out across the border into Sudan. The doctor told him about the drought, the quality of the soil, the nutritional conditions, and so forth that fit into a whole basket of information which Gersony instantly grasped—especially after the doctor casually mentioned that a recent TPLF military offensive, which everyone at the Acropole assumed had been a success, had in fact been a failure. The doctor was a perfect source: he was naïve politically so didn't comprehend the significance of what he was saying, thus he was objective and disinterested. Gersony wrote a classified cable about it, which the DCM, David Shinn, was delighted with.

Some days later, around midnight, there was a hard, angry bang on Gersony's door. It was Abadi Zemo, who represented the TPLF and the Relief Society of Tigre (REST) in Khartoum. Abadi was among the most recognizable figures at the Acropole because he had only one arm. He used the stump of that arm to bang at Gersony's door. Gersony opened the door and Abadi came in shouting and threatening. How dare Gersony report that the TPLF had lost the offensive against the Ethiopian government! Then Abadi quoted back verbatim a sentence or two of Gersony's cable. It was a complicated situation. Both the ethnic Amharas who dominated the Ethiopian regime and the TPLF were Marxist, so that the real fight was about blood and territory, not ideology, and the Amhara regime in the capital of Addis Ababa was using food as a weapon against its enemies, the ethnic Tigreans and Eritreans. In any case, Gersony suspected that there was a leaker at the State Department. How else could Abadi have gotten that cable? But Gersony said nothing to the U.S. Embassy at the time. It would have caused an uproar amid fierce denials, hurting his credibility. He would quietly investigate the matter the next time he was in Washington.

And he did. Going down the line of offices of the refugee programs bureau in the State Department some months later, he met a guy, an amiable, inoffensive networking sort of bureaucrat, who casually told him that he had shared a cable with a TPLF liaison. Gersony burned up inside. He felt betrayed. After all, this was not a cable revealing an atrocity or a scandal that the public had an interest in knowing about. Sharing this cable served no higher purpose. But he stayed silent: nothing could be gained by igniting a controversy over a single, classified cable, the sanctity of which even in the 1980s few would take seriously, given how many leaks there were to journalists. But he resolved never again to put anything in a cable that could endanger him or a source. Instead, he would phone Dewey directly with that kind of sensitive information.

There was one person at the Acropole with whom Gersony did trade information, though. That was Fred Cuny, whom Dewey (as I've said) sometimes employed as a private relief consultant. Gersony and Cuny had crossed paths in Guatemala and Dominica, but it was in Sudan at the Acropole where they really got to know each other. They were both competitors in the same field and opposites in personality, so there was a certain amount of rivalry and tension built into the relationship, which their long late-night bull sessions in Gersony's room partly alleviated. "We were wary friends," Gersony says.

"Bob and Fred were certainly opposites," observes Bill Garvelink, whom Gersony had traveled with in Bolivia, and who spent a lifetime in relief assistance. "But they had one thing in common. They knew how to talk to real people, the farmers and herders affected by disaster. They were the two gurus of the humanitarian field, in my opinion."

Whereas Bob Gersony was at heart an introvert and bookkeeper type, making him throughout his career a fish out of water among NGOs and journalists, Fred Cuny was the ultimate extrovert and, as one person said, "twice the size of Bob." Tall, imposing, a little overweight, Cuny, with his hand-stitched cowboy boots, was a real Texas character—a pushing, hectoring man of action and a "first-rate engineer," in Gene Dewey's words—who consequently fascinated journalists and relief workers. When he disappeared under mysterious circumstances in 1995 during the First Chechen War (perhaps the Russians had a hand in murdering him), the elite media and humanitarian worlds were full of encomiums. Cuny always did have a fascination with war and guerrilla groups, the very groups which Gersony, a self-confessed coward, was afraid of and sought to avoid. Maybe Chechnya, with its altogether brutal warrior bands, the effect of both Stalin and militant Islam, constituted one risk too many for Cuny. In the end, Cuny, according to war correspondent Scott Anderson in a detailed biography, was a real hero who imagined he could always save places, even a place like Chechnya, which it turned out he couldn't.[7]

Just as Gersony was a pessimist, both obsessive and methodical, Cuny, who harbored a "congenital optimism," was impulsive and improvisational, a risk taker who flew gliders and small planes himself, and this only added to his swagger.[8] "Fred brilliantly saved thousands of lives in eastern Sudan by delivering water and advising young U.N. relief workers," Gersony says. "Fred didn't go anywhere just to get along with people and be nice to them." To the contrary, Cuny could be the nightmare of complacent aid bureaucracies, and Dewey used him occasionally to light a fire up the backsides of UNHCR and others.

Cuny, born in 1944, was a year older than Gersony. He grew up in Texas and started a private relief and reconstruction outfit in Dallas.

Getting his start during the Nigerian civil war in Biafra in 1969, thereafter hardly a humanitarian disaster occurred anywhere that did not involve him. A civil engineer, his specialty was developing systems for the construction of refugee and displaced persons camps that held hundreds and thousands of people with latrines, sanitation, and so on.

Gene Dewey says, "We needed Gersony's systematic, in-depth analysis and assessment to identify options for the best, needs-based humanitarian response from the U.S. government and the multilateral system. After getting Gersony's workup, we needed to parachute in Fred Cuny, with his 'lone-ranger' style, to oversee the start of operations and run things."

That is, Dewey—with his own, action-oriented military manner—would have liked to use Gersony and Cuny as a one-two punch. Gersony, by listening and writing silently in his notebook, would figure out the difficult, hard-to-admit truths of a situation. Cuny would then storm in and try to alleviate it all. It was a case of realism followed by idealism, even as both men harbored elements of the other tendency.

Whenever Gersony reminisces about Cuny, a smile often crosses his face. Summing up Cuny, Gersony says: "I like people who are good talkers because I like to listen, and Fred was one of the greatest talkers I ever knew."

Eastern Sudan, with its panorama of refugee camps filled with ethnic Tigreans fleeing war and famine in neighboring Ethiopia, had sparked an NGO industry on its own, one essentially run out of the Acropole Hotel. Meanwhile, approximately 120,000 refugees from eastern Chad had tramped over the border into western Sudan and almost no one knew anything about them, or why they were really there. From faraway Khartoum it all seemed a mystery. One day in July 1985, DCM David Shinn called Gersony into his office and asked him if he would go out to the Sudanese-Chadian border area and "check on the situation." Gersony readily agreed. He instinctively hated following the crowd, which meant in this case reporting on the ethnic Tigreans, and much preferred to strike out on his own.

He went to the embassy motor pool and insisted on the best car and the best driver-mechanic-translator-fixer, all in one, who was available. This meant a new Land Rover and Andrew, a tall thirty-year-old Dinka who was a fluent English speaker and a virtual genius at maneuvering in difficult situations. He and Andrew loaded up on food, extra tires, and as many large plastic jugs of gasoline as they could fit in the trunk. They drove for more than three days almost straight westward, across 890 miles of the Sahara, through the vast and naked provinces of North Darfur and West Darfur. The roads were badly rutted. "It was the kind of really bad trip that your back will never forgive you for," Gersony recalls.

It was the rainy season and Andrew taught Gersony how to identify and navigate around "black cotton soil," a loamy cross between mud and quicksand, in which the wheels of a car would sink two feet into the muck, stranding you in the middle of nowhere. Gersony's habit of eating only once a day was a blessing in such circumstances. In addition to the snacks they brought with them, they ate camel liver and fried onions at local guest houses where they spent the night. One restaurant was merely a stifling room with a big table and a small table. While they ate at the small table, a group of Libyans in white robes and wound turbans stormed in and occupied the big table. This was an era when Colonel Muammar Gaddafi's Libya was a radical, anti-Western regime that excited fear and mystery. Libyan convoys often crossed into western Sudan and the pro-Western Khartoum government was powerless to stop them. Gersony remembers being shocked at the way the Libyans spit watermelon seeds all over the table and floor with no regard for him and Andrew.

Their arrival in the Sudanese town of El Geneina, on the border with Chad, brought no letup in discomfort. Summer in the Sahara meant temperatures well over 100 degrees and the feeling of no oxygen to breathe. There were no air conditioners. The lonely relief workers at the UNHCR outpost appeared to have no idea why the Chadians kept crossing into Sudan. They told Gersony that he and Andrew could not travel in the area or visit the makeshift refugee camps without the permission of the local sheikh, who invited Gersony and Andrew for a Saturday lunch. There was no refrigeration. Bugs were everywhere on the table and the food itself seemed to be moving. But the iron laws of local hospitality commanded that they eat what was put in front of them, and the food was generous and splendid in the eyes of the host. It was like the famous dinner scene in *Indiana Jones and the Temple of Doom*. Gersony was no Indiana Jones. He always had a sensitive stomach and was sick for two days afterward.

With the sheikh's permission, the two drove north for two hundred miles along the Chadian border, sleeping and staying in each of the six refugee camps along the way. This time there were no roads. The conditions in the camps, with their wattle huts, makeshift shelters, and tents in a whirling sea of sand and dirt—with hardly any landscape features—were worse than on the journey west from Khartoum to El Geneina.

It came to Gersony, still a bit sick, as well as filthy and exhausted, that this was an opportunity to try something new. Not totally new, just a further elaboration of what he had been learning about, in regard to how to talk and listen to refugees and displaced persons from Guatemala to El Salvador to Uganda to southern Thailand. He required a more methodical, comprehensive, and persuasive version of what Roland Bunch had done when Bunch had wandered around earthquake-devastated Guatemala. It was awkward since he was teaching himself—the ultimate autodidact who had never finished high school. He decided he would collect the ages, home villages, and other details of everyone he interviewed. "If I could collect enough information from enough eyewitnesses, I could put a picture together of what was happening. After all, here I was working with a tabula rasa. Practically no NGO had interviewed these people."

He resolved to ask no leading questions. "How many goats did you have? How many cattle? Tell me what happened the day you left your village. What was the first thing you heard, the first thing you saw?" touching and pulling on his ear, and then pulling on his eye, to give the subject faith in the translation. "You said you were running," pumping his arms. "What was the next thing you did? And the next?"

Soon the subject would begin to speak spontaneously, with confidence, learning the cadence, so that there was no need to ask more questions. He would just listen.

"The most sensitive things they told me on their own. Had I specifically asked, they never would have told me." And "no breaks!" he adds. "If you give them breaks, they start thinking about all the implications for their security of what they have just told you and henceforth may clam up."

There were often two translators present: from the local dialect to Arabic, and from Arabic to English. This gave him time to write notes during the conversation. But it was broiling hot in the wattle huts, with not enough water to drink. He was dizzy and only wanted to doze off. Yet he had to act interested during the translations, even when nothing useful was said—and when so much of what was said had been said before by other refugees. To look disinterested was to show disrespect. He began training himself to do this in the same obsessive-compulsive way that he took notes and did so much else.

"I always said to the person, 'You are my teacher, explain to me what happened.' Because I was taller and white, it was a way for them to be less intimidated of me. Who in the past had ever asked them their opinion of anything, especially of the women? Thus I wanted my interviews to be cathartic and satisfying for them."

All of this was as much the traveler's technique as that of the journalist. It involved no tape recorder, no camera, no electronics. It was still a time in Africa when such devices often made people suspicious and on their guard. And when soldiers searched you at roadblocks, or in your hut even, they would be less suspicious of a pen and notebook than they would be of a camera and tape recorder. He was starting to learn how to collect the kind of absolutely vital *humint*—human intelligence—that the cyber and digital age has increasingly rendered obsolete. Again, he learned this all on his own. He had never studied journalism or associated much with journalists. And he had usually kept his distance from the NGO community, even at the Acropole, to the degree that was possible.

He hated it. It was grueling, skull-crushing. He had to concentrate for hours on end. And it was just so hot and the air so heavy. The dust was like a paste on your skin. You were regularly breathless. He interviewed roughly sixty people in western Sudan, each for hours, then ran out of steam. The stories were mainly identical and it only increased the tedium, and therefore his fatigue. But the repetition was a good thing. For it allowed him to form general assumptions about what had happened to these people. That is when he started to take pride in his method, when he finally began to feel less insecure about himself. He knew he was on to something.

He kept hearing the same word, over and over again: "Goran . . . Goran . . . Goran."

"Goran warriors on horseback arrived at my house. They stole all our goats and whatever else there was. They raped my wife. They burned my house down. So we fled." It was the same story, with variations, over and over. They never disemboweled anyone. There were no roundups. There was a drought. The Goran, among other things, were desperate and under pressure, and they just ravished the local population. Anyone who opposed them was killed.

Gersony was out in Darfur by the Chadian border for three weeks. He returned to the Acropole, spoke to no one, and went to the embassy, where he wrote a mega-cable to the State Department. It was cleared by DCM David Shinn, with a copy sent to the U.S. Embassy in the Chadian capital of N'Djamena.

Two days later, Shinn called Gersony into his office and said, "Look at this." It was a cable from the U.S. Embassy in N'Djamena that literally accused Gersony of inventing facts. The embassy had excellent sources, the cable said, and it knew, therefore, that Gersony had made everything up. If Gersony had guts, he would come through N'Djamena and travel to eastern Chad with embassy officials. "It was a totally intemperate cable and uncalled-for," says one Washington-based source. The cable, written by Ralph Graner, the American chargé d'affaires in the Chadian capital, was copied to Princeton Lyman, the deputy assistant secretary of state for African affairs. Gersony had intellectually usurped the U.S. Embassy in Chad's territory and invaded its prerogative.

But there was more going on than that.

It takes a bit of explanation.

This was the Cold War. Chad's leader, Hissène Habré, was America's and France's ally against the mercurial, radical firebrand Muammar Gaddafi of Libya, who fit perfectly into Moscow's anti-Western design. And Gersony's cable had played against Washington's counterstrategy to Gaddafi. Five years earlier, in July 1980, Gaddafi had invaded northern Chad's Aouzou Strip and annexed it to Libya. The Aouzou Strip was a mineral-rich band that extended Libyan territory sixty-five miles south into Chad along the border of the two countries. Except for a narrow column of mountains the Aouzou was a sandbox. Libya claimed it had been a southern outpost of the Ottoman Empire and thus was rightfully inherited by Libya. In 1982, Habré came to power in Chad with CIA and French support, which provided him with arms, financing, and military training for his troops to contain Gaddafi. By the time Gersony visited the Sudan-Chad border, the United States was providing Habré with the full gamut of paramilitary support. This would pay off in 1987 when Habré's "technicals"—perhaps the first time the once-famous phrase was used—driving Toyota Land Cruisers with machine guns mounted on them, would defeat Libyan tanks, which couldn't maneuver in the Aouzou's sands. Yet Habré, an ethnic Goran from northern Chad, remained weak. Among his perceived enemies in Chad's centrifugal ethnic and tribal politics were the Zaghawa of eastern Chad. In fact, an ethnic Zaghawa, Idriss Déby, would go on to topple Habré in 1990. Gersony, in 1985, had stumbled upon a case of ethnic cleansing by the pro-American and pro-French Hissène Habré. In 2016, Habré would be found guilty of crimes against humanity and sentenced to life imprisonment by a court in Senegal. "Habré was one tough desert warrior in a part of the world where coercive power often has an ethnic base," Chester Crocker, the assistant secretary of state for Africa during the Reagan years, explains.

Gersony accepted the challenge of the U.S. Embassy in Chad with pleasure. He would leave Khartoum within a few days and head immediately to N'Djamena to meet with Graner and his staff. His emerging methodology had given him real confidence for the first time in his professional life, and this challenge would give him an opportunity to validate it. "I knew that what I found could not be wrong."

When Gersony arrived in Chad, he had another advantage. Tony Jackson from Guatemala was now the representative for Oxfam in N'Djamena. With his fluent French, he promised to help Gersony in the eastern part of this former French colonial territory. He also gave Gersony the hope that the local NGO community would cooperate with him.

Chad was "flat, huge, dry, brilliant. I loved it," Jackson says with his typical enthusiasm. N'Djamena was bare, dusty, with the odd tree and camel, and with broad avenues: an intoxicating emptiness. There was a massive Roman Catholic cathedral to make the point of France's colonial resolve, even as its design carried a hint of the spare desert geometry all around. Large flies lay on the food of the local eateries. But there was a gourmet French restaurant or two and, even in a postcolonial Islamic country, plenty of red vermouth and beer to be

Tony Jackson in Chad in 1985.

had. And in the local market you could buy ceiling fans or any other convenience you required. The U.S. Embassy in N'Djamena was small but spread out. The chargé, Ralph Graner, was short with a stubby round face. Graner treated Gersony like a barking dog. The hostility was palpable. Graner had a sidekick whom he relied upon, Leslie McBride, a former Peace Corps volunteer and contractor for USAID. McBride was short and thin with glasses. He had married a local Chadian woman and lived permanently in N'Djamena, and thus, analytically speaking, was to some extent compromised. "You've made a huge mistake," he told Gersony. Gersony wasn't bothered. He had encountered hostile embassy types before, notably in La Paz, Bolivia, where FSOs were administering, as it turned out, a flawed drought relief program in the Altiplano there.

Graner and McBride told Gersony that he would be accompanied by an official of the Chadian interior ministry on his visit to the eastern border area. Gersony replied that no one would be honest with him in the presence of such an official. They also said that official translators would be provided him. Gersony said he wanted Tony Jackson to be his French translator. They said there would be no room on the small plane for Jackson. Gersony drew a line and insisted. They relented. Gersony left N'Djamena at six the next morning. On the small Cessna-type plane were Gersony, Jackson, McBride, the CIA station chief, and the interior ministry official. There had been no time to first interview local NGO workers in the capital.

The plane landed in Abeche, roughly seventy-five miles west of the border with Sudan. McBride had insisted on seeing the prefect there. The prefect served strong black coffee. Gersony knew he would not sleep that night and didn't. The prefect said he was mystified by the claim that Goran warriors were razing the area and driving tens of thousands of locals across the border into Sudan. McBride then began berating Gersony for his inaccurate cable.

The next morning the six crammed into a Toyota Land Cruiser that had been provided them and drove due north toward Biltine, about thirty-five miles away. There was not a human being in sight. Jackson by this time had been charming the interior ministry official in French.

"You say you do interviews. You haven't interviewed anybody yet," McBride said to Gersony in the car.

"We haven't seen anybody to interview on this road," Gersony replied.

In the distance they saw a human being. As their vehicle approached, it turned out to be an old, short, bent-over, grizzled man in rags. "Why don't you interview him?" McBride said to Gersony.

They all poured out of the car like circus clowns and surrounded the old man. Gersony was worried that the man, whatever he knew, would be too intimidated to tell the truth.

Gersony began in his usual way. "How are you? We are pleased to meet you. May we ask you a few questions? By the way, where are you walking to?"

Suddenly the man exploded into a fast verbal torrent, unable to be interrupted, and Gersony picked out the words "Goran . . . Goran . . . Goran."

It was a cumbersome, interminable process. First the entire speech had to be translated from the Chadian dialect into French, for Jackson to translate into English. The old man said that the day before, Goran horsemen had come to his house, beat him, raped and killed his wife, stole his food and his goats. Since he couldn't survive without his goats he was going to walk to Sudan. Then the interior ministry official started questioning the old man and it emerged that all the man's neighbors had already fled over the border. "Why do you think there is nobody here!" the old man said.

McBride turned ashen. Gersony felt like kissing him for picking out this man for him to interview. "We can't spend all day with this man, we have a meeting with the subprefect in Biltine," McBride said. The six of them poured back into the Land Cruiser and continued north: sand, scrub, and desolation. Not a single human being.

In Biltine at the subprefect's office, they all sat on a round couch.

Tea was served. McBride announced that he would conduct the interview. The subprefect told McBride that there were no problems in his region. McBride turned to Gersony and said, "You see!"

But after a pause of a few seconds, the subprefect said, "Unless you mean the Goran horsemen," who he then said for months had been pillaging the area and driving people over the border into Sudan.

The next morning they drove due east on a dirt track toward the town of Guereda, near the border with Sudan. About halfway there, they came upon black cotton soil. Gersony recommended that they make a hard right turn in order to drive around it. McBride said he was in charge and they would drive straight through it, without turning. Gersony and Jackson left the Land Cruiser and took their dry food and sleeping bags with them. The Land Cruiser proceeded and promptly sunk over a foot into the muck. Gersony and Jackson watched as McBride and the driver dug the car out.

By now it was noon on the desert in eastern Chad. The sun pounded like a sledgehammer. They began driving again and soon came to a wadi, halfway between Biltine and the Sudanese border, where water was flowing from some recent freak rain. Gersony said they should not go through the wadi, since the water was deeper than it appeared. McBride disagreed. This time everyone except McBride and the driver got out of the Land Cruiser and took their sleeping bags and other personal effects. McBride then got out of the car and directed the driver to inch forward into the wadi. At first the Land Cruiser had no trouble crossing the wadi. Then suddenly it dove at about a thirty-degree angle and became partially submerged in deeper water. Gersony and Jackson watched as they ate a lunch of dried food with the others.

It was theater.

Jackson recalls that he never encountered anyone as stubborn as McBride in his life. Meanwhile, McBride's own recollection of the journey avoids any mention of its real purpose—to discover if there were large-scale human rights violations by the Goran tribesmen—and instead focuses almost entirely on the challenges of driving through the difficult terrain.

At this point the embassy station chief was frequently laughing. Eventually some nearby villagers, who had not fled to Sudan, came with ropes to haul the car to the other side.

Gersony said they should "drive to Dodge," that is, to Guereda, since the desert was no place to be at night. Ignored by McBride, they kept driving and around ten P.M. unrolled their sleeping bags on the desert, waking up in the morning, not bitten by scorpions or snakes, but with flies all over their faces. All Gersony wanted to do at this point was escape into a nice hotel room, bathe, clean his gear, have a soft drink, and sleep properly.

At the station chief's recommendation, the group drove to Adré, a market satellite of El Geneina, on the border with Sudan, where there was an official crossing point. Again, at McBride's insistence, they met with the subprefect there, who had invited almost two dozen people to the meeting, including the local field representatives of the international relief charities. Everyone denied that there were any problems with the Goran. Gersony praised the subprefect for his hospitality and information, and then asked him for a tour of the town and the displaced persons camp. Gersony assumed that once they started walking around, the group would gradually break up and he or Tony could talk individually to the local aid workers who had come to the meeting. Jackson, of course, was quick to pull aside the representative of Médecins Sans Frontières, who immediately and profusely apologized for staying silent about the Goran at the meeting. But he asked for understanding since he had to live and work in the town, and needed the subprefect's cooperation. He then talked about the Goran in the same way as did the old man, the other subprefect, and everyone Gersony had interviewed on the other side of the border.

On the plane back from Adré to N'Djamena, the day before the Muslim Friday holy day, the station chief assured Gersony that he wouldn't change as much as a comma in the cable that Gersony would soon write about the trip, as long as Gersony downplayed the number of people affected by the ethnic cleansing, since the station chief believed that the number was closer to 30,000 rather than the figure of 120,000 that Gersony had used in his cable from Khartoum. Gersony agreed, even though he still thought the number was closer to 120,000.

Back in N'Djamena, Gersony immediately went back to his hotel, showered, put on a suit, and went to see the chargé, Ralph Graner, to ask for permission to work over the weekend in the embassy writing his cable. Graner said no. So Gersony appeared at the embassy two days later, wrote his cable, which he had composed in his head and with notes over the weekend, and sent it to Washington, with copies going to the Africa bureau and the embassy in Khartoum. Not a comma was changed.

As for McBride, he has remained in Chad for half a century, directing American humanitarian efforts for USAID, the State Department, and the Peace Corps. He and his wife raised five children in Chad, all of whom went on to serve in the U.S. military. McBride, his long-ago encounter with Gersony notwithstanding, went on to live a meaningful and exemplary life.

CHAPTER 7

Honduras
1985–1986

"That Camp's Got to Be Moved."

When Bob Gersony returned to Washington from Sudan in the fall of 1985, Gene Dewey immediately had yet another assignment for him.

"A real hot one," Dewey said. "Honduras."

Gersony lifted his eyes in dismay. On the one hand, he was being temporarily dragged back into Central America, which he didn't like; on the other hand, Central America was the center of the action for the Reagan administration—and to a significant extent for the world—during the 1980s, with the ongoing conflicts between the Sandinistas and the contras in Nicaragua and between the right-wing death squads and leftist revolutionaries in El Salvador: in short, here was the Cold War in all its inhumane, zero-sum extremes. For all anybody knew at the time, the Cold War was destined to go on forever. Eastern Europe might have been undergoing subtle changes throughout the 1980s, pointing to the end of the conflict. But that was not the case with Central America. And the Reagan administration saw the leftist provocations in Central America as the Soviet-inspired counter in America's backyard to what the Americans were doing in the Soviet backyard of Afghanistan.

Mountainous, relatively tranquil Honduras was trapped in the middle of it all: located between densely populated El Salvador, which even before the 1980s had one of the highest murder rates in the world, and Nicaragua with all of its ideological madness. Honduras

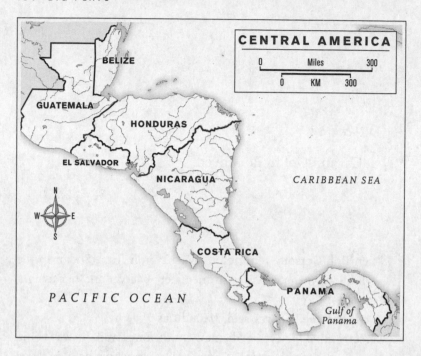

became the rear base for the CIA-supported contras. Also by then, the drug wars were beginning to come to Honduras, along with their attendant gangs, whose leaders the Honduran military literally fed to the sharks.

Gersony was world-weary about the whole subject. He spoke fluent Spanish and had spent the better part of a decade living in Central America. So it was the one place where he was an expert. And he knew that when it came to Central America, "everything was just so polarized, there was almost nothing and no one between Mussolini and Lenin." You either were a committed and bloody Cold Warrior against the communists, or a morally preening leftist committed to the struggle against American imperialism.

After all, the region had been an ideological battleground even before the arrival of the Soviets, the Cubans, and Ronald Reagan. Gersony hated the entire debate, since for him, Central America was so much more than that. Indeed, concealed within this narrow land bridge connecting the North and South American continents was a truly baroque political geography.

To start with, there were the highlands in the middle and the north toward the Atlantic (or Caribbean) coast, where most of the labor was: the small peasant farmers who grew corn, beans, onions, garlic, and squash. The bottom lands near the Pacific coast were defined by a sugar and cotton agro-industry, as well as by shrimp and tilapia farms. Tension—real historic animosity—lay between the inhabitants of these two geographical belts. The peasants in the northern highlands, who barely scraped by, sold their labor to the wealthy agro-businesses on the southern coast on a seasonal basis. The country capitals—Guatemala City, San Salvador, Tegucigalpa, Managua— were generally part of the Pacific-based power structure, which these northern highland peasants deeply resented.

There were, too, cultural differences. The Indians of Mayan extraction were among the poorest in the highlands. Meanwhile, the Ladinos of mixed European and Indian blood, who ambitiously identified with the modern Spanish culture, were the teachers and shopkeepers in the cities closer to the Pacific; and they also composed the army officer corps and senior enlisted ranks, which were sometimes complicit in murder, drug smuggling, and corruption. Above them was an authentic German-Spanish oligarchical elite from the colonial era. On the periphery were the Miskito Indians and descendants of black migrants or slaves of the thinly populated, riverine Atlantic coast. These blacks and Indians were culturally influenced by a two-century-long British protectorate, and had become further marginalized by the ideological upheavals inland and toward the Pacific.

Also on the Atlantic coast were the *maquilas* or *maquiladoras,* processing plants for export goods that paid salaries and benefits. These factories were hated by the Latin American Left as pillars of ruthless capitalism, even as every peasant wanted a job in one. Central America's core geography was thus a place of complex economic and social divisions, which provided a somewhat obscure foundation for the far more visible ideological divisions that the world and Western journalists were so obsessed with.

To make matters more complicated still, there was the split between the traditional Catholics and the fast-multiplying Protestant evangelicals, who would ultimately compose as much as a third of the population, making Central America one of the most dynamic areas for the evangelical movement in the whole world. The fact was that traditional Catholicism, with its fatalistic sensibility and emphasis on having lots of children, was a prescription for poverty in Central America, and the population, buffeted by the battle of political ideologies as well as by creeping social and technological change, was becoming more ambitious by the day.

Protected from much of this turbulence, as Gersony also knew, were Costa Rica and Panama: the former being largely middle class without the big plantations of the other countries; while the latter had been part of Colombia for much of its history and whose highly entrepreneurial population serviced the isthmus of Panama—a geographical feature conquered by mule packs and rail lines long before the Panama Canal. Indeed, it was the Panama Canal that truly anchored America's interest in all of Central America, especially during the Cold War. The Spanish oligarchies of the region protected American interests. And these oligarchs were themselves protected by the right-wing militaries. These elites basically told the Americans: *Don't worry, we'll take care of things here for you.*

Gersony processed all of this in his mind in an instant as Dewey repeated himself: "I need you right away in Honduras. You've got to move Colomoncagua."

Colomoncagua?

Colomoncagua, named for a nearby town of the same name, was a refugee camp within walking distance of Honduras's southern border with the north-central part of El Salvador, making it practically part of El Salvador's civil war. The province of Morazán, which made up this northern part of El Salvador, was the most radicalized province in that entire country. It was home to the Ejército Revolucionario del Pueblo (the "People's Revolutionary Army"), the most extreme faction of the leftist FMLN (the Farabundo Martí National Liberation Front). There was also another refugee camp in Honduras near the

Salvadoran border, Mesa Grande. But Mesa Grande, far to the west of Colomoncagua, was not quite as close to the international frontier and faced a less politically extreme region of El Salvador. Thus Colomoncagua was the real problem: an important rear base for the left-wing Salvadoran guerrillas that was a refugee camp in disguise.

"Do not come back to Washington until you've moved Colomoncagua further away from the border," Dewey ordered Gersony in his trademark, eyes-lowered military style.

Gersony couldn't believe what he was hearing. He, a lone contractor, was supposed to convince the Honduran government together with UNHCR to move a refugee camp of 8,000–10,000 people? But the big shots in the bureaucracy were hot and bothered, it turned out. Edwin Corr, Deane Hinton's replacement as ambassador in El Salvador, was now effectively beating the war drums against Colomoncagua. Corr claimed that if it were not for Colomoncagua providing a rear base for leftist Salvadoran guerrillas, the Salvadoran army might be doing much better in the field than it was.[1] According to this narrative, Colomoncagua was a transit point for arms coming to the Salvadoran guerrillas by way of Cuba and Nicaragua. The camp maintained a factory for explosives, and provided medical help and rest-and-relaxation facilities for the guerrillas, who were also getting food and fertilizer siphoned off from the refugees. Colomoncagua, in its own little way, was the heart of the Cold War.

Consider that the year before, a military helicopter was shot at by Salvadoran guerrillas from the vicinity of Colomoncagua. Aboard were two Democratic senators, Lawton Chiles of Florida and Bennett Johnston of Louisiana, as well as Diana Negroponte, wife of John Negroponte, the U.S. ambassador to Honduras at the time. So Dewey and Corr were not alone in their opinions. Consider Elliott Abrams, who had moved jobs from being assistant secretary of state for human rights to the more critical, line-bureau post of assistant secretary of state for inter-American affairs. Abrams bluntly told Gersony that he had just informed the United Nations High Commissioner for Refugees, Poul Hartling, that if Colomoncagua was not moved, UNHCR risked losing its funding from the United States, which would cripple the organization. This was the Cold Warrior Reagan administration—and this was high policy. Gersony had been selected as the point man for these bureaucratic heavy hitters and their threats to withhold money from the United Nations.

The fact was, Gene Dewey simply trusted him, not only because of his record thus far, but because in Dewey's eyes and also in Gersony's own, Gersony fit in well with George Shultz's State Department: Gersony, like Shultz, was a moderate conservative with moral convictions, lacking the ideological blinders that would later destroy conservatism. Indeed, Shultz's genius was to nuance and further humanize Reagan's own foreign policy inclinations. Shultz helped Reagan win the Cold War by supporting anti-communist guerrilla groups around the world, otherwise known as the Reagan Doctrine. But he also paid close attention to refugee and other human rights matters. The fact that Reagan is now considered a great president, lionized by old-fashioned Republicans and accepted by Democrats, is significantly due to Shultz's influence.

As for Gersony, he describes his own belief system thus: "I came from a family steeped in business and the grain trade. My father was a real hustler. It was the commodity trade that formed me. In Guatemala I ran what I would describe as a business, not a charitable institution. I was helping to *conserve* a culture with its many languages, not leading a revolution. Though I came back from Vietnam knowing that the war could not be won, I was alienated from the antiwar movement because of its disrespect for the soldiers. And then there was Ed Koch's influence on me. Koch was a Scoop Jackson Democrat, that is, a real hardline anti-communist who was pro-Israel. And though Koch was a liberal in everything else, he was sick and tired of being bullied by the Left to waste money on programs that just didn't work. He hated cant."

But now Gersony really felt the pressure from those he considered his allies. "I was really nervous about Colomoncagua."

He well understood that the Salvadoran guerrillas were a ruthless bunch of people. But it wasn't as if they didn't have cause to hate their government and its army. As Gersony would later tell me, "The massacres at El Mozote [so famously detailed by *The New Yorker*] were a world-class atrocity. It was a real radicalizing experience for the population and the guerrillas in northern El Salvador."

In the back of his mind he knew that the ground-level reality would prove to be far more complicated than the State Department's polarized view, and far more intractable. So he already dreaded the translating he would have to do for his superiors once he returned from Honduras. Gersony may have been a conservative, but he was one who never let that get in the way of what he found in the field.

TEGUCIGALPA, HONDURAS. Cool, hilly, picturesque, high mountains in the background. So quiet and safe, with the feeling of a backwater by the standards of the congested, war-torn core of Central America. A panorama of clay tile roofs. The Honduras Maya Hotel sits at the top of a hill with a bar and swimming pool, where CIA contractors mingled with the Honduran upper class giving their kids swimming lessons. The contra war was being run out of not only the U.S. Embassy and the border areas, but also from this hotel. It was the kind of place—paradise with a hint of sex and danger—where you might have filmed an early James Bond movie. Gersony had no appreciation for the setting, though. He was a nervous wreck, his thoughts screwed tight in preparation for his embassy briefings. Following his meeting with the ambassador, John Ferch, who had replaced John Negroponte, Gersony met with the deputy chief of mission, Shepard Lowman.

"Shep" Lowman was a legend, Gersony knew. It had been Shep, along with Lionel Rosenblatt and Hank Cushing, who had stretched Henry Kissinger's State Department instructions beyond the breaking point in order to rescue hundreds of Vietnamese employees and friends of the U.S. Embassy in Saigon, as South Vietnam was being overrun by the communists a decade earlier, forever earning the gratitude of the Vietnamese-American community and human rights advocates in general. But Shep offered Gersony no sympathy. Like Ambassador Ferch, the DCM said, "That camp's got to be moved."

Joe McLean, the embassy's refugee coordinator, a straightaway likable guy who reminded Gersony of Tony Jackson, was more tentative in his beliefs. Caught in the vortex of demands by Shep, Ferch, Ed Corr, Elliott Abrams, and Gene Dewey, the refugee coordinator was actually glad that Gersony was there to relieve him of some of the burden. As for the local UNHCR office, the people there felt caught in the middle, too: because Colomoncagua was located in Honduras, UNHCR-Honduras felt that it had to defend the status quo and leave the camp in place.

As usual, Gersony had learned relatively little in the Honduran capital, which in terms of insights had been an extension of Washington. So he left for Colomoncagua itself to spend the better part of a month.

The town of Colomoncagua was nestled in the mountains, composed of about fifty adobe houses with clay-tiled roofs.

The local UNHCR representative took Gersony from the town to the camp, and warned him at first that "people are not allowed in and out. Even I am not allowed to speak with anyone inside. I can't even approach people. That is the decision of the camp committee. They run the camp. They hire anybody who needs hiring."

In that case, Gersony asked to meet with the camp committee. The setting was a small building of processed lumber and corrugated iron, like the other dwellings, all lined up in military style. Everything in the camp was neat and pristine, though dusty, and with no greenery. There were six members of the committee, headed by a woman. It was a radicalized group. Some were actual survivors of El Mozote and similar massacres. "They had every good reason not to like me, though they were also seized with their own authority," Gersony says.

"They were not friendly," he goes on. In fact, "they were seething with hostility. They refused to answer my questions about conditions in the camp. They had been warned about me, and so there was only one issue for them: *you're not moving this camp*." The whole meeting was punctuated by long, embarrassed silences. "I asked if I could walk around the camp and talk with the refugees. I was told no. I walked around anyway with the UNHCR guy. People averted their eyes and walked away from me. UNHCR told me that the same rules applied to them and the other NGOs. They always had to be accompanied by a member of the camp committee. Food was only distributed by the committee. The camp was like a gulag, under strict enforcement. The monopoly of power was clear."

So Gersony improvised.

He began conducting one-on-one interviews at his humble pension back in town with all the NGO workers, both international and locally hired, who worked in the camp or were in contact with it in some way. Médecins Sans Frontières (MSF, or Doctors Without Borders), arguably the most prestigious of the non-governmental organizations, later to win a Nobel Peace Prize, had recently pulled out of the camp, on principle, the group claimed. That gave him a hint that there was really something wrong there. (Years later, MSF would publish an online confessional admitting to similar issues with Colomoncagua that Gersony would soon discover.)[2] Every NGO that Gersony interviewed emphasized that the camp should not be moved. But they avoided answering the sensitive subjects that he had brought up in his questions, regarding the camp's complicity in aiding the Salvadoran leftist guerrillas. Several NGO workers, however, as an act of conscience, told him that two people had been executed by the camp authorities: one for simply wanting to go back to El Salvador; the other for challenging the committee about cutting food rations to dissenters—letting them starve, in other words. Their bodies were buried outside the camp.

Nevertheless, Gersony concluded that there was no evidence that the camp was being used as a transit center for weapons and fertilizer-based explosives. There was no evidence of tunnels under the border, or anything like that. But food and medicine were being diverted into El Salvador, and in terms of Marxist indoctrination Colomoncagua was very much a "Khmer Rouge–style camp inside Honduras." Because Gersony had also gone during this period to visit Mesa Grande, further west along the border, where he was able to interview anybody he wanted, the contrast between the two facilities was stark.

Flying back to Tegucigalpa from Colomoncagua in November, he asked himself, "What did I miss?" All he knew was that he was headed for a "shitstorm" at the embassy in Tegucigalpa and in Washington. The embassy in San Salvador was claiming that Colomoncagua was a guerrilla rear base. "What kind of big rear base? Are they crazy? However, what was it that I didn't know?"

He decided that the first person he needed to see was the CIA station chief in Tegucigalpa. He wanted to leave no stone unturned, and the CIA might know things, many things, about the camp that he didn't know and which "the Agency" was not sharing with the State Department. And if he was going to get into a battle with Ed Corr, the ambassador in San Salvador, and with Gene Dewey and Elliott Abrams, he wanted the CIA alongside him.

Honduras was the center for running the contra war against the Nicaraguan Sandinistas. Not surprisingly the station chief, in addition to being measured and analytical, had the rugged, craggy looks to demonstrate that he had been around, fighting many battles, bureaucratic and otherwise. He loaned Gersony a young subordinate: a working-class guy, with every kind of security clearance imaginable. This guy read everything in the CIA files. He came back after a few days and told Gersony: "You nailed it. We have nothing to indicate that Colomoncagua is a major transit point for the Salvadoran guerrillas."

There had never been a reason to use it as a transit point in any case. Honduras's southeastern coastline by both El Salvador and Nicaragua was much better suited. The fact that the State Department heavy hitters did not know these obvious truths was sadly typical of a vast imperial capital—Washington, D.C.—where one part of the bureaucracy was not informed about what to another part was obvious, and where ideology often blinded people to facts inherent on many maps.

Gersony and the station chief concluded that, in any case, the Honduran government would never move the camp; and that if the camp were moved, the camp committee would make sure that some of the elderly and young children were killed, so that they could blame it on the Reagan administration. It would make for a great propaganda tool. For the next few years, the "massacre at Colomoncagua" would play in the world media. And what would the U.S. government gain from all this?

Gersony's recommendation was to tightly patrol the camp from the outside with trusted Honduran troops, and then half of the smuggling that the camp committee was involved in would immediately dry up. And get UNHCR inside the camp. Mere presence would help further. After all, wasn't that UNHCR's mandate?

Gersony provided a long brief to the Tegucigalpa embassy staff. The CIA, the political section, and the refugee officer all approved the plan. Ambassadors love whenever a whole team approves a plan, since it often doesn't happen and it gets them somewhat off the hook. Furthermore, the new ambassador, Everett Ellis Briggs, was pleased not to have to recommend moving the camp, which would have caused the embassy untold complications. Briggs, a towering, Dartmouth-educated son of an ambassador himself, was a real conservative Brahmin whom the influential Republican senator from North Carolina, Jesse Helms, really liked. Thus, Briggs had clout with the rabid anti-communist crowd on Central America.

"But in addition to briefing the refugee and Latin America bureaus in Washington, you will have to go to San Salvador to brief Ambassador Corr," Briggs told Gersony. Gersony dreaded having to brief Corr, who he thought already hated him.

The same day he flew to San Salvador and briefed Corr, along with his DCM, David Dlouhy. Gersony spoke for less than a minute when Corr interrupted: "What's the bottom line?"

"It doesn't make sense to move the camp. It's not necessary. The camp is not strategic. What is going on in the camp doesn't justify it. There are better solutions."

For the next few minutes Corr was angry at Gersony. Corr claimed the Hondurans were ready to move the camp and that Gersony was undermining U.S. policy in Central America. Then Dlouhy was angry at him, too. Gersony was thrilled. After all, not only had Ambassador Briggs, the Jesse Helms favorite, backed him up, but he felt that Gene Dewey, the moderate Republican military man, and Elliott Abrams, the neoconservative, would as well.

Gersony went back to his New York apartment for a few days. But as soon as he arrived home that night, the phone rang. It turned out that Gene Dewey was in New York at the United Nations and wanted to see him, at six the next morning for breakfast. It was typical Dewey, like in Khartoum.

At six A.M., the cafeteria at the United Nations building was completely empty. Dewey stormed in and they went to sit by a window.

"Have you moved the camp yet?" Dewey said.

Gersony began to brief his trip, his visit to Colomoncagua, and so on, but Dewey kept interrupting, "Have you moved the camp yet?" Gersony wasn't eating his breakfast. He was tired, a bit sick, and nervous. Finally, Gersony said: "Gene," looking Dewey in the eye, "it would be a big mistake to try to move this camp." Gersony quietly walked Dewey through his logic. And this time Dewey listened.

"All right then," Dewey said. "You'll have to brief Elliott." Abrams took the news with good grace. The Honduran government and UNHCR were obviously relieved that the U.S. government was not going to force them to relocate the camp, even as they now had to patrol and occupy it.

Decades later, Dewey tells me: "Looking back, I have a twinge of guilt for presupposing from my Washington perch the solution to the problem. This was a camp we learned from Bob to be run not by the Honduran government (or even by UNHCR, since none of its local staff had ever spent a night inside), but by El Salvadoran insurgent leaders who wielded total power, including capital punishment, over the camp residents. It was an insurgent justice system, devoid of the most basic human rights guarantees central to UNHCR's own protection mandate." Thanks to Gersony's reporting, Dewey had the upper hand when he told the high commissioner Poul Hartling that UNHCR would have to do much more to protect the refugees. Gersony's mere visit to Colomoncagua had concentrated the minds of the State Department bureaucracy, which in turn was able to bring more pressure on UNHCR to actually force its way inside the camp. And that is what happened.

"Everyone in the Reagan administration assumed we would have to move Colomoncagua further away from the border," Elliott Abrams tells me. "But Bob explained why that wouldn't work. It would have just meant more expense, more misery. Bob reversed the policy completely on his own. He told us things the whole bureaucracy was ignorant of."

Gersony really hadn't done much. He had merely walked around inside the camp, then interviewed maybe two dozen NGO workers one-on-one outside it, and then conferred with the CIA in the embassy. It wasn't like his work in western Sudan, and it certainly wasn't the kind of epic, thorough reporting that would dramatically affect high policy, as he would later do in Mozambique, Rwanda, and elsewhere. But high policy can end in tragedy when the policymakers are ignorant of some of the basic, little things that any reporter picks up as a matter of course. This is how ground-level fieldwork, even of a minor sort, triumphs over the discussion of big abstract ideas with which Washington remains enamored. The Washington foreign policy community is marked here and there by affable operators with all the right degrees and résumés and connections to their names, who often know very little about the factual minutiae on the ground in farflung places. Gersony was the opposite of such people in every way.

What nobody could know then was that three years later the fall of the Berlin Wall would help take the momentum out of the Central American Left, and change history.

Meanwhile, around the same time that Gersony had been busy with Colomoncagua, followed by an assignment on the Honduras-Nicaragua border, there were personnel changes at the State Department's refugee programs bureau in Washington. These changes were a normal bureaucratic rotation, but constituted prologue to assignments much more dramatic than any others he had had so far. For Gersony was about to go back to Africa for a long stretch.

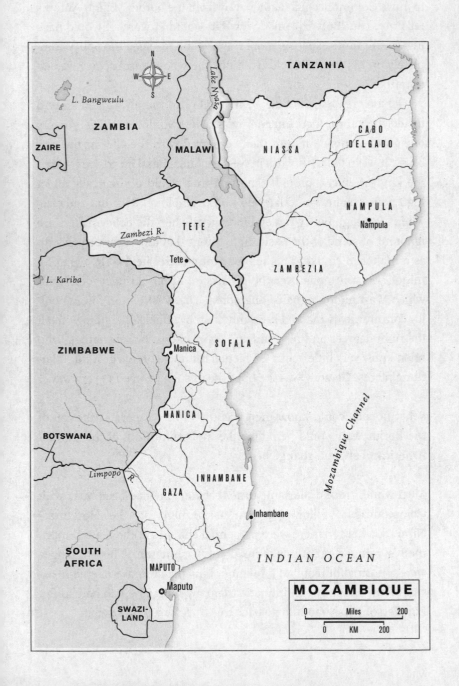

MOZAMBIQUE

CHAPTER 8

Mozambique
1987–1988

"I Was Now in the Zone."

After Colomoncagua was settled, Gersony turned his attention for almost six months in 1987 to the Miskito Indians on the Atlantic coast straddling Honduras and Nicaragua, whose territory constituted a sideshow of the Sandinista-contra war. While there he got a message from the Bureau of Refugee Programs at the State Department that he was needed in Mozambique. His handlers this time would be different.

Gene Dewey and his boss, Jim Purcell, had by now left the bureau. Dewey had become the United Nations deputy high commissioner for refugees in Geneva. Coming in as both President Reagan's refugee coordinator and director of the Bureau of Refugee Programs was Jonathan Moore, whose new office was located on the State Department's seventh floor adjacent to Secretary of State George Shultz himself. In other words, the refugee bureau and its boss had both been dramatically upgraded in importance.

Jonathan Moore, who died in 2017, was an intimate friend and bureaucratic colleague of the eminent liberal Republican Elliot Richardson, who, like Moore, had served several presidents in a wide variety of key positions: both being the ultimate, selfless public servants of the kind that are now all too rare, the kind who are deeply moral without being ideological, while operating at the top of the power structure. Moore worked with Richardson at the Departments of Health, Education, and Welfare; Defense; Justice; and State. They both stood up to President Richard Nixon and subsequently resigned in the famous Saturday Night Massacre, but not before laying the groundwork for exposing the corruption of Vice President Spiro Agnew. Richardson was famously an old-fashioned Massachusetts patrician, and Moore—an unusually feisty Protestant of Italian and Irish background with ties to Dartmouth and Harvard, who used to love big, smelly cigars—was Richardson's kind of guy.

Moore was deeply spiritual without being specifically religious. He was funny, argumentative, loved a good political fight, but in the heat of battle was calm in the moment. He could think a problem to death through endless analysis, poring over every last detail, making him later on a great teacher at Harvard's John F. Kennedy School of Government. Moore at this time was on his way to becoming legendary in the human rights community, and would later be lionized by Samantha Power, the great campaigner against genocide, who is also tied to Harvard.

Moore, who believed it was only through fieldwork that you could truly understand a situation,[1] did not know and had never heard of Bob Gersony. But someone he deeply respected, Sheppie Abramowitz, did. Sheppie and her husband, Mort, were emerging as the first Washington power couple of the human rights community in a practical, operational, and diplomatic sense. Mort was a heavy-hitting ambassador and assistant secretary of state close to Shultz. Sheppie dedicated her professional life to refugee issues. They were, like Gersony—albeit on a much more prestigious level—able to combine a deep commitment to human rights with the necessities of national interest. Baked into their worldview was the notion that realism without a sufficient dose of idealism was not realistic at all. Sheppie went to see Jonathan Moore and told him that he simply had to utilize Bob Gersony. Margaret McKelvey, who worked on the Africa desk at the refugee bureau, told Moore the same thing.

And that was that.

Moore told Gersony that he wanted him to go to Mozambique, where a civil war was raging and a million refugees had fled into half a dozen neighboring countries—in addition to another million who

State Department refugee coordinator Jonathan Moore, who sent Bob to Mozambique in 1988 and supported his work all along. On the other side of Bob is Moore's wife, Katie.

were internally displaced inside Mozambique itself. But the problem was that the Africa bureau had yet to grant Gersony permission. After all, Gersony had created difficulties for the Africa bureau in Uganda, Sudan, and Chad. Chet Crocker was still the assistant secretary of state for African affairs. But he now had a new principal deputy assistant secretary, Chas Freeman, the former DCM in Bangkok who had been so supportive of Gersony's work on South China Sea antipiracy. It was Chas who broke the logjam at the Africa bureau, and so Gersony prepared to go off to Mozambique.

It was an assignment that would launch Gersony's reputation as a humanitarian into the stratosphere among Washington insiders.

But the assignment did not at first excite Gersony. Gene Dewey had imbued Gersony with a concern for root causes. For example: Why were refugees fleeing a country in the first place? What exactly had happened to them? But root causes did not seem to be part of this new assignment. He was told only to check on how UNHCR and the other NGOs were dealing with the Mozambique exodus: were the refugees getting enough food, sufficient basic health care—mundane stuff. Little did he know what he was getting himself into.

Before leaving he paid a ten-minute, meet-and-greet courtesy call on Chet Crocker, the assistant secretary of state for Africa. Chester Arthur Crocker, four years older than Gersony, was the ultimate upper-crust Brahmin, the son of a New York investment banker and a descendant of Chester Alan Arthur, America's twenty-first president. That being said, he harbored a fiercely independent Holden Caulfield streak in him, having dropped out of Andover and lived on his own, before enrolling in Ohio State University. He would ultimately turn out to be a real theological Republican of the old school, straight out of early- and mid-twentieth-century Americana, who with his owlish glasses and balding head had the tweedy looks to match. Alternatively, as Chas Freeman recalls, Chet Crocker was "a European conservative rather than an American conservative," meaning he had an "elegant vision of how to produce change" as opposed to a nativist one, and was a moderate as opposed to a radical.[2]

Crocker, a reserved man who often seemed slightly annoyed, was at the moment a deeply embattled assistant secretary of state. His policy of constructive engagement toward the apartheid regime in South Africa was being torn apart by the entire American Left and

U.S. Assistant Secretary of State for African Affairs Chester A. Crocker, who sent Gersony to Mozambique in 1988.

liberal senator Ted Kennedy in particular. Meanwhile, hard right-wing Republicans completely distrusted him because of the demands for liberalization he was making on the apartheid regime as part of his constructive engagement policy. It was a no-win situation. Senator Jesse Helms hated Crocker as much as Ted Kennedy did. The North Carolina Republican had even held up Crocker's nomination for assistant secretary for months, and after he was confirmed kept trying to have him fired. And then there was the epic war in Angola that Crocker had to deal with, pitting pro-Cuban Marxists against Western-supported guerrillas who were a component of the Reagan Doctrine to roll back communism. Crocker's goal, which few at the time believed he could accomplish, was to get the Cubans to withdraw from Angola in return for South Africa granting independence to sprawling Namibia, located between South Africa and Angola. The fact was that after the Portuguese had left southern Africa, the Soviets and their east bloc allies were desperately trying to fill the vacuum—and the white South Africans had no intention of letting them do so. Fighting raged. This made the region a bloody hot zone of the Cold War, and the Washington policy battles were almost as brutal as the actual fighting itself. "Africa divided Washington in the 1980s to a degree that few can imagine in our own era," says Frederick Ehrenreich, a longtime Africa specialist at the State Department's Bureau of Intelligence and Research.

Indeed, "Crocker was a stoic, with no friends in Washington," Chas Freeman recalls, "but George Shultz believed in him and that was enough."

Crocker, unsurprisingly, appeared to Gersony as distracted throughout the short meeting, and therefore had no guidance for him. None. This seemed to Gersony like a little fact at the time, but it would prove to be of crucial significance later on, when Gersony would come under attack from the right wing as a tool of Crocker for his Mozambique report.

"I would not have presumed to give someone like Bob Gersony instructions," Crocker says now. "We operated on totally different planes. Bob was in a position to get information that a diplomat would never get. A diplomat's life is highly constrained. In eight years as assistant secretary of state for Africa, I was lucky if even once I got to see an elephant. A diplomat, if he or she is any good, wants to be in touch with the Bob Gersonys of this world."

So with the approval of Moore and Crocker, Gersony now turned his mind to the whole subject of Mozambique.

To read the history of Mozambique is to experience a particular kind of sadness and ennui. This is not a land of spectacular atrocity and mass murder like Rwanda or Nazi-occupied Poland; nor of utter ungovernability like the dense forest tracts of the Congo; nor of vain and stupid politics for decades on end like Argentina; nor of repeated invasions like Romania. It is simply a land whose human and topographical makeup did not suit the strictures of the modern nation-state, a fate made worse by having suffered the least enlightened form of European colonialism: that of the Portuguese, a nation that because it lacked a robust and modern middle class until relatively late in its history had a cadre of colonials even less humane and competent than other European empires. Mozambique thus constitutes a spectacular land and seaboard with a rather dreary modern story behind it. It is emblematic of Africa, not underdeveloped so much as merely awaiting a new phase of history when the nation-state will not matter as much: when political and economic borders will be more flexible and subtle, thereby liberating its people more than any president or prime minister can do.

It begins with climate. Despite the Indian Ocean monsoon, a pattern of irregular rainfall culminates in droughts that can last for years, bringing, in turn, epidemics and locusts. Because of the tsetse fly, it was always difficult for a cattle-based economy to adapt and flourish. This put an emphasis on agriculture and agricultural labor, encouraging slavery—and the capture of women especially—to work in the fields.

The early modern era in Mozambique was a time of petty kingdoms, twelve in number, complicated further by at least seventeen and as many as forty-two languages and dialects. Until the 1960s, there was no direct road or rail link between the north and the south, or between the major port cities, of this long and rambling country. Portuguese rule over this immense geography was burdened by poverty, instability, quasi-fascism, and the lack of a sturdy middle class in Portugal itself. As it happened, the Portuguese inhibited the development of any national identity by dividing Mozambique into concessions, with no central planning or much infrastructure at all. Only in 1942 did the territory come under a single colonial administration.

The Frente de Libertação de Moçambique (Mozambique Liberation Front), or FRELIMO, took power upon independence from the Portuguese in 1975, and was defined by a non-tribal, non-racial modernist agenda as part of its Marxist ideology. But FRELIMO had little presence except in the extreme south and extreme north of the country at the time that the Portuguese left. This led to a brutal, heavy-handed policy in which FRELIMO went after the Catholic Church in central Mozambique, treating it as the historical arm of the Portuguese. FRELIMO confiscated church properties and closed church schools, and then installed political commissars in place of traditional tribal leaders, who, too, were seen by FRELIMO as fixtures of Portuguese rule. Upon independence, FRELIMO also announced its solidarity with the indigenous African political parties fighting the white settler governments in Rhodesia and South Africa. The effect was to encourage the hostility of nearby powers upon which Mozambique's economy intimately depended.

Mozambique immediately got sucked into a vast regional war as South Africa attempted to topple the new Marxist regime that had emerged in Angola following that oil-rich, former Portuguese colony's independence (also in 1975). It was a Rhodesian policeman and intelligence officer, Ken Flower, a character straight out of the mold of Bob Astles and Bill Kirkham in Uganda, who helped establish an opposition military force to FRELIMO called the Resistência Nacional Moçambicana (the Mozambican National Resistance), or RENAMO, whose support and training would be taken over by white South Africa upon white Rhodesia's demise.[3] RENAMO—composed of indigenous black Africans—was also supported by Portugal, and at the time of Gersony's arrival in Mozambique, when the civil war was more than a decade old, was strongly vying for diplomatic and military assistance from the Reagan administration, as part of the so-called Reagan Doctrine, a strategy to roll back pro-Soviet regimes around the world. RENAMO was tribally based in the center of the country, with much less of an ideology than FRELIMO, and became known to peasants as the Matsanga or the Matchanga, after its first field leader, André Matsangaissa, who died during a raid in central Mozambique in 1979.[4]

Grinding on for years, the civil war between pro-Soviet, pro-Chinese FRELIMO and the South African–supported RENAMO had displaced and taken the lives of millions of innocent civilians by the late 1980s, when one of Mozambique's great droughts hit the country, driving the fighting into even higher gear, as both sides became desperate for food that had to be extracted from peasants. Though Mozambique was a major battleground of the Cold War, ideology was becoming less and less a factor internally. To wit, FRELIMO, by 1988 when Gersony arrived in Mozambique, was already in the process of dropping its emphasis on Marxism-Leninism and the command economy. But this fact was little known at the time and therefore disputed, even as it would become tied up with the fate of Gersony's work.[5]

Mozambique was a war-torn, sprawling, fragmented, and irregularly shaped puzzle piece on the map of southern Africa. Therefore, reporting on what was going on in the refugee camps meant covering great distances around the country's borders. Mozambique's capital, Maputo, tucked away as it was at the very southern extremity of the country, might as well have been in South Africa; in the days before email and mobile phones it was even more isolated from the interior than most African capital cities. It was not Gersony's first stop.

In January 1988, Gersony flew first to Lilongwe, the capital of Malawi, a small, peaceful, albeit very repressive pro-Western country, with a prominent salient reaching deep into central Mozambique: bordered by Mozambique on three sides. It seemed to him that every street and building was named after President Hastings Kamuzu Banda. Many women wore dresses embroidered with his portrait.

The USAID director in Lilongwe was John Hicks, an incisive, dynamic, and extremely smart African American who made all of his contacts available to Gersony. Gersony by this time was cemented into the Foreign Service network, even as he himself was not an FSO, and thus the fact that people reached out to help him was no longer unusual.

"I want you to meet somebody," Hicks said to Gersony, introducing him to Steve Shumba, a grandfatherly and charismatic African in his fifties with white hair who immediately put one at ease. Gersony liked the fact that Shumba spoke all the border dialects and was also an embassy agricultural officer, since most Mozambican refugees were small peasant farmers. Hicks assigned Shumba to Gersony for his counterclockwise travels around the southern Malawi salient, where Mozambican refugees were pouring in from all sides. The third person on the trip was Gilbert Ilimu, the driver, a young and enthusiastic fellow who unfortunately had a habit of accidentally running over chickens as they passed through villages.

The first refugee camp that Gersony and Shumba stopped at was located on the grounds of the Catholic mission church of Mtendere. It was a well-organized camp with UNHCR, MSF, and many other leading NGOs represented with health and feeding programs. Gersony found no problems with their operations. No aid groups appeared overwhelmed by the influx. Officially speaking, given Gersony's limited instructions from Washington, his job was over at Mtendere. But Gene Dewey's words about root causes nagged at him and he became curious: Who were these people? He was interested in more than how many calories they were ingesting daily. And after his experience in western Sudan, he knew that surprises always lay in store.

So he and Shumba began selecting refugees at random and pulling them aside for one-on-one interviews. The stories he heard were all identical. It was like being back in western Sudan and eastern Chad, except instead of *Goran . . . Goran . . . Goran,* it was pro-Western *RENAMO . . . RENAMO . . . RENAMO,* and *Matsanga . . .*

Matsanga . . . Matchanga. "They attacked my village . . . They killed . . . They raped . . . They forced people to be load-bearers [porters]."

This was interesting, but Gersony drew no conclusions. It was only one camp and a few interviews, with so much more Mozambican frontier territory to cover. He spoke with the parish priest at Mtendere. The priest, with his neat collar, was very articulate, neutral-sounding, affable, and accessible: an American who was a favorite of the diplomatic and donor communities; the go-to man for Westerners in Lilongwe who wanted to be able to say that they had gone out into the field and interviewed an expert source. "Father, what are all these people doing here?" Gersony asked him.

"Oh, they are all running away from FRELIMO," the parish priest said.

"But the people I met said they were running away from RENAMO. Can you find people for me to interview who ran away from FRELIMO?"

"No problem."

It took a while, but he eventually found Gersony two such people. The first was an old woman who had fled five years earlier and was still at the camp. The second was a young man who had fled across the border as a child with the same woman.

Gersony asked the priest for more people to interview who said they had fled FRELIMO but the priest never managed to produce any, though he kept promising. Gersony stayed at the camp several more days interviewing people. Every interview was virtually the same. *RENAMO . . . RENAMO . . . Matsanga.*

Gersony now decided to be extraordinarily careful. It occurred to him that the parish priest had been handling multiple cycles of Western visitors, conditioning their vision of the Mozambican conflict. The priest's was the closest refugee camp to the capital of Lilongwe, and thus the one most likely to be seen by journalists and international officials on short visits. It was a typical story. Diplomatic and media accounts of many a conflict often sound similar for reasons both good and bad, the bad being that the authors of these reports all talk to the same people. So Gersony and Shumba began pulling people aside for interviews right at the border, before the refugees could receive "guidance" from camp officials—whether that guidance be anti-FRELIMO or anti-RENAMO. And he resolved to say nothing about what he discovered once back in Lilongwe, one of the few places in sub-Saharan Africa that had a close relationship with apartheid South Africa. Thus, blaming the pro-Western RENAMO guerrillas for the attacks on civilians would be distinctly controversial and unpopular in this particular diplomatic setting.

After spending a week at Mtendere, Gersony and Shumba now proceeded to spend more than another two weeks on the road, stopping at every refugee camp down and up the Malawi salient, interviewing all day, each day, Mozambican refugees. The accounts never altered: *RENAMO . . . RENAMO . . . Matsanga.* Shumba would later tell AID colleagues that he had never worked with anyone who had such a magical ability to talk and listen to people, and to extract information from them, as Gersony.

"I was now in the zone," Gersony reflects. "I was doing exactly what I was made for. I was without further ambition. I sensed that the stories of these people truly mattered. The atmosphere while they talked was *charged*. This was what I always wanted to do—not to be a bureaucrat in Washington. This was realism: the material at hand, and at ground level. I would rather talk to these people than be president of any country. I had reached the top of my game in Mozambique."

He was forty-three years old. By now he had perfected his methodology. He systematically collected the basic data of every refugee he interviewed, except their names, which he deliberately never asked for, assigning them numbers and distinguishing characteristics instead. By not providing their names, they felt safer from retribution and were more likely to talk; by assigning each refugee a distinguishing characteristic—a birthmark, a piece of clothing, a way of talking—he was able to remember them better from memory. Thus (and this was very important to him) he was able to preserve their individuality. It was all an elaboration of a process he had consciously begun in southern Thailand and on the Sudan-Chad border.

He had other rules as well. He never worked as part of a team. Team efforts reduced everything to the lowest common denominator, he believed. He cleared his mind of everything he knew. He trained himself not to know, that is, to have no assumptions beforehand. He made sure no one was able to reach him. He believed in total immersion in his work, something very possible to do in the predigital age. He never went down rabbit holes. He kept his mind only on the specific questions at hand, since it was easy to get distracted by related issues that others would tell you were just so fascinating. Finally, he always slept with his notebook under his pillow.

He would begin each interview with his basic checklist:

1. Name of the camp where the interview took place
2. The age of the refugee
3. The sex
4. The tribe and ethnicity
5. His or her occupation
6. His or her home village, district, and province
7. The personal identifying characteristic
8. His or her assigned code number, and the date of the interview
9. The name of the translator

The checklist was a good icebreaker with the person, especially as it made clear he would never ask their names. But he was transparent about who *he* was, and *his* name: "I am Robert Gersony from the U.S. Embassy." It was very important to conduct each interview in complete privacy: in a shack, in a shed, or under a tree. If anyone wandered toward them he would chase them away. Those being interviewed liked that. If there was a chair he used it. The translator and the interviewee were more comfortable sitting on the ground.

As in western Sudan, he worked from seven A.M. to nine P.M. He brought candles with him for the evening interviews, as the sun went down in the tropics around six and there was usually no electricity. He never wore shorts, as he considered that impolite. He ate one meal daily: before sleep, often rice and beans with purified water. There was dust not only in the food, but in his nose, throat, and ears. The heat was like a heavy cloak over his head that partially smothered him. There were all sorts of insects and rodents. It was the kind of environment where you needed a stiff drink to fall asleep, except that he never drank, not even beer. Because he was a man of few pleasures anyway, it made the ordeal easier on him than on someone else.

The ones with the least education were the most useful, because they were the least calculating, he discovered. Again, he never asked *Who did it?* They will tell you anyway. Don't ask sensitive questions. They will tell you, and only if you never ask. When they stop talking, don't ask a question. The silence allows a person to think and then they prompt themselves. And again, use your hands. *What did you see?* Pulling down an eye. *What did you hear?* Tugging an ear. *Was it big?* Holding his hands out wide. For they had to trust the translator. After each interview was concluded, the translator escorted the person away from the site, so that there would be no contamination with the next interviewee who was approaching. The old rules still carried forward: Gersony used no tape recorder, no electronics of any kind, just a pen and notebook. When he got back to Lilongwe, he holed up in his hotel room typing out the contents of his notebook.

He was God's own witness, listening to the stories of those most affected by history—by wars and conflict—in order to communicate those same stories to high officials when he got back to Washington.

From Lilongwe, Gersony flew to Harare, the capital of Zimbabwe, the successor state to white-ruled Rhodesia, which had a long border with Mozambique where he could interview more refugees. In 1988, the degradations of Robert Mugabe's kleptocratic rule had not yet begun to visibly settle in, so streets were clean, streetlights and traffic signals still worked, and street signs had not yet been stolen to be sold as scrap metal. Stores were still well stocked with local and imported products, and race relations were startlingly good. Tall cande-labra trees were about to burst into bright yellow blossoms when Gersony arrived, if he noticed them at all. Evenings were cool and the days temperate, thanks to the mile-high elevation.

The hotel was especially luxurious. The ambassador, James Raw-lings, a former chairman of Union Carbide Corporation, was a po-litical appointee of the Reagan administration. He and his DCM, Ed Fugit, were willing to be helpful, but Fugit warned Gersony that he, Gersony, "had a problem." Zimbabwe's Central Intelligence Organi-zation (CIO) did not want any foreigners in the border area, since Zimbabwe's leader, Robert Mugabe, was helping FRELIMO protect the railroad from Zimbabwe across Mozambique to the Indian Ocean at Beira, which functioned as the main export route for Zimbabwean goods. Gersony met with local officials, trying to convince them oth-erwise, but they were having none of it. Finally, they agreed to have two CIO agents accompany Gersony and his embassy translator on all of their interviews of refugees from Mozambique. Gersony gam-bled that the two agents would not have the funds for three weeks of travel, with the expense of gasoline and occasional hotels.

By the second day in the border area southeast of Harare, observ-ing one interview after another in a miserable, dusty place, the CIO agents were bored stupid, wasting away their own per diem. Gersony was deliberately asking questions about the availability of water, the quality of the soil, and so forth, both in order to fulfill his original mandate from the refugee bureau and to demonstrate to the CIO that he was doing nothing of interest to them. On the second day the CIO agents excused themselves and went back to Harare. Gersony and his translator then continued their journey to several other refugee camps strung along the Zimbabwe-Mozambique border, interview-ing people about why they had fled.

He was by now getting reports from people in areas not in com-munication with each other, but who had experienced the same or strikingly similar events. *RENAMO . . . RENAMO . . . Matsanga.* There would be the shooting at dawn by RENAMO in the undefended villages. People would run. The atrocities included rape, disembowelment, mutilations, forced portering, and beatings to death while on long marches, with single-file lines of hundreds of people bearing heavy loads for the right-wing guerrillas. People showed him their cuts and bruises as proof. RENAMO organized their areas in concentric circles of trust, with the inner circle a slave encampment. Gersony's mind was beginning to work like an old-fashioned calculating machine, with each of the columns-slash-categories filling up on his mental charts. He couldn't sleep. The hundreds of data points had to be sorted out.

Back in Harare, he typed up all his notes verbatim, spending days in the embassy and his hotel room. Over and over again, he thought, his professional life was an assault on the Washington way of doing things, with its executive summaries, which dangerously simplified situations: enemy number one in his mind.

In such a lonely life, Gersony was probably never more lonely than in that Harare hotel room. He had nobody to talk to about his information. He forced himself to tell no one at the embassy about what he had found, which was that RENAMO—about to be included as a large recipient of military aid as part of the Reagan Doctrine—was the real culprit in this brutal war.

Then Roy Stacy suddenly showed up, stuck in Harare for a few days, because of a problem with a plane connection. Stacy was the new deputy assistant secretary of state for Africa, number three in the bureau after Chet Crocker and Chas Freeman, specializing in humanitarian and refugee affairs. More importantly, Stacy had the softest and sincerest of bedside manners.

Gersony couldn't hold back.

"Can I confide in you?" he asked Stacy.

"Sure."

Gersony told him what he had discovered in the refugee camps along the Mozambique borders with Zimbabwe and Malawi.

"Do you have any idea how important this is?" Stacy said to Gersony calmly. They migrated to the nearby botanical gardens where they could talk out of earshot of anyone. Stacy added that nobody in Washington had any notion of what was going on. Therefore, Gersony's reporting would ignite a big debate in a city gearing up to add RENAMO to the list of pro-Western guerrilla groups receiving weapons and funding.

"What can I do to help?" Stacy then asked.

"I need to go everywhere inside Mozambique, and then to the border areas of Swaziland, South Africa, and Tanzania."[6] Gersony knew that if there was going to be a big debate about his evidence, he needed to have all his ducks in a row, so to speak. Mozambique, because of the thousands of miles separating its border areas, could offer differing refugee accounts depending upon where he was. He still wasn't convinced that he was anywhere near having a complete picture.

Roy Stacy immediately called Chet Crocker by secure embassy phone. Crocker immediately called Jonathan Moore. They all gave Gersony carte blanche. Moore, who loved a good fight in order to do good, was especially delighted with Gersony's plan of action. Crocker instinctually trusted Stacy's advice because the latter had so much credibility owing to his previous work for USAID. Stacy, in turn, recalls Gersony's news from the vantage point of three decades later as a "game-changing ray of sunshine" amidst the confusion of the southern African wars.

Gersony flew to Maputo, the capital of Mozambique, formerly known as Lourenço Marques, after the Portuguese explorer who sailed into the bay there in 1544. Gersony stayed at the Polana Hotel, where his father used to go to play bridge while he was stuck in Lourenço Marques for several months after jumping a ship bound for Shanghai, and waiting for another ship that would take him to the United States. His father always talked fondly about the Polana. This fact gave Gersony quiet pleasure.[7]

In 1988, the Polana, with its cagelike elevator redolent of the Pera Palace in Istanbul, was in a state of real dilapidation. It was thirteen years after the Portuguese left and almost two decades before an international luxury chain would renovate it. There was not even air conditioning, and so Gersony kept both the room door and the door to his balcony open to let in the wonderful Indian Ocean breeze: the architecture and the vast panel of sea bore all the suggestive ambience of Africa, India, Persia, and the Arab world. Moreover, there was a fancy veranda facing the Indian Ocean where excellent seafood was served. Still, he worried constantly. RENAMO was tied to the South African clandestine services, which he assumed had to have informants in the Mozambican capital.

Maputo was as modern as Harare, but far more cosmopolitan, in the way of all port cities. It was also, in addition to the great heat, a more humid place because of the Indian Ocean. In a cultural sense, Maputo was Portuguese, that is, Latin, with a smoky, beguiling mestizo culture, and a soft and gracious atmosphere that the former capitals of British Africa lacked. A lot of white South Africans came over the border to vacation in Maputo, for an edgy experience in racial mixing. In fact, the U.S. Embassy was located on the second floor of a building in the red-light district where security was virtually nonexistent, the roof leaked, and electricity cuts were common.

Because his mother was Viennese and his formative professional years had been spent in Latin America, Gersony was very polite and old-fashioned for his generation: *Be indirect, don't contradict* was his motto. He felt at ease in Maputo, despite its bad roads, shanty towns, intermittent squalor, shuttered restaurants, and beaches littered with land mines. But he didn't know the lingua franca as he did in former British Africa. Portuguese reads as quite similar to Spanish. But when you hear Portuguese spoken, with the consonants elongated and the vowels quickly swallowed, it might as well be a Slavic language.

The DCM at the American embassy was Mike Ranneberger, an intense, hyperactive guy who was constantly in motion. He put people off, but not Gersony.

"What can I do for you?" Ranneberger said over and over. He and Gersony became fast friends.

The ambassador was Melissa Wells, tall, stately, with beautifully coifed salt-and-pepper hair. Jesse Helms had held up her nomination for ten months until she came around to mouthing words of support for RENAMO. During that time she played the proverbial game of twenty questions with the folksy and infamous North Carolina senator, who long presaged the neo-isolationism of Donald Trump: she would answer a set of his questions, then he would give her another set to answer, and so on. Like Ranneberger, she was as supportive as could be. Both were top-of-the-line FSOs and Africa area experts. Gersony felt at home with them, as if he were back with Allen Davis and John Bennett in Uganda.

Wells and Ranneberger were then working hard to move the FRELIMO government from the left to the center left, a distinction often missed in the black-and-white political and media bubble of Washington. The U.S. Embassy's efforts were being helped by FRELIMO's own realization that it had made blunders during its thirteen years in power, and with a civil war still on its hands. Furthermore, Mozambique's president, Joaquim Chissano, the former foreign minister, was a relative moderate within FRELIMO ranks who had replaced the hardline Samora Machel, after the latter was killed in a plane crash in 1986. "Chissano was like Gorbachev after Machel. The plane crash, which could have led to chaos, turned out to be fortuitous," Ranneberger says.

Ranneberger sent Gersony to see the USAID director, Julio Schlotthauer, who, like Ranneberger and Wells, could not have been more cooperative. This friendliness wasn't just a matter of instructions from Crocker and Moore at the Africa and refugee bureaus. The truth was, Gersony was fast gaining a reputation throughout Foggy Bottom as someone *who would always find the truth* about a situation.

Julio Schlotthauer put a small two-engine charter plane and a Tanzanian pilot at Gersony's disposal, since the roads throughout the country were potholed and full of land mines and ambushes. Suddenly the whole magnificent geography of Mozambique opened up for Gersony: stretching 1,500 miles along the Indian Ocean and half as far inland in places, blanketed with extremely lush jungle—excellent guerrilla country. Julio also gave him two translators from the AID pool. "Now let's go for a drink tonight," Julio said. Julio drove Gersony at high speed throughout the city in his Cadillac with fins.

Gersony hated it. He was afraid of an accident and the police, and late-night drinking was his idea of hell. But he said nothing. "The guy is laying on a plane for me, so don't complain," he said to himself.

Gersony made the rounds of the NGO community, asking their advice on where to go and what to see in the country, while not telling them what he had learned in the Malawi and Zimbabwe border areas. He was well aware that Maputo wasn't the real Mozambique. Mozambique beckoned *inside,* in the towering bush with its sluggish brown rivers, swirling through the green monotony like a lazy knife. In this matter there was one man in the NGO community who had the aura of knowing everything about it. That man was Peter Stocker, the Maputo office director of the Swiss-run International Committee of the Red Cross, or ICRC.

Peter Stocker was an old-time ICRC type: mysterious, deeply knowledgeable about culture and landscape, with a commanding presence, and armed with Scotch and cigars. Stocker wasn't cynical since he was beyond cynicism, as well as completely uncommitted. He reminded Gersony of Kurtz, the ivory trader in Joseph Conrad's *Heart of Darkness* (1899). Pierre Gassmann had vouched for him, and so Gersony decided to trust him. Gassmann recalls, "Stocker had trouble getting along with his superiors, but he had excellent relations with truck drivers and every manner of person who could actually get things done in a place like Mozambique"—a bit like Jerry Weaver in Sudan, in other words.

Stocker sat at a simple spare table with two of his field guys, facing Gersony. Stocker was a devotee of feng shui, and thus his office had an unusual harmony to it. Gersony unloaded on them with his preliminary findings, emphasizing that he had so far only interviewed refugees in two border areas and had yet to meet any displaced persons within Mozambique itself.

Stocker turned to his two field guys and asked, "What do you think?"

"Identical," they said cryptically.

Stocker said that the ICRC had people all over the country and their accounts matched Gersony's. Few aid officials were focusing on the atrocities, though. It was all about sending in assistance, not about root causes. And of course, the ICRC, as part of its mandate, had to remain neutral.

Gersony, along with his two translators, flew to Beira, Mozambique's third-largest city, located several hundred miles north along the Indian Ocean. In Beira there was an important Roman Catholic archbishop. Gersony wanted to see him, since it was assumed that the Catholic Church was backing RENAMO.

Archbishop Dom Jaime Pedro Gonsalves received Gersony after dinner in his private book-lined quarters. Clearly, the discussion would be off the record. The setting, the archbishop's demeanor, all manifested a studied elegance. Like an embassy or an NGO office, there was an aura of extraterritoriality about the place, as if Gersony had left the squalor of a Third World country behind. Gersony wanted from the archbishop a letter of introduction to priests around the country. He was also desperate to hear the other side's point of view, which he assumed he would get from the archbishop. But to get the other side's point of view, he had no choice but to confide a bit in Archbishop Gonsalves about what he had learned in the field. "Was I hearing all those refugees' stories right?" he asked.

Archbishop Gonsalves was quiet for a moment, then said: "Unfortunately, you're not wrong. That's what I've been hearing from parish priests around the country."

Gersony thought: "The most pro-RENAMO institution in Mozambique is telling me, with sadness and disappointment, that I am basically right. I have real political dynamite that could blow up in my face."

He saw Gonsalves as an African version of papal pro-nuncio Josef Rauber in Uganda, who also had a soft, whispering voice, and was also deeply committed to human rights.

It wasn't as if reports of RENAMO atrocities were completely new. The details that Gersony was gathering did not exist in a vacuum. For example, the year before, on July 18, 1987, there had been a massacre of almost four hundred civilians in the coastal town of Homoine, north of Maputo, almost halfway to Beira. A FRELIMO detachment had been wiped out and several hundred civilians were, according to reports, subsequently murdered by RENAMO. But nobody could reach a definitive, investigative conclusion about what exactly had happened. And so the incident became politicized, as had others. Because RENAMO's behavior had not been comprehensively studied, its supporters both in Washington and Pretoria could always claim that criticism of the group was a mere tactic of the Soviet bloc and the American Left. In Washington, in particular, not only Jesse Helms but other right-wing stalwarts such as Pat Buchanan and Pat Robertson were beating the war drums to support white South Africa and arm RENAMO. This further incentivized Gersony to be thorough in his research.

For three weeks following the meeting in Beira, he flew all over Mozambique, staying at every displaced persons camp he could possibly find, amid the green sameness of a tropical landscape that was both grim and beautiful. Much of his energies were taken up with logistics: finding the next camp, finding a place to sleep, obtaining fuel for the onward plane journey. Usually he shared a bare room or shack with his two translators. He quickly filled up his handwritten notebooks. When he finished typing up the notes from each book, he triple-sealed the notebook in a manila U.S. government envelope with clear packing tape over which he signed his name, so there would be evidence if the seal was broken. He would later put it in an embassy safe for classified documents and subsequently send all the packages by diplomatic pouch to the refugee programs bureau in Washington.

Even with a plane, the journey was harrowing, since it was precisely the displaced persons camps that RENAMO liked to attack, along with schools, health centers, and villages that the refugees had returned to from camps in Malawi, Zambia, and Zimbabwe. In one village Gersony actually saw smoldering grass as well as huts on fire: RENAMO had just been there and set fire to the place. The guerrilla group was sending a message to the rural population: *The government can't protect you.*

He would conduct lengthy interviews with 196 refugees and displaced persons in all, throughout his travels in Mozambique and the border areas of neighboring countries. As in so many other places where he had worked and would still work, his documentation and analysis was deeper than that provided by almost any journalist. It is possible that no journalist or relief worker ever equaled his output.

Though all the people he interviewed touched him, naturally a few stood out.

There was the very dignified, quite "self-possessed" Sena-speaking lady with the black kerchief and blue blouse. She had been a farmer in Chemba district, Sofala province, near the great Zambezi River and a tributary she called the Tunga in central Mozambique. She had seen her niece and other villagers executed by RENAMO soldiers before RENAMO closed in on her, her seven-year-old daughter, and more villagers, forcing them all into the rough waters of the Zambezi, in the direction of which the soldiers began firing. She told Gersony that "she tried as best she could," but in the panic of a split-second decision to save herself, she let go of her daughter, "who was swept away by the current and drowned." The moment she told me of letting go of her seven-year-old daughter's hand in the great river, "her hand slowly waved in the air, as if she were letting go again, and again."

Gersony says, "That woman was a turning point for me in this assignment. I said to myself that I've really got to do a good job to put all this across for the people in Washington. The seal of detachment in my mind was broken then and there. I became a human being for a moment. This is a task that has been given to me to do." She was the 143rd person he interviewed out of 196.

Another refugee, this one a man, from the village of Sekwa, also in Sofala province (his 123rd interview), told Gersony how the Matsanga came into his village, took people's "clothes, goats, sorghum, and burned the houses." He said, "The only job I did was carrying loads for the Matsanga," who always beat him. Once the Matsanga stole a car, dismantled it, and made people carry many of the parts to a RENAMO base. He also carried guns, ammunition, and sewing machines. The trips were sometimes as much as six days each way. He estimated that he portered two or three times a month. "You had to serve as a porter unless you hid in the bush. There would be no food and almost no water given on the journey. When there was a stop, you had to find your own food. People I met along the way would sometimes give me maize and water." He saw two porters beaten to death. Once the Matsanga found a FRELIMO soldier living with a family. "They cut the FRELIMO soldier's ears off and made him eat them. Then they put him in a sack and beat him." It was one of the few cases of mutilation that he heard about. He was always careful not to exaggerate.

One interviewee, Gersony's 163rd, seemed especially strong and smart, with a jazz-type goatee. He said he was a "technician" from Namarroi district in north-central Mozambique. RENAMO abducted him and used him as a porter. He said he had made thirty trips the year before, showing Gersony the deep cracks in his heels. He would march sixteen hours per day, carrying ammunition in metal boxes, in addition to guns, cases of beer, and blankets. He estimated that each column was composed of dozens of porters and many more RENAMO soldiers. Porters who could not keep up with the pace were beaten with a *shamboko*, a special stick. When two men refused to continue, they were shot on the spot. Women, including wives, were frequently raped by the Matsanga, he said, and their husbands beaten. On one occasion, he and about sixty other men had their hands tied behind their backs by RENAMO, and then were left in a compound for several days without food and water. Finally, RENAMO soldiers threw pieces of cassava over the wall and the prisoners struggled on their knees to eat, unable to use their hands. Four men died. After he was released, he made his escape to Malawi in three days of walking. This refugee, who was at a RENAMO base in Mongola in central Mozambique several times during his portering treks, said he had seen white advisers there, presumably South Africans, a confirmation of the apartheid regime's support for what RENAMO was doing.

Every story had been told to him in isolation. Yet each story added weight to, rather than contradicted, the others. And thus Gersony had no choice but to believe them. After a lifetime of interviewing people uprooted from their homes, Gersony explains that refugees come in the following three categories:

1. Émigrés: Refugees settled in usually comfortable economic circumstances abroad. These people, he says, have "little or no credibility, mainly because they are years removed from what is happening now in their homelands, and in addition have a political agenda of their own to push." One thinks of the czarist sympathizers in Europe in the decades following the Bolshevik revolution, or the Iraqi exiles who fooled American officials in the run-up to the Iraq War.
2. The exiled intelligentsia: They, too, have little credibility because their accounts are full of political calculation.
3. The ordinary people with whom Gersony has spent a lifetime in Mozambique and elsewhere on several continents: "These people have no agenda or ability in political calculation. They are at the end of the chain of events set in motion by more powerful and educated classes. They are the eyewitnesses to history in real time, literally staggering across borders and across districts within their own country. They are also the ones," he goes on, "with real get-up-and-go like my parents. There is a big assumption out there that lack of education means you're not smart. That's not true. Uneducated people can still be very good observers, with very good memories."

Back in Maputo after weeks in the Mozambique bush and savanna country, and saying goodbye to his pilot and two translators, Gersony flew 1,500 miles north to the Tanzanian capital of Dar es Salaam. From there he headed south to near the border with Mozambique, to interview people in more refugee camps. He spent almost a week along the Tanzania-Mozambique border, a region hundreds of miles away from all the people he had thus far encountered. But he kept hearing the same story: RENAMO`... RENAMO ... Matsanga.

At one camp in southern Tanzania officials insisted he stay in the "VIP quarters," even though it was so hot that he wanted to spend the night outside in his sleeping bag. The "VIP quarters" was a thatched hut like most of the others, but with a table and cot. It was malaria territory, so he placed two mosquito coils by the cot. He was exhausted and fell into a deep sleep. Suddenly in the middle of the night he awoke. Something was not right, he felt. He reached over for his flashlight and saw that his body was covered in ticks that had fallen from the ceiling, drugged by the mosquito coils. With his box of matches, he burned each off, one by one, then took his sleeping bag outside and fell asleep for two hours.

Next he flew more than 1,500 miles back south to Swaziland, which like South Africa bordered the southern extremity of Mozambique. Despite the colorful, birdlike traditional costumes of the inhabitants, he got a hint of next-door South Africa from the high-performance cars parked outside the bars and nightclubs of Mbabane, the Swazi capital: like Maputo, wealthy white South Africans came here to sample interracial sex, still forbidden at home. He ignored it all and concentrated on visiting more refugee camps, where he heard more horrifying stories about RENAMO ... RENAMO ... Matsanga.

In Mbabane, Swazi officials insisted that he meet the king, Mswati III. "I was exhausted. The meeting was a real pain in the ass. I have no memory of it. I just wanted to work. I was afraid that meeting the king would make RENAMO agents aware of what I was doing." As it happened, nobody bothered about him.

Finally he flew to Pretoria, the capital of South Africa, the belly of the RENAMO beast. His research was practically done. His notebooks were in a classified safe in the U.S. Embassy in Maputo. So he was much less afraid of being exposed, and he wanted to be able to report that he had investigated the war from the other side. It would give him street cred, he figured.

PRETORIA, SOUTH AFRICA, 1988. "Whites only" signs slung over restaurants, government buildings, and the many parks. Wide streets lined with jacaranda trees, laid out in an austere grid pattern, and swept clean by black laborers in blue coveralls. Reddish-brown Union Buildings of this executive and administrative capital, reflecting the staid and stolid mentality of the city's Afrikaner founders.[8] For Gersony this sterile city, so hushed and orderly, was a shock (as well as a bit depressing) after the cheerful cacophony of car horns, roaring mini-buses, shouts of market vendors, and loud conversations in several tribal languages that characterized the other capitals he had visited. The lingua franca was Afrikaans, a Dutch dialect brought by Protestant settlers in the seventeenth century, rather than the English and the softer Portuguese to which he had become accustomed.

Because of the enormous size of the U.S. Embassy in Pretoria, and with so much else going on there, he was considered just another contractor, not central to embassy concerns. Thus, he saw no one higher than a political officer. The AID office got him a translator. But there was a CIA guy, young with a pencil-thin mustache, who seemed impressed by his methodology, and so Gersony had an idea. He knew he was headed into a firestorm in Washington. He knew his work, despite the almost two hundred interviews and six countries covered, would not be judged on its merits. Washington, after all, was less about deep reportage than about opinions held by policy grandees who never went anywhere except for conferences and CODELS (congressional delegation tours). In the midst of this buzz saw, the one organization that the White House would be sure to have check out his reporting with was the CIA. Thus, a CIA endorsement, from Pretoria especially, would be a boost.

"Why don't you come along with me?" Gersony asked the CIA officer casually.

After getting his per diem approved, the CIA officer agreed.

The three of them, including the translator, drove east several hundred miles on the best roads Gersony had seen in sub-Saharan Africa. They passed through Kruger National Park and saw the wild animals in the game preserve. It was the closest Gersony got to real tourism.

At a refugee camp on the South Africa–Mozambique border, Gersony asked the CIA guy to pick out a few people for him to interview. He did, and the story from each was the same: *RENAMO . . . RENAMO . . . Matsanga.* Gersony, satisfied, knew that the guy would file a cable to headquarters in Langley, Virginia.

At the embassy back in Maputo, Gersony spent several days typing up his last 12 interviews in South Africa, and going through the entire 196 of them with yellow, orange, and blue highlighting markers, with the blue denoting the highest order of significance. He knew he had Ambassador Wells on his side, but she was already suspect in the eyes of Jesse Helms and the rest of the right wing. Thus, he also wanted the support of Ambassador James Rawlings, the Reagan political appointee, in Harare. So he asked the DCM in Maputo, Mike Ranneberger, if he would fly with him to Harare where he would deliver the full brief first as a dress rehearsal to both Ranneberger and the DCM there, Ed Fugit. Both were experienced Africa hands and they would constitute a good murder board. Ranneberger, "that hyperactive son-of-a-bitch, actually said 'yes.'"

Ranneberger explains: "I saw the trip to Harare as a way to build regional support for what Bob was doing. His report was an opportunity not to be missed, since it would allow the embassy in Maputo greater leverage with the FRELIMO government," owing to the political ammunition about RENAMO the embassy could supply.

Gersony took a day to brief Ranneberger and Fugit in the latter's house in Harare. "I remember Bob going through page after page of a yellow legal pad. The thoroughness of it all, there was so much attention to detail," Ranneberger remembers, closing his eyes for a moment.

The next day Ambassador Jim Rawlings gave Gersony two hours

of his time. Cables went out from Maputo and Harare to Jonathan Moore and Chet Crocker in Washington.

In Washington, Gersony delivered the long, six-hour version of his brief to Jonathan Moore, complete with maps. Moore, delighted, was excited about the policy battle to come.

"Don't speak to anybody about this," he ordered Gersony.

Meanwhile, Moore called Chet Crocker, who offered Gersony one hour of his time. Gersony refused, saying that "Chet's neck will be on the line over this, so he will need to know all the details." Gersony was by now acting a bit like a prima donna. But Crocker relented and gave him two consecutive two P.M. to five P.M. slots in his office, to be joined by Chas Freeman and Roy Stacy, the deputy assistant secretaries. Though both briefings were after lunchtime, nobody nodded out for even a moment. Crocker, grinning at the end, said he wanted the written report on his desk in a week. Gersony pleaded for several weeks, since he still hadn't analyzed all the data from the 196 interviews.

"No, I need it in a week," Crocker said. "Because if word leaks out about the report, the Left will accuse me of suppressing it."

"Give him two weeks," said Moore quietly, a tone of voice somewhat rare for him.

"All right," said Crocker.

Gersony knew he needed help. Specifically, he needed someone who could collate on a computer all his systematic data from the interviews—the total number of rapes, murders, and so on that people had seen with their own eyes, meshing it all with time frames and geographical locations, and then using these numbers to project fatality rates for the whole Mozambican population.

He asked a friend at USAID from his Guatemala days, Jane Kochman, if she knew anyone who could help. "Well, there's Cindy Davis," Jane said. Cindy was ten years younger than Bob, the adopted daughter of a Naval Academy graduate. She had been educated at Wellesley and was now a contractor for the Office of Foreign Disaster Assistance (OFDA) in the State Department. She was also part of an OFDA committee to decide what kind of computer system to introduce there, this being the early days of widespread computer use. "I was very good with information management," she says. Bob will never forget his first memory of Cindy Davis: a cute girl with a miniskirt and high heels. "I really need your help!" he pleaded. "No, I can't," she answered, explaining that she already had a full-time job, while also working on a master's degree at George Washington University. "I wouldn't give up. I kept working on her, and she relented."

"Bob was really in a state of nervousness," Cindy recalls. "He took me down to the State Department cafeteria and told me he had sensitive data that had to be extracted and organized into an analysis. It sounded fascinating and I always cared about refugees and human rights, and he already had a reputation."

Cindy and Bob began pulling all the data together from his typed notes in Moore's seventh-floor office. "It was a drama that emerged in the silence of data analysis," she says. "This person in this refugee camp talking about the same incident as that person in a displaced persons camp many miles apart. I became attracted to Bob. He was smart and compelling."

A few days after they had begun working together, Cindy passed a handwritten note on a small piece of paper to Bob. It read: "From Chet to Bob: meet me tomorrow to brief Shultz in his office." He had moved up another peg, he momentarily thought to himself.

The office of the secretary of state is long and ornate with a fireplace. On the afternoon of March 28, 1988, Gersony saw Jonathan Moore and Chester Crocker waiting for him at the entrance. Then George Shultz arrived with a woman. "I'd like you all to meet Maureen Reagan," he said. The president's eldest child was particularly close to him, and also active on policy issues. Gersony was shown to a small couch. Directly facing him in two chairs as they all sat down were Maureen Reagan and the secretary of state. Crocker and Moore sat to the side, a bit in the background. They had arranged the seating so that the secretary of state and the president's daughter would get the full-bore Gersony treatment.

"Go ahead," Shultz said.

Gersony unloaded with his methodology, description of his refugee interviews, and his conclusions. The woman with the black kerchief who had let go of her daughter's hand, the forced portering, the
rapes, the mutilations, the killing of babies, were all crammed into the
one-hour brief: the grim highlights of his six-hour talk. He was never
interrupted. The president's daughter was visibly moved. Shultz was
angry at the substance of the material, and occasionally shook his
head slightly. Neither was accustomed to this sort of brief. Shultz bore
down on Crocker with his typical Buddha-like, chairman-of-the-board
face: "Is there anything the South Africans won't stoop to?"[9] The secretary of state then turned to Maureen: "What do we do?"

"I'm having dinner with Dad tomorrow night. This is what I'm
going to talk about," she said.

Shultz actually met twice with Reagan over the next week.[10] Following that came an April 12 meeting in the White House attended
by the president, Secretary of Defense Frank Carlucci, National Security Adviser Colin Powell, Deputy Chief of Staff Kenneth Duberstein,
and many other officials and conservative luminaries who filled every
seat at the vast cabinet table.[11] The subject was the Afghan peace
agreement[12] and the unfinished business of the Reagan administration, particularly the Reagan Doctrine, that required attention in the
final nine months of the president's second term. What other guerrilla movements in the world required Reagan Doctrine help? Someone reportedly raised the question of RENAMO, requesting that
those "freedom fighters"—a term both romantic and deceptive—
finally get support.

According to one source, Reagan put up his hand, and armed with
his trademark, deadly serious half smile, said:

"Hold it right there, fellas. We have a report coming out next week
showing that RENAMO is a bunch of murderers." He then recounted
some of their atrocities. "Don't ever mention RENAMO again in my
presence. And if you're smart, you'll drop the subject."[13]

In fact, Shultz had just a few days earlier slipped into Reagan's
hands a one-page "out-of-system breast-pocket memo" that Roy Stacy

and Chet Crocker had drafted about the substance of Gersony's report.

The conservative luminaries were stunned. The president had spoken. Policy had been made. It was that simple. This was a big vindication for Crocker, helped by the fact that the CIA and embassy cables from southern Africa were now vouching for Gersony, who was able to state in the ensuing media debate that Crocker had sent him out to Mozambique with no instructions or agenda of any kind, further buttressing the Africa bureau's claim to objectivity. More help had come from British prime minister Margaret Thatcher, who had previously met FRELIMO leaders Samora Machel and Joaquim Chissano and was impressed by their moderation. Crocker explains that it was the trio of Bob Gersony, Maureen Reagan, and Margaret Thatcher that ultimately convinced Reagan not to support RENAMO.

Meanwhile, Gersony was working feverishly in Moore's office and in his New York apartment on his IBM Selectric, with extra white-out and ink ribbons, on the final draft of his report, leaching out of the copy any word that might indicate emotion of any kind. Even words such as "but" and "only" were sometimes suspect, because of the way they could create emphasis. He wanted the writing to be flat, clinical, without a hint of politics, thus stripping the copy down to facts and the statistical analysis that Cindy Davis had helped him with.

Moore liked every word of the report except for the recommendations at the end and the title that Gersony gave it, "Why Mozambicans Flee." The recommendations Moore felt would merely distract from the heart of the report, which was about the crimes of RENAMO. Moore also complained that the title "sounded too much like an advocacy report." He advised Gersony to come up with a dull bureaucratic title, to further enhance the objectivity of the material. The final published title would be "Summary of Mozambican Refugee Accounts of Principally Conflict-Related Experience in Mozambique." It was barely grammatical. Because no one could ever remember such a title, it would become well known as simply "the Gersony report." No one knew at the time that there would be a more famous "Gersony report" having to do with Rwanda six years hence. Moore's advice succeeded beyond his imagining, so much so that Moore himself would be forgotten in the affair, with Gersony getting all the Washington media attention, even though Moore had been the bureaucratic driver behind Gersony's work in Mozambique from the beginning.

The forty-page report begins and ends with statistics. The author states that he visited 42 locations in five countries, which included 25 refugee camps separated by as much as 1,500 miles. The 196 refugees and displaced persons interviewed came from 48 different districts of Mozambique, each of which Gersony names. "The relationship between RENAMO and the population," he writes, "appears to revolve solely around the extraction of resources, strictly by force, without explanation, with no tolerance for refusal, and without reciprocation." He adds that "the possession of new clothes, a radio, any type of army issue apparel such as a belt or cap—perhaps even a bag of salt—may be enough to trigger torture or death." There were, too, reports of "targeted retribution against small children," involving "mutilation and subsequent killing . . . in retaliation against parents who fled a RENAMO visit or attack against their homes." The overwhelming majority of the refugees and displaced persons "cited RENAMO actions as the reason for their flight."[14] Forty percent said they had personally witnessed the murder of civilians by RENAMO. Ninety-one percent said they had a "very negative" impression of RENAMO; 7 percent had a "very negative" impression of FRELIMO, and 2 percent were undecided.

The refugees observed that RENAMO appeared to have no ideology or program. There was "almost no reported effort to explain" the purpose of the insurgents' actions or the nature of their goals, or to enlist the loyalty of the population. "The only reciprocity the captives appear to receive or to expect is the opportunity to remain alive."

Gersony writes that the refugees and displaced persons he interviewed lacked two basic skills that hindered their own observations. They could not identify the month and year of an incident. Therefore, the author had to work back through "seasonal agricultural thresholds" like rainy and dry seasons to establish rough timelines. And most could not accurately count above the number 10. Beyond the number 10, the only word used was "many." Thus, in quantifying casualty reports the term "many" was assigned a maximum value of 10 by Gersony. Deliberately lowballing casualty rates by this and other means, Gersony said that RENAMO was responsible for the deaths of at least 100,000 Mozambicans. "I knew the figure was low," he says. "But I did not want anybody to undermine my analysis with an even lower number." Nobody ever did. UNICEF would later put the figure at 600,000.[15]

The State Department's refugee bureau could not print up several thousand copies fast enough, given the demand within and outside the building. Once the news circulated that Shultz and Maureen Reagan had met with Gersony, everyone wanted to be briefed, from Deputy Secretary of State John Whitehead and Undersecretary of State for Political Affairs Michael Armacost on down. It was his briefing on Mozambique to Assistant Secretary of State for Intelligence and Research Morton Abramowitz that permanently anchored Gersony's friendship with Mort and his wife, Sheppie.

Mort had been ambassador to Thailand in the late 1970s, when there were hundreds of thousands of refugees in the country, and a future ambassador to Turkey during the First Gulf War. He would help found the International Crisis Group, committed to ending deadly conflicts. Abramowitz had not only a deep heart but a ready sense of humor. "Boy," he said, laughing during Gersony's briefing, "is there going to be a shitstorm with Helms over this." Abramowitz tells me thirty years later, "Gersony always had fascinating information about how high policy was affecting ordinary people's lives. He knew many things that people at the high levels missed. Every time I talked to him I learned something vital. And he wasn't a pain in the ass."

Of course, the right wing as well as military circles were in an uproar as word spread that one lone contractor helped upend pending administration support for RENAMO. At a Pentagon briefing, attended by uniformed personnel and civilian defense bureaucrats from the building and the Defense Intelligence Agency (DIA), Gersony had barely got started explaining his methodology when a DIA official interrupted, saying, "We've all read the report and know what's in it," before tearing into Gersony and assailing his motives. It appeared that elements of the defense community had gotten ahead of the policy: that is, they were leaning too far over the handlebars and had already begun the planning stages for how to assist RENAMO when Gersony's report suddenly landed on their laps. (Indeed, the year before, the DIA had already downplayed the RENAMO massacre of hundreds of civilians in Homoine, noting that "damage to buildings was limited."[16]) The DIA had been relying considerably on the CIA's directorate of operations for its information about RENAMO, and the CIA's directorate of operations was relying on information provided by the South African security services, which wanted the Americans to believe that RENAMO would eventually win against FRELIMO troops.[17]

But it was more than that. The DIA official, who admits "the extraordinary quality of Gersony's accomplishments over the course of an exceptional career," had an intellectual disagreement with him on this particular issue. His colleagues genuinely thought that FRELIMO bore an equal share of the blame for the flight of Mozambican refugees, despite what the refugees and displaced persons had told Gersony. Moreover, RENAMO represented an authentic "nationalist movement," making it more than just a bunch of thugs and killers. Clearly, FRELIMO forces were not angels, being brutal and incompetent in their own right. The few journalists who were able to visit the parts of Mozambique held by RENAMO during the war all reported a more ambiguous human rights situation than the one portrayed by the refugees that Gersony had interviewed. It was a messy and confused war, and Gersony knew only what the victims of it had told him.[18] Still, even if instead of 90 percent of the atrocities in Gersony's report were attributed to RENAMO, the real number was only 70 percent, the policy implications would be unchanged. RENAMO was clearly not a group that the U.S. government should support.

By this time, Helms and the conservative *Washington Times* were aiming their cannons in Gersony's direction.

The Washington Times published an editorial accusing the State Department of mounting a "guerrilla war" against the Reagan Doctrine. The editorial called out Gersony by name, as a tool of Crocker's "propaganda blitz." The editorial quoted longtime RENAMO advocate and analyst at the right-wing Heritage Foundation, William Pascoe, as saying that Gersony's report "should be dismissed by those concerned with understanding the true nature of the conflict in Mozambique." Pascoe, who, like the *Washington Times* editors, had never called Gersony for a briefing, claimed that Gersony did not speak the "language" of the refugees. Of course, there was no such "language," but rather eighteen different languages and dialects, often mutually unintelligible, necessitating eleven translators from vastly different regions, unknown to each other, that Gersony employed in order to get a cross-section of viewpoints. Pascoe also accused Gersony of interviewing only refugees guarded by FRELIMO soldiers, forgetting the many interviews Gersony conducted in five countries bordering Mozambique, where obviously no FRELIMO troops were present. The lengthy editorial lamented that "President Reagan himself may have swallowed" Gersony's analysis and the "illusions" of Crocker and Foggy Bottom.[19] As it would turn out, though, others much closer to *The Washington Times* would soon swallow those so-called illusions as well. The editorial was a case of ideology and rank partisanship slandering meticulous reporting and fieldwork, something that would only become more typical in Washington in the decades following.

In Washington, even during the Cold War, having the president and the secretary of state behind you only created more enemies. Gersony knew he needed help. He called Robert Hunter, a born-again Christian active in the national prayer breakfast circuit, whom he had met at one of his briefings about the Luwero Triangle in

Uganda. Hunter arranged for Gersony to speak at a prayer breakfast attended by Helms's staffers and other followers.

The prayer breakfast was held at the beginning of May at Fellowship House in Washington, later described by *New Yorker* writer Peter J. Boyer as a "frat house for Jesus."[20] Gersony arrived in the sumptuous, flower-bedecked dining room, decorated with paintings and religious books, at 6:30 A.M., half an hour early as usual, always terribly insecure throughout his life about being late. Roughly twenty people filed in without introducing themselves or shaking his hand. The atmosphere was noticeably hostile. Everyone held hands and squeezed their eyes shut to pray before beginning to eat their bacon and eggs. Hunter introduced Gersony as "a friend" on matters relating to Africa, whom he hoped everyone would listen to with an open mind.

Gersony related his methodology to the group, the numbers of people he interviewed and how he had interviewed them. Then he spoke about the gratuitous murders, the killing of children, the forced portering, and so forth. Silence. Finally an old portly gentleman stood up, seconded by others, and said: "I want to apologize to you on behalf of everyone in this room. I had no idea you were so serious. We are going back to talk to the senator." Everyone walked over to Gersony and shook his hand before departing. Helms soon abruptly withdrew his support for RENAMO. It may have been the only time Jesse Helms reversed himself on a major symbolic issue for the right wing.

It still wasn't quite over, though. A number of congressmen, notably Senator Bob Dole of Kansas, then running against Vice President George H. W. Bush for the Republican presidential nomination, announced that if elected he would immediately fund the RENAMO "freedom fighters" against communism. Gersony phoned Elliott Abrams, telling Abrams's secretary that he needed to give her boss a briefing about Mozambique. Abrams agreed, knowing that if Gersony insisted on talking to him, it must mean that there was some trouble. Abrams was still the assistant secretary of state for Latin

America, but because he was so immersed in directing the contra war in Nicaragua, he had a lot of influence among movement conservatives throughout Washington.

Gersony ended his briefing for Abrams by saying that Dole didn't know what he was talking about. Abrams briefly smiled, then called Dole's chief of staff while Gersony was still in his office, announcing into the phone that "we've got to walk this one back up the branch, or else there could be a big problem for the senator." Dole henceforth dropped the subject of RENAMO. Gersony marveled at how Washington worked. He himself would have had to deliver at least an hour-long briefing to convince anyone of what to do about an issue, whereas if you were trusted in the right circles one sentence without any specifics would do.

Abrams's trust in Gersony was absolute. He had recently written a letter to Gersony's father, saying: "Your son Bob is a national treasure, and for years now, we have been relying on him for courageous and absolutely straightforward analyses of some of the most difficult humanitarian problems our country faces."[21]

Abrams explained his thinking to me this way: "For years we [conservatives] had made heroes out of Jonas Savimbi and the anti-communist resistance in Angola. Helms, Dole, [Pat Buchanan, U.N. ambassador Jeane Kirkpatrick, CIA director William Casey] were all supporting RENAMO, which was viewed as an analogue of UNITA, Savimbi's force.[22] So we all assumed that published attacks on RENAMO were merely propaganda from the Left. Then Bob shows up, and guess what: we learn that the Left is right on this one!"[23]

Crocker immediately sent Gersony back to southern Africa, accompanied by the principal deputy assistant secretary, Chas Freeman, to brief the leaders in the region about what the United States had learned about RENAMO, and to drive home the point that the United States, contrary to assumptions, had no intention now of backing RENAMO. Rather than fly directly home, Gersony flew from southern Africa to Portugal to link up with Jonathan Moore.

After briefing Portuguese officials, who were formally backing RENAMO but were not surprised by what Gersony told them, Moore insisted on taking Gersony out for a celebratory dinner, now that Gersony's report had raised the status of the refugee bureau. Moore got pleasantly loaded on Portuguese wines, whose quality he extolled, while Gersony drank ginger ale. Moore would later tell his wife, Katie, that Bob Gersony was the finest of all fieldworkers he had come across. "This man was *it*."[24]

History pivoted in southern Africa thanks to Bob Gersony.

If you accept the fact that Gersony's figure of 100,000 dead because of RENAMO's war against the FRELIMO government was a lowball estimate, then his report probably saved the lives of hundreds of thousands more civilians, who would have been killed had the Reagan Doctrine been applied to Mozambique as it had been to the Afghan mujahideen, the Nicaraguan contras, and other groups, perhaps dragging out the war in Mozambique for another fourteen years, as in the case of Angola, where half a million people perished. Instead, because of the political effect of the Gersony report in Washington, Crocker and his counterpart on Africa at the National Security Council, Herman Cohen, were immediately able to move into high gear facilitating peace talks between RENAMO and FRELIMO, which culminated successfully in 1992.

In turn, dramatically calming and then ending the war in Mozambique—which perhaps constituted Crocker's fiercest interagency battle—helped facilitate the demise of the apartheid regime in South Africa, with Nelson Mandela elected as the country's first black president in 1994. For suddenly the white rulers in Pretoria did not have a hot guerrilla war on their hands right on their border that they were promoting, and consequently they felt less besieged in regard to their overall strategy. The end of the Mozambique conflict made it easier for Chet Crocker, in Chas Freeman's words, "to rearrange the strategic geometry in southern Africa."[25] By moving closer to apartheid South Africa, while also pressuring it by opening peace talks with Cuba over Angola, Crocker's high-wire diplomacy resulted in an end to the civil war in Angola and the end of white South African colonialism in Southwest Africa (Namibia). Both developments would help catalyze the end of apartheid itself.

Crocker, along with Henry Kissinger, George Shultz, James Baker III, and Richard Holbrooke, was one of the great diplomatic masters of the age, however underappreciated he remains compared to the others. And he received a stroke of luck with the Gersony report. In Crocker's diplomatic memoir, he writes that a significant reason "why we prevailed was the outstanding humanitarian research undertaken by . . . Gersony," whom he goes on about at some length.[26]

On October 2, 1992, the government of Mozambique and RENAMO signed a formal peace treaty. One of the two chief negotiators, the Italian diplomat Mario Rafaelli, called the Gersony report a "fundamental turning point in the peace process." Because of Gersony, "Mozambique remained an internal conflict and did not become internationalized."

There is a fitting coda to Gersony's work in Mozambique.

One of Gersony's interviewees was a woman, a farmer, whose left hand was deformed and who spoke Shangani. She told him that in late December 1985, the people of her village had dug a network of tunnels to hide from the Matsanga. When they heard RENAMO was coming, they would disappear into the tunnels and would cover the narrow entrances with a carpet of leaves and dirt. The ploy worked a couple of times. But RENAMO found out about the tunnels by interrogating a boy who showed them the entrances. The soldiers then suffocated the occupants by lighting stacks of bush and throwing them down every hole. When the villagers burst out of the holes to escape, RENAMO shot them. Hundreds of villagers died, the woman claimed. Gersony could not use the story in his final report because it was based on a single source and strained credibility.

But after Gersony had left the region, the DCM at the U.S. Embassy in Maputo, Mike Ranneberger, who was traveling around the country at the time in a small plane, met a woman in a displaced persons camp who told him the exact same story. Ranneberger went to the village in question with her and saw the tunnels himself.

"This is why you must always believe refugees," Gersony says. "Their stories have a literal truth that is hard to replicate."

In fact, as the Cold War went on and reached its later stages, the issue of refugees increasingly penetrated the sanctums of top policymakers, helped by the likes of Shepard Lowman, Lionel Rosenblatt, Mort Abramowitz, and Elliott Abrams, to say nothing of Jim Purcell, Gene Dewey, and Jonathan Moore. And most of these men had been, in turn, dramatically sensitized on the subject by the fieldwork of Bob Gersony. Indeed, the humanitarianism of the 1990s did not emerge out of a vacuum, a product exclusively of the end of the Cold War and the consequent liberation from realpolitik. It had important roots in the Cold War itself, of which Mozambique was a prime example.

CHAPTER 9

Ethiopia and Somalia
1989

A Giant Table That Had Just Tilted Over

With Mozambique behind him, Gersony's methodology and place in the world was fully established and articulated. So it is a good moment to pause and take another, deeper look at him—and at myself, too.

"The great success and wealth of Bob's father, coupled with Bob always being an insecure outsider in the State Department bureaucracy, was what ultimately drove Bob's ambition," observes Peter Kranstover, a USAID lifer who first met Gersony in Guatemala back in the seventies. "And Bob's success at State and AID over the decades," Kranstover goes on, "was built on sheer fastidiousness. He just wears you down." Indeed, Gersony, a high school dropout, sought acceptance in a world where he lacked the educational pedigree for admission, even as he realized he was the intellectual equal of almost anyone in the room. His obsessive-compulsive approach to work may have derived from this insecurity.

"Mozambique was the big turning point in Bob's professional life, when he became a star," says Dennis King, the senior humanitarian analyst at the State Department's Bureau of Intelligence and Research. However, even before Mozambique, Gersony had acquired a certain reputation among State's normally cautious civil servants.

"Bob and Fred Cuny, though very different from each other, were each seen as mysterious mavericks," King explains. "Bob and Fred

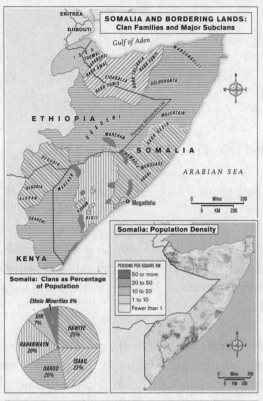

SOMALIA AND BORDERING LANDS: Clan Families and Major Subclans

ERITREA
DJIBOUTI
Gulf of Aden

I·S·S
TOUMAL
SAMARURSI
HABR AWAL
EIDAGALLA
HABR YUNIS
WARSANGELLI
HABR TOLJAALA
HABR YUNIS
DOLBOHANTA

ETHIOPIA
OGADENI
MAJERTAIN
MARENAN
HABR GEDIR
HAWIDTE
MUDSUSUADE
MURDSADE
HABAR
ABGAI

Provisional Administrative Line

SOMALIA

ARABIAN SEA

DEGODIA
MARENAN
DEGODIA
AJURAN
OGADENI
AJURAN
DIGIL

○ Mogadishu

KENYA

| 0 | Miles | 200 |
| 0 | KM | 200 |

Somalia: Clans as Percentage of Population

Ethnic Minorities 6%

- DIR 7%
- HAWIYE 25%
- RAHANWAYN 20%
- ISAAQ 22%
- DAROO 20%

Somalia: Population Density

PERSONS PER SQUARE KM
- 50 or more
- 20 to 50
- 10 to 20
- 1 to 10
- Fewer than 1

| 0 | Miles | 200 |
| 0 | KM | 200 |

ETHIOPIA-SOMALIA BORDER REFUGEE CAMPS

Gulf of Aden

△ Darbihore

Bulhar
Berbera ●
Gelokor
Daragodleh
Bihendula
△ Bixin
Biyoley
Gabile
Adiades
Sheikh

△ Darimaan
△ Ohamuk
● Boroma
Agabar
△ Las Dhure
Darboruk
Darweina
Dubato
Adadle

Dila
Gebile
Daawale
Calabeid
△ Tug Wajale
Arapsio
Aubakhadle
△ Saabad
Dam
Hargeisa ●
Hahe
Odweina
Burao ●

Jijiga ●
Hartesheikh △
● Kebreh Beyeh
△ Harshin

NORTHWEST SOMALIA

ETHIOPIA

Cam Aboker △
Rabasso △
Aware ●
Daror △
Duruksi ●

△ Refugee Camps

| 0 | Miles | 20 |
| 0 | KM | 20 |

● Degeh Bur

didn't tell people what they liked to hear. Bob's reports especially carried an aura of credibility because they were so long and detailed. There were those in the bureaucracy who resented them both" as private contractors, who had walk-in privileges with assistant secretaries of state. "Unlike Fred Cuny, Bob's personality was very closed. He didn't let people in. That only added to his mystique. Of course, Bob and Fred are types that no longer exist," King goes on. "Now State uses Beltway bandit firms [big corporate consultancies] who charge a lot of money because they have a high overhead, and their people rarely tell you anything interesting."

Contrary to Beltway bandit firms, says King, "Bob Gersony was a big believer in not going to secondary sources. He based his research on those who were at the end of the chain of events and decision-making. Thus, it was the refugees who were the real chroniclers of history, in Bob's view."

As I have already said, because I am writing about Gersony, I will never have to write an autobiography (not that I am important enough for such an endeavor). For we truly have led parallel lives, covering the same countries and crossing paths periodically. I started out as a freelancer living out of youth hostels and cheap hotels for some years, discovering my path largely on my own without connections or professional mentors: except for a short stint as a reporter on a Vermont newspaper. To make a living I was always looking for what "the crowd" wasn't reporting on, and making that my subject. I was lonely in the way that Gersony was. I listen to him describe his methodology to me, which he discovered completely on his own, and I flash back to what I wrote in my very first book, about interviewing ethnic-Oromo refugees from Ethiopia in 1986 in a camp in northwestern Somalia, unaware then of how Gersony was doing things:

> I interviewed fourteen refugees at Tug Wajale B and another nearby camp in three days at the end of October 1986. Almost all of the interviews were done in isolation; the refugee was moved by Land Cruiser to an area out of earshot from his or

her compatriots, where I spent, on the average, about ninety minutes talking to the person. The translator I used was not a member of the Oromo Liberation Front or any other political organization I know of, and he had been highly recommended to me by several foreign relief officials. I tried hard to avoid asking leading questions, and I sought constantly to ferret out inconsistencies in the stories I heard, so much so that one of the women I interviewed accused me of being hostile. Despite all of these precautions, I was impressed with the consistency of the accounts [of rape, persecution, and forced resettlement].[1]

Neither Gersony nor I ever used a tape recorder. We are devotees of the pen and notebook. I have filled several notebooks listening to Gersony and nearly a hundred of his colleagues talk about his life. Like me, he is by nature conservative and skeptical of elite opinion, a realist by temperament if not by conviction. In fact, he has never belonged to a community of believers. He has been a realist, humanist, interventionist, and noninterventionist, depending upon what his ground-level research in each situation and each location has revealed to him. The truth is in the field, not in Washington.

For Gersony, the truth emerges from the bottom up, in the specificity of each conflict zone: places that people in the nation's capital with their grand schemes only see in shadows. That is ultimately why diplomats and policymakers believed him. Like me, he has always been a freelancer in the spiritual sense: a contractor who has had to get himself hired over and over again by different people throughout his career. He has always been an outlier, never really part of any institution—not an NGO worker, nor part of USAID, the Foreign Service, or any other group. This made him perennially insecure and anxious, as Peter Kranstover says, but it is also perhaps a reason why he never developed an ego, and why he had periodic physical and spiritual breakdowns. But it is also what made him independent-minded. No bureaucracy ever captured him.

Gersony and I are both introverts who crave solitude, even though we have been forced by circumstances to be extroverts. I love reporting and interviewing people; but I love reading and being alone even more, and so I have always infused my reporting with what I learn from books.

Gersony likes to think of himself as primarily a great listener. But he has also been a great briefer, and a bit of a sly bureaucratic operator. We both feel ourselves to be cowards, even though we have been forced to continually take risks, both physical and intellectual. Like Gersony, for decades coming home from assignments, I wanted to kiss the ground of my house; even so, we both are away constantly and married women who were comfortable with us being away not days, but weeks or months at a time. We are generalists, not globalists, with quite similar libraries that emphasize books on specific landscapes and human terrains. We both had old fathers who loved us and imparted much vital knowledge to us, but who also didn't know how to be fathers, and whose own families, by the way, both came from Latvia. And we both "could have gone wrong" early in life, as Ursula Strauss puts it. I wandered around the globe for years in my twenties before I found a direction.

Gersony is a character out of a Saul Bellow novel trapped in settings depicted by Joseph Conrad. Like Bellow's heroes—Artur Sammler and Moses Herzog, for example—he is fearful, neurotic, deliciously ironical, and haunted by guilty memories: a hypochondriac of the spirit who takes nothing for granted; someone with an abnormally dark mood, partly a consequence of the circumstances of his work, but who is also deeply warm, considerate, and loving; a sufferer who internalizes the suffering of others. He is full of confessions with a rich, baroque interiority, and humorous in his very Jewish identity. But rather than inhabit New York or Chicago, the scene of Bellow's great novels, Gersony spent his professional life in Africa and Latin America, among other such places: locations often deemed hopeless. The characters with whom Gersony had to deal early in his career— the cynical Lucas Garcia in Guatemala and the superficial Perry Seraphin in Dominica—evoke nothing so much as the characters in the desperate backwater of Costaguana, the setting for Conrad's *Nos-*

tromo (1904). And as with Conrad in *Heart of Darkness* (1899), the truly appalling conditions of life and the savage nature of the violence in a place like Mozambique only quickened his sense of humanity, and his realization of the interconnectedness of all humankind, and with it the blunt fact of moral responsibility. He was continually horrified by what he saw, but he was never cynical. He dug and dug for facts, so as to hold people and policymakers to account. He has never succumbed to saying "What's the use?" In that and related senses, he is not like me at all.

I can listen to Gersony for hours. He holds you, as with the stories told by sailors in Conrad's *Lord Jim* (1900). I trust him. Almost everyone else he met did, too.

Gersony's assignments had taken on a pattern. He flew economy class and stayed at modest hotels, as did I for many years. He ate alone, and sparingly. He worked twelve-hour days, seven days a week. He squeezed in as many meetings as he could in the capital city: with government officials, foreign embassy officers, and the gamut of the NGO community, in addition to interviewing many dozens and hundreds of refugees and displaced persons in remote and dangerous locations far from the capital. And he fed it all into a rigorous analytical framework. As I have observed, he usually avoided journalists. After all, he was filing confidential reports for the U.S. government, and wanted to come to his conclusions on his own; without having them influenced and conditioned by the ideas of other outside observers. The whole point of his investigations was always to be in firsthand contact with the evidence, while at all costs avoiding groupthink.

Gersony told me that his role model was Philip Habib, a thirty-year veteran of the Foreign Service, who constantly flew around the world, troubleshooting for successive Cold War presidents, and coming back to Washington with real-time strategic analyses of crises in the Middle East, Southeast Asia, and elsewhere. But whereas the boisterous Habib worked at the rarified heights of presidents and prime ministers and secretaries of state, Gersony's analyses came from encounters with refugees and relief workers. It was fascinating, excruciating, grueling, and lonely, but he didn't know how else to live. Whereas Fred Cuny, Gersony's friend and competitor, was like Red Adair, the flashy oil well firefighter from Texas, whom the media lionized, Gersony was like a much calmer version of Philip Habib, the deliberate influencer hovering in the background.

Though it wasn't only Bernard Fall and Philip Habib that provided Gersony with a compass point. There was also a certain category of foreign correspondent that over the years he privately admired—and which I did, too: men and women who spent their lives abroad, becoming expert on one region after another, whose work periodically overlapped with his own, and who were so dryly objective that you could never figure out how they voted. In particular, he would mention James Brooke, Alan Riding, Shirley Christian, and Jane Perlez, all of *The New York Times,* who, taken together, roamed all of Africa, Latin America, and East Asia over the past few decades. For Gersony, these men and women were great precisely because they did not usually break front-page stories, but, in his words, "owned page A3 of the *Times,*" and were therefore even more important because page A3 often featured lengthy, savvy, ground-level situationers of critical and complex countries: again, the realities that Washington overlooked. Because Gersony's was a lonely professional life, his spiritual comrades in arms were a select and somewhat obscure few who never sought or achieved fame, and were the more serious because of it. He admired them from afar, since, with the exception of Alan Riding, he never met them.

But whereas these men and women had each other as colleagues to exchange trade secrets with, Gersony had only his method. Again and again, he goes back to his conversations with refugees, the moments when he has always felt most at peace with himself:

I had to put the person at ease and keep them confident and talking. So I began, as you know, with eight or ten easy questions. I could see they were pleased with their answers. I believe their greatest fear was not being able to answer well, not to be able to hold up their end of the discussion. I employed translators who were empathetic and respectful, who sent the message that it was all right for people to say things that could come back to harm them and their families, even to cause harm to their relatives still living in the country they fled.

I had to listen carefully to each sentence, understand what the person was saying through a translator, about an environment that was new to me, with place-names it took a while for me to become familiar with. I had to clarify or ask for details sometimes without appearing hostile or doubtful, assess what they said, try to keep the chronology straight when their narrative jumped around in time, or the translator used the wrong tense in his translation.

I had to think quickly about how a location, a type of event, a type of victim, a type of weapon, a time of day, might match up with another account I had heard elsewhere. It got complicated, especially as the number of persons interviewed went up into the hundreds in each conflict zone. I made careful, almost verbatim notes, which had to be clear enough so I could read them later. I was constantly thinking about topics I wanted to ask about when the flow of their spontaneous, mostly unimpeded account ended.

Since I had only one opportunity with each person, I had to make sure I asked every question, cleared up every loose end, did not miss some important clue about some insight or topic that they themselves might not emphasize. Was the person being truthful? Did certain questions make him or her nervous? I had to pace the interview, make sure not to exhaust the person, let them go at their own speed, but not so fast that we missed important details. I couldn't probe too hard, or make them nervous. I had to be reassuring but not too much. I had to remember that they were exhausted to begin with. Some had just staggered into camp from Mozambique or from wherever, emaciated, having escaped with only their lives.

Gersony also needed to encourage and appreciate the translator, who was concentrating even harder than he was on the dialogue and on getting it right. He or she was working twice as hard as Gersony, actually. Gersony tried to make sure he or she wasn't pursuing questions or clarifications of his own that might affect the person's account. He always had to make sure the translator had enough food, water, and regular small breaks. He had to keep an eye out for anyone who might wander around, or into the room, or to the place behind the tree, and interrupt the flow of the conversation or spook the interviewee. As an interview went on, he had to decide how much more of a benefit the particular interviewee could be in providing information, or whether he should continue to the next person.

Usually the person warmed to the conversation. He or she liked being appreciated and respected, listened to, with follow-up questions asked at the end showing their message had gotten through. They realized they had something important to say. The tragedies and hardships they had experienced would be used to help their people somehow, they must have believed. There were a few who never wanted to leave, who wanted to just keep talking. During the interviews, he was always thinking where the next stop on his trip would be, where he'd get dinner, where he'd sleep.

Each person, he told me, required 100 percent concentration. It was a mental strain. At the same time, he had to keep himself detached, not get too absorbed into, or influenced by, the emotional dimension of what he was hearing: not let the drama and heartbreaking events of their accounts move him off an objective center. He usually received reports of abuses by both sides, though in Mozambique it was mostly by RENAMO. The travel was tough, and listening to the accounts of so many traumatized people all day long was a strain.

At night, he was exhausted, but his mind was running through what he had heard that day, processing it. Sometimes he couldn't sleep for hours. There were cycles of understanding that affected his sleep. He would have epiphanies, usually after several weeks of interviews, that kept his mind racing for hours.

I was often living inside the interviews, rather than in the physical environment, picturing what I was being told about. I was not especially conscious of the landscape or living arrangements, which were simple: a cot, a dirt floor, a tent, a room in a school, a sleeping bag, sometimes just a bowl of water to wash and shave with. There were heavy rains. I was often never in one place long enough to clean clothes. I made notes by candlelight, alone in the late evenings with lots of bugs and ticks, and occasional snakes.

Mozambique marked the culmination of his interview technique. Afterward he made adjustments, but he never substantially improved upon it. He was now at the top of his game, and all his assignments henceforth took on an importance that the previous ones had not quite had.

Yet the loneliness had only intensified as the years went on. It was the very consequence of his methodology. Interviewing thousands of refugees with whom he could not have personal conversations only worsened the situation. In his letters to his girlfriend Ann Siegel he went on about this all the time. After all, he usually could not tell people what he knew, and because he was clumsy at small talk, it was better for him to simply keep away from people, period. He became antisocial. He stayed in his hotel room and ordered room service. Out in the field there were the military roadblocks and the 24/7 security threat. The bad food, the fevers, diarrhea, and exhaustion all added up to frequent depression.

Oddly, given his life's work, he was not a very good traveler. Great travelers all possess more optimistic, even happy-go-lucky frames of mind. Great travelers are connoisseurs of landscape who can have an engaging conversation with anybody, and who love fine food and drink, even as they revel in the dangers and deprivations. Gersony, who was all work and bone-dry analysis, was the antithesis of that.

• • •

Gersony returned home to New York from his trip through southern Africa and Portugal in August 1988, and a few days later his Mozambique assignment officially ended. There were no follow-ups. Nobody ever called to inform him of further developments or to ask his advice about Mozambique. That's the way it usually was with freelance contract assignments at the State Department. One day you were the center of attention and the next day you didn't exist.

Jonathan Moore at Refugee Programs had no new assignment for him at the moment, so Gersony journeyed to the Dominican Republic and soon afterward to the Honduran border on USAID assignments, the later one having to do with the families of U.S.-supported Nicaraguan contra guerrillas. But while Gersony was once again immersed in Latin America, events culminating in the Horn of Africa were of increasing interest to Jonathan Moore.

The Horn of Africa was where my scattershot relationship with Gersony had begun in 1985. We met in Khartoum, when the Sudanese capital functioned as the principal listening post for the wars that racked Ethiopia and the Somali borderlands next door. The Horn, much of whose landscape was like the forbidding, inhospitable surface of a distant planet, a place for only nomads and camels, had been for many years in the 1970s and 1980s ground zero for the Cold War.

The Cold War may have started and ended in Europe, but the blood was shed in the Third World. And outside of the Korean peninsula and Vietnam, where Americans themselves had fought in large numbers, the Horn of Africa may arguably have been the most dramatic and clear-cut case of strategic positioning and competition for the two superpowers.

The strategically located Horn, at the confluence of the Indian Ocean and the mouth of the Red Sea by the Strait of Bab el Mandeb, formed one of the world's most critical and vulnerable shipping lanes, as vessels going to, and coming from, the Suez Canal had to practically hug the coastlines of Djibouti, Somalia, and Ethiopia. For decades, until 1974, the United States had a firm ally in Ethiopian emperor Haile Selassie, the small bearded man with a pith helmet and bedecked with medals who was larger than life, and who ruled a country of 32 million people back then; the Soviet Union had a firm ally in Somalia's president Mohamad Siad Barre, a tough desert warlord who ruled a much poorer and much less urbanized population of only 3.6 million at that time.

Courtesy of Haile Selassie, Ethiopia had granted the United States permission for a crucial military communications complex near Asmara, the capital of the province of Eritrea. The evils of Haile Selassie's reactionary misrule certainly were well known to U.S. policymakers, and generous economic aid was designed to mitigate the backbreaking poverty of the Ethiopian masses. Haile Selassie's downfall began with the 1973–74 famine in the regions of Tigre and Wollo, news of which filtered back, despite local censorship, to radicals in Addis Ababa. And so in early 1974 the "creeping coup" began, starting with a strike by taxi drivers in the capital. Events soon cascaded. It wasn't as if Haile Selassie's picture was abruptly removed from the city's ubiquitous high walls; rather, the image imperceptibly changed, day by day, a line at a time, until the emperor's face was wiped out and the face of Mengistu Haile Mariam, a remorseless, thirty-two-year-old army captain, emerged out of the dim background.

By the end of 1974, as Ethiopia came under the rule of the shadowy clique or Dergue and Mengistu methodically eliminated his rivals, students were being forcibly dispatched to the countryside to revolutionize the masses. The Soviets were duly impressed, and dispatched East German security advisers to help Mengistu plan his next moves. Mengistu was now emerging as the most lethal sort of dictator: the kind with stores of ascetic discipline and therefore not distracted by greed.

In May of 1977, the Red Terror began, when soldiers gunned down hundreds in the streets of Addis Ababa, including university students and children. The new U.S. president, Jimmy Carter, washed his hands of Ethiopia, cutting off arms deliveries, because of its human rights violations. Mengistu responded by flying to Moscow for a weeklong state visit. It was then that the Soviets began one of the most massive arms transfers ever in the history of the Third World. Castro sent soldiers direct from pro-Soviet Somalia to Ethiopia, and tanks and armored personnel carriers began arriving from Marxist South Yemen, as Moscow orchestrated a brazen and dramatic switch: trading up from an alliance with empty and impoverished Somalia to one with the far more populous and consequential empire of Ethiopia. Late in 1977, the Somalis expelled their Soviet advisers and came running to the United States for help. The great superpower flip-flop of the Cold War was under way.

Moscow got a better ally in Mengistu than Washington had had in Haile Selassie. Mengistu turned out to be not merely a pro-Soviet African leader, but a full-fledged Marxist who turned Ethiopia into an African version of an East European satellite, as the Ethiopian countryside became a version of Ukraine during the terror famine of the 1930s. As in Ukraine, untried, theoretical principles of collectivized agriculture were inflicted on a peasantry burdened by centuries of feudalism. The result was the death and starvation of tens of thousands.[2]

Meanwhile, the war between Ethiopia and Somalia—two perennial enemies—dragged on for years and years, leaving hundreds of thousands of refugees on each side of the border in the Ogaden Desert. In 1981, Somali exiles of the Isaaq clan, living in Ethiopia, established the Somali National Movement with Soviet help, in an effort to topple the pro-American Somali government in Mogadishu. Siad Barre responded with a directive to his army to utterly destroy all Isaaq communities and their watering holes in northwestern Somalia. Seven years later, in April 1988, the Ethiopian and Somali leaders finally signed a peace agreement. Consequently, Mengistu told the Isaaq-dominated Somali National Movement, which had been using eastern Ethiopia as a rear base to attack Siad Barre's ethnic-Ogadeni forces in northwestern Somalia, to leave and go back home. The Somali National Movement, loaded with guns and ammunition, decided to make a last stand and launch a full frontal attack on the towns of Hargeisa and Burao in the northwestern end of the bent vertical hot dog that is Somalia on the world map. The upshot was a mass movement of refugees crossing into Ethiopia in the late spring and summer of 1988 to escape the fighting. While Gersony was in Honduras, Mengistu and the other members of the Ethiopian Dergue were complaining that UNHCR was doing an inadequate job minis- tering to the new hordes of refugees now flooding into Ethiopia from Somalia.

It was as if the African Horn were a giant table that had just tilted ever so slightly with all of the marbles (Isaaqs and Ogadenis both) rolling down onto one side.

At this juncture Jonathan Moore dispatched his deputy, Kenneth Bleakley, to travel to the affected region and investigate. Bleakley was the real deal of an FSO (foreign service officer), a former president of the American Foreign Service Association, in fact. But with all of his operational and diplomatic skills, he and the U.S. mission in Addis Ababa could not convince the Dergue to give him permission to travel outside the Ethiopian capital to the Ogaden region, near to the border with Somalia: just as Siad Barre would not let the ICRC and the other NGOs travel to northwestern Somalia to investigate the situation from the other side of the border.

With nobody in the international community having any idea what was actually happening on the ground in this vast desert no- man's-land, famous for Dervish revolts against the British and one of the world's largest camel populations, Moore and Bleakley decided to send Bob Gersony out there, in the hope that he could break through.

So from Honduras, Gersony traveled through Washington and New York to UNHCR headquarters in Geneva, Switzerland, where he met up with Gene Dewey, as well as with International Red Cross operations director Jean-Pierre Hocke, whom he knew from his work on the Luwero Triangle. They promised to send messages to the UNHCR offices in the capitals of Addis Ababa and Mogadishu, say- ing that Gersony should receive all possible assistance. But neither they nor their colleagues in Geneva had any idea about what was really happening on the ground in the Ethiopia-Somalia border re- gion, in this pre-Internet, pre-social-media age.

• • •

ADDIS ABABA, ETHIOPIA. The name is Amharic for "new flower," a city built by Emperor Menelik II in 1889. Though occupied by Mussolini, Ethiopia was never actually colonized by Europeans, and was always less a state than a sprawling empire of different peoples— Amhara, Tigrean, Eritrean, and Oromo. At eight thousand feet in altitude, Menelik's new capital lacked wood. In 1900, the introduction of the fast-growing eucalyptus tree from Australia solved the problem. Consequently, the first sensation one felt in 1988 upon arrival was of bodily well-being, brought about by the invigorating mountain climate and the shade and ubiquitous fragrance of the eucalyptus trees. After the blinding sunlight and leaden heat of other African capitals, "Addis" was like a godsend, as though arriving at a hill station in the Himalayas after weeks on the steamy plain of the Indian subcontinent.

Surrounding Addis were broiling desert badlands and *Lord of the Rings*–style mountains. In the African Horn, only Addis and Asmara, also at a high elevation, were truly pleasant. Gersony has no recollection of any of this. As usual, he was intent on getting his embassy and NGO briefings, and then heading out into the field to start listening to refugees.

He put up at the Hilton, which with its bar, swimming pool, and the ambience of a large, enclosed compound had been a famous hangout for journalists and relief workers during the great Ethiopian famine of the mid-1980s: you would fly up to the famine zone for the day, and fly back at night to file your story by telex and eat at the Hilton. When Gersony arrived there a few years later, there was no official ambassador because of the tense relationship between Washington and the Marxist regime. The American chargé d'affaires was Bob Houdek, whom Gersony knew from his work on Uganda. Gersony's Mozambique report was fresh not only in Houdek's mind, but also in the mind of the Marxist Dergue, which liked the fact that an American official had exposed the abuses of an anti-communist guerrilla group. This helped Gersony to succeed where Bleakley had failed: getting permission to travel to the Ogaden border area.

But the Ethiopian regime insisted that Gersony travel with a minder, that is, a government security agent. It so happened that USAID had in mind a certain FSN, a Foreign Service National: an Ethiopian citizen who worked for USAID. His name was Ato Makonnen Ture, and he was dignified, professorial, in great physical condition, and with indefinable charm. The embassy convinced the Ethiopian authorities to deputize Makonnen as Gersony's minder.

Gersony and Makonnen were outfitted with a four-wheel-drive vehicle bearing diplomatic plates, extra tires, fan belts, oil canisters, an industrial jack and chains, and a winch in front of the car. The driver was also a mechanic who had a full tool set. It was what you needed for a scrappy, dun-drab desert where barely a tree loomed, only anthills.

Gersony and Makonnen drove east to Dire Dawa, entering the forbidding territory that the French poet Arthur Rimbaud and the British traveler Richard Francis Burton had explored in the nineteenth century, Rimbaud as an arms merchant and Burton as a heathen in the Muslim bastion of Harar. In 1930, the British traveler Wilfred Thesiger and the novelist Evelyn Waugh would also pass through here, having attended Haile Selassie's coronation. Waugh would have an acute attack of boredom in these parts, spending days reading a French dictionary and old weekly magazines cover to cover.[3] But Gersony knew little of these literary associations until much later.

At Dire Dawa, the regional capital, Gersony and Makonnen went to the government security office with Gersony's letter of introduction. That was the way he always did things, formally and transparently. Then they went on, through Harar, to Jijiga, where he visited the UNHCR office to announce himself. Finally, another few hours eastward—the vehicle got stuck in black cotton soil on the way—brought him to the vicinity of the Somali border and the refugee camp of Hartesheikh, the largest of five camps in the region, which would become his base for the next three weeks.

He and Makonnen ate all their meals together and shared a hut, where they slept on the desert floor. Every day constituted twelve to fourteen hours of work, of interviewing and typing.

Gersony conducted 120 separate interviews with Isaaq refugees from Somalia in five camps. There was Hartesheikh, where half of the refugees were located, and the satellite camp of Harshin, literally right on the border; roughly a hundred miles to the east lay the three camps of Cam Aboker, Rabasso, and Daror. In typical Gersony style, he began the painstaking documentation, broken down into villages and time frames, of rapes, lootings, shootings, knifings, beatings, regardless of age and sex—what would later become known on the Internet as the Isaaq genocide between 1987 and 1989, conducted by Siad Barre's nominally pro-American Somali Armed Forces, in which up to 100,000 people died.

Gersony wasn't briefed on any of this, but discovered it interview by interview, breaking down the percentages of how many had witnessed a violent incident, where and when, and extrapolating from there. Yet after twenty-one days he still didn't know all this. For by then all he had was raw data in one region that he hadn't as yet analyzed, though he did have a rough awareness of what had transpired.

On March 29—he will never forget the day, as he kept a diary— Gersony was interviewing a man in Harshin into the early evening, something he tried never to do. His rule was to always get back to base camp before dark. But because of his obsession with detail he got caught up in the interview. This old shrunken man, a sixty-five-year-old Isaaq farmer with no education, huddled near a fire with two starving kids, was absolutely credible. He was good with figures, and when Gersony asked him, he guessed correctly the number of people in the camp. The man and his family had escaped from Somalia only five days before. The Somali army had arrived in his village of Beye Gure, he told Gersony, and herded people into trucks without their belongings. He was taken to Berbera on the Gulf of Aden to do forced labor for four months, unloading cargo at the port. The women were made to sew food bags. They were surrounded by soldiers. It was difficult to escape. He told Gersony that he saw many people killed and many dead bodies lying about. He gave the names of seven people he saw murdered. His seven-year-old son died of starvation, as did ninety others, mainly children.

Finally, the story ended.

Gersony and Makonnen headed west back to Hartesheikh. Again, they got stuck in black cotton soil: he was tired and hadn't been paying attention to the road. They found themselves stranded in the middle of an Ogaden Desert security area in utter darkness. It took hours for the driver-mechanic, working with flashlights, to drag the car out of the pit. In the process, the underside of the vehicle hit a rock and the oil case snapped, springing a leak. The driver entered Hartesheikh with his lights off but with his interior lights on. Gersony and Makonnen held their hands up in the air: all this was to reassure the Ethiopian soldiers guarding the camp, since a curfew was in force. Nevertheless, the soldiers began firing their AK-47s in the air, and one bullet hit the car. The soldiers moved in and pointed their assault rifles at Gersony's head. He was almost weeping with fear. Makonnen, talking fast and diplomatically, quickly managed to clear things up.

In April, their last day in the field after the better part of a month, they headed back to Addis Ababa late in the day from Cam Aboker. Again, he had gotten caught up in an interview. They should have spent the night in Hartesheikh, but Gersony was restless to get back to the capital and the comfort of the Hilton, so he stupidly insisted on leaving before dark. Just before arriving in Jijiga, Makonnen told Gersony, "You and the driver sit in the car with the door locked. I will look for a place for us all to stay this night in Jijiga." Gersony, as usual, worried. At last, after about half an hour, Makonnen returned and directed the driver to a stone gate with a wall and double iron door, not quite wide enough for the car. They walked into the compound in the pitch-black and Gersony was shown a room in the back that smelled of perfume with a dirty mattress and a twisted sheet.

"This place is a brothel," Makonnen told him. "But no one is going to bother you."

Left alone, Gersony looked up at a rotted ceiling that he was afraid was about to collapse on him. It had been another fourteen-hour day and he was twitching with fatigue. He had never learned how to relax and pace himself. He took his red Kipling bag with his notebooks inside and used it as a pillow, like he always did, and fell asleep. A cat rubbed against his leg, and he snuggled with it between his legs. (He has always loved animals, and in his home today there are two dogs and two parrots.) But he felt no fur on the tail and wondered what kind of cat has no fur on the tail. It must have been a hundred degrees Fahrenheit. He was filthy and drenched in sweat. He slowly grabbed his flashlight beside him and looked.

It wasn't a cat. It was a rat!

He must have levitated a foot in the air and so did the rat. He gasped in terror. He couldn't sleep the rest of the night. He packed up and counted the minutes till dawn.

They left at six A.M. and were back at the Hilton in Addis Ababa that night after three weeks in the field. He may have taken the longest shower of his life and washed all his gear in the bathtub, had his laundry done, and ordered sandwiches from room service. He never appreciated a hotel as an extraterritorial life-support system so much.

At this point Gersony had a good sense of what had happened to the 300,000 Isaaqs from Somalia who had fled to the camps in Ethiopia that he had just visited. But in Somalia there were hundreds of thousands of Ogadenis who had escaped from Ethiopia during the fighting between the two countries. In fact, Siad Barre was propping up his government with UNHCR money stolen from these refugees in his country. Just like Siad Barre, the Ogadenis were Marehans, a subclan of the Darods. But rather than put them in southern Somalia close to his base and the capital of Mogadishu, Barre put these Ogadeni refugees, his kinsmen, among the Isaaqs in northwestern Somalia. He had recruited these Ogadeni refugees for his army and used them to fight and terrorize the Isaaqs. It was this factor that had led the Isaaq-controlled Somali National Movement, sheltered in Ethiopia and aided by the Dergue and the Soviets, to invade Ogadeni refugee camps in northwestern Somalia. With the cache of weapons given to them by Mengistu as a severance package before kicking them out of Ethiopia in 1988, the Somali National Movement also attacked the towns of Hargeisa and Burao in Somalia.

If the reader is overwhelmed by all of this, he or she is supposed to be. Gersony had never been so confused in his life. Nobody in Addis Ababa, not even Houdek, the consummate Africanist, could explain much of this to him. He had to learn all of it by himself, piecing the story together from the individual refugees he had already interviewed on the Ethiopian side of the border, and those he would soon interview on the Somali side. It was a classic case of how only the victims knew the story, and he was required to hear them out and tell it to the world. Whereas from a distance it carried the complications of theoretical physics, up close it was pure Hobbes: anarchy, the war of all against all.

As he put it: "By the time I had returned to the Hilton I knew what I didn't know. I had made a start."

He was, in effect, writing history from the original source material: refugee accounts. Thus, he needed to know more about such things as the role of the Ogadeni refugee camps in Somalia before the conflict had intensified, the details about Somali army recruitment, how food was diverted from the camps by the Somali government, the exact sequence of all the events, and so on.

He decided that before leaving Ethiopia for Somalia he would travel southeast into the ethnic-Oromo area of the country to interview more Ogadeni refugees, who were not in the border zone and were consequently less scared. He hoped that they could explain more to him. But Makonnen told him that the Ethiopian authorities insisted on his traveling with a security accompaniment. This baffled Gersony. The Dergue had just let him travel to a sensitive war-torn border area with only Makonnen, but now they wouldn't let the two of them travel alone into the heart of Ethiopia, far from the border. Perhaps it was because the authorities were genuinely curious about him, owing to his recent Mozambique report and his foray into Isaaq refugee camps near Somalia. So he and Makonnen traveled southeast with a security detail, and Gersony consequently filled in more pieces of his emerging story by listening to more refugees.

They were away in the southeast almost a week: more twelve- to fourteen-hour days, dealing with refugees and the overbearing hospitality of people met along the way. He was exhausted. Getting shot at in Harshin, the incident with the rat near Jijiga, and the nervousness of the government security detail had all worn him down. He headed back to Addis Ababa with a massive amount of typing to do. There were not only the refugee accounts to work on, but "thank-you" letters to write to diplomats and NGOs as he prepared to leave the country. He was a real obsessive-compulsive, always forcing himself to finish all the preliminary work and formalities before he departed anywhere, which often was simply not possible.

After a long day working at the embassy, he went back to the Hilton at night to pack for his flight to Nairobi, Kenya, at ten the next morning. He overslept, waking at nine. He rushed to the airport without properly washing, but missed the flight. There wouldn't be another one until the next day and he had already checked out of the hotel. All of a sudden his spirit was broken, completely broken.

Like an automaton, he took a cab back to the U.S. Embassy. It was a Saturday and the grounds were deserted, without the security of the post-9/11 era. He sat down on a bench with his bags on either side of him, like a homeless person, on the brink of tears. He didn't know what to do. Most anyone else would simply have gone back to the Hilton, checked in again, relaxed, and rebooked his flight. But anyone who has experienced a nervous breakdown of even a mild sort knows how the simplest tasks loom insurmountable and overwhelming.

Gersony just sat there, his mind vacant. The whole world had gone dark for him. Then Bob Houdek walked by in shorts. It was his day off and the chargé d'affaires' residence was right on the compound.

"I've had it," Gersony announced tearfully.

"You come home with me," Houdek said.

Houdek and his wife, Mary, took care of him. They showed him to a room with a private bath. They told him to stay there, rest all day, and come down only for dinner. They rebooked his flight, and arranged for an embassy car to drive him to the airport the next day.

And so Gersony flew south to Nairobi. He was no fearless explorer like Wilfred Thesiger, who always sought out so-called barbaric splendor. Yet Gersony was like other travelers in one profound way: at difficult moments he required the sympathy and hospitality of others.

. . .

He spent only a day or two in Nairobi enjoying the many conveniences that this urban crossroads of sub-Saharan Africa had to offer. He soon felt physically and psychologically renewed. It was time to fly northeast, to Somalia, to immerse himself once again with refugees, in order to fill out the other half of the picture of this overwhelmingly complicated border war—which he barely understood, even though he probably understood it better than anyone else at this point.

MOGADISHU, SOMALIA. Crenellated lemon-and-white bastions, rocketlike minarets, all leprous; rotting fruit in alleyways; a silent white sand beach without a breeze where sharks gathered, on account of a slaughterhouse that discharged entrails into the ocean; air so thick and hot that it could light a match. Ebony, wraithlike, fine-featured people in flowing multicolored robes. There is an insubstantiality to everything here, as if the whole ratty town could be blown away in a dust storm. For this is a country of nomads where the city has no place. A feeling of insecurity everywhere, and this was years before the actual chaos. (Indeed, Somalia was a place where the term "failed state" originally came into vogue.) At the Croce del Sud, the hotel where foreign relief workers stayed, amid the bougainvillea and geraniums, they served warm Italian white wine with the lobster. Gersony did without the white wine.

As usual, Gersony began with the U.S. Embassy. The DCM, David Rawson, and the USAID mission director, Lois Richards, were especially friendly. Rawson was an enthusiastic fan of the Mozambique report, and acted at the time like Gersony's best friend. Richards, a tall and imposing woman who swore like a truck driver, reacted similarly to Gersony's arrival. She assigned him an FSN, Ashur Warsangali, a Darod in his sixties, who had ulcers and, because it was Ramadan and he couldn't eat during the day, was especially irritable. The two would travel for weeks together.

Somalia is a sprawling country with a particularly ungainly shape because it was composed of a former Italian colony in the south and a former British protectorate in the north. Even during the years of Siad Barre's supposedly iron rule, large swaths of the country were unsafe and given to semi-anarchy, and transport from the formerly Italian part to the formerly British part usually meant hitching a ride on a U.N. plane.

Gersony and Ashur flew from Mogadishu directly to Boroma, tucked into the northwestern corner of the country right on the border with Ethiopia, where there was a cluster of refugee camps that the United Nations was active in administering. At Boroma, a car and driver awaited them. Gersony had dozens of lengthy interviews to conduct with a largely non-Isaaq population: fifty-seven interviews, as it would turn out. It was grueling work. He forced himself to start from scratch, to empty his mind of everything he had learned so far, and to see in Somalia if he could both corroborate and put in context what he had been told by Isaaqs in eastern and southeastern Ethiopia just across the border, regarding Somali leader Siad Barre's depredations.

The eleven refugee camps clustered around Boroma, which included Tug Wajale (where I had interviewed refugees three years earlier), contained inhabitants from a variety of clans, only 18 percent of whom were Isaaqs. These people formed a cross-section of the hundreds of thousands who had fled Ethiopia for northwestern Somalia. They spoke to Gersony of mass roundups and systematic executions that began only days after the Isaaq-led Somali National Movement (SNM) forces crossed the border from Ethiopia and penetrated to an area southeast of here. SNM soldiers attacked Ogadeni refugee camps; and in the towns of Hargeisa and Burao, where Somali government troops were lodged, deliberately put civilians in the crossfire. One Isaaq refugee told him that her brother, who was mentally disabled, had been executed by a rival clan in retaliation for SNM predations. It was always the individual incident that rescued the statistics from inhuman abstraction.

Almost two weeks went by. In the early afternoon of May 8, Gersony and Ashur were packing inside their guest house in Boroma, shaking out the dust from their gear and preparing to leave, when they heard shooting outside. They walked out into the devastating heat. A group of young men with assault rifles, hopped up on *khat*, the mild narcotic that everyone in the region chewed after the midday meal, demanded the keys to the car from Ashur. Ashur hadn't eaten because it was Ramadan, and he was in a foul mood. He screamed at the young men. They pointed their guns at him. Ashur threw the keys in the dirt, and screamed again:

"You want these keys, pick them up like dogs."

The young men drove off with the car.

Gersony, very shaken, was awestruck at Ashur's courage.

Ashur stormed into the office of the local commissioner and demanded that the commissioner find the young men and get the car back: cleaned and gassed up. A few hours later the car was returned in good condition. But the day was lost.

The next day they drove fifty miles southeast to the town of Hargeisa, where the SNM attacks had been concentrated, and which contained another cluster of refugee camps. (They were shot at twice en route.) In the Hargeisa region, Gersony conducted twenty-two interviews over four days. Since leaving Mogadishu he had been eating one meal per day: fried camel liver with onions, which he considered the safest food. The onions, desperately needed for flavor, were particularly hard to obtain and he was constantly searching local markets for them.

In Hargeisa, he and Ashur literally wandered amid the rubble. The year before, SNM troops had dispersed into Hargeisa, fighting government forces. Then Siad Barre retook the town, using Rhodesian mercenary pilots who bombed Hargeisa into smithereens. Barre wanted to send a message to the Isaaq inhabitants.

Thousands were killed in Hargeisa and Burao, another camp fifty miles to the east. But Gersony in his report did not consider these people "murdered" in cold blood, as in the case of individual shootings and executions. Thus, his death estimates for human rights purposes were low. He always deliberately worked to have the lowest possible numbers in order to maintain his credibility. He was interested in premeditated human rights crimes, as a category separate from the habitual cruelty of war, in which civilians were targeted as well as killed in the crossfire. He didn't excuse the latter. He just dedicated himself to the former, since it provided a more precise motivator for the U.S. government to act.

Getting from Hargeisa northeast to the port city of Berbera required several hours of driving. There Gersony came upon a single runway, the longest in sub-Saharan Africa at the time, which U.S. military aircraft had used for surveillance of the Gulf of Aden and the Indian Ocean ever since the Soviets departed. It was that runway and where it was located that constituted the main U.S. interest in Somalia, and why Washington was putting up with the depredations wrought by Siad Barre's government. Alas, another Cold War contingency.

At the edge of the runway were several one-story, air-conditioned shacks where a handful of American nationals—buttressed by imported food, cold soft drinks, and back issues of *Sports Illustrated*—maintained radio contact with the outside world, even as the desert right behind them was now a land of mass executions and utter anarchy, as Gersony was finding out, interview by interview.[4]

Stepping into one of the shacks, after a few weeks away from Mogadishu, the air conditioning hit Gersony like a benediction. Then there were the hot shower and the cold American soft drinks. Whatever the absurdity of this outpost and its situation, he felt revived. Over the coming days, based in this luxury hotel-of-sorts, he and Ashur conducted seventeen interviews with Ogadenis and Oromos at four displaced persons camps to the southwest and the southeast. Here he reconfirmed that while the Isaaq-dominated Somali National Movement never actually attacked Berbera, it had attacked Hargeisa and Burao, and so Siad Barre's government army conducted a mass roundup of Isaaq civilians in Berbera, torturing and executing them by the hundreds, accusing them of being Somali National Movement sympathizers. The army buried the victims by the dozens in different places; one burial place was at the end of the runway used by the American military. Gersony confirmed this not only by interviews with displaced persons, but by speaking with one of the American military contractors who saw the trucks filled with bodies being unloaded.

Gersony and Ashur now left the comforts of Berbera and drove for a few hours to Burao, thereby making a triangle formed by their journey from Boroma east to Hargeisa, then northeast to Berbera, and finally southeast to Burao. In the Burao region, fifteen separate interviews with displaced Ogadenis informed Gersony that forces of the Isaaq Somali National Movement entered the town, rounded up all the local officials—representatives of the Barre regime—and simply executed them. In other words, there were no good guys here. The Somali National Movement was not executing and bombing civilians on the scale of Siad Barre's modern army, but while the scale was not comparable, the manner of the killing was.

"This was intense, altogether brutal, total warfare, even if the numbers were not that great—not enough to garner front-page news worldwide, I mean. And it was all so complicated, my head was spinning. Though I had filled up several notebooks, I could barely explain it to myself," Gersony recalls.

To see it through a Cold War filter, this is what it was all about:

The Soviet Union was backing the Marxist regime of Mengistu Haile Mariam in Ethiopia, which, in turn, was backing the ethnic-Isaaq Somali National Movement, so it could attack the American-backed regime of Siad Barre over the border in Somalia. The Somali National Movement invaded the northwestern Somali towns of Hargeisa and Burao and killed Somali government officials there. Siad Barre's response was to commence a mass killing of Isaaqs. But because the Somali National Movement dispersed its fighters in civilian areas of Hargeisa and other towns, even more droves were killed in the chaotic, house-to-house fighting between the Somali National Movement and Barre's forces. Meanwhile, the Americans kept flying their surveillance planes, with Siad Barre's permission.

Gersony and Ashur drove back to Mogadishu, covering the seven hundred miles east and then south in several days, gaining an appreciation of the flimsy, sprawling polity that was modern-day Somalia,

where everything seemed to vanish in clouds of wafting and horrendous dust, rendering you almost blind. By now Gersony had been on
the road for 11 weeks and had conducted 302 interviews with refugees and displaced persons in 31 locations in three countries (including several interviews in Kenya). The DCM in Mogadishu, David
Rawson, instantly became Gersony's biggest cheerleader, and later
on, when Gersony's Somalia report was released, the State Department would refer to Gersony's "long and excellent record" as a human
rights investigator. This would prove of great significance in the coming years, when Gersony came under fierce and widespread attack
over his reports regarding Rwanda and Bosnia, including attacks
from David Rawson himself about the Rwanda report.

All that lay in the future, however.

For the moment, Gersony was just thankful to get home. He had
a case of amoebic dysentery, which he alleviated by eating cans of
sardines from Zabar's in his Manhattan apartment.

Partially recovered, in late July 1989 he flew to Washington and
went straight to the State Department, where, as in the case of the
Mozambique report, he begged Cindy Davis for help in organizing
all the statistics he had gathered. Soon the two of them were dating.
(He had recently broken up with Ann Siegel.) It began with drinks at
the Watergate, and continued afterward back at the Howard Johnson's hotel across the street, the place where five years before he had
spilled his story about Uganda's Luwero Triangle to Caryle Murphy
of *The Washington Post*. Inspired by him, Cindy soon went to Antigua, Guatemala, to study Spanish.

Of course, he also went immediately to the Bureau of Refugee Programs, where Ken Bleakley, the bureau deputy who had himself failed
to get permission to leave Addis Ababa for the field, invited Gersony
back to his house, where Gersony briefed Bleakley and Margaret
McKelvey, the head of the bureau's Africa office. They sat out on the
back deck of Bleakley's house in northwest Washington. "I can't do this
in an hour," Gersony began. The briefing would last several hours. By
now, of course, Gersony was in a position to demand whatever time he
needed. That was followed by another interminable brief to the new

assistant secretary of state for African affairs, Herman ("Hank") Cohen, who had replaced Chet Crocker. Everyone was impressed, overwhelmed, and baffled by what Gersony had told them.

Uganda and Mozambique may have constituted epic chapters in Gersony's professional life, but the story lines in those other places were relatively simple: mass atrocities where there was a single culprit. Somalia, to the contrary, had multiple culprits and story lines that were both complex and opaque. What had begun as a binary, Cold War struggle between a Soviet-supported regime and an American-supported regime had started to crumble into obscure fissures. And Gersony had to put it all together for his colleagues based purely on refugee and displaced-person accounts.

The result was "Why Somalis Flee: Synthesis of Accounts of Conflict Experience in Northern Somalia by Somali Refugees, Displaced Persons and Others." It was sixty-five pages long, an exhaustingly detailed analysis involving tribes and languages and places. Gersony "conservatively estimated" that in 1988, Siad Barre's Somali Armed Forces had killed five thousand ethnic Isaaqs, while the Isaaq Somali National Movement executed at least several hundred ethnic Ogadenis and others. But while Gersony was briefing people up and down the bureaucratic food chain at the State Department and the National Security Council, back in Mogadishu, U.S. ambassador Frank Crigler was taking weeks to decide whether the report should be released at all. And the State Department did not want to move without the approval of the ambassador of the country in question.

As the U.S. ambassador to Somalia, Crigler had a primary responsibility to manage the relationship with this Cold War ally. Though it was the summer of 1989, few as yet had a notion that the Cold War was going to end so abruptly in such a dramatic fashion only a few months later. Crigler's legitimate concern was that the publication of Gersony's human rights report would signal to Siad Barre that "we're done with you." Thus, the very act of publishing "Why Somalis Flee" would be a political act that sent a strategic signal to the regime, especially as that regime was beginning to come apart. Gersony's report had also embarrassed Crigler, whose embassy had not been reporting very much about the human rights violations that Gersony had unearthed.

The DCM in Mogadishu, David Rawson, as well as Hank Cohen, the assistant secretary, were inclined to release the report, especially as "this guy Gersony" was already a big name in the refugee assistance community and so suppressing the report would eventually lead to an even bigger controversy. In any event, the deputy secretary of state, Lawrence Eagleburger, approved the release of Gersony's "Why Somalis Flee" in August, with several thousand copies going to Congress, U.S. diplomatic missions, and the media.

On September 8, 1989, the front page of *The New York Times* carried a story by Jane Perlez, headlined "U.S. Says Somali Army Killed 5,000 Civilians," which quoted extensively from Gersony's report. Within days, similar articles appeared in *The Washington Post, Los Angeles Times,* and *Houston Chronicle,* in addition to the *International Herald Tribune* and other newspapers in Europe. Perhaps, more significantly, six years later, Oxford University released a survey of refugee literature, decrying how "unbalanced, emotive, and highly polemical" accounts had marred the study of Somali refugees, but singling out Gersony's "Why Somalis Flee" as "one of the very few exceptions that provides objective evidence" of the events of 1988.[5]

Gersony's report certainly weakened Siad Barre's regime, undermining what little international standing it had left. But it was the collapse of the Berlin Wall in November 1989 that would change the whole context of power dynamics in the Horn of Africa, just as it did in Central America. In 1991, Mengistu's Marxist regime in Ethiopia unraveled, even as Siad Barre was toppled without the United States coming to his aid. Somalia then fell into a deeper level of chaos, leading to the famine of 1992 that spawned America's ill-fated military intervention there.

As it happened, Gersony's report, which unmasked what would later be termed the Isaaq genocide, was a harbinger of the greater role played by human rights in U.S. foreign policy in the period between the end of the Cold War and 9/11.

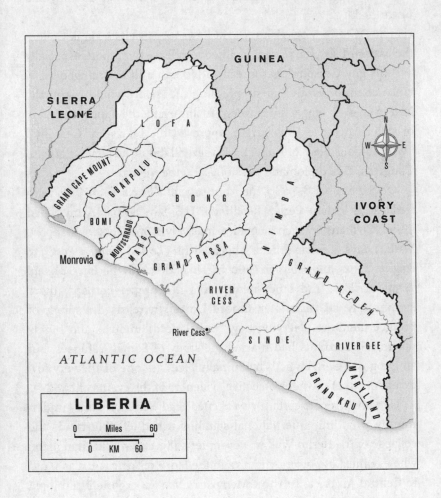

CHAPTER 10

Liberia by Way of Nicaragua
1990–1993

"It All Grew Out of the Methodology."

B ob Gersony was turned off by the exultations about the coming age of democracy and stability that followed the collapse of the Berlin Wall and the end of Moscow's communist empire in Central and Eastern Europe, because the world he knew in the far-flung corners of the earth was not stable at all. He saw no democratic pattern emerging in the Horn of Africa, sub-Saharan Africa, Central America, and so on. Thus, he never bought into the optimism of the 1990s. It was another example of Washington elites manufacturing a theory, a theory born of dramatic events in Central Europe that they mistakenly applied to the whole world. As for humanitarianism, the end of the Cold War was a double-edged sword: it removed the strategic self-interest to care about human rights in many a country, even as it allowed humanitarianism as a cause to replace the obsession with strategic interest.

Gersony had a lot of time to think about these things, since, for reasons entirely unconnected with the geopolitical upheaval in Europe, he was suddenly out of a job.

It was the same old story, which any private contractor or freelance operator of any kind knows only too well. Your survival is always tied to patrons who support your work, and when someone replaces them as the boss—someone who is less sympathetic to you—suddenly half a dozen valid bureaucratic reasons emerge about why your services are no longer required. Officially it's never personal, but it often is. You just have to force a smile, say polite things you don't really mean, and move on to find another patron somewhere else.

This is sort of what happened when Princeton Lyman took over the Bureau of Refugee Programs following the change of administrations, from Ronald Reagan to George H. W. Bush: from George Shultz as secretary of state to James Baker III.

But in this case, it really wasn't personal. It was just that Princeton Lyman, a former upper-level official in the Africa bureau and former ambassador to Nigeria, had a decidedly more conventional view of the role of the refugee bureau than Jim Purcell, Gene Dewey, and Jonathan Moore had had.[1]

The Bureau of Refugee Programs had its origins in the great cataclysms that befell Indochina in the 1970s.[2] When Vietnam and Cambodia came under communist and Khmer Rouge rule, millions streamed across land borders and sought to escape by boat. As a result of this pressure, which brought 14,000 Indochina refugees into the United States each month during the Carter administration, the refugee bureau was carved out of a financially scandal-plagued human rights bureau, and set up as a stand-alone division of the State Department on July 31, 1979. Chas Freeman had drawn up the original plan, and Jim Purcell, a Tennessean who was friends with the moderate Republicans George Shultz and Wyoming senator Alan Simpson, came over from the Office of Management and Budget to run it. Following Reagan's election, Purcell chose Gene Dewey as his right-hand man. Both men were activists who believed in crisis response, and Shultz gave them considerable running room when he became secretary of state. As it would turn out, Bob Gersony—and to a much lesser extent, Fred Cuny—became the tip of the spear for Purcell and Dewey.

Jim Purcell remembers working with Gersony after he and Dewey had just discovered him:

"He was quiet, intense, meticulous, and turned over every rock. When he did speak, sparks would fly."

But the Africa bureau had often quietly chafed as the refugee bureau and particularly the human rights bureau stole part of its thunder. The Africa bureau had openly tried and failed to take away ownership of Jerry Weaver's Falasha rescue operation from the refugee bureau. So when Princeton Lyman, one of the stars at the Africa bureau, took over the refugee bureau, there was an element of a hostile takeover about it, even as Lyman himself was dedicated to refugee work.

Whereas Purcell, Dewey, and Moore had wanted the refugee bureau to contribute active human intelligence and have a seat at the table when the geographic "line" bureaus made daily policy, Lyman did not want Refugee Programs stirring the pot quite as much, with forward operators such as Gersony and Cuny. And while Lyman was deeply impressed with Gersony's work in Mozambique, he was also at the Africa bureau when Gersony caught the bureau off-guard with his reports about the Luwero Triangle that made it into *The Washington Post*. In the back of his mind, too, might have been the cable dustup between the Sudan and Chad embassies over Gersony's reporting about the predations of the Goran tribesmen, in which Gersony was unintentionally undermining a pro-American regime in Chad.

Nevertheless, Lyman told me from the vantage point of a third of a century removed, several weeks before he died, that "Bob's reports enabled us to lay down markers on human rights in areas where we had competing interests." In other words, while the Africa bureau, as opposed to the refugee and human rights bureaus, was concerned primarily with national interest and bilateral relations between specific African regimes and the United States, Gersony helped provide a deeper perspective on human rights for the bureau, so that the bureau could better balance our values with our interests.

Yet at the time Gersony represented an irritant and an unorthodox force who could always discover things that the bureau couldn't control. There was also the matter of Gersony's self-negotiated pay, quite high for a contractor since he billed for seven days a week, which only Purcell, Dewey, and Moore were willing to fork out. The State Department comptroller may also have been concerned that the refugee bureau kept certifying, again and again, that only Gersony could do these consulting jobs. Perhaps, too, for such a smooth, old-school FSO like Princeton Lyman, Bob Gersony was just too much of an outsider.

Finally, there was an element of coincidence about it. In 1989, the news focus shifted dramatically to Europe, even as the military conflict in Yugoslavia would not begin in earnest for almost another two years. So there was a temporary lull in high-profile humanitarian emergencies that required the talents of someone like Gersony.

Whatever the reason, in late 1989 and the beginning of 1990, the phone line from the refugee bureau to Gersony went dead. No follow-up requests, nothing, despite all the work he had done in Uganda, Thailand, Mozambique, Chad, Sudan, the Horn of Africa, and elsewhere. It's like that in life. You're a star until a moment later, when management changes at the top, and you're gently or not-so-gently nudged aside.

Finally the phone rang.

It was USAID.

The December 1989 invasion of Panama by the United States to oust dictator Manuel Noriega had displaced the population of one slum neighborhood and USAID was providing these people with temporary housing. Would Gersony go down to Panama to do an assessment of how the relief operation had been handled, and how it was progressing? Gersony said sure. He was out of work and had no other options. He made several trips to Panama during the first half of 1990, interviewed scores of displaced persons there, and was able to give a seal of approval to the USAID mission. It was a no-sweat assignment.

Then he continued unemployed.

The phone rang again in December 1990. It was Janet Ballantyne, the USAID mission director in the Nicaraguan capital of Managua. Ballantyne, who died in 2017, was a truly formidable woman, with a doctorate from the Cornell School of Business, who had worked like Gersony as a private contractor before becoming an FSO. Tall and imposing, she was a realist, committed to privatization, who was also a liberal Democrat, even if it had been Republicans who usually put her in key positions throughout her career. People just loved her and were charmed by her, including the so-called Sandalistas, aging and scraggy former hippies who always wore sandals and streamed into her office with grim expressions, demanding that USAID do more for the left-wing Sandinistas.

Ballantyne would rise to become the most senior woman in the Foreign Service and be a counselor to the administrator of USAID himself, the third-highest person in that bureaucracy. In her, Gersony would find another loyal patron to replace Jonathan Moore, Gene Dewey, and Fred Schieck. In fact, it was through Schieck that Ballantyne had found out about Gersony's work for USAID in Central America.

Janet Ballantyne, the official for the United States Agency for International Development who brought Bob to Nicaragua for years of work in the early 1990s.

Ballantyne now had a challenge on her hands that Schieck convinced her only Bob Gersony could deal with.

Nicaragua is the most sparsely populated country of core Central America, with only four million people by the mid-1990s. Most of the population, the descendants of Spaniards and other Europeans, live close to the Pacific coast, while the vast forests close to the Atlantic or Caribbean coast are populated by only a few hundred thousand Miskito Indians and descendants of African slaves: 5 percent of the total population, as it happens. Relevant contemporary history in Nicaragua begins in 1934, when the forces of National Guard commander Anastasio Somoza García, who went on to establish a despotic dynasty, assassinated the revolutionary Augusto César Sandino, who had led a seven-year rebellion against the local oligarchic order and American imperialism, symbolized by the presence of U.S. Marines. Thus began the decades-long struggle between the Somoza family, supported by the United States, and the political heirs of Sandino, known as Sandinistas, which was made more intense by the insularity and inbred nature of politics in a former colonial backwater where every dispute was personal.

Somoza family rule was famously disrupted by a series of earthquakes that hit Managua in December 1972, destroying or damaging about 80 percent of the capital's buildings and killing ten thousand people. The inadequate response would undermine the rule of Anastasio Somoza Debayle, the second son of the dynasty's founder. The election of Jimmy Carter as U.S. president in 1976 convinced Somoza to liberalize and lift the state of siege. But by 1978, the assassination of a prominent newspaper publisher convinced the local elite that Somoza could no longer protect them, a view encouraged by a successful Sandinista siege of the National Palace. Following heavy fighting and the failure of the Carter administration to forge a political compromise, the Sandinistas took power in 1979.[3]

Despite Sandinista promises, as *New York Times* correspondent Shirley Christian reported at the end of 1979, "A government that had been put together to look civilian, moderate, and pluralistic just

six months earlier . . . now looked far less that way." The media was
politicized and many hundreds of Cubans poured into the country
to perform military, security, and public health functions. Indeed, as
the first successful leftist insurrection in Latin America since Castro
had come to power in Cuba twenty years earlier, the Sandinistas
galvanized the attention of both official Washington and leftists
throughout the Western Hemisphere. Still, just as Somoza was not
particularly repressive compared to other autocrats, the Sandinistas
were not particularly repressive compared to other leftist dictatorships. Nicaragua, partially through sheer disorganization, was supremely ideological without being overwhelmingly oppressive.[4]

In 1981 the Reagan administration received information that the
Nicaraguan Sandinistas were involved in east bloc arms shipments to
the leftist guerrillas in El Salvador. The following year, the so-called
contra war against the Sandinistas began. In truth, the contras were
mainly highland mestizo peasants, with a smaller contingent of
Black Creoles and Miskito Indians, who had turned against the low-
land, urban Pacific *españoles,* whom these highland peasants roughly
identified with the Sandinistas. In the eyes of the peasant contras, the
Sandinistas were trying to control their way of life, whereas the So-
mozas had to a larger extent left them alone.[5]

It turned out to be "the strangest of wars," according to *New York
Times* correspondent Shirley Christian, in which human beings
fought for specific reasons of belief, personal experience, and geographical turf divides, but whose portrayal in the outside world was
dominated by public relations hacks of both the Left and Right in
Washington who helped turn it into a binary Cold War saga.[6]

Gersony in 1988–89 came to the same conclusion about the contra war soon after Shirley Christian did. USAID had tasked him to
visit the Yamales salient of Honduras, surrounded on three sides by
Nicaraguan territory, where the contras occupied a rear base. Because
the Reagan administration was supporting the contras, USAID had a
feeding program for fifteen thousand contras and their family members there. He found the camp as neat as a pin, with properly dug
latrines and drainage, and people washing their clothes: what guerril-

las around the world do when in a safe place. Having done the routine assessment, Gersony decided to interview the contras themselves, to get *underneath,* as it were, the ideological battles raging in Washington and learn who these people really were.

He interviewed sixty-two combatants randomly, breaking them down according to age, education, religion, and so on: his usual method. He learned that because of the introduction of state farms, work brigades, state-run agricultural co-ops with fixed prices for tools and fertilizers, and involuntary military service, these peasants had simply had it with the Sandinistas. Gersony became frustrated. It wasn't only the Left, which considered the contras mercenaries, that bothered him, but the Reaganite Right, too, which had not adequately told the true story, obsessed as they were with the fight for democracy. These contra peasants had little particular interest in democracy. "For them," he explains, "democracy meant only a tangible memory of what had happened to them and wanting just to be left alone. They never once mentioned elections to me." It was again a case of subtleties that became rigid black-and-white nostrums in the imperial capital of Washington.

Yet in February 1990, in the immediate wake of the fall of the Berlin Wall, Nicaragua indeed did hold national elections and the opposition candidate, Violeta Chamorro, won a surprise victory over the Sandinista leader Daniel Ortega. Chamorro was now taking over a country wrecked by east bloc socialist ideas, and the elder Bush's administration wanted her to succeed. USAID mission director Janet Ballantyne was spurred on by Fred Schieck. He, in turn, was worried about latent Cuban influence in the sparsely populated, riverine eastern half of the country, which was populated by Miskito Indians in the northeast and Blacks in the southeast. He wanted something done immediately. The Cubans had built an airstrip and had sent in all manner of relief experts and political agents over the years under the cover of the Sandinista regime. Now the area was filling up with returning war refugees from Honduras: mixed in were returning

Miskitos who had fought the Sandinistas, rubbing shoulders with other Miskitos who had supported the Sandinistas. Then there was the disbanding of displaced persons camps that were leftovers from the contra-Sandinista conflict. The Cold War was officially over, but its aftershocks would go on for years.

Janet Ballantyne's orders to Bob Gersony were "Go down there and figure out what we need to do to stabilize the area. I don't want any more assessments or bureaucratic studies. I want a plan of action."

Gersony literally spent forty days and forty nights hiking through a bush veined with rivers where people lived and farmed out of their canoes. Because of his Spanish fluency, he was more adventurous in Nicaragua than in other parts of the world. But he, being Gersony, still had his limits. His adventure had begun at Managua airport, where the flight to Puerto Cabezas on the Atlantic coast departed from the most ramshackle and distant part of the terminal. All the other passengers on the plane were peasants with "bundles of crap tied up in bolts and all sorts of rope." He found Puerto Cabezas practically cut off from the outside world, rickety and magical in those days, composed of wooden houses on stilts except for a concrete center. Using Puerto Cabezas as his base, he would visit thirty-five villages and interview literally hundreds of residents. He had to be thorough with each one. It was an altogether boring and yet useful exercise, since everyone told him the same things, proving the truth of the situation: everyone needed rice seed, simple tools, and ready cash.

It took him twelve hours to traverse sixty-five miles of one deeply rutted road. There were several feet of mud in many places. He traveled a hundred miles on a river against the current. *Bam, bam,* the canoe slapped against the surface of the water in a storm. He was nauseous. He felt like his back was going to collapse. "It was raining frogs and razor blades," he says. "At least that's how it felt."

He discovered banditry, instability, zero employment, no currency in circulation, insufficient food (since farmers had been dislocated by armed conflict), and bridges and roads in catastrophic conditions. Eastern Nicaragua was so close to the United States, but it might as well have been in the most underdeveloped part of Africa.

He began zeroing in on the details. As always, it was about understanding the situation at the granular level. He knew from his interviews that he couldn't give the peasants just any kind of rice seed, it had to be *cica-ocho*, a miracle seed from Colombia. And not just any machete would do. It had to be the twenty-eight-inch *corneta*. He was also formulating a plan to repair all the roads and bridges by hand without heavy equipment, in order to create mass employment.

He had nothing to do one day in Puerto Cabezas, since the flight back to Managua wasn't until the next morning. So he wandered into the office of the local forestry commission. In the dingy, ratty, tumbledown office he saw two crusty middle-aged men sitting at a table chain-smoking. They were both hard and lean, without a muscle wasted. The two dark-skinned old-timers, along with the dusty, grimy brown and lava-colored surroundings, reminded Gersony of the scene in Cézanne's *The Card Players*.

Gersony began asking one of the taciturn men about his plan to import *cica-ocho* seed and create mass employment in eastern Nicaragua. The man's answers were sharp, direct, and without any dissembling. To be sure, some of the man's comments were downright inappropriate. The man seemed ignorant about how to be a diplomat with a stranger. He also seemed a man accustomed to authority, who understood the region down to the smallest detail; he knew the name of every bridge, it would turn out. Gersony recognized him as a fellow like himself, with realism ingrained in his bones. "He was our guy," Gersony thought. The man's name was Rodolfo Jaentschke, a former boxer, and he was a forestry engineer of mixed German, Spanish, Creole, and Miskito extraction: a character straight out of Conrad's *Nostromo*. His sidekick was Miguel Abella, an accountant who also knew all about the region.

"Would you run my entire project here?" Gersony asked Jaentschke. As incredible as it seems, he had instantly decided he could trust this man with millions of dollars. It testified to his ability

Paul Cézanne's *The Card Players*, which reminded Gersony of a critical memory from Nicaragua.

to spot talented people in random encounters without going through conventional channels.

"Yes," Jaentschke answered.

"I don't know why, but I had a firm instinct that I could have faith in this man," Gersony says.

Gersony returned to Managua the next day and recommended to Ballantyne a labor-intensive transportation infrastructure program to go along with a reforestation project to plant eight million trees. There would also be the purchase of twenty thousand machetes to clear the bush—and put even more people to work—as well as the importation from Colombia of *cica-ocho* rice seed for planting.

"The international community is still dividing up aid among the warring groups," he told Ballantyne. "With my plan, everyone who wants a job will get one, reducing criminality and repairing the underlying causes of dissent."

Ballantyne hired Gersony for six months to start the project, and

Gersony promptly hired Jaentschke to be his foreman. The $5 million project was all done on a handshake. Only someone as self-assured and charismatic as Janet Ballantyne could have pulled it off. It would have been altogether impossible to do in today's Washington.

The six months would stretch into four years, with Tony Jackson soon brought in as Gersony and Jaentschke's assistant. Tony settled into a wooden Miskito house on stilts in Puerto Cabezas, where he worked together with a relief worker for MSF-Holland, Rose-marie de Loor, with whom he would fall in love and adopt two malnourished children. Every visiting international journalist wanted to meet and be briefed by Tony, partly on account of his charming theatrical manner and British accent.[7]

Gersony, as usual, stayed in the background. Ballantyne shrewdly got Cindy Davis a job helping in the demobilization of the contras, so that Gersony would be, for personal reasons, stuck in the country. Cindy, fresh from studying in Antigua, Guatemala, now spoke passable Spanish. Bob and Cindy would later be married on Halloween 1992, at the Rainbow Room in Rockefeller Center, with Janet Ballantyne in attendance, presiding as the virtual godmother of the festivities.

In effect, Violeta Chamorro, Nicaragua's new leader, had subcontracted the eastern half of her country to Janet Ballantyne, who in turn subcontracted it to Bob Gersony, who then further subcontracted it to Rodolfo Jaentschke and Tony Jackson. Chamorro and Ballantyne had instantly liked each other, and Ballantyne had instantly liked Gersony. With only a small overhead in emergency relief, crime dramatically decreased and commerce blossomed in eastern Nicaragua while Gersony was there. Thanks to Tony and Jaentschke, everything was accounted for with receipts. By the end of the project, Tony would become Jaentschke's virtual factotum, as though they were brothers in the womb.

The project, which employed over three thousand people, received the highest USAID audit rating: "no findings, no recommendations."

By the time the project was completed four years later, 500 miles of road would be repaired with picks and shovels, and 411 wooden

One of the bridges that Bob, Tony Jackson, and Rodolfo Jaentschke had built on Nicaragua's Atlantic coast.

bridges would either be built from scratch or rebuilt using eight-foot saws. Gersony forbade chain saws, which encourage clear-cutting and would have led to fewer people being employed. Six million pine trees and one million hardwoods, including mahogany, teak, and oak, would be planted. For a moment in time there was a visceral identification on the part of the people of eastern Nicaragua with the United States of America. The United States had supplied the money, but the indigenous people built everything with their own hands. At the ceremony marking the end of the project in January 1995, Ambassador John Maisto's wife would operate an enormous tractor to officially open a road, a photo op that would run in the national newspapers back in Managua.

"It all grew out of the methodology," Gersony explains, "listening, in interview after interview, to the felt needs of the people themselves. We never imposed our values on them."

During these four years in Nicaragua—the first half of the 1990s— Gersony, with Ballantyne's approval, got called away for urgent assignments in Liberia and Rwanda, which, like Nicaragua though in radically different ways, demonstrated how the fall of the Berlin Wall in Europe carried little meaning elsewhere. Gersony's base in Central America and his forays to Africa put him completely outside the mindset of those describing a new world order.

It was the end of July 1993. Gersony was sitting in his large and well-appointed USAID mission office offering a panoramic view of Managua, the nicest office he had ever had. But he was bored out of his mind with the Nicaraguan project, which, thanks largely to Rodolfo Jaentschke and Tony Jackson, was essentially running on autopilot.

The phone rang.

A woman was on the line, an assistant to United Nations Secretary-General Boutros Boutros-Ghali, inquiring about Mr. Gersony's availability to be on a three-person panel investigating a recent massacre in Liberia.

Gersony was interested.

"Does the job pay?" he asked.

The woman said it shouldn't be a problem. The next day she called back. A fee with expenses was arranged.

Gersony left Tony and Cindy in charge of the eastern half of Nicaragua, and flew to New York to meet the U.N. secretary-general. It turned out that Melissa Wells, who had supported Gersony's work in Mozambique as the American ambassador there, was now the U.N. undersecretary general of administration and management, and she had recommended Gersony to Boutros-Ghali. Gersony's meeting with Boutros-Ghali was perfunctory. Boutros-Ghali barely knew who Gersony was. But with the meeting began Gersony's engagement with a massacre in Liberia that defies polite description; which involves realities about people and places that Western elites have trouble dealing with, unless they can twist them into a simple morality tale of good and evil.

For in Liberia, as V. S. Naipaul once wrote about an imaginary African country, "To talk of trouble was to pretend there were laws and regulations that everyone could acknowledge. Here there was nothing. There had been order once, but that order had its own dishonesties and cruelties . . . We lived in that wreckage," since without law of some kind, there was no meaning to anything.[8]

It had all started in April 1980, when Master Sergeant Samuel Doe, an ethnic-Krahn tribesman, led a group of disaffected soldiers into the presidential mansion in the Liberian capital of Monrovia and stabbed to death President William Tolbert, Jr., in his bed. Tolbert was an Americo-Liberian, a descendant of American and Caribbean slaves, a group that had ruled the country since independence as a back-to-Africa movement. Doe's rule was the first to introduce indigenous West Africans into the top of the power structure. But Charles Taylor, a leading ally of Doe, had a falling-out with him and, after some years in exile, involving an escape from a Massachusetts correctional facility, reentered Liberia from the Ivory Coast in 1989 in order to lead an insurrection with his newly formed National Patriotic Front of Liberia.

Soon a certain Prince Yormie Johnson broke away from Taylor to form his own militia group to topple Doe. It was Prince Johnson who captured Doe in September 1990 and immediately tortured and mutilated him. There is a video on the Internet showing the entire spectacle, in which Johnson is sipping a beer while one of Doe's ears is cut off. Doe's naked body was then carried through the streets of Monrovia, while his limbs and other body parts were hacked off, to prove to the population that he wasn't protected by black magic, as the late leader had claimed. The macabre event ended with Doe's decapitation.

While Taylor's and Prince Johnson's forces then vied for control, a conference of Liberian notables, meeting outside the country, anointed Amos Sawyer as an interim president. Nevertheless, Doe's ethnic Krahns still dominated the Armed Forces of Liberia, the semi-official national army. Meanwhile, Taylor's forces of ethnic Gios and Manos absorbed Prince Johnson's little army, with Taylor forming a base of operations in Gbarnga, inland in central Liberia. Keeping Taylor's troops from overrunning Monrovia on the Atlantic coast was the Krahn-dominated Armed Forces of Liberia, which had been subcontracted to do so by the Nigerian-led ECOMOG, the Economic Community of West African States Monitoring Group, a regional peacekeeping force. Prince Johnson was now out of the picture.

Charles Taylor's territory in central Liberia was a ghoulish hell of armed, drug-crazed teenagers with bizarre wigs, painted faces, and decorated, semi-naked bodies, who had mutilated and dismembered their victims. Stalking the area was General Butt Naked, a nom de guerre, who wore only a loincloth and was associated with child sacrifice and cannibalism: he worked for an allied warlord, Roosevelt Johnson. As a reporter in the region the same year, encountering such forces, I learned that the most controversial thing you could put in your story was merely describing what you saw in front of your face. Joan Didion had described the frontier territory of war-torn El Salvador as hovering close to the "cultural zero."[9] Well, Liberia, along with neighboring Sierra Leone in the 1990s, was closer still to that baseline.

Unlike Taylor's soldiers, the Armed Forces of Liberia were dressed normally. They wore battle fatigues but were more systematically brutal than the rebel groups. On the evening of July 29, 1990, in Monrovia, they murdered several hundred men, women, and children with knives, guns, and machetes—people they assumed were Taylor supporters, because they were members of the Gio and Mano tribes.[10]

Carter Camp, where another massacre occurred—the one Gersony would investigate—was located just outside the town of Harbel, forty miles east of Monrovia along an excellent tarmac road by the coast. Carter Camp was at the edge of the Firestone rubber plantation, the biggest employer in the country. ECOMOG troops, with the help of the Armed Forces of Liberia, had cleared Taylor's soldiers from the area. But the Krahn-dominated Liberian government army believed that the local inhabitants remained Taylor sympathizers, and had therefore moved them into work camps, of which Carter was one. The people in Carter Camp were harassed constantly by government soldiers, who accused them of passing information to Charles

Taylor. The government troops, only nominally controlled by Amos Sawyer, warned the camp inhabitants of a day of reckoning.

At about midnight on the night of Saturday–Sunday, June 5–6, 1993, armed soldiers systematically massacred and mutilated nearly six hundred Carter Camp residents, mainly women, children, and elderly persons. Some forty-five bags of rice and beans were removed from the camp, apparently carried by a hundred or more survivors abducted by the attackers. Roughly a thousand other survivors escaped and fled in several directions.[11]

Three days later, Trevor Gordon-Somers, a Jamaican, the special representative in Monrovia of the U.N. secretary-general, decided to personally conduct an investigation. He set up tables in the market square of Harbel, using soldiers from the Armed Forces of Liberia as a security detail. He interviewed a few dozen survivors in front of a large crowd. The survivors all said it was too dark to identify the perpetrators. Within days Somers, along with the national coroner, Dr. Isaac "Skeleton" Moses, and several other investigators, formally announced that Charles Taylor's forces were guilty of the massacre. But there were enormous contradictions in each of their reports. One report said there had been a pitched battle near the town, another said there had not been. There was no crime-scene work: no photos taken or maps made, and no one had picked up the spent cartridge shells for analysis.

Meanwhile, Charles Taylor, in his base in Gbarnga, sent a message to James Jonah, the U.N. undersecretary-general for political affairs (and a native of Sierra Leone), categorically denying guilt. The United Nations had little choice but to conduct a full-bore investigation, instead of the deeply flawed charade that the U.N. official Gordon-Somers had casually conducted.

Gersony was officially made a member of the investigative panel on August 4, 1993. The first thing he did was fly to Washington to get his own briefing at the State Department. A desk officer there matter-of-factly told him that Charles Taylor was guilty, since the department had "intercepted radio messages" to prove it. Gersony figured that

Taylor was no angel, the State Department had intercepts, it was a foregone conclusion, this would be an easy assignment.

In Geneva at the Palais de Nations, Gersony met the other two members of the panel, S. Amos Wako of Kenya and Mahmoud Kassem of Egypt. Amos Wako was of medium height, stout, strong, always smiling, but beneath the smile lay a very serious countenance. He was the attorney general for Daniel arap Moi, the veritable dictator of Kenya. He was essentially Moi's private lawyer: someone who, as the cliché went, "knew a thing or two because he had seen a thing or two." Kassem was an Egyptian diplomat, natty and well-coifed, who seemed very protocol-oriented and process-driven. He had been Boutros-Ghali's colleague in the foreign ministry in Cairo. Rounding out the team was the "secretariat," that is, the secretary and fixer, Gianni Magazzeni, a career U.N. officer from Italy whom Gersony instantly liked.

The first decision was where to conduct the investigation. Kassem, the natty diplomat, said they should summon the witnesses to Monrovia. Gersony said no, the whole team should go out to the field, to Harbel and Carter Camp. Wako, the chairman of the panel, agreed with Gersony.

En route to Monrovia from Geneva, they all fell into conversation. Gersony wondered aloud, Why would Taylor murder his own supporters? Kassem suggested that maybe Taylor killed his own people to embarrass the government, to show that the government could not protect civilians. If that was the case, Gersony thought, why not kill other civilians rather than his own people? And then Gersony added, Why did many of the survivors flee to Taylor's lines, in the direction of Gbarnga, rather than toward Monrovia? In truth, though, Gersony only half believed what he was saying. His main thought was that the State Department had intercepts that implicated Taylor: this is a cut-and-dried affair.

About two dozen excited local journalists greeted the panel members upon arrival at Roberts International Airport in Monrovia. They shouted questions. Wako handled it expertly, Gersony thought. Wako told the reporters in a stentorian tone that the panel would have nothing to say about the investigation until it was all completed, then the findings would be made public.

MONROVIA. A mishmash of shanties and corrugated iron roofs covered in orange rust, vegetation bleeding out of the gaps between the shanties; piles of trash in the middle of the roads, the "slapping, striding press of people"; teeming markets, mildewed modern buildings, all patrolled by jumpy soldiers.[12] The whole place oozed incipient chaos and insecurity. A place that could be safe in one instant might be a murder scene the next. Little electricity unless you owned a diesel generator. No streetlights, no mail delivery, a telephone system covering only a few blocks of downtown. The panel members were driven to the United Nations compound at the edge of the city, secured with armed guards and gates. They slept and ate most of their meals there.

After dinner the first night they met with Trevor Gordon-Somers, the local U.N. official who had already conducted his own, quick investigation. Gordon-Somers acted annoyed by the very creation and presence of the panel. Gersony asked Gordon-Somers if he had worried that interviewing survivors in front of the Harbel townspeople might affect their answers. Gordon-Somers became more annoyed.

The next morning Gianni Magazzeni drove the panel members in a U.N. car to Harbel, a small market town of wooden shacks with corrugated iron roofs. There was no damage to the structures, no spent cartridge shells or any other sign that a battle had been fought here, as one of the government investigations claimed.

They walked to Carter Camp. It was littered with spent cartridge shells. They ordered a collection: the shells with their serial numbers could tell them what type of weapons were used. They also ordered a diagram made of the camp. The next day they split up into two teams to interview survivors. Wako and Gersony constituted one team, Kassem and Magazzeni the other.

Wako and Gersony trusted each other at this point, and they agreed to conduct interviews according to Gersony's methodology. They found every survivor, interviewed in isolation, to be authoritative and detailed in their answers, provided in excellent English by these native Bassa speakers. They could even identify and name the perpetrators.

Gersony thought that such people, if only given a chance, could do well anywhere. They just happened to have been born in a place without any institutional base, so that thugs and liars ruled. In a world of no real government like Liberia, there was no right and wrong, because there were no consequences for any act.

According to the eyewitnesses, the timeline of what had happened was the following:

On May 27, almost ten days before the massacre, the World Food Programme began to stop food distributions to government soldiers. Some days after this, government soldiers, now furious and threatening, began confiscating food from the Carter Camp residents. In the days immediately prior to the massacre, an Armed Forces of Liberia private, twenty-three-year-old Zarkpa (pronounced "Zagba") Gorh, who ran the camp as the commandant—and who had taken one of the girls in the camp to live with him—began showing a new group of government soldiers wearing black berets all over the camp. The government army then ordered a tight curfew for the night of June 5. That afternoon, one of the new soldiers, a Lieutenant Kollie, had told a gathering of camp residents:

> We suspect you people in the camp of being NPFL [Taylor's] soldiers because we don't know the difference between you people and the NPFL soldiers. So if anything happens, we'll come and kill everyone here. . . . You people will die, but we military people will know how to save ourselves.[13]

Another government soldier said, "You are feeding and keeping the rebels . . . we shall deal with you tonight."[14]

The differences in what would turn out to be thirty-three individual survivor accounts (in addition to fifty other interviews conducted in the vicinity) were based solely on where exactly in the sprawling camp of tiny wooden and iron dwellings the eyewitnesses happened to be at the time of the violence.

There was considerable moonlight the night of June 5. Camp residents were awakened near midnight by the rumble of arriving vehicles and the sound of gunfire, which soon became deafening. Krahn-speaking soldiers—more corroboration that it was the government army—began ordering people out of their houses. Six witnesses said they saw or heard Private Zarkpa Gorh leading the soldiers from house to house and ordering people outside to their deaths. One witness reported seeing Zarkpa himself killing a camp resident. The soldiers did most of their killing with machetes. No rapes were reported. Not a single survivor identified the perpetrators as members of Taylor's army, the National Patriotic Front of Liberia. In any case, there was no possibility of NPFL vehicles being able to drive through ECOMOG and government lines—the only way for them to get to the camp. One survivor, who was ordered to carry a heavy bag of rice to the nearby government army camp, gave this account:

> "Come outside!" the soldiers shouted. They said, "Why do you need this cap, this belt, these shoes?" and took them from me. I saw two of my children and seven others dead in front of my house. There were many, many dead all around the camp. I saw a baby with the head cut off. . . . There were many soldiers in the camp, the same army soldiers that always came to the camp. . . . They put a whole bag of rice on my head. . . . "If you put this down, we'll kill you."[15]

Gathering all this information with Wako through one interview after another, and learning that the other team of Kassem and Magazzeni was hearing the very same stories, Gersony kept wondering: What about those intercepts that Washington said it had, and which he had been briefed on? Something was not adding up.

Walking back from Camp Carter to Harbel after another day of interviewing, Gersony let Wako, Kassem, and Magazzeni get ahead of him, so that he could quietly slip off by himself into an area of shacks just before the town, a tactic he had used in eastern Chad and other places. Gersony saw an old man and asked him, "Was there ever a battle here between government and rebel soldiers [like one of the previous investigators had claimed]?

"No, there was no battle. The government soldiers just moved into the camp."

He spoke to two other people. Same answers. These people were under the protection of the government army, yet corroborated the survivors' accounts that government troops had committed the massacre.

It was time to interview Charles Taylor.

Gianni Magazzeni drove the group in their U.N. car over a hundred miles inland through some of the wettest, densest forests in West Africa, in a northeasterly direction to Gbarnga. Now there was roadblock after roadblock manned by "these creatures," in Gersony's words: young men bearing assault rifles and practically naked with wigs and paint all over them, stimulated by drugs and alcohol. This was all Taylor-controlled territory.

Gbarnga was a sprawling encampment. There was no electricity and they had to use flashlights. Charles Taylor's house was at the top of a hill. He kept the group waiting for many hours until he received them at one in the morning. His office was a vast room filled with ornate, overstuffed furniture in the French style, dripping with gold leaf, a monument to bad taste given the milieu.

Taylor was very direct. He again categorically denied any role in the Carter Camp atrocities. "I've done many bad things in my life. But I did not do that massacre." This rebel leader, who would later be convicted of war crimes in Sierra Leone, appeared urbane and rational. "You can walk around here all you want, for as many days as you want, and interview anyone you want, unescorted. No one will follow you."

Taylor was as good as his word. There was no interference. Out of sight and out of hearing, they interviewed one displaced person after another who had fled Carter Camp to come to Gbarnga. It was the same story that they had heard from survivors on the other side of the battle lines. One man cried about his lost son. When Gersony told him that his son was alive and he had interviewed him in Carter Camp, the man cried again. Every detail of Trevor Gordon-Somers's conclusion was contradicted by everyone.

The conclusion was becoming inescapable.

"The four of us were talking to each other all the time in intimate conditions for days, probing each other's thoughts and opinions, and the stories we kept hearing were highly credible," recalls Gianni Magazzeni. "Bob, especially, was gathering every single thread of information and sequencing them. And his typing was amazing."

But what about those intercepts?

They went back to the coast near Monrovia, this time headed to ECOMOG headquarters. It was not an easy trip. They got stuck alongside a river in the rainy season and had to radio Monrovia for another vehicle. But they never felt unsafe. "These were still the days before the Iraq War when the U.N. flag really protected you," Magazzeni says, referring to the attacks on U.N. personnel in Iraq. Reaching the ECOMOG camp, they met a Nigerian general. He was all British-style spit and polish, a universe removed from the Liberian soldiery. He casually mentioned that Taylor's men must have committed the massacre; after all, he said, "We have the [transcribed] conversations."

"Can I see them?" Gersony asked.

"Of course," the general answered.

Gersony read them carefully. He could not believe his eyes. The cables were dated days after the massacre had already taken place. All they contained was a mention of a lack of food for the soldiers of Taylor's NPFL and the possibility of having to kill a few people.[16]

Gersony felt relief. The panel was on the right track and the State Department had gotten it wrong. Because by Foggy Bottom standards Liberia was a secondary matter, probably nobody in an upper-level position had read the intercepts and compared the dates with

those of the massacre. It was nothing that the bureaucracy was paying close attention to. Once again, he thought, the situation on the
ground was opposite to what officials in Washington believed. As for
the opinion of the ECOMOG general, the panel assumed that because ECOMOG was now allied with the Armed Forces of Liberia, it
had no incentive to blame government soldiers for what had happened at Carter Camp.

The last day of the investigation they interviewed Private Zarkpa
Gorh at the U.N. compound in Monrovia. Sullen, looking down and
away, disdainful of the panel's purpose, he denied everything, even
that he had lived in the camp.

They flew back first-class. Only with the United Nations would Gersony ever do so. In the cabin they began the drafting of the report,
with Gersony doing the typing and essentially the writing, too. He
was always meant to be the workhorse of the panel, with Wako and
Kassem there to provide the expertise, as well as a ceremonial impri-
matur. "I always thought of the U.N. investigation as the 'Gersony
report,'" remarks Jeff Drumtra, the Africa policy analyst for the U.S.
Committee for Refugees and Immigrants at the time. "Bob's strength,
when it was all said and done, came down to his exhaustive methodology, which was like that of the best journalists on steroids."

The panel members met with Boutros-Ghali in New York. A few
days later, on September 10, 1993, the United Nations published the
executive summary of the report blaming the Liberian government
army for the massacre; however, the full, seventy-five-page document, again written by Gersony and Magazzeni, was never actually
released. The New York Times and The Washington Post gave it prominent coverage.[17] The State Department, in a reversal of its previous
view, endorsed the findings, backed by the U.S. Embassy in Monrovia. The Liberian interim government of Amos Sawyer challenged
the findings but removed the government army from the Harbel
area. Neither ECOMOG nor a single NGO disputed the report.

Charles Taylor was later vanquished and his ragtag murderous
army dissolved. As a tenuous peace took hold, one task of the Libe-

LIBERIA BY WAY OF NICARAGUA

rian establishment was to absolve themselves and their political predecessors of any responsibility for past actions. Liberia's Truth and Reconciliation Commission, funded by international donors, became a vehicle for this. In a report riddled with vast amounts of plagiarism of the U.N. report's own language—where blame was merely shifted to Charles Taylor—the Truth and Reconciliation Commission absolved the Armed Forces of Liberia of any wrongdoing. Once the plagiarism was pointed out, the commission's report on the Camp Carter massacre disappeared from its website. Charles Taylor was guilty of legions of crimes, but not this particular one.

"And the guilty went unpunished, bringing shame on themselves and their enablers," Gersony concludes, shaking with anger decades later, his voice cracking. He still refuses to accept the Hobbesian state of affairs in Liberia, in which, because there were no responsible institutions to enforce order, there was no practical way to separate right from wrong and thus erect a moral community, however rudimentary.

Liberia was, in a way, the saddest place he would ever go because while people went on suffering, there were never any consequences for the perpetrators. There was no higher authority to appeal to.

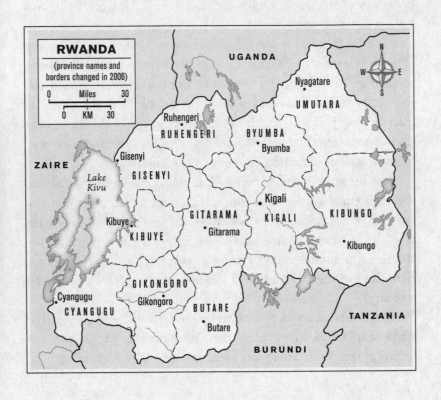

CHAPTER 11

Rwanda
1994

"You Told the Truth. . . . Let Me Worry About the Rest."

The genocide against almost a million ethnic Tutsis in Rwanda in east-central Africa, perpetrated by the majority Hutus in the spring of 1994, was one of the most important events of the twentieth century; and constituted an additional, monumental piece of evidence that the world had not changed nearly as much as American triumphalists and other starry-eyed proponents of globalization and democracy believed following the collapse of the Berlin Wall.

Perhaps no one understands better how the Rwandan genocide transpired and how it was misunderstood than the French expert on Africa, Gérard Prunier. Prunier's classic work, *The Rwanda Crisis: History of a Genocide,* published in 1995, contains a sharp criticism of Bob Gersony's field research in post-genocide Rwanda. But in a postscript, copyright 1997, Prunier disavows that earlier criticism and praises Gersony. What happened to change Prunier's mind and make close friends out of intellectual enemies is its own epic story, which involves Gersony in a controversy reaching up to the highest officials in the United Nations. But this saga must begin with the genocide itself, and Prunier's interpretation of it.

The Rwanda genocide, writes Prunier, was not a factor of biology: of tall and thin people with sharp features from some vague Semitic extraction (the Tutsis) and shorter, stockier ones of Bantu extraction from east-central Africa (the Hutus) predestined "to disembowel each other" like "cats and dogs." It was the result of a process rooted in specific human choices that can be studied and analyzed. Nor, for that matter, is Rwanda as a landscape some dense, interminable jungle like Liberia. It has beautiful vistas and four seasons, so that the whole country looks like a "gigantic garden," with very few tsetse flies and malarial mosquitoes. This engendered, as Prunier explains, "centralized forms of political authority" and a "high degree of social control," the very opposite of the sort of chaos often associated with Africa.[1]

Belgium, the colonial power, created a modern Rwanda that was efficient and brutal in the 1920s, with the native population under constant mobilization for the purposes of construction and working in the fields. Rwanda, it emerges in Prunier's telling, was more a place of plans and systems and hierarchies than of spontaneity. And by favoring one group over the other—the Nilotic Tutsis over the Bantu Hutus—the European colonialists, in particular the Belgians, fostered at every dimension of the church and state an attitude of resentment and inferiority on the part of the Hutus, thus lighting a very deliberate, slow-burning fuse.

It was precisely because of the many years of Belgian harping on the superiority of the Tutsis that the lethal idea of "race" came to define the differences between one part of the Rwanda population and the other part. Consequently, in 1959, the Hutus toppled the Tutsi monarchy and over 100,000 Tutsis fled to neighboring countries. This intercommunal violence continued into the early 1960s.[2] In 1963, writes the journalist Philip Gourevitch, "a band of several hundred Tutsi guerrillas swept into southern Rwanda from a base in Burundi and advanced to within twelve miles of Kigali before being wiped out by Rwandan forces under Belgian command." In response, Hutus massacred tens of thousands of Tutsis in southern Rwanda.[3]

In the decades that followed, the Tutsis formed their own invasion force in exile. Now that the Belgians were long gone, the French, particularly the French army, became deeply invested in supporting the Hutu regime against this Tutsi invasion force, which had originated in the violence begun by the Hutus themselves. The French army justified its strategy by telling itself that the Hutu regime was democratic. But with the Hutus making up 85 percent of the population, what really existed was not the spirit of democracy but merely the tyranny of the "tribal" majority, wrapped up in a phony moralism against the so-called feudalistic Tutsis. Prunier does not use the word "tribal" in a pejorative sense, by the way. As he writes, "if tribes did not exist, they would have to be invented." In a world of illiteracy and parochial interests, where philosophies are abstract inventions restricted to intellectuals, "solidarity is best understood in terms of a close community."[4]

This close community brought together the Nilotic Tutsis with the Banyankole of southern Uganda, Ugandan leader Yoweri Museveni's tribe, which helped make allies of Museveni and Tutsi leader Paul Kagame. This is how Kagame's RPF (Rwandan Patriotic Front) was able to utilize Uganda to invade Hutu-led Rwanda from the north. In fact, when Museveni was in the bush fighting the Ugandan government of Milton Obote, Paul Kagame acted as Museveni's chief of military intelligence. Thousands of Museveni's fighters were actually Rwandan Tutsis. This is how the Tutsi RPF came to be formed in Uganda after Museveni came to power there in the 1980s, sending shivers down the spine of the Rwandan Hutus next door. They knew back then that sooner or later they might be invaded by the very people who had oppressed them for so many years. Another thing that terrified them was the 1972 slaughter of many tens of thousands of fellow Hutus by Tutsis in neighboring Burundi to the south.

Nevertheless, history is not only a matter of large impersonal forces, but of contingency—of unpredictable incidents that can ignite such large forces. To wit, in the beginning, two personalities vied for control of the Tutsi RPF, Paul Kagame and Fred Rwigyema. Rwigyema was a moderate whose vision was to employ the Tutsi force not to invade Hutu-dominated Rwanda at all, but merely to use it as a means of leverage for concessions from the Hutu regime in Kigali. The hardliner here was Paul Kagame, who always envisioned a full-scale invasion. Rwigyema was killed in 1990 in a military operation during a dispute over tactics, and thus it would be Kagame's vision that prevailed, without which the genocide of 1994 might simply not have happened, or not have happened in the way that it did.

The French military was now fiercely backing the Hutu regime in Rwanda with the Americans, a bit more vaguely, backing Kagame's Uganda-based Tutsi force (the upshot of America's alliance with Museveni, which Bob Gersony had an indirect hand in forging in 1984). By 1993, Kagame's RPF had pushed deeper into Rwanda. The United Nations sent peacekeepers to occupy the space between the Tutsi RPF forces in the north and the Hutu government forces just to the south. The head of that U.N. force was General Maurice Baril, a French-Canadian: a name that will come up prominently later in this story about Gersony's Rwanda odyssey.

At this point the Americans, especially the U.S. ambassador in Kigali, David Rawson (Gersony's cheerleader from some years back in Somalia), were promoting a power-sharing agreement between Hutu and Tutsi elements in Rwanda; even as diplomats were making increasing demands on a Hutu regime terrified over the prospect of an RPF invasion. In this beehive of an overpopulated country, the bees were humming louder and louder, and the Hutus, angry at concessions made by their own regime, began organizing their militias to slaughter the minority Tutsis.

The country was on edge, and the Rwandan genocide was sparked by another unpredictable contingency: a Falcon 50 corporate jet carrying Rwandan president Juvénal Habyarimana and Burundian president Cyprien Ntaryamira (both ethnic Hutus) back from peace talks was shot down over Kigali the evening of April 6, 1994, at almost the same moment that the Tutsi RPF was about to march on the capital.

Thus began the killing of the minority Tutsis by the majority Hutus, both of whom were emboldened and petrified by both the plane crash and the RPF invasion. What made the Tutsis particular objects of hate was the fact that they were wealthier and better educated, a consequence of having been favored by the Belgian colonial system. In Rwanda, Prunier writes, "all the pre-conditions for a genocide were present: a well-organized civil service, a small tightly-controlled land area, a disciplined and orderly population, reasonably good communications and a coherent ideology containing the necessary lethal potential." The remnants of the Hutu regime and the militia authorities set up roadblocks, ordered house-to-house searches, drew up detailed lists, and closed off neighborhoods, with the killers using AK-47 assault rifles but mainly machetes (*pangas* in Swahili). Pogroms multiplied. The relative absence of wild country, unlike so much of Africa, made it harder for people to escape. It was a cascading tsunami of bloodshed. Mutilations and rapes were common. Corpses and limbs were heaped in separate piles. Radio Mille Collines ("a Thousand Hills"), an extremist Hutu media network, exhorted the Hutus to keep murdering. In Washington, Chas Freeman, by now assistant secretary of defense for international security affairs, pleaded with the U.S. military's joint staff to jam all fixed and mobile radios inciting racial violence in Rwanda: but to no avail.[5] Roughly 800,000 to 850,000 people—11 percent of the total population, mainly Tutsis—were killed. Around 2 million fled across the border to Tanzania, Burundi, and Zaire, and another 1.5 million or so became internally displaced.[6]

In the same time frame in Kigali, the RPF Tutsi invasion force managed to topple the Hutu-led regime that had been perpetrating the genocide, with General Paul Kagame installed as the de facto head of government by July. Moreover, the RPF's 157th mobile division, commanded by General Fred Ibingira, was quickly moving in a clockwise fashion through the Rwandan provinces of Byumba, Kibungo, and Butare, pacifying the eastern, southeastern, and southern parts of the little country. The Hutu perpetrators of the genocide had by now fled into refugee camps in Zaire, Burundi, and Tanzania.

In sum, the majority Hutus had committed genocide against the minority Tutsis, but the Tutsis themselves were now on their own warpath as they took over the country from the terrified Hutus. Yet in the outside world it was still a black-and-white situation: the Hutus were like the Nazis, plain and simple, with no mitigating circumstances.

As for Paul Kagame, he was technically only the vice president under a Hutu president, making the character of the new Rwandan regime somewhat ambiguous. Yet it was he who was really in charge. Kagame is "a cold fish, about as cheerful as a kamikaze pilot," according to one expert observer. Kagame was good organizationally, but without a moral compass: a bit like Mengistu Haile Mariam, the former Marxist dictator of Ethiopia, himself a passionless, ruthless killer. All Kagame ever had to offer was efficiency and results.

Kagame had been in charge, and RPF general Ibingira had been sweeping clockwise through Rwanda for several weeks already when Bob Gersony and his three-person team, consisting of himself, his wife, Cindy, and Tony Jackson, touched down in Kigali in a German cargo plane from Nairobi on July 30, 1994.

Bob Gersony's own involvement in the Rwanda crisis would not have happened at all without a great coincidence.

He and Cindy had been married for almost two years in July 1994, yet they had never really gone away together. Bob and Cindy found themselves alone in a house in the French village of Chens-sur-Léman, just across the border from Geneva, Switzerland. Pierre Gassmann, Bob's old ICRC friend from his Uganda assignment, had lent them his place. It was late morning, Bob and Cindy had just woken up and were settling down to their first exquisite breakfast, sampling the hot bread, fresh butter, and pâtés from the village, amid the vines, trellises, and the expectation of rich coffee and fine wines for Cindy, as Bob eschewed caffeine and alcohol.

Then the phone rang.

It was Bill Garvelink, Gersony's old traveling companion in the Bolivian highlands who now worked for J. Brian Atwood, the administrator of USAID. Atwood had just returned to Washington from Goma in Zaire (now the Democratic Republic of Congo), where a million refugees from the Rwandan genocide and political crisis had fled.

In fact, Cindy had been with Atwood in Goma and traveled to this French village by way of Nairobi and Geneva for their vacation. Cindy was on a temporary duty assignment in East Africa for the Office of Foreign Disaster Assistance, and actually had not been invited to accompany Atwood from Nairobi to Goma, when suddenly the regional director for Africa in OFDA, Katherine Farnsworth, learned that her father had died. So at the very last minute, Cindy was asked to travel with Atwood to Goma on July 18, 1994, in place of Kate Farnsworth.

Cindy mentioned to Atwood that her husband, Bob Gersony, had once briefed him on Nicaragua. Indeed, did Atwood ever remember that briefing! Gersony had spent literally hours informing Atwood about all the issues involved in reconstruction on Nicaragua's Atlantic coast. Not only was this news, but the manner of the brief itself had inspired Atwood. This Gersony, Atwood thought, wasn't just another bureaucrat. When Atwood had asked him whom he respected most, Gersony answered, "Agronomists, because agronomists know how to relate to peasants."

For the first time in some years, Bob Gersony was at the forefront of Brian Atwood's thoughts, thanks to Cindy being accidentally on the plane to Goma and seated next to him.

Atwood was appalled at the situation in Goma, where there was widespread cholera, little potable water, and Hutu genocidalists mixed in with the mainly Hutu refugees. "Kids with dead eyes mobbed the runway. The water was so dirty it was as dark as Coca-Cola. Hutu military vehicles were still patrolling the refugee camps. Hell, it was worse than hell," Atwood recalls. Though the Hutus had perpetrated the genocide, the Tutsi-led Rwandan Patriotic Front had meanwhile taken power in the capital of Kigali at roughly the same time, driving Hutus out of the country en masse. In one sense it was a case of good and evil; on another level it was messy and complicated. The messy and complicated part would be something Gersony was destined to discover on his own, to his great horror, interview by interview.

Atwood, Garvelink said over the phone, wanted Gersony to go immediately to Geneva, the headquarters of UNHCR, and meet with Sadako Ogata, the United Nations high commissioner for refugees, about the situation in Goma. Atwood then wanted Gersony to travel to Goma and "straighten things out there."

Gersony thought to himself, "Straighten things out! Is he crazy?"

U.N. High Commissioner for Refugees
Sadako Ogata, who sent Gersony to
investigate the situation in Rwanda in 1994.

Goma was a vast conflagration of human suffering and the United Nations and other agencies were doing all that they could just to cope with the mess.

"If I go to Goma, I would only be a fifth wheel, a busybody parachutist telling the U.N. and the NGO workers what to do. I would be worse than useless. I would be a distraction."

Gersony told Garvelink in no uncertain terms that if he did go to Rwanda as well as Goma and the other refugee camps over the border in whatever capacity, he would only do so accompanied by Cindy and Tony Jackson: this was Francophone Africa, and Jackson spoke fluent French. Jackson was also Gersony's lifetime "ambassador to the left-wing," as he always liked to put it, someone particularly useful in an international emergency with so many NGOs on the ground.

"Whatever you want," Garvelink answered. ("Negotiating a contract with Bob Gersony had always been a nightmare," Garvelink recalls.)

It so happened that Gerald Walzer, the deputy U.N. high commissioner for refugees, the number two person in UNHCR under Mrs. Ogata (it was always "Mrs. Ogata" or "Madame Ogata"), was a friend of Gersony's from Bangkok, when Gersony had worked on the South China Sea piracy problem a decade earlier. Walzer was a charming Austrian from Vienna just like Gersony's mother. Gersony decided he would make a day trip to Geneva to see Walzer.

In Geneva, Gersony told Walzer about Atwood's idea to send him to Goma. Walzer rolled his eyes. Nevertheless, Gersony advised that the most important thing to do now was to get the refugees home as soon as possible. He remembered the reconciliation-without-revenge strategy of Yoweri Museveni in Uganda in 1986, which had helped bring peace to that country after years of mass killing, a formula that the new Rwandan government might follow.

"We need to pull hundreds of thousands of Hutus back into Rwanda from camps in Zaire, Uganda, and Tanzania, in order to deprive the Hutu genocidalists of their population base in the camps. Even though the Tutsi RPF controls the new government," Gersony went on, "Rwanda is simply not viable without the Hutus who make up 85 percent of the population, many or most of whom are not murderers."

That was Gersony's "optimistic thesis" at the moment, a moment when many assumed that the genocide was simply a case of the Hutus killing the Tutsis, sort of like the Germans killing the Jews: the Tutsis being totally innocent and the Hutus totally guilty, in this case. And thus it was not a bad thing that the Tutsis had taken effective power away from the Hutus.

Of course, the situation was full of far more twists and turns—and of far more tragedy—than that. It was the process of discovering, bit by bit, just how much more convoluted and just how much more tragic the Rwandan catastrophe actually was—how naïve his original thesis was—that Gersony's greatest professional and personal crisis would begin to unfold.

Walzer liked Gersony's thinking and immediately took him in to see Mrs. Ogata, someone as diminutive in size as she was towering in willpower and the ability to make tough decisions. Indeed, she had a very un-Japanese way of saying, in impeccable English, exactly what she thought.[7] Mrs. Ogata instantly liked Gersony's idea of a three-person repatriation force, given that she was under pressure from the new Rwandan government and other parties to stop spending money on genocidal Hutus in refugee camps when Rwanda itself was suffering.

Gersony, by this time, was well known, and positively so, in the UNHCR family.[8] In fact, he was referred to as "a friend of the house." This most important of U.N. agencies knew of his work in Uganda and Mozambique, and also in Sudan, where he had repaired the relationship between the U.S. government and UNHCR following the rushed departure of Jerry Weaver from Khartoum. There was also Colomoncagua on the Honduras–El Salvador border, where Gersony had kept that refugee camp from being moved and thus ended the State Department's threat to cut funds to UNHCR.

The arrangement would be thus: USAID was engaging Gersony to work for—and only report to—UNHCR, so that Tony, Cindy, and Gersony would be completely under United Nations supervision, even as USAID paid Bob's consulting fee.

A few days later Bob, Cindy, and Tony got U.N. passports in Geneva as well as UNHCR survival kits: small trunks filled with basic necessities for three weeks in the field.

There was no passport control at the airport when the three of them arrived at the end of July. Kigali was littered with broken glass. Many buildings were without windows. Electricity and water were uncertain. The city constituted a war zone just beginning to rebuild.[9] Roman Urasa, the UNHCR representative in Kigali, gave Gersony a hard stare upon meeting him at his office. He had made no plans, no sleeping arrangements for the new arrivals, even as he cautioned them not to stay at a hotel. Urasa, a Tanzanian, bore a grudge against Gersony dating back to Mozambique. It was Gersony's report criticizing the human rights record of RENAMO that had spoiled Urasa's carefully laid-out plans to repatriate Mozambican refugees from neighboring countries. At over 5,000 feet in altitude, the nights could be chilly in Kigali. The three slept on the cold stone floor of UNHCR headquarters that first night without their survival kits, which were supposed to have been sent ahead but which never actually arrived. No matter, Gersony thought. With Atwood, Mrs. Ogata, and Walzer all behind him, "I had juice."

The next day they moved to the Hôtel des Mille Collines, the famous hotel that had served as a sanctuary for hundreds of Tutsis during the genocide. But the place had been trashed. The toilets were clogged. There was no power or water. Cindy and Tony talked by flashlights with other humanitarian workers at the hotel.

The three sought help at the USAID office, which they also found in a state of disarray: looted, with furniture toppled, and a calendar page still turned to April, the month the genocide began. But it would be USAID that eventually provided them with a vehicle, driver, and supplies, to which they attached U.N. logos with magnets.

Gersony figured he needed a very impressive-looking official letter, or laissez-passer, from the Rwandan government in order for the trio to travel throughout the strife-torn country and conduct interviews. He learned that only Jacques Bihozagara, the minister of rehabilitation and a co-founder of the RPF, could provide such a letter. He asked Urasa to arrange a meeting with the minister. Urasa said sullenly that he would work on it.

Gersony was having dinner one evening in the UNHCR dining room when the UNHCR protection officer for the southern Rwandan province of Butare, Kofi Mable, came over in a frantic state, insisting that he had to talk to Urasa. Mable, a Togolese, told Urasa that a report had come in of hundreds of Hutus being slaughtered in a field by a church. Gersony suggested that, in this case, maybe his team should start their investigations in Butare to the south. But Urasa recommended that Gersony not change his original plan to drive first to the northwest. Gersony was not particularly surprised by what Mable had told them. He had always figured that there would be a certain amount of revenge killings after the genocide. As for Urasa's lack of interest in the report, Gersony said nothing.

Days went by, as Gersony waited for Urasa to arrange a meeting with the Rwandan government minister. Gersony used the time to talk with as many NGO workers as he could.

Finally, Gerald Walzer phoned UNHCR's Kigali office from Geneva, and was surprised to learn that Gersony's team was still not in the field.

"I can't go," Gersony told him. "I need a letter and Urasa has been unable to get me an appointment with the minister."

"Put Urasa on the phone," Walzer said.

Urasa took the call alone in his private office. Gersony asked no questions. But before the end of the day, Urasa told Gersony that they would meet with Rehabilitation Minister Jacques Bihozagara the next morning, August 9, at eight o'clock.

The minister appeared unfriendly and skeptical.

Gersony assured him that his team was only interested in the best way to handle the repatriation of refugees, and he promised that nothing would be made public until the minister and others in his government were briefed on what the repatriation team had found. Gersony wore an extra-earnest expression, something that was easy since that's how he looked most of the time anyway.

The minister agreed to provide the laissez-passer. Gersony then asked that at the bottom of the letter, it should be noted that a copy had been sent to "Vice President Paul Kagame." The minister shrugged and agreed. The laissez-passer with Kagame's name at the bottom arrived that afternoon. Gersony knew that Kagame had only been copied. But that wouldn't matter in the field, where merely having Kagame's name on the document would work magic.

Bob, Cindy, and Tony left the next morning, driving northwest to the province of Ruhengeri, bordering Uganda and Zaire. They would cover seven hundred miles inside tiny Rwanda over the coming weeks, four hundred miles of which would be on dirt laterite roads, from which they were officially barred, supposedly because of the danger of land mines.

Ruhengeri constituted a labyrinthine swirl of hills, wreathed in a complex pattern of narrow dirt paths, making the earth appear even more beautiful. Here and there were tea and coffee plantations, adding to the dignity of the landscape. Gersony looked up at the hillsides and will never forget the sight: of vast numbers of people silently walking home, single file, their possessions on their heads—men, women, children, old people—from Goma, the refugee camp over the border in Zaire. He thought of the organization of ant columns. The pageant contradicted the operating assumption that no one was returning home because the Hutu genocidalists were not permitting them to. But here were all these Hutus reversing their original exodus, after the new Tutsi-led regime had taken power in the country. Cindy and Tony did house counts: how many were occupied, reoccupied, or empty. Meanwhile, Bob did one-on-one random interviews. They found that 60 percent of the houses were again occupied. People told Gersony that they had seeds to plant and required nothing else.

"Do you feel safe?" he asked.

"Yes."

"Has anyone bothered you?"

"No."

The three went from commune to commune in this regimented, hierarchical society. In some areas there were 90 percent occupancy rates.

Gersony felt deflated. "I'm the repatriation strike force and these people don't need my help," he thought.

Then they drove off the main roads and headed still further north. At the village of Kinigi, they came to a roadblock filled with mean-looking government troops. He showed them the laissez-passer. The soldiers told him that they didn't care about any letter, and that the U.N.-emblazoned vehicle could not pass, no matter what. "We're de-mining," a soldier explained. "De-mining," Gersony thought, "on a small dirt road leading nowhere?"

He kept the roadblock at Kinigi in mind. The mystery would soon be solved.

They headed south throughout the province of Gisenyi. There were cows with big horns known as Ankole cattle. People stood by the sides of the roads washing down goat brochettes with banana beer. Cindy and Tony tried the brochettes with piri-piri sauce, which Bob avoided, afraid at first of getting sick. He disapproved of lunch anyway. "If we skipped lunch, we could interview one more refugee, and each refugee was precious—you never knew which one would yield a breakthrough in understanding."

Here, though, there were no columns of people returning for him to interview. The atmosphere seemed tenser than in Ruhengeri to the north. Only 15 percent of the houses were occupied, and those returning were mainly doing so for a brief look-see. The people he did find filled Gersony's notebook with stories of beatings, arrests, and disappearances perpetrated by Tutsi RPF regime troops. Hutus began asking him nervously if they should leave and go back to Goma over the border. They spoke of RPF troops arresting groups of a dozen or two dozen people at a time, and killing them in the nearby Gishwati Forest.

"I was still not surprised at this point," Gersony recalls. "Many hundreds of thousands of Tutsis had just been murdered by the Hutus. What I was hearing, given what had transpired, still fell into the category of revenge killings."

But he kept hearing of whole families disappearing, and in southern Gisenyi, even more people were preparing to flee to Goma.

Goma lay directly over the border from where they were at this point. Bob and Tony crossed the border on foot to Goma, while Cindy headed south with the car into the province of Kibuye to conduct more house counts.

Goma, in Zaire, was a vision out of hell, coated in white lime, used to prevent decay of dead bodies, where there was insufficient potable water and the hard volcanic soil made it difficult to dig latrines. A million people stretched out along roads in squishy mud, barely able to move, with few or no provisions, and disease ubiquitous. Of the thirty-six individuals interviewed by Gersony there, half said they had personally witnessed RPF violence and the other half said they had heard about it. Naturally, these people were afraid to return home. Meanwhile, the Hutu genocidalists were regrouping within this sprawling refugee encampment.

"Is the RPF hunting down actual perpetrators [of the genocide] or just shooting fish in a barrel?" he asked himself. He still wasn't convinced that all of this was much more than revenge killings that had gotten out of hand.

He met the UNHCR representatives in Goma, Filippo Grandi and Joel Boutroue. Filippo, a tall and aristocratic Italian, would go on to become the head of UNHCR. It was mid-August and the two officials were working under unbelievable stress. Gersony was glad he hadn't agreed to simply parachute into Goma in order to be a fifth wheel. They showed him a just-received report that the RPF had killed 150 men, women, and children with machetes in the village of Kinigi in northern Ruhengeri. Gersony was heartened by the news—heartened, that is, that his suspicions about the de-mining excuse the soldiers had given him about the roadblock there were well founded.

"We're getting very granular," he thought to himself. "It's hard to miss things here, the country is too small." Still, he wasn't altogether pessimistic. There was the overall positive situation in Ruhengeri, while Gisenyi to the south was what you would expect: killings by the new Tutsi regime in the scores, maybe hundreds, yet still not mass killings. The new de facto Tutsi government simply had to discipline its troops more. Until then, the situation was not quite ready for Hutu refugees to return home.

In fact, there were some repatriations of Hutus from Goma already in progress. People would sign up the night before and be taken by bus back to Rwanda the next morning. But even those numbers were rapidly diminishing, Gersony learned. The Hutu genocidalists were beating up the people who had signed up to go back and live under the Tutsi regime, and later the Hutu who was in charge of the operation was found beaten to death, his face barely recognizable.

Crossing the border from Zaire back into Rwanda, they linked up with Cindy, who told them that she could hardly find any Hutus in Kibuye. The houses there were nearly empty of occupants. A pattern had developed. The situation was getting grimmer as they moved south into Rwanda's southwestern corner. They were in fact retracing from the opposite direction the sweep of RPF General Ibingira's 157th mobile division through the country.

Just as they were about to continue across the south of Rwanda, from the southwest to the southeast, Gersony got a message that he was wanted immediately back in Kigali. He was angry. Capital cities always catch you in a spiderweb of official responsibilities where you learn nothing compared to what you learn in the field, even as they corrupt you with their creature comforts. "Just as I was getting into a rhythm, this damn thing happens," he told Tony and Cindy. "Just as I was getting used to the bad food, to the harsh conditions and sleeping arrangements, and filling up my notebook, I now have to break the spell."

He had been summoned back for a meeting with Michel Moussalli and Kamel Morjane. Moussalli had been named by Mrs. Ogata as her special representative for the Great Lakes region of Africa. A decade earlier he had treated Gersony to a memorable, expensive dinner by Lake Leman in Geneva when Gersony was burning up with the news he had of atrocities in Uganda's Luwero Triangle. Morjane was the head of Africa for UNHCR and was Mrs. Ogata's most trusted colleague in this crisis. He would go on to become the defense minister and later foreign minister of Tunisia. But as soon as he got back to Kigali, Gersony first tackled the basic necessities: he showered, ate sandwiches in his room, and handed in his laundry. Then he had met with Moussalli and Morjane. Cindy and Tony had remained in their hotel rooms.

Gersony briefed them for half an hour. He expressed doubts about his earlier plan for the repatriation of Hutu refugees to Rwanda, now controlled by the Tutsis. Seeing how sympathetic both Moussalli and Morjane were, Gersony then decided to really trust them, the way he had trusted Roy Stacy in Harare about what he was discovering about RENAMO. Opening his heart, he said to them to make a decision. He had heard rumors, and also had a feeling, that as he continued to travel across the south of the country, in the opposite direction of RPF General Ibingira's Tutsi army, he might find out things that could put UNHCR in a very difficult position.

Gersony explains to me twenty-five years later: "I knew they couldn't say no to me. But I had to have it on the record, that it was their decision that I continue my journey. For the reigning assumption in the West was still that the Hutus were simply the perpetrators and the Tutsis only the victims."

Moussalli and Morjane did, in fact, say yes. They told Gersony that he should continue his travels. Moussalli and Morjane simply wanted to know the truth. They wanted "field-based, quality-of-information," that's all. Gersony reveres them to this day.

On August 22, 1994, Bob, Cindy, and Tony left Kigali for the southwest to pick up where they had left off.

They planned to travel from the province of Butare eastward to the province of Kibungo in Rwanda's southeastern corner. Only 25 percent of the houses in Butare were occupied. There was the unmistakable odor of human flesh. Everywhere fat dogs were hanging about: always a bad sign. But the start of the genocide was already four months past, and it was four months since the RPF had swept through here, pacifying the province. Whereas Gersony had been pleased by what he saw in northwestern Rwanda and had been concerned by the situation in western Rwanda, here in the south of the country he became truly alarmed. There was a real atmosphere of tension. The three crossed the border into Burundi, where Hutu refugees told them that they had been invited back home by the Tutsi authorities, but after they had witnessed large-scale arrests and killings, they came back to Burundi as refugees a second time.

The three returned over the border into Rwanda and then headed east, to the province of Kibungo: a true step into hell.

Kibungo was flatter with fewer trees. There were no goat brochettes or other food available, so they survived on a wheel of cheese that Bob and Tony had bought at a makeshift stand in Goma. Soldiers were everywhere, not letting their vehicle through at a main roadblock, despite the laissez-passer and the U.N. logo on their car. It was the first time since Kinigi that this had happened. They finally managed to enter a military headquarters. It was buzzing with activity. Some kind of major operation was ongoing. The RPF soldiers all had fresh uniforms and expensive Motorola phones and radios. The three obtained a quick meeting with a snarly, arrogant major from military intelligence, who had a real command presence. He had no time for polite conversation. Yes, he knew they had a laissez-passer, but nobody goes into the area of the operation. Gersony pointed out Kagame's name at the bottom of the letter. The major said: "I'll let you in. But don't be a reporter. Things happen to reporters here."

They drove further inside Kibungo.

It was all deserted, no civilians; "there were more people in the middle of the Gobi Desert," Gersony thought. But there were quite a few military outposts: again, soldiers with neat uniforms and expensive Motorola radios. There was no sense of a looming battle or engagement with another army. The province was truly pacified. The RPF was in complete control.

Once in a great while they saw an old man or old woman sticking his or her head out from behind a tree or hut. Gersony interviewed them deep in the bush, disobeying the order not to be a reporter. They told him about mass killings. Cindy and Tony did house counts: there was nobody in the houses. They saw what appeared to be a brick schoolhouse surrounded by about half a dozen fat, greasy dogs. The smell was overpowering; it had even seeped into their car. Bob went inside the small building. Stacked up against all the walls, with hands tied behind their backs in kneeling positions, were fresh human bodies, all executed within the past few days: thus the smell.

On one wall, smeared in red, presumably blood, Gersony read:

"Hutu can [sic] home to die."

He interviewed a man on the road, who told him:

"The army is killing everybody they can find."

Further down the road was a Catholic church. Strewn throughout the churchyard were bodies, but these were shriveled and desiccated, and thus emitted no smell. Inside, in the pews, they counted sixty more bodies in the same condition. These people had been dead for some months: victims of the original genocide. Here there were no dogs prowling about. They could easily tell the difference between the bodies in the church and the bodies in the school building. The two scenes told the story of Butare and Kibungo.

They were driving down a dirt road in Kibungo when they came upon a surreal sight: a long line of stocky Hutu men in bright pink medical scrubs, carrying picks and shovels, being force-marched by

Tutsi RPF soldiers with assault rifles at the front and the rear of the line. They stopped the U.N. car to shake hands with the RPF soldiers, in order to show deference. Later they saw another such column, and then another. Finally they slowed the U.N. car to a crawl and asked one of the men in the middle of the column, far from the soldiers at the front and back, "What are you all doing?"

"We're burying fresh bodies."

Another day they passed large groups of men in pink scrubs digging long pits. The armed RPF soldiers around them looked relaxed, none in defensive positions. There were evidently no Hutu militias anymore to guard against. But they did occasionally encounter RPF troops packed into the backs of trucks screaming and chanting. Their excited mien was unlike the other soldiers that they had seen.

They spent eight days traveling about southern Rwanda, sleeping at night in abandoned homes.

Gersony became terrified of what he knew, of what he had accumulated in his notebooks the past few weeks, and the possibility of having his notebooks confiscated; or of being arrested, or worse, by the RPF. The fact that he was protected by his U.N. status did not alleviate his paranoia.

He was overcome with relief as their car crossed the Akagera River bridge into Tanzania on August 30, 1994. They passed through a drier, more open landscape and soon arrived at the vast refugee camp of Ngara. They headed for the UNHCR headquarters there, with its clean latrines, hot showers, mouthwatering buffets, and general ambience of glamping. They slept on army cots, a luxury after Butare and Kibungo, despite the bedbugs. Cindy and Tony relaxed, drinking Primus beer. Bob shared their findings with the local UNHCR officials. They told him that all the evidence about large-scale killings by the new Tutsi regime that they had gathered from the refugees there was identical to his, and that they were fishing dozens of bodies with machete and gunshot wounds out of the river daily. He conducted interviews with randomly selected refugees in Ngara and its satellite camps for several days.

By this time they had conducted over two hundred one-on-one

interviews, and one hundred one-on-two-or-three interviews at ninety-one locations, including nine refugee camps in three countries. Within Rwanda they had covered 41 of 145 communes, and gathered some material from 10 others, totaling about a third of those in the country.[10] The stories they had heard were corroborating each other. While those in the refugee camps might have been influenced by the propaganda of Hutu genocidalists, their stories, nevertheless, tracked with those of the many more people he interviewed inside Rwanda itself. Moreover, UNHCR workers in the refugee camps had been hearing the same stories from refugees just as they stumbled across the border, before they could be influenced by the genocidalists.

Gersony knew he had to get back to Geneva and brief Mrs. Ogata about what was going on. His plan was to drive for several days southeast across Tanzania, from Ngara to the capital of Dar es Salaam, where the three of them could fly back to Geneva. He was frightened of reentering Rwanda. He called Gerald Walzer on the UNHCR satellite phone. Afraid of being monitored, he casually mentioned to Walzer that he had something important to tell him. Walzer insisted that they return first to Kigali, only four hours away to the northwest, so as not to insult their Rwandan hosts.

So they returned to Kigali, spent one night there, said their good-byes, and flew to Nairobi with all the notebooks. For Gersony, every minute back in Rwanda was nerve-racking. In Nairobi they camped out in a luxury hotel for a week, organizing and analyzing all the interviews, which Gersony typed up, working all day, every day they were there, internalizing the results of his reporting through the typing process, and going out periodically for BLT sandwiches.

"I had previously hated Nairobi," Cindy explains. "I always found it congested and unfriendly. But coming out of Rwanda with all of its horrors, Nairobi was like paradise, a place where we could comfortably work."

The more than three hundred accounts of the interviewees told the following story:

The RPF had met little resistance at first, as it wheeled its army through Rwanda, so that the countryside was occupied by relatively friendly Tutsi soldiers with Hutus among them. Weeks went by. These soldiers were replaced by others: all Tutsis, the kill units, the soldiers that Gersony had observed chanting and screaming from the backs of trucks, their legs draped over the sides.

They would call people to meetings: something common in such a hierarchical and well-organized society. The soldiers would deploy in a semicircle, open fire, and slaughter everyone; or sometimes order people into a church and set the building on fire with the help of grenades; or separate people into groups and kill them with machetes in the bush. They would hunt down escapees in the swamps and banana plantations. The army then went from village to village conducting mop-up operations. Machetes were preferred because they were silent. All of the murders were done by uniformed RPF soldiers.

May and June were the big kill months, before the population widely understood what was happening and hid or escaped over the borders. One hundred percent of the victims were Hutus. The original genocide against the Tutsis had begun in early April and lasted through the end of June, so this second mass killing occurred both in the immediate aftermath and also somewhat parallel to the genocide.

Gersony estimated that May and June saw a minimum of 20,000 murders of Hutus in Butare and Kibungo, with a minimum of 10,000 in July and August. In sum, the Tutsi RPF committed a minimum of 30,000 murders in order to create a Hutu-free strategic rear base in the south and southeast of the country: to counter the genocidalist center of gravity for the Hutus in the west and over the border in Zaire.

Despite the safety and luxury of Nairobi, Gersony was in a foul mood during the whole week there. He admits, "I was ungrateful, very unpleasant with Cindy and Tony. I was always snapping at them." Cindy remembers: "When Bob gets worried and nervous, he lashes out. It was the worst I've ever seen his behavior in more than twenty-five years of marriage. All he did was question the results, blaming Tony and me. But he couldn't escape from the evidence we had compiled."

Though the conclusions of the research were no real surprise to him, for the first time he was faced with the documented reality of it all. In the back of his mind he had kept hoping that the accounts would add up to a more muddled outcome: revenge killings that had gotten way out of hand. But here in the neutral, antiseptic environment of a Nairobi luxury hotel, the awfulness of his predicament nakedly stared him in the face.

"I knew no good would come of this for me," he says, still full of intensity. It was hardly the truth he wanted to share with the world. "There was this genocide in which close to a million people had been murdered only weeks and months ago and the West had done nothing to stop it, so that the immensity of the guilt was overpowering. The Hutus were the Nazis and the Tutsis were the Jews in the minds of concerned and influential people in the outside world. And now I'm the one bringing them news that the very victims of the genocide were killing the perpetrators of it, on a large scale, in an organized and premeditated way. No one would make the distinction between the RPF and the innocent Tutsis, I knew. The messenger of this news would be reputationally ruined, I thought. No one is going to be happy to get this information. I knew our report was going to be attacked and taken apart," he continues, "and that I would be the one assailed personally: since I am accusing the Tutsis of mass murder right after a genocide against them. It doesn't get any worse than that. I have always made the distinction between the mass murder of tens of thousands of people and the genocide of hundreds of thousands. But no one attacking me will make that distinction. I really thought this was going to be the end of my career."

In bed at night he was plagued by racing thoughts. He took an extra Xanax, a prescribed medication against anxiety, which he had been taking since the mid-1980s.

He arrived at the Ramada Renaissance Hotel in Geneva healthy but in psychological turmoil. Pierre Gassmann came over the first night for drinks with him, Cindy, and Tony in the hotel bar. Gersony, sipping juice, poured his heart out to Pierre. Pierre will never forget the meeting. "Bob was a complete wreck, paranoid, biting his finger-nails. I simply told him: 'All you can do is give them the facts.'"

The meeting with Mrs. Ogata took place September 12, 1994. Beside her around a small table in the corner of her vast office were Gerald Walzer, the deputy high commissioner; François Fouinat, her chief of staff; Kamel Morjane, UNHCR head of Africa; and three other officials.[11] Gersony spoke in dense detail, aided by a frayed, dirt-stained, cruddy map of Rwanda: a real map. He began with his positive impressions of Ruhengeri in northwestern Rwanda, in order to build credibility, and then as he narrated his travels around to the south and southeast, his briefing gradually turned darker. After three hours he still hadn't finished. A second meeting of the same group was scheduled for the next day. At the end of the second briefing, he made clear the distinction between the genocide of the Tutsis and the mass killings of the Hutus that followed soon after.

He was in no way diminishing the magnitude of the former crime because of the latter, he said.

Mrs. Ogata spoke.

She said she would immediately halt organized repatriations of Hutus to Rwanda from neighboring countries. "Mr. Gersony, you've done a great job, but this problem goes higher than me." She then asked him to brief Kofi Annan, the U.N. undersecretary-general for peacekeeping, a Ghanaian, and more importantly a leading candidate to be the next U.N. secretary-general.

But before he left the room, Mrs. Ogata, explaining that she had nothing on paper regarding this staggering report, asked Gersony for a copy of his briefing notes. He hesitated, then handed them to her reluctantly. His notes were full of all sorts of points of emphasis and personal comments, as these things often are. *She has given me her trust and so I will give her mine,* he thought. "Don't worry, I'm putting your notes in my safe, no one will see them," she said.[12]

With Cindy and Tony flying back to Nicaragua, Gersony next trav-

eled to London, where Kofi Annan was at the moment. Gerald Walzer accompanied him there for the sake of support from the head
office.

The two-hour meeting with Annan on September 14, at a hotel
near Heathrow airport, went well. After all, Gersony had been recommended *by the house*. Annan didn't appear particularly surprised or
even perturbed by what Gersony had to say. Annan's own "moral cha-
risma," in the words of one journalist, emanated from his self-
awareness of the United Nations' own limitations in such a tragic
world,[13] though this very attribute could also make him a fatalist. At
any rate, Annan already seemed to be strategizing about how to handle the information Gersony had given him. Annan had to be very
troubled at this moment, or he should have been. It was Annan, who
as head of U.N. peacekeeping, was in the main bureaucratically responsible "for assuring that the UN Mission to Rwanda remained
small and weak," and thus did not do nearly enough to prevent the
genocide of the Tutsis.[14] Redemption for Annan in conventional
terms had to mean standing up for the new Tutsi government. But
here was this American contractor telling him that the new Tutsi
leaders were themselves guilty of killing a large number of people.

Both the United Nations and the Americans were backing
Kagame's new government in the face of no other alternative, and
Annan was also Washington's emerging candidate to be the next
U.N. secretary-general. However, by this time Mrs. Ogata had sent to
him and other top U.N. officials cables that had come from UNHCR's
own field offices at refugee camps in Tanzania and elsewhere, which
corroborated Gersony's findings. Thus, Annan asked Gersony to immediately brief U.N. Secretary-General Boutros-Ghali's inner circle
in New York.

Gersony told officials at U.N. headquarters in New York that he
needed several hours for the briefing. There was no pushback. The
meeting took place September 16, 1994. It was a Friday, he remembers. The meeting was chaired by Marrack Goulding, the U.N.
undersecretary-general for political affairs, a truly formidable British
presence in U.N. circles who apologized to Gersony for the absence

of Secretary-General Boutros-Ghali, who was away in Japan. Goulding sat opposite Gersony. Packing the table on all sides were six others, including the legendary Algerian negotiator Lakhdar Brahimi; the Peruvian diplomat and Boutros-Ghali's senior political adviser, Álvaro de Soto; and the Tunisian diplomat Hédi Annabi.[15]

Gersony, with the aid of his frayed map, spoke for two hours without interruption. At the end, Hédi Annabi, who would later be killed in an earthquake in Haiti, said, "Nothing Mr. Gersony has said surprises me. I have heard these kinds of reports." There were no challenges, just requests for clarification. There was never a question of *whether,* only a question of the protocol for taking action. Goulding immediately wrote to Boutros-Ghali that Gersony would be instructed to return to Rwanda to brief its effective leader, Paul Kagame. Without explicitly endorsing Gersony's findings, the United Nations would use his report to demand "that if such killings are indeed taking place, they be immediately stopped."[16]

Kofi Annan, who was in Burundi by this time, would be diverted to Rwanda in order to accompany Gersony to the meeting with Kagame. The United Nations was playing it straight at this point in the Rwanda crisis. But as with many international crises, the United Nations was not really in control of the policy to the extent that the United States was.

Before the meeting ended, Gersony asked Goulding's permission to brief the USAID administrator Brian Atwood in Washington, merely as a courtesy since it had been Atwood who originally initiated his reporting trip to Rwanda. Goulding consented. Gersony called Atwood to ask if he could meet alone with him the very next morning. Atwood agreed.

Though it was a quiet Saturday morning, Atwood ambushed him. While Atwood remembers meeting first alone with Gersony, Gersony remembers entering Atwood's large, intimidating office and being met by a large group. Gersony had a quick decision to make: Should he give them all the long, no-holds-barred brief? He decided he had no choice.

At the meeting were eight others besides Atwood, including the deputy USAID administrator, Carol Lancaster; George Moose, the assistant secretary of state for Africa; and Donald Steinberg, the director for Africa at the National Security Council.[17] This group's reaction to Gersony's brief was quite different from that at the United Nations the day before. Here no one was pleased with Gersony. The reason: Kagame was more of an American-supported ruler than a United Nations one. The United States, having failed to take action to prevent the original genocide against the Tutsis, now embraced the new Tutsi regime as a means of moral self-absolution; moreover, Kagame was a close ally of Uganda's Yoweri Museveni, another U.S. client. Gersony was being driven crazy by the constant need of American officials to simplify a complex situation and put into neat semantic categories what was going on. George Moose in particular, according to Gersony, delivered a rambling, semi-coherent monologue, criticizing minor aspects of the brief.

Gersony rolled his eyes, and was blunt: "I don't see your point."

Gersony longed for the days when Chet Crocker and Hank Cohen had held that same job in the Reagan and elder Bush administrations.

But there was a lot more going on than that. Gersony, for all his attributes (and precisely because of his attributes), could also be, in the words of a colleague, "annoying, persistent, and somewhat overpowering." Moreover, "it was the very nature of his work that required a 'trust me' element. For there was always the possibility that he didn't get it all right." This came to a head in Rwanda, where an early presumption of absolute truth had existed that Gersony exploded with his methodology. And yet as impressive as his methodology was, being a methodology that dealt with human experience in the midst of war and chaos, he was dealing with Shakespearean elements that even the best methodology could not quite capture.

Maybe some of his interviewees had lied to him; maybe some were genuinely confused. He clearly got the big picture right, but beyond that, there could have been nuances that he missed. It's possible that he also didn't have the full story.

"A lot of people lost it over Rwanda. Rwanda led to a lot of soul-searching, which often results in bad analysis," one State Department official says.

Margaret McKelvey, a veteran of the Africa desk at the refugee bureau, adds: "The skepticism about Bob's analysis was somewhat ironic. Six months earlier Kagame's RPF had been our enemy, its representatives not even allowed to enter the State Department building. Now, after the Hutu-led genocide, the RPF went suddenly from being bad guys to being heroes. So the RPF was the enemy until they weren't. But Gersony brought us back to reality about the RPF."

In any case, Arlene Render, office director of central African affairs in the State Department, sent two cables to all U.S. embassies the following week about Gersony's Saturday morning briefing, stating that "the team found that systematic killings by the RPA [RPF] were taking place . . . and the team will inquire what steps Kagame plans to take to halt these abuses." The entire matter, the cable said, would be taken to the U.N. Security Council.[18]

Gersony, thoroughly tense and exhausted, having gotten little rest since he had originally left for Africa from Pierre Gassmann's French villa two months earlier, flew back to New York and then on to Nairobi, where he met up with Kofi Annan and Kamel Morjane, the very sympathetic Tunisian deputy to Mrs. Ogata. From Nairobi, the three flew to Kigali, a place that Gersony now dreaded, where he was to deliver the same briefing of several hours' duration to one hostile audience after another. It was September 20, 1994.[19]

The first such briefing he gave at Annan's insistence was to Shahryar Khan, Boutros-Ghali's special representative to Rwanda and a former Pakistani foreign secretary. Also in the room was Major General Guy Tousignant, the latest in a line of French-Canadian officers who had led UNAMIR, or the United Nations Assistance Mission to Rwanda.[20] Both Khan and Tousignant were uncomfortable with Gersony's findings, which put them on the spot. In such a small country, how could they not have known what was going on? But Gersony was blunt with them, telling his audience exactly what he had told every audience thus far:

"I stake my twenty-five-year reputation on my conclusions which I recognize are diametrically opposite to assumptions made by U.N. and other observers on the ground here."[21]

Major General Tousignant simply remarked when Gersony had finished: "Now I understand why the Rwandan government wouldn't let UNAMIR into Kibungo."[22]

Paul Kagame was at this time in South Africa meeting with the recently elected Nelson Mandela. In fact, Kagame might actually have extended his visit there by a day or two in order to avoid seeing Annan and Gersony. Thus, Gersony ended up briefing Faustin Twagiramungu, the figurehead Hutu prime minister in the Tutsi-controlled state. At the rectangular table Twagiramungu sat at one end and Gersony at the other. Annan and Morjane sat on the side closer to the prime minister. The room was packed with RPF military intelligence figures and soldiers who spoke English: all allies of English-speaking Uganda's Yoweri Museveni. Twagiramungu was probably the only Hutu in the room, and he also spoke French. The scene was testimony to the political distance that this former Francophone colony had traveled away from its Belgian and French roots.

Gersony felt like he was at the wrong end of a firing squad.

As with all his briefings, Gersony had his map and began with the positive developments in Ruhengeri that he had observed at the start of his field trip and his conflicted appraisal of Gisenyi, which helped build credibility for a comprehensive, balanced analysis. After all, no one at this date had randomly interviewed as many people in as many locations as he had. Ninety minutes later, after he finished, there was a moment of quiet.

The prime minister said: "I myself am a Hutu and I don't believe these reports are true." But he then proceeded to ask softball questions. What emerged was a non-denial denial of what Gersony's research showed. Twagiramungu would flee Rwanda into exile in Belgium the following year.[23] Cutting off the prime minister, a member of the Tutsi military intelligence team asked Gersony:

"How can you be sure the people you interviewed were Hutus?"

"Why would hundreds of Tutsis, selected randomly and interviewed alone in different locations, all pretend to be Hutus and then give false information?"

The prime minister asked: "How did you arrive at the figure of thirty thousand killed?"

Indicating the figure was "an order to magnitude," Gersony explained his methodology. Crucially, the killings were large-scale and systematic.

At the end, Annan privately signaled to Gersony some concern over the numbers question.

Kamel Morjane told Gersony, "You did fine."

Next, Gersony went to the home of Roman Urasa, head of the UNHCR office in Kigali, to brief him. Urasa told him at the end, "You've made our life very difficult." The truth seemed to affect Urasa less than the political complications that the truth would cause for the local office. Gersony was by now getting reactions from two types of people: the *protection*-oriented officials, who concentrated on the truth and its implications for innocents still at the mercy of the RPF; and the *politically* oriented officials, who jumped immediately to what it meant for their own positions, and those of their governments and organizations.

The U.S. ambassador to Rwanda, David Rawson, had helped Gersony enormously and heaped praise on him during the Mozambique and Somalia episodes of his life. But Rawson was now a different man: he must have been because of what he had witnessed. The son of medical missionaries in the region, he had grown up a speaker of Kinyarwanda. He was one of the State Department's exemplary Africa hands, akin to the Arabists and China hands of old. But because he had played a significant role in the diplomatic process that forced political concessions on the Hutus, just prior to the genocide they committed against the Tutsis—and because he had personally witnessed the piles of bodies along the roadsides—Rawson may have been seeking atonement by championing the new Tutsi regime. At the end of the Rwanda tragedy, Rawson would seem to have no friends, only detractors. Gersony, who was no stranger to personal trauma, recognized the turmoil Rawson was in.

Rawson insisted on seeing Gersony alone, without any other embassy officers present. Gersony was very wary, afraid of a "he said, she said" report of their meeting. After listening to Gersony and praising him for his work elsewhere in Africa, Rawson suggested that the Hutus he had interviewed may have been victims of a collective hallucination.

"We interviewed hundreds at random in ninety-one locations in several countries. Are you saying they all had the same hallucination?" Gersony asked him.

A quarter century later Rawson recalls to me:

"While I thought Gersony's sampling technique somehow captured the story of Somalia's nomadic clansmen, who are independent and difficult to pin down, I wondered if his sampling technique worked in Rwanda with its dense population, and history of outward conformity to expected behavior. In Rwanda, stories quickly spread, and became internalized and repeated as one's own."

Gersony shoots back:

"Rawson had no problem with our sampling technique in northwestern Rwanda—Ruhengeri and Gisenyi—where he liked the results: the sampling technique in his mind was only flawed in southern and eastern Rwanda—Butare and Kibungo—where he didn't like the results."

Rawson may have been less than candid with Gersony when they met in Kigali in 1994. It was late September and the previous month, August 5 to be exact, he had been one of those officials receiving a secret cable from Frederick Ehrenreich of the State Department's Bureau of Intelligence and Research, which stated:

> Despite RPF professions of support for human rights, it will take "justice" into its own hands . . . There have been numerous recent reports of systematic killings of Hutus by the RPF . . . The continuing flow of thousands of refugees into Tanzania suggests that significant human rights violations are occurring in eastern Rwanda, an area which has been under RPF control for several months . . .[24]

More significantly, on August 11, Rawson's ambassadorial colleague in Burundi, Robert Krueger, fired off a secret five-alarm cable mentioning a "conscious [RPF] policy of terrifying Hutus in southeastern Rwanda, encouraging their exile. . . ." Krueger wrote of "intentional cruelty" of the RPF, and added:

There are repeated reports . . . made by Hutu refugees from Rwanda that: after having occupied a certain area, the RPF had called together a "peace meeting" at which many men were taken away who subsequently disappeared. At times it is said that all participants at such meetings, including women and children, have been liquidated.[25]

Then on August 17, Rawson met with Kagame himself and raised the issue of Hutus fleeing south into Burundi and Tanzania. When all this is taken into account, Rawson's skeptical reaction to Gersony's briefing appears somewhat inexplicable.[26] But in another sense it doesn't. As Rawson told a colleague who had raised the issue of RPF human rights abuses: "There is no path out of this mess except by helping the Rwandan RPF government," even as he knew that the RPF couldn't stand him, as they associated him with the diplomatic context that had led to the original genocide against the Tutsis.

Undeterred, yet full of fatigue and a growing anxiety, the next day Gersony delivered yet another multihour briefing, this time to Seth Sendashonga, Kagame's interior minister, a Hutu. At the conclusion, Sendashonga said, "I am already aware of all these killings. I have sent many letters to the vice president [Kagame] and haven't gotten an answer. Your report is going to be a great help to me." The following year Sendashonga fled into exile in Kenya after criticizing Kagame. In 1998, the RPF assassinated him in Nairobi.[27] Before he was murdered, Sendashonga would tell the Africa expert Gérard Prunier that the repercussions of Gersony's reporting had stopped the RPF killing machine in Rwanda's south and southeast. (This would be confirmed years later by another scholar, writing that the diplomatic pressure initiated by Gersony's report, in addition to other factors, led the RPF to order soldiers to stop killing civilians after late September.)[28]

Following Sendashonga, Gersony, accompanied by Kamel Morjane, briefed Kagame's chief of staff, Lieutenant Colonel Andrew Rwigamba.

"Are you saying that these murders have been systematic?" Lieutenant Colonel Rwigamba asked Gersony.

"Yes, they could not have occurred without senior officials of the army knowing," Gersony replied.

General Maurice Baril, the military adviser to the U.N. secretary-general, was also in the room. He remembers how "livid" Colonel Rwigamba became at Gersony's remark. "The atmosphere was tense, with armed guards at the door," says Baril. Speaking truth to power was not a mere phrase to Gersony. At this point he began to really worry about his safety. But Kamel Morjane didn't blink.

Gersony stumbled back to the UNHCR office, out of energy. Urasa wasn't there. So he just sat alone, enjoying a moment of downtime. Then who walks in? Ambassador Rawson, along with Prudence Bushnell, a deputy assistant secretary of state for Africa ("the DAS" in Washington bureaucratic lingo), and Timothy Wirth, the former Democratic senator from Colorado and now the undersecretary of state for democracy and global affairs. Rawson had a deer-in-the-headlights look upon seeing Gersony. Gersony had the presence of mind to ask the three, focusing on Bushnell and Wirth, if they would like a briefing. Rawson hesitated but Bushnell and Wirth both said yes, the latter carefully so. A former politician and smooth operator, Wirth may have quickly calculated that he should never be on record as refusing such an important brief. In fact, Gersony's report was a main purpose of Wirth's trip to Africa.

So Gersony performed yet again, with his map, and beginning with the good news from Ruhengeri in order to disarm them. Indeed, as he told this and every previous audience, Ruhengeri constituted incontrovertible proof that where the RPF permitted safe return and did not conduct mass killings, Hutu refugees streamed back into Rwanda in the tens of thousands. But it wasn't happening elsewhere in Rwanda because of the actions of Kagame's troops in more strate-gic areas, to which both the United States and the United Nations were turning a blind eye.

Gersony directed his eyes throughout to the DAS, Pru Bushnell, a sparkling, intelligent, high-church WASP. Her father had been a ca-reer Foreign Service officer and she was viewed by some as the real brains and power in the Africa bureau.[29] When Gersony finished talking, Wirth thanked him but was noncommittal. Bushnell knew, however, that everything Gersony said was true. This became appar-ent in a carefully worded confidential cable that the embassy sent out immediately afterward, on September 23, which also included Wirth's assessment that there was "potential for serious damage to interna-tional support" for the new Rwandan government on account of Ger-sony's report, which "could greatly complicate" American diplomatic efforts.[30]

Indeed, three weeks later in Washington, Wirth would personally express doubts about Gersony's reporting to a group of NGOs. Wirth, according to several people involved with the issue, was still acting like a senator, hard-charging for a policy of repatriation, which meant consciously undermining the results of Gersony's research. Sheppie Abramowitz, representing the International Rescue Committee, would fire back at Wirth: "Some of us have known Gersony for years and we take his reporting seriously."

Wirth and ultimately the State Department would publicly have none of it, even as privately they used Gersony's fieldwork to bring pressure on Kagame.

Translation: The United States was behind the new Tutsi govern-ment in order to stabilize Rwanda and to atone for its own failure to prevent the genocide against the Tutsis. There appeared to be simply no practical alternative to Kagame's RPF regime at this point. After all, who else was going to rule Rwanda if not Kagame? Kagame, it must now be said, went on to become an exemplary modernizing dictator, accomplishing wonders with the economy, infrastructure, and bureaucracy. There is no unity of goodness: a murderer can indeed go on to lead a nation out of conflict and underdevelopment, history shows. But nobody dealing with Rwanda knew that then. Moreover, Gersony had upset this whole decision-making process and confused the narrative. He had, merely by methodically listening to people and writing down what they told him, inserted a moral complication into a *raison d'état*.

"The last thing the donor countries and the United States wanted to hear at this juncture was that the victims of the genocide were taking large-scale, systematic retribution against the perceived perpetrators," said an international official. "They preferred a morally black-and-white situation." Moreover, since the RPF leaders were all English speakers and impressive as individuals, "some American officials in particular just ate it all up."

Pru Bushnell, looking back from a vantage point of twenty-five years, says that "Bob Gersony, like others in the aftermath of the Cold War, was intent on making human rights into a national security issue, whether or not it complicated things for us."

On his last night in Kigali before flying home, Gersony was dragged to a reception by Kamel Morjane at the residence of Shahryar Khan, Boutros-Ghali's special representative in country, someone Gersony had instantly disliked and who he felt had been blindsided by his report. The reception was in honor of Kofi Annan, who everyone assumed would be the next U.N. secretary-general. Gersony's fears and hatreds of these occasions proved accurate. In the house filled with United Nations and Rwandan government officials, no one wanted to talk to him, or even to be seen in his company. He wandered outside to the garden and sat down at the top of three flagstone steps alone: weary, upset, and scared for the security of his career, intending to take an extra dose of Xanax before bed. All along he knew intellectually that the evidence he and his team had accumulated would prove to be his undoing, but it was at this moment, with everyone else enjoying themselves over drinks inside, that the full force of it hit him emotionally on this cool, high-altitude tropical night.

Suddenly, General Maurice Baril came over in his Canadian army summer uniform and sat down beside him. General Baril, after heading UNAMIR, had become a military adviser to Boutros-Ghali and was often at U.N. meetings with Gersony, but usually stayed quiet.

"I know you've been telling the truth," Baril said in his French-Canadian accent. "I was getting constant reports back in 1993 that the RPF in areas it controlled in northern Rwanda was acting identical as you describe. I should not worry, Bob. We all know you've done a great job."

Decades later, Baril would reiterate to me that "it was difficult for the rest of the world to believe the truth: that Kagame and his leadership could allow such horrors after what had happened from April to July 1994."

Gersony flew out the next day. With him at the airport VIP lounge in Kigali were Kofi Annan, Kamel Morjane, and Shahryar Khan. Annan called him over to a huddle with Khan.

"There's going to be a one-day [Rwandan] government investigation of what has been happening" in the southeast, Annan told him.

Gersony called it a "whitewash." Officials would drive out in a convoy of RPF vehicles, return the same night, and discredit him.[31]

Annan snapped angrily:

"You're lucky there's going to be an investigation at all!"

"It's a sham."

"That is not your concern!"

"Okay," Gersony meekly answered.

Gersony wandered off alone next to a panoramic window and curled up into a Rodin thinker's position, utterly dejected. According to Gersony, Annan then came over and sat beside him, saying in his trademark mellow, patrician voice:

"Bob, I'm very sorry I snapped at you. You did the right thing. You told the truth, and I want you to continue doing that. Let me worry about the rest."[32]

Annan understood the politics of the situation in a way that Gersony, who took everything so personally, did not. Annan knew that merely by conducting an investigation, however phony, the Rwandan government was conceding a point to the United Nations and to Gersony. In other words, the RPF government had been put on notice. And without endorsing Gersony's findings, Annan was already putting pressure on Kagame's regime to stop the killings.[33] Again, given how, over the decades, Kagame has both stabilized and economically developed Rwanda, albeit in an authoritarian fashion, one might defend the United Nations policy at the time as the wiser course to take. Simply because Gersony's report was true did not mean that anyone was under any obligation to publicly praise him. The point was only to use his report toward a good purpose.

At the end of September, Mrs. Ogata asked Gersony to write a long memo, a synopsis for her file only, of his investigation and the results, to "be treated as confidential."[34] The result was a drab yet succinct fourteen-page account, with the bureaucratic title of "Summary of UNHCR Presentation Before Commission of Experts: 10 October 1994; Prospects for Early Repatriation of Rwandan Refugees Currently in Burundi, Tanzania and Zaire."[35] It lacked the depth and complexity of his much longer published reports on Uganda, Mozambique, and elsewhere; or of the reports he was later to write about such subjects as the Lord's Resistance Army in Uganda and the Maoist revolt in Nepal. Yet precisely because his Rwanda report was never released by the United Nations, it attained a legendary aura over time as "the so-called Gersony report," which many in the human rights community tried to get their hands on and henceforth proclaimed had been suppressed. Some even denied it ever existed, yet spoke about it in conspiratorial terms as if it did.[36]

All in all, it was Gersony's "biggest play," in Gene Dewey's recollection of Gersony's career.[37]

Finally there is the case of that French Africa expert, Gérard Prunier, with whom I began this chapter.

In the fall of 1994, Prunier started hearing of a certain "Gersony report" that nobody had as yet seen, which only lent more power and mystery to it. Bizarre rumors abounded among journalists and the human rights community regarding its contents and its author.

"When I heard that this so-called Gersony report attributed mass kill-ings of Hutus to the [Tutsi-dominated] RPF, I immediately assumed French army manipulation in order to develop a pretext to topple the RPF, given the French army's historic support of the Hutus. 'Get me this report,' I told people." Going on, Prunier recalls, "Gersony be-came in my mind some ghost manipulated by French military ex-tremists who only wanted to restart a war: a son of a bitch who was a disinformation tool of both the French security services and the CIA." Prunier writes in his book *The Rwanda Crisis,* which would be pub-lished the next year, that the Gersony report, which he had not seen, nevertheless "tended to obscure rather than clarify the problem," and that "there must be strong doubts about its reliability."[38]

It soon dawned on Prunier, however, that he already knew Ger-sony intellectually through the latter's study of five years earlier, "Why Somalis Flee," which Prunier had employed in the footnotes of his own research on the Horn of Africa. So he was at least prepared to listen to him. Through a mutual friend, Prunier and Gersony were able to meet at Gersony's New York City apartment in late 1995. In the interim nothing had happened to allay Prunier's suspicions of Gersony because Gersony himself had not been permitted by the United Nations to speak publicly. For after he returned from Rwanda, Gersony had gone immediately back to Nicaragua, and then on to other assignments in the West Bank, Bosnia, and elsewhere. And as for Prunier, he had not followed completely the vindications of Ger-sony that had begun to appear in the English-language press.[39]

Prunier remembers a tiny apartment with a distinctive radical-bohemian air. This prepared him further to find a naïve and out-of-his-depth human instrument of larger forces. His first impression of Gersony-in-the-flesh was of "a total Anglo-Saxon, very rigid and grounded, in a good way, like an accountant." Given the surround-ings, Prunier couldn't quite place him. "But within a few minutes I saw that he was honest and had no hidden agenda."

As Gersony began to talk, first about his methodology, then about what he had found in Ruhengeri, Gisenyi, Butare, Kibungo, and the refugee camps across the border, and how he had originally been a supporter of the RPF (just like Prunier), and how he had, step by step, come to his conclusions, Prunier got "this horrible, nauseous feeling" that he and everyone else writing and talking in New York, Washington, and Paris had been wrong about the RPF up until that moment. For it turned out that "the good guys were really quite bad guys."

In a rush of revelation, Prunier went from disdain to compassion for Gersony, as he saw how full of tension the real Gersony—now sitting a few feet away from him—actually was: he could see vividly how Gersony had been psychologically crushed by the suave and intimidating politics of top U.N. operators swirling around him, only because he was simply being honest, and what he had to say was so shocking and inconvenient to the world's political elite. Gersony was a blunt, truthful, very nervous man among these sly, high-class operators, educated at the best schools, on the diplomatic cocktail circuit.[40]

Prunier, exactly like Gersony, had desperately wanted to find better people on the victims' side. Prunier, defending Gersony later on, would write in 1997 that Gersony "was shocked at his own findings."[41] Prunier would also subsequently admit that it "was my sympathy for the RPF and my refusal at the time to believe" this organization "could be cold-bloodedly killing people" that blinded him to the dreadful truth that Gersony had uncovered.[42]

It was all something that the liberal imagination, with its belief in the basic goodness of humankind, had difficulty contending with. Once it was proven that both sides were capable of mass killing (even if one side had killed many times more people than the other), then one confronted the horror of there being something intractable in the very human landscape itself, with all the determinism and essentialism that such thoughts bring to bear. Gersony was neither a determinist nor an essentialist: he never succumbed to fate and he didn't stereotype people. He could not have done what he did over the decades if he were such a person. His personal bible had always been André Schwarz-Bart's *The Last of the Just*. But he did have a great reverence for facts, unlike some officials at the State Department and the United Nations, who did not want him to write up and publish his report; who, indeed, would have found it more convenient had his research never come to light in the first place.

"Bob and I have a great respect for the factual truth. The world is not just an interpretation or a place for competing narratives. That is our fight," Prunier says.

THE WORLD IS WHAT IT IS

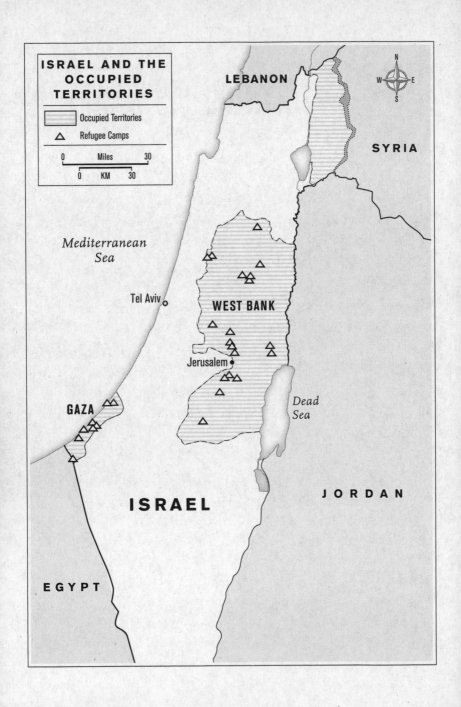

ISRAEL AND THE
OCCUPIED
TERRITORIES

Occupied Territories
△ Refugee Camps

0   Miles   30
0   KM   30

LEBANON

SYRIA

Mediterranean
Sea

Tel Aviv

WEST BANK

Jerusalem

Dead
Sea

GAZA

JORDAN

ISRAEL

EGYPT

CHAPTER 12

Gaza and the West Bank
1995

"I Wish I Had Gotten to Know Him Better."

Rwanda traumatized Bob Gersony. He refused to talk to journalists who were contacting him about his report since he had made a commitment to United Nations High Commissioner for Refugees Sadako Ogata that he would not do so. Although articles began emerging in the major media that supported his version of events, they were intermittent, and in significant cases would take years to see the light of day. In fact, it would be decades before he was fully vindicated. Thus, he felt isolated and betrayed. He hadn't known at the time that Assistant Secretary of State for Africa George Moose and Deputy Assistant Secretary Prudence Bushnell were utilizing his report to pressure Paul Kagame's Tutsi regime to stop the mass killing, and that together with United Nations efforts to secretly threaten the Rwandan government with releasing his report, the overall effect would be to halt the killing in its tracks. Yet in the halls of the State Department he was treated as if he had the plague, especially by the ambitious careerists and political types like Tim Wirth. So once again Gersony felt that his career was over.

It would take weeks for his wounds to even begin to heal. Meanwhile, he returned to Nicaragua and buried himself in his work. Whereas Rwanda was high international politics and the universal issue of genocide, Nicaragua was the more parochial world of Latin American development economics: no one there outside of Cindy and Tony really cared or understood what he had just gone through.

But by January 1995, only a few months after he returned from Rwanda, the four-year development project in eastern Nicaragua was over. Bob and Cindy, after almost half a decade in Nicaragua, with Bob working seven days a week as a paid consultant, suddenly found themselves back in his small apartment in Manhattan. Bob was depressed. Cindy complained how rude people were at the supermarket compared to the Nicaraguans.

The phone rang.

It was Toni Christiansen from USAID, who knew Bob from Barbados, where fifteen years before he had worked on Dominica hurricane relief. She had money for a jobs project in the Gaza Strip and Janet Ballantyne had just recommended Bob to her.

"I'm your guy," Gersony said.

He needed work, and because he was still ambitious at fifty, he recognized that Gaza would get him to the Middle East, adding another region to his résumé.

En route to Tel Aviv he stopped in Washington to see Carol Lancaster, the deputy administrator of USAID, right below Brian Atwood. She told him that USAID had $25 million and was looking for impact in order to ease tensions in the occupied territories, but the mission was stalled. There was the usual, hideous Palestinian-Israeli politics—despite the Oslo peace process—made worse by the fact that the State Department did not trust the Israel-based USAID mission for the occupied Palestinian territories. Gersony didn't care. It was an employment project, and therefore he could apply his experience in Nicaragua, El Salvador, and elsewhere.

He arrived in Tel Aviv, his brain overloaded with logistical questions. He needed an apartment for himself and Cindy since he would be there for six months. He needed background briefings from both the U.S. Embassy and USAID mission in Tel Aviv, as well as a briefing from the U.S. Consulate in Jerusalem, which dealt with the Palestinians. He had just so many new people to meet and a new region to learn about. He was in shut-his-mouth-and-listen mode, again working long days, seven days a week.

As for Israel itself, it curiously remained only in the background of his thoughts, despite his family history—such a workaholic was he. Tel Aviv itself didn't help. It was a sterile modern city on the Mediterranean, without the grace, sensuality, and indigenous cultural allure of a Barcelona, Nice, Tunis, or Palermo. The USAID mission was in Dizengoff Tower, an ugly, brutalist twenty-nine-story building with a Sbarro fast-food restaurant in the basement. Visually, being in Tel Aviv was not like being abroad at all.

The USAID office was run by Chris Crowley, the mission director, and Maureen Dugan, the project director for Gaza. Chris Crowley was calm, amiable, very good-looking in a conventional CEO sort of way. He seemed like a guy who was going places in the bureaucracy. The chemistry between him and Gersony was instantaneous: similar to that between Gersony and Mike Ranneberger in Mozambique.

"I liked Bob immediately," Crowley recalls. "He was serious and full of analytical rigor without being a wonk."

As for Maureen Dugan, she had chronic back pain and often spoke while lying supine on the floor of her office. She was another one of the great women of USAID, like Carol Lancaster and Janet Ballantyne, who had virtually adopted Gersony, and were less stodgy than the men. At the embassy a few blocks away, the political and economic officer, Norm Olsen, who made constant trips to Gaza—and who was fiercely sympathetic to the Palestinian cause—had one overriding message for Gersony:

"Find things for the kids to do after school."

Otherwise, Olsen implied, those kids would constitute a breeding ground for Palestinian radicalism. Olsen, a talkative Mainer, knew of what he spoke. He had previously worked for USAID in Gaza and had an intimate knowledge of the territory. Gersony had made a strong impression on him. "A lot of people were always coming out to the Tel Aviv embassy from Washington. Bob was the only one who hadn't already written his report in his head. He let the evidence on the ground drive his conclusions," Olsen says.

After meeting his new colleagues at the embassy and the USAID mission in Tel Aviv, Gersony started exploring a bit. He first experienced the visual drama of the Holy Land when he traveled from Tel Aviv to Jerusalem, quickly passing by the Old City with its monumental sixteenth-century Ottoman walls built by Sultan Suleiman the Magnificent, which enclosed the Temple Mount, Wailing Wall, Church of the Holy Sepulchre, and so much else. The sunlight seemed to blind him, further sharpened by the ubiquitous stone, which changed from warm rose to cream to dazzling white, depending upon the time of day. He saw a pageant of Gothic, Romanesque, and Moorish arches: the entire panorama crowned by the octagonal Dome of the Rock, with its gold cupola and Hellenistic blue faience frontage. Whereas Tel Aviv was the drab architectural expression of a new and raw Western-oriented settler society, Jerusalem suddenly brought history in a visual sense into the equation for him.

"I'll have to come back here with Cindy," he thought.

His car swept by the Rockefeller Museum, built during British rule in Crusader style. The nearby visa section of the U.S. Consulate, with its stone facade, arched windows, and tiled roof, conjured up the period of the late Ottoman Empire and the British Mandate: before the creation of the State of Israel.

The political offices of the consulate, located in West Jerusalem close to the Arab eastern section of the city, operated virtually independently of the embassy in Tel Aviv, and reported directly to the State Department in Washington. The U.S. Embassy in Tel Aviv, though it included Gaza as part of its responsibilities, was immersed in the world of the Jewish state. The consulate, whose area of representation was predominantly the West Bank and the Jerusalem municipal authorities, was generally immersed in the Arab Palestinian side of reality, and point of view, therefore. The embassy dealt intimately with the Israeli government; the consulate tried to have nothing to do with the Israeli government. Though close geographically, the two missions were far apart politically and at a deep emotional level truly distrusted each other: this little diplomatic turf war mirrored the Israeli-Palestinian conflict itself.

For all these reasons, in addition to being overwhelmed by Jerusalem's visual pageantry, Gersony was anticipating his meeting with Ed

Abington, the U.S. consul general, who Gersony assumed would be a fount of gritty, streetwise wisdom on the Palestinian territories. Abington even bore a vague resemblance to Chester Crocker, with his round glasses and tight WASPy looks, which Gersony over the years had learned to appreciate.

But Abington proved a letdown, filling the time with broad generalities that Gersony felt he could have gotten from the most basic textbooks. "He's a cold fish," Gersony thought.

Meanwhile, Norm Olsen, despite being based at the embassy in Tel Aviv, appeared to have a better feel for the occupied territories than Abington. Olsen fixed a meeting between Gersony and retired Israeli brigadier general Fredy Zach. General Zach was the deputy head of the civil administration in the Palestinian territories, and therefore had the job of making the occupation work on a daily basis. He was a bit of a slick operator, but one who knew his subject. He immediately launched into a dense economic briefing, rife with statistics, of the kind that Gersony, given his own background, appreciated. Gersony thought, "He speaks my language. This nuts-and-bolts military guy has been forced to understand the Palestinian situation because the lives of his own people depended on him not being a bullshitter." In fact, General Zach, born in Basra on the Persian Gulf, was a native Arabic speaker who had spent a year living in a tent with his family in Israel, having just been expelled from Iraq in 1948. Though an ardent Zionist, Zach knew what expulsion was all about and therefore could empathize with the Palestinians.

Zach repeatedly emphasized to Gersony that the Palestinians did not want temporary, make-work jobs. They wanted real jobs in a real economy. Don't be condescending toward them, he warned. He was one of those high-ranking Israeli officers who had a visceral sense of reality, based on experience, that many of Israel's own politicians lacked. Gersony was impressed, but was hesitant to become emotionally attached to a former general in the IDF (Israel Defense Forces) so soon after his arrival. Picking sides in the Israeli-Palestinian conflict when it wasn't necessary could ruin a State Department or USAID career.

It came time to pick a guide and translator. Chris Crowley in Tel Aviv introduced Gersony to a number of FSNs (Foreign Service Nationals). One stood out: Dr. Jamal Tarazi, a Palestinian medical doctor from a prominent Christian family in Gaza, who had what appeared to be a good bedside manner. Jamal would prove to be an excellent facilitator; he knew everybody in Gaza and was "smart as hell." Likewise, Jamal's first impression of Gersony was "of an absolutely good personality with immense experience. And I could judge," Jamal goes on, "since my father worked in relief assistance for many years for the U.N." Gersony and Jamal would spend five weeks together in Gaza, conducting 137 one-on-one interviews, going to the homes of ordinary Gazans from all walks of life, in addition to interviewing officials from the United Nations Relief and Works Agency for Palestine (UNRWA). Jamal would make sure that Gersony also got to meet and give a fair hearing to the territory's leading opinion makers. "We went into some risky neighborhoods," Jamal recalls, "which even back then were Hamas strongholds. People would gather around us. But Bob was unfazed. He just kept asking questions."

Gaza then comprised 900,000 people, mainly refugees and their descendants from the vast population movements that accompanied the creation of the State of Israel in 1948. It was an extremely hot, humid, and crowded place—an Arab version of Soweto. One journalist described it as a "dense, gray concrete shantytown" with black sewage water, crude septic tanks, dingy food stalls, all without greenery.[1] It was the kind of physical environment that would turn anybody radical. People were often in a bad mood and out of hope. The water was brackish; not a lemon tree was left. And now, in the spring of 1995, it faced an acute economic and employment crisis, arising from tectonic shifts in the Middle East that were the following:

For decades, arguably the biggest booster of the Palestinian Arab cause against Israel had been oil-rich Kuwait. Hundreds of thousands of Palestinians worked in the wealthy Persian Gulf sheikhdom— 20 percent of its population—earning hard currency in Kuwaiti dinars. They sent much of this money back in remittances to relatives in Gaza, the West Bank, and Jordan. The taxes they paid in Kuwait went not to the Kuwaiti government, but straight to the Palestine Liberation Organization, the PLO. This was in addition to direct aid, hundreds of millions of dollars, that the Kuwaiti government sent to the PLO.

But in August 1990, Iraqi leader Saddam Hussein invaded Kuwait. The Arab League, famous for issuing lowest common denominator platitudes of little value, uncharacteristically united with a firm and nearly unanimous statement of support for the Kuwaitis and condemnation of Saddam. There was only one complete holdout: PLO leader Yasser Arafat. It may have been the most unfortunate and inexplicable decision of Arafat's life, even if Saddam had been giving $10,000 to each of the families of Palestinian suicide bombers. (Saddam, though not supporting al-Qaeda, was in fact supporting many other terrorist groups such as Islamic Jihad and the Arab Liberation Front.)[2] Perhaps it was the innate radicalism of Saddam's invasion of the land of these rich and complacent Gulf Arabs that appealed to Arafat's romantic sensibility, in addition to widespread support for Saddam in the Palestinian street.

The reaction was swift.

The Kuwaitis called Arafat a "traitor."[3] Not only Kuwait but other wealthy Arab Gulf kingdoms deported their Palestinian populations, many of whom had nowhere else to go, other than Gaza and the West Bank. Everything was lost: the remittances in hard currency, the tax rebates to the PLO, and the direct aid to the PLO, even as the population of the occupied territories swelled. The financial damage to the Palestinian territories was $405 million in 1990 alone.[4]

Simultaneous with these events was the Intifada, the general Palestinian uprising against the Israeli occupation authorities that began in 1987 and fully ceased only in 1993. Because of the deterioration of the security situation, Israel dramatically reduced the number of Palestinians it allowed to cross its borders daily for work inside Israel. The number of Gazans allowed to work in Israel fell from 50,000 in 1987 to 10,000 in 1995. This mattered, since at the high point of these border crossings, as many as one-third of Gazan families had somebody earning a decent wage in Israel. Finally, Israel allowed large numbers of foreigners, mainly Thais and Romanians, to replace the Palestinians, signaling that there would be no going back to the previous status quo.

One step at a time, the Palestinians, especially the Gazans, had alienated their principal employers—Kuwaitis and Israelis both.

When Yasser Arafat shook hands with Israeli prime minister Yitzhak Rabin on the White House lawn on September 13, 1993, it was not a triumph for him, but the ultimate humiliation, culminating the train of events that had begun with his fateful decision to back Saddam Hussein three years earlier.

Because the PLO, under the Oslo Accords, recognized Israel's right to exist, the U.S. Congress appropriated $25 million to Gaza and $100 million to the West Bank.

The money was to be administered by USAID, which had eventually dispatched Gersony to Gaza to help figure out how best to spend it.

What did Gazans think? Gersony asked himself.

As Gersony found out in the course of his 137 interviews, they wanted permanent jobs and small business expansion, based on importing raw materials that they would process and ship out. Everyone from unskilled workers to teachers told him that temporary jobs were getting them nowhere.

"We want jobs measured in person-years, not in person-days," people repeatedly said.

In other words, the Israeli general's analysis had been right.

A United Nations official backed this up, telling Gersony:

"I've not come across a single Palestinian who agrees with the donor analysis"—that what was needed was more temporary jobs, such as clearing fields of garbage and whitewashing graffiti-strewn walls.

Keeping his thoughts to himself, Gersony could not agree. For despite believing in the essential truth of what people told him in interviews, by now he had decades of experience in similar situations and knew a thing or two. He had seen in Latin America how getting people to work immediately, no matter how menial the jobs, did in fact help to stabilize the political situation. He felt that the hostility to temporary jobs had more to do with the Palestinians' self-image as a First World people than with the actual needs of Gaza at the time. Yet he kept telling himself, "My job is to be a human listening device. I've got to document what people here think." After all, as his thoughts ran, "This was a sensitive political thing, much more so than Latin America. It's the first significant, official interface between the U.S. government and the Palestinian people. My survey is more than a survey. It's a question of relationships before a global audience, unlike with the Miskito Indians."

As the days and weeks in the concrete slum of Gaza went on, Gersony became gradually more impressed with UNRWA, whose presence was felt everywhere he went. It employed 116 Palestinian engineers, and any project it took on it did properly. Whatever UNRWA had evolved into by the second decade of the twenty-first century, in the mid-1990s UNRWA was a first-class organization, far superior to the European NGOs also working in Gaza. It was the only politically neutral organization with decades of experience in the territory, since the Israelis were always disliked, and even the PLO was seen sometimes as distant and corrupt.

And UNRWA led him to a factor invisible to the outside world: the basketball courts.

UNRWA had built many basketball courts made entirely of concrete slabs and completely enclosed. They were bleak and ugly to look at, but there was little wood in Gaza with which to build courts with proper backboards and so on. These basketball courts also served as spaces for volleyball and other sports, and were wildly popular during school hours. Gersony discovered that the cliché about Arab girls and women not liking sports was false. Because these courts were enclosed, girls and young women could play matches as often as the boys and men.

It got him thinking.

He also noticed UNRWA's successful small business loan program, which administered $4.5 million annually with a 98 percent repayment rate, creating 450 jobs at salaries of $3,000. It had limited capacity, sure, but might be something to build on, he thought.

He was under no illusions about the overall situation. Visiting those schools with the concrete basketball courts, he also heard students chanting, for up to half an hour sometimes, "It's an honor to die for the state of Palestine." The school corridors were plastered with regional maps where "Israel" did not appear. The conflict was unending, so it was a matter of finding partial, stop-gap solutions.

The years of the Intifada meant curfews and continued security lockdowns. There had been few opportunities for safe, after-school activities. Now, in the wake of the Oslo Accords, there were no more lockdowns, but the basketball courts remained unused after midafternoon, when school ended. This meant that the young guys hung about in the streets and the girls were confined in their houses.

In Gaza City, he saw Zainab al-Wazir, the director of physical education in one of the ministries. She was the sister of a famous PLO martyr, Khalil al-Wazir ("Abu Jihad"), and so he felt that he was talking with the heart of the resistance against Israel.[5] He asked her why all the basketball courts were going unused in the afternoons and evenings. "I would play there myself if they were open!" she exclaimed, explaining that they were closed only because there were no security personnel or coaches available. "More security people, that's more jobs created," he thought.

He returned to the USAID office in Tel Aviv with a plan.

Ten people crammed into the small conference room to hear his briefing, including Chris Crowley and Maureen Dugan. He began by saying: "Let's all be humble. It's only $25 million, and this conflict has been going on for a long time. If the Israelis would merely allow 722 more workers from Gaza across the border daily, it would have the same impact as our $25 million. Also, for us it's an emergency, since we believe in creating jobs fast. But for the Gazans, who go home every day at 2:30 P.M. as they have for years, life goes on."

At the words "let's all be humble," the scales fell off people's eyes. Because he was speaking a somewhat new language, he had a rapt audience.

These were his recommendations:

1. USAID should work with UNRWA to repair schools damaged in the Intifada.
2. Add 50 more all-purpose, concrete basketball courts.
3. Give UNRWA $1 million to hire 200 Gazan security personnel and sports coaches to keep the courts open throughout the afternoons.
4. Appropriate money for nighttime lighting, since the best time to play sports was in the cool evenings.
5. Give UNRWA $4 million to expand its small loan program.
6. Expand the reach of the United Nations Development Program (UNDP) to tile the streets and create even more jobs.

"You can own Gaza by making kids and parents happy," he concluded. "I stake my reputation on it." He didn't mean that literally, since little or none of this would matter without political progress at the top.

Nothing Gersony said was remotely original or ambitious even. It was all about humility: the recognition of how little could be accomplished by USAID alone. UNRWA was doing great work already, so USAID should build on it, rather than compete with it. What else could you do with only $25 million, anyway? Chris Crowley felt at the time that Gersony, without saying it, had identified a key political-demographic problem of the Arab world, the male youth bulge, and had a plan, however small and partial, to deal with it.

But by USAID standards, Gersony's ideas were actually controversial, since the AID bureaucracy at the time normally frowned on having anything to do with sports: sports stadiums and the like were the kind of things the Russians and Chinese preferred to build. "But if you dropped a thousand soccer balls from helicopters into Gaza, you might actually cut down on terrorist attacks," Gersony now quips.

A year later, on June 13, 1996, a USAID public affairs officer, Suchinta Wijesooriya, sent out an email, saying:

"The after-school program is going great guns and is now all over Gaza . . . everybody loves it. . . . Next to [the] water [project], it is one of the most worthwhile things we are doing."

After the $25 million was spent, the Danish government picked the program up and kept it going.

But on September 28, 2000, the Israeli opposition leader at the time, former general Ariel Sharon, visited the al-Aqsa Mosque on the Temple Mount in Jerusalem, one of the holiest sites in Islam. He was accompanied by 1,500 armed Israeli police, anxious for his security and to prevent a riot. The upshot was another Intifada against Israeli occupation. Whatever impact Gersony had in Gaza was completely overtaken by events.

Upon Gersony's completion of the Gaza project, Chris Crowley had a real problem on his hands. Congress had given USAID $100 million to spend in the West Bank, but Crowley did not trust the consultant teams that Washington had sent out to tell him how to spend the money—the teams that unfailingly served up the least creative, boilerplate analysis. He was frankly suspicious of their recommendation to spend all the money on roads, schools, and education. It just seemed too easy and obvious. So he sent Gersony out on a fact-finding trip to investigate the teams' recommendations. Gersony took with him the USAID mission engineer Carl Maxwell, an extremely taciturn man who was part Eskimo. He rarely talked or smiled, and always seemed withdrawn.

At this point Cindy had arrived, and she and Bob were living in a small apartment in downtown Tel Aviv. For a week, Gersony drove from Tel Aviv into the West Bank with Carl Maxwell to inspect the roads, schools, and health centers that the USAID consultants wanted to spend $100 million improving. After Gaza, the West Bank was sheer paradise to Gersony, an utterly different country and plane of existence. It was more prosperous, more normal, not as hot, and people seemed much less aggravated. The gaunt and dizzying hillsides, which burst out in lemon green after the rains, were truly majestic and suffused with biblical associations. Gaza, a generic, baking-in-the-heat-and-humidity shantytown, was not meant to carry the population it did. That, combined with its sealed-off isolation, had the effect of creating monsters. The West Bank was beautiful: it had cobblestones, old houses, Roman arches, archaeological sites, and so forth. The West Bank, like Jerusalem, was rooted in history, whereas Gaza seemed rootless.

Gersony and Maxwell found no problem with the roads, which were in pristine condition and perfect for access to the villages: to widen them, as the USAID consultants wanted to do, would have involved destroying olive groves, cutting into the rock, and threatening landslides. Bigger wasn't necessarily better. The schools and health centers were also in decent shape. By this time, watching Gersony work till late each evening writing up his daily reports, Carl Maxwell began warming to him. They went back to Chris Crowley and told him that they couldn't fathom why USAID wanted to spend $100 million to fix things that did not need fixing. Gersony told Crowley:

"Why don't you let me and Jamal [Tarazi] go out for a week just to talk to villagers in the West Bank and get a sense of what's going on, to see what they feel they need?"

For a week, he and Jamal conducted open-ended conversations with village sheikhs, local teachers, and others throughout the West Bank, traveling in both Samaria in the north and Judea in the south. All he and Jamal heard from everyone was one word: "Water!"

Most water came from rain, which ran down the corrugated iron roofs into plastic buckets. Because there were no proper storage facilities, the villagers explained, each family paid up to $240 per season for periodic deliveries of water. You could see the water trucks traveling up and down the roads of the West Bank, especially in the warm, dry months. There were natural springs, but they were often contaminated by livestock. Where clean water did exist in abundance, it was often located several miles away from each village. There was a desperate need to collect, store, and efficiently distribute water.

Gersony went to see the chief engineer and project officer of the UNDP in Jerusalem, Lana Abu-Hijleh. She immediately made a life-long impression on him. "Lana was terrific, young, attractive, thoroughly professional, alluring, fastidious, and a perfect English speaker." When Gersony told her that everyone he had met in the West Bank said water was the big issue, she shot back that she had a $4 million water project at the proposal stage, and had already gotten all the permits from the Israeli occupation authorities. At the micro level, she wanted to do the same thing as Gersony. Carl Maxwell, despite his reserve, actually smiled.

"Here is where the rain falls," Lana remembers telling Gersony. "He immediately understood what I meant," Lana now explains. "Bob had an open mind to the facts and wasn't blinded by the [Israeli] propaganda machine that always managed to twist them. He knew that control of water and the underground aquifer was an essential reason for the Israeli occupation [since water was scarce in the region and was therefore a strategic resource]. Bob was an unusual USAID consultant because he was so concerned about people's suffering in Gaza and the West Bank. He always listened intensely because he cared, and thus he understood everything I told him. I wish I had gotten to know him better."

Lana took Gersony and Carl to her ancestral village, Deir Istiya, in central Samaria, south of the big West Bank town of Nablus. In 1995, it had 370 families, of which hers was among the most prominent. The architecture, as in so many places in the West Bank, conjured up the historical ages from the Romans to the Mamluks, with stone archways and cobbled streets. Gersony loved cobblestones, since for him it meant a solution to mud and flooding, even as laying the cobblestones gave people jobs. Carl took out a notebook and pencil and designed an overhead water storage tank on the spot, complete with cladding appropriate to the village architecture.

Gersony reported back to Chris Crowley.

He told Crowley and his team that the Palestinian Arabs of the West Bank needed water, pure and simple. And that the UNDP should play a significant part in implementing the project. The

USAID mission in Israel and the territories could not oversee roads, schools, health systems, and so on as the consultant teams wanted to do. It was too extravagant and multifaceted for one mission. "USAID here should spend the whole $100 million on water, with help and advice from the UNDP." He told Crowley that USAID needed to hire a few water engineers in order to become the go-to intermediary for anything having to do with water for the West Bank.

Crowley sat silent for a minute, then for two minutes. A big smile gradually formed on his face. "That is exactly what we're going to do," he said.

"All my instincts said *yeah*," Crowley now remembers. "I knew enough about the Middle East to know that water was the key to everything."

Of course, whereas Gersony was thinking about all the details below him—working with the engineers, with Lana and the UNDP, and with the Palestinian Authority—Crowley was thinking about all the politics above him: which constituted a yawning universe of big shots with big egos, given the world media attention lavished on the West Bank. Yet water was an elemental, powerful symbol. It was about life itself. Thus, it was an idea he felt that he could sell in one sentence to his ambassador in Tel Aviv, Martin Indyk. Crowley's assessment proved accurate. He also sold the project to the Middle East peace process team led by Dennis Ross. But he had some difficulty convincing the consul general in Jerusalem, Ed Abington, whom Crowley felt harbored resentments both political and personal against Indyk: it was a typical case of a career diplomat sympathetic to the Palestinians versus a political appointee sympathetic to the Israelis.

Partly as a result of the success of Gersony's water project, Crowley was able to stay in Israel for another four years, and then would go on to become USAID mission director for Iraq from 2010 to 2013; after that he became the senior career official for USAID throughout the whole Middle East.

Gersony brings all of these high politics down to earth, though.

"When you listen to ordinary people, there is so much wisdom," Gersony explains. "That is what Jamal and Lana and myself did all over Gaza and the West Bank. That is what Chris Crowley, Norm Olsen, and General Fredy Zach did. We talked to real people who told us about their problems and what they needed. Chris was a seasoned USAID diplomat. Jamal and Lana were Palestinians. Norm was pro-Palestinian. Zach was an ardent Zionist, and I was sympathetic to Israel because of my own family background. But I feel close to all these people, as if we were all on the same side. Because we believed in applied common sense issuing from the ground up, in all its granularity, rather than imposing our beliefs and assumptions, however idealistic, on others."

Years later, after Egyptian president Hosni Mubarak was toppled in the Arab Spring in early 2011, Chris Crowley tried to get Bob Gersony to do an assessment of what the Egyptian population needed at the mundane, ground level for further development. But the Washington bureaucracy turned him down. The bulk of the development assistance would be spent on democracy promotion programs, all of which turned out to be wasted, and which in fact backfired. Egypt, a complex, poverty-stricken, ancient civilization with its very own historical experience different from America's, easily fell back into dictatorship.

Their home in Israel constituted among the happiest periods of Bob and Cindy's life together. Bob liked living in Tel Aviv. He felt a revival of his Jewishness there. He liked Palestinians like Jamal and Lana. He liked working with UNRWA and UNDP. He loved the weather. And he felt very close to Chris Crowley. He felt settled in Israel in a way he hadn't elsewhere since Guatemala, and he assumed that Crowley would have continuous work for him there.

Unbeknownst to Gersony, immersed as he was in his work in the Palestinian territories, in Dayton, Ohio, the U.S. assistant secretary of state for European and Canadian affairs, Richard C. Holbrooke, was orchestrating a complex arrangement of accords among the warring parties in Yugoslavia that was to be hailed by the media as the greatest diplomatic achievement of the post Cold War. Under the assumption that Holbrooke would succeed, USAID administrator

Brian Atwood wanted his agency on the map first in the former Yugoslavia—quickly, visibly.

Doug Stafford, the head of humanitarian operations for USAID and former deputy U.N. high commissioner for refugees, who had been so impressed with Gersony's work in Rwanda and elsewhere, told Atwood: "Gersony's the one you want to send to Bosnia." Carol Lancaster, the deputy administrator of USAID, who had mastered six languages in her own legendary career, seconded Stafford's suggestion, even though Atwood needed no convincing on the matter. Bill Garvelink was tasked to get in touch with Gersony.

Garvelink called Gersony in Tel Aviv:

"Atwood wants you back in Washington now. You've got to get to Bosnia right away."

Gersony thought of the sunshine in Tel Aviv and the frigid, dismal cold of Bosnia, with winter approaching.

He went to the Western Wall with Cindy and wrote a note: "Please God, give me the wisdom to understand what the ordinary people of Bosnia are saying." He rolled the note up tight and stuck it deep between the great ashlar stones.

While he was in Washington for briefings on Bosnia, Cindy called him on November 4, 1995, with the news that Israeli prime minister Yitzhak Rabin had been assassinated by a right-wing Jewish extremist. It would begin a chain of events that would overtake the work Gersony had done in the occupied territories. "It may have been one of the most successful political assassinations in history," Norm Olsen observes. "The assassin wanted to stop the entire Oslo peace process in its tracks, and he did."

On October 11, 2002, Lana's mother, Shaden Abu-Hijleh, a peace activist no less, was quietly sitting outside the family home by the garden in their well-to-do neighborhood in Deir Istiya, knitting, when an Israeli patrol stopped, and shot her dead for absolutely no reason, with no advance warning. It was an utterly stupid, senseless killing. "When I heard about it, I was overcome with grief for Lana and with absolute fury at the Israeli military," Gersony says.

But despite these dark and overwhelming forces of Middle Eastern politics, Bob Gersony still left a legacy, however slight. Jamal Tarazi, now a group leader for cancer research at the Pfizer pharmaceutical company in the San Diego area, made a return trip to Gaza in 2012 to visit relatives. There, by the beach in Gaza City, he happened to see the lovely cobblestone streets that one of Gersony's projects had created, which had recently been extended to other areas. Sometimes the legacy Gersony left behind was pivotal, and many more times it clearly was not. He was only one man, after all.

CHAPTER 13

Bosnia
1995–1996

"Columbo Meets Indiana Jones"

Up until now, the pattern of Gersony's travels in recent years had not been dictated by the end of the Cold War. Exactly as he had sensed upon returning home from the Horn of Africa just as the Berlin Wall was about to fall, the world simply continued with its crises and upheavals no matter what was going on in Europe. Since the autumn of 1989, which the media had defined as a new era, Gersony had worked in Nicaragua, Liberia, Rwanda, and the occupied Palestinian territories: dealing with state failure, rule-of-law breakdowns, genocide, and long-standing ethno-nationalist conflict. Indeed, the world through his eyes at ground level was unchanged from the 1970s and 1980s. After all, there had been little qualitative difference between the pre-1989 reality and the one afterward in Central America, sub-Saharan Africa, and the Middle East. Democracy, capitalism, and the other themes championed by the Washington elite were distinctly second-tier issues in Bob Gersony's world—the world of much of humanity, in fact—compared to the far more basic issue of the absence of legitimate authority itself. The problem wasn't authoritarianism, but the dearth of governance in its most basic form. The world was quite real to him; it was the ongoing debate in Washington that was unreal.

Bosnia, though, marked a bit of a turning point for Gersony. In Bosnia the issues still were ethno-national conflict, mass murder, and the absence of legitimate authority. But now such issues were

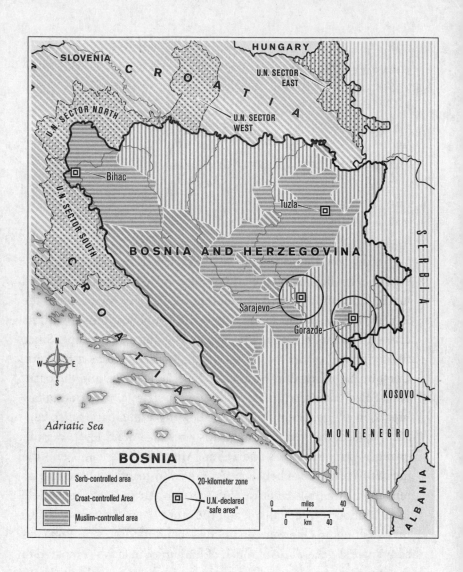

SLOVENIA

HUNGARY

C R O A T I A

U.N. SECTOR
EAST

U.N. SECTOR NORTH

U.N. SECTOR
WEST

Bihac

Tuzla

U.N. SECTOR SOUTH

BOSNIA AND HERZEGOVINA

S E R B I A

C R O A T I A

Sarajevo

Gorazde

N
W   E
S

KOSOVO

Adriatic Sea

MONTENEGRO

ALBANIA

BOSNIA

Serb-controlled area

Croat-controlled Area

Muslim-controlled area

20-kilometer zone

U.N.-declared
"safe area"

0   miles   40

0   km   40

relevant inside Europe itself, as a direct aftershock of the collapse of the Berlin Wall. The carapace of communist rule along with the Cold War security structure had crumbled, and the result in the sprawling multiethnic federation of Yugoslavia was secession and institutional breakup. Rather than the United States and Europe having conquered the Third World with Western democracy, the Third World had arrived inside Europe itself. Indeed, throughout its existence, USAID never had a geographical division dedicated to Europe, since it hadn't needed one. But with the outbreak of the Yugoslav war in 1991, it suddenly did.

As with Uganda, Mozambique, and Rwanda, not to mention other places, Bob Gersony had no particular wish or intention to go to Bosnia, or much advance notice either. And as in those places, he had no idea what he was getting into, believing that Bosnia would be a mere reconstruction assignment similar to the Palestinian territories.

Keep in mind that Gersony never sought or got caught up in *causes*. His suit was math and business, not the humanities. And with that came his methodology, which meant listening in isolation to dozens and hundreds of people in every place he visited, collating their stories and attitudes—all the while believing in the innate wisdom of the common person—and letting the reality of the situation emanate from the ground up. In his mind, ideas, no matter how grand, were not always valuable in their own right; they had first to emerge from facts discovered in the field. In this, though a generalist, he was spiritually akin to the area experts: the Arabists, the China hands, and so forth, who worshipped the granularity of cultures and situations, and whose knowledge and wisdom were often ignored.

Rushing home from Israel, Bob and Cindy spent well over a thousand dollars on winter clothes at Eddie Bauer on Broadway in Manhattan. They had never worked in a cold climate before, and Cindy was going with him to Bosnia. She herself had become well known in the humanitarian community for her longtime work in the Office of Foreign Disaster Assistance (OFDA), and for backing up disaster assistance response teams (DARTs) around the globe from her office

in the State Department. A graduate of Wellesley College, Cindy is a
detail person happiest doing research in the library, who reads several books at a time. She first worked with Bob on his Mozambique
and Somalia projects, applying her computer skills to analyze his
hundreds of interviews in those places. She overcame her shyness
doing fieldwork in Central America, talking to ordinary people. They
just liked her, sensing her vulnerability, and this made her an effective interviewer. She felt she had been granted an unusual privilege:
the privilege of listening to people in their huts or under a tree, rather
than remaining deskbound in Washington the rest of her life. She
first blossomed in the southern Atlantic coast of Nicaragua, distributing seeds and packing bags.

From New York, Gersony headed next to Washington to meet
with Brian Atwood, the administrator of USAID. Atwood was a tall,
imposing Bill Clinton–style moderate-liberal Democrat who was a
polished political operator, someone who knew how to speak to all
sides in any intense philosophical debate and how to get buy-in. He
quickly went through the usual with Gersony: in the immediate aftermath of the Dayton Accords, Gersony needed to find out how to ex-

Brian Atwood, administrator of the U.S. Agency for International Development in the Clinton
administration, who used Gersony to investigate crises in Rwanda, Bosnia, and so on.

pedite the return of war refugees, how to get job creation going, how to build and reconstruct housing and infrastructure. Then, leaning back in his chair, Atwood said:

"Well, you know, under Dayton, we're going to have this policy of conditionality and cross-ethnic return. While you're out in the field, you just might want to look into how all of this is going to work," particularly in the Muslim and Croat areas under U.S. military control.

It was a subtle way of suggesting that the Dayton Accords that had stopped the war in the former Yugoslavia might be difficult to implement, and thus he wanted Gersony's own, outside opinion on this matter, despite all the heavy hitters and other experts that Atwood already had at his disposal within the USAID bureaucracy. After all, this was Europe, not Africa or Central America. And European affairs especially in the State Department had always attracted the most ambitious, intimidating sorts of people. Gersony really had no idea what he was being parachuted into, not to mention his having absolutely no idea what the "conditionality" that Atwood was referring to actually meant.

Bosnia, the most rugged and war-torn of the former Yugoslav republics, at this moment in time was a place littered with vacant villages: bony mazes of walls and foundations without roofs, since the lumber structures had been firebombed and the clay tiles had collapsed inward. There were giant empty shells of houses. Water systems and schools had been destroyed. People had recently experienced all manner of inter-ethnic atrocities. Outside observers, especially the international humanitarian community, were obsessed with learning not only how but why all this had happened.

I had begun covering Yugoslavia in late 1981 and went back there frequently throughout the 1980s, as I was based in nearby Greece. On my first visit as a reporter there, I noticed how the cut in subsidized fuel from the Soviet Union had led to electricity blackouts and other hardships, which set the various ethnic republics within the Yugoslav federation against each other, so that long-standing historical grievances merged with more recent political and economic ones. Generally, the further south one traveled in Yugoslavia, from Slovenia, once a part of the Habsburg Austrian empire, to Kosovo and Macedonia, once parts of the Turkish Ottoman Empire, the poorer it became. This was a federation that in the early 1980s began undergoing enormous economic and political strains. To make matters worse, Yugoslavia stretched across several imperial and developmental legacies, making unity always a tenuous affair. The federation's ruler for decades, Josip Broz Tito, a half Croat, half Slovene, kept Yugoslavia at peace through a combination of benevolent dictatorship and a low-calorie version of communism. After he died in 1980, Yugoslavia suffered a revolving door of dull and forgettable leaders, mired in collective constraints and bureaucratic formulas, who essentially kicked the proverbial can down the road. The economy kept deteriorating, and ethnic and religious strains among the various groups and republics worsened.

They were further inflamed by the fall of the Berlin Wall in 1989, which, while encouraging democracy in all the other, more cohesive communist states of Eastern Europe, only quickened the federation's breakup along ethnic and national lines by serving to undermine the legitimacy of the Marxist central government in the Yugoslav capital of Belgrade. Whereas the fissures following the fall of the Berlin Wall in the other countries were vertical, dealing with the nature of central government itself, in Yugoslavia they were horizontal—dealing with the relationship of one ethnic and national federation with the other.

Then there was the matter of individuals. The leaders of the various ethnically based republics, foremost among them Slobodan Milošević in Serbia, cynically migrated from communism to nationalism in order to preserve their power bases and perks—their villas, hunting lodges, and so on. The wars of the Yugoslav succession began in late June 1991 when Milošević's Serbia violently tried to prevent the secession of Slovenia from the federation. When Slovenia bolted, being the richest and most philosophically influential of the republics throughout the twentieth-century history of Yugoslavia, the whole house of cards began to fall apart. War would spread south throughout much of the country. And war meant a civil war of mass atrocities in which the civilians of one ethnic group became the victims of the army of another ethnic group. Precisely because Bosnia was home to several of the ethnic groups—Serbs, Croats, and Muslims—war there was particularly intense and barbaric. And the killing of men, women, and children often happened en masse, in a planned, methodical manner.

Yugoslavia was the first hot war in Europe since World War II. Moreover, it erupted soon after the conclusion of the Cold War and constituted its greatest individual reverberation. It was a time when many intellectuals and journalists, feeling suddenly free of the burden of great-power politics, assumed foreign policy would henceforth be dedicated to the achievement of universal human rights. Yugoslavia violated this sensibility with its unspeakable ethnic violence and civilian atrocities—the mass murder and expulsion of Muslims at the hands of the Serbs, to say nothing of the violence by and against Croats. Indeed, "ethnic cleansing" was coined by the media as a new-old phrase, both chillingly modern and antique at the same time. The world at the conclusion of the Cold War, which itself was but a tail-piece of World War II, was not supposed to be like this. For this to happen on the same continent as the Nazi Holocaust, so soon after the conclusion of the Long European War (1914–1989), was, to say the least, unacceptable.

Because this war was unacceptable, it was a matter of taking moral action, that is, a matter of "human agency" in the parlance of the intellectuals and committed journalists. As the saying went, evil only triumphs when good men do nothing. For it was evil men, primarily the Serbian leader Slobodan Milošević and his band of war criminals, who had caused this mini-Holocaust in the first place. Truly, as these intellectuals and journalists argued, evil does not happen on its own, it is not a matter of dull and inexorable historical processes: rather, it must be a matter of the actions of individuals, who had thus to be defeated and punished.

Of course, there was also the issue of ethnic animosities tied to history, geography, and economics. While there were a substantial number of intermarriages in Bosnia, and people there were not weaned from birth to hate, ethnic groups in Yugoslavia and the Balkans could often recall an era of historical greatness when their own kingdoms had spread across southeastern Europe and dominated others, so that territorial claims, real and imagined, overlapped and contradicted one another. After all, hadn't Yugoslavia experienced an ethnic civil war between Serbs and Croats in the midst of World War II? And communism, even Tito's diluted version of it, was enough to keep a preponderance of rural Serbs, Croats, and Muslims in a relative state of freeze-frame poverty throughout the Cold War decades, so that, rather than be assuaged by middle-class prosperity, those ethnic animosities had been allowed to fester.

There assuredly were evil men, responsible for great crimes, but they arose out of a context of already inflamed ethnic divides. Yet for many in the intellectual, journalistic, and relief communities, one had to emphasize the former over the latter. For to do the opposite, to put too much emphasis on the ethnic and historical divides, was to submit to determinism and essentialism, academic buzzwords for fatalism and the acceptance of ethnic stereotypes.

And fatalism led to doing nothing to stop this war while it was happening.

Action was needed, therefore, according to the intellectuals and committed journalists, including military action. And that meant— went this logic train—to downplay the historical backdrop of ethnic rivalry, even if the Yugoslav war was a matter of both things, evil men *and* difficult historical processes.

I myself ran afoul of this dialectic when I published a book in 1993, *Balkan Ghosts: A Journey Through History*, excerpted in *The Atlantic* beginning in 1989, four months before the Berlin Wall fell. It was a product of my own reporting on the ground almost everywhere in southeastern Europe throughout the 1980s, where I recorded interviews with many scores of people—as I had been doing on the Ethiopia-Somalia border—detailing their tendency to think in terms of religious and national identities, as well as individual ones. In July

1989, I wrote in *The Atlantic:* "In the 1970s and 1980s the world witnessed the limits of superpower influence in places like Vietnam and Afghanistan. In the 1990s those limits may well become visible in a Third World region within Europe itself. The Balkans could shape the end of the century, just as they did the beginning."[1] On November 30, 1989, less than three weeks after the Berlin Wall fell, I wrote in *The Wall Street Journal:* "Two concepts are emerging out of the ruins of communist Europe. One, 'Central Europe,' the media is now beating to death. The other, 'the Balkans,' the media has yet to discover. . . ." Thus, I devoted the article to considering the ethnic fissuring of Yugoslavia.[2] War broke out there nineteen months later.

Gersony stepped unknowing into this heated argument, armed only with his methodology: conducting random, one-on-one interviews in isolation, without asking leading questions, and making sure to include a large, representative cross-section of people. Let the facts of the situation emerge by themselves, and speak for themselves, he believed.

Unknowing as he was, one of the first things he did was to read the Dayton Accords, in particular the critical Annex 7, signed in November 1995:

> All refugees and displaced persons have the right to freely return to their homes of origin.[3] They shall have the right to have restored to them property of which they were deprived in the course of hostilities since 1991 and to be compensated for any property that cannot be restored to them. *The early return of refugees and displaced persons is an important objective of the settlement of the conflict in Bosnia and Herzegovina.* The Parties confirm that they will accept the return of such persons who have left their territory, including those who have been accorded temporary protection by third countries.
>
> *The Parties shall ensure that refugees and displaced persons are permitted to return in safety, without risk of harassment, intimidation, persecution, or discrimination, particularly on account of their ethnic origin, religious belief, or political opinion.* [Italics mine]

In other words, despite the worst mass atrocities with an ethnic and religious basis in Europe since the Holocaust, people—Serbs, Croats, and Muslims—were expected to set aside what they felt in their hearts—and what had happened, really—and move back to the places where they had lived before the war: for example, with a Muslim family or two mixed in among Croats, with a Croat family or two mixed in among Serbs, and so on. After all, an international elite, led by Assistant Secretary of State for European and Canadian Affairs Richard C. Holbrooke—a force of nature at once inspiring, dominating, intimidating, and infuriating—had decided it was the right thing to do.

And it was the right thing to do.

The question was, Could it be done?

As for that so-called conditionality, it meant that in every case no funds for reconstruction would be dispersed unless moves were made to ensure the safe return of refugees and displaced persons as outlined in Annex 7. Thus, if you wanted a new health facility in your village, you had to let the minority families return to their homes. Conditionality codified a rejection of ethnic cleansing. And because ethnic cleansing was inherently evil, to question the logic or even the practicality of conditionality was self-evidently immoral. In this way, conditionality ran the risk of becoming an intellectual trap. "The likelihood of Annex 7 working completely was not much more than zero," says Ambassador Brunson McKinley, who came out to Bosnia as a humanitarian coordinator after a long career in the State Department working on refugee affairs.

Of course, Gersony himself knew too little at this point to form an opinion on the text of Dayton after reading it. As elsewhere, he would be driven by what the dozens and hundreds of ordinary people he was to interview would tell him.

Bob and Cindy flew first to the Croatian capital of Zagreb. Tim Knight, who ran USAID's disaster assistance response team inside the U.S. Embassy and worked closely with UNHCR, was their initial point of

Timothy R. Knight with a Bosnian woman (name unknown) who was a recipient of assistance from the housing program Bob Gersony designed.

contact. Tim Knight was charismatic, good-looking, and supremely plugged in. He was someone perennially reassuring and who spoke with authority. It was a July 9, 1993, unclassified cable that Knight had written from Zagreb, after a field trip to Sarajevo about the dire situation in Bosnia—he had described Sarajevo as a veritable concentration camp run by the United Nations—that was passed on to President Clinton, who then issued an ultimatum to the Serbs, getting them to restore gas in the city.[4] Most crucially, Knight had the ear of the powerful, extraordinarily accomplished U.S. ambassador to Croatia Peter Galbraith, a friend and ally of Holbrooke.[5] Though Galbraith and Knight were rough opposites—the former was the product of a prominent liberal family and elite schools from the North; the latter was a moderate conservative and the product of state schools in the South— they got along famously, mainly because Knight's frequent trips to Bosnia from Croatia gave Galbraith informational access to what was occurring in the war zone. Galbraith wanted little more than for Knight to continue his adventurous forays.[6]

There was nothing Tim Knight would not do for Bob and Cindy Gersony. He had first met Bob in Piura in northern Peru in 1983, when they both were doing fieldwork for USAID there. "Bob's energy was unmatchable, always taking copious notes with his pen that hung from his neck. He never tired of interviewing people. I've always been good at noticing inconsistencies in what people tell me, but Bob was a master at it. So there was an obvious professional attraction between us. Bob avoided huge, grand programs that could never be implemented in the real world. His approach was methodical, commonsensical, anthropological. As for Cindy Davis," Knight goes on, "I met her before she knew Bob. She was a whiz in the disaster assistance community. The two of them together constituted the greatest synergy."

Knight found Bob and Cindy an apartment in Sarajevo. He convinced the regional security officer (RSO) to allow them to travel wherever they wanted, something RSOs generally hate to do. With the help of Galbraith, he got them a "soft-skinned" (unarmored) vehicle to give Bob and Cindy the latitude of doing what they needed to do. He essentially put his whole office at their disposal.

From Zagreb, Bob and Cindy drove southwest and then south along the great lower jaw of Croatia for several hundred miles, parallel to the Adriatic coast, all the way to Mostar, the famous old Ottoman town tucked inside Herzegovina, with a historic arched bridge destroyed in the 1990s fighting. On the Adriatic, they found refugees and displaced persons with whom to conduct their first sample interviews in peaceful, secure settings: getting their feet wet, so to speak.

From Mostar, they struck northeast and inland over the mountains to Sarajevo.

SARAJEVO, BOSNIA-HERZEGOVINA. Fog-strewn streets with neo-Gothic and neo-baroque facades, exuding the subtle colors of a dying autumn leaf, overseen by Ottoman-style domes and pencil-thin minarets—a place where you could admire Islamic architecture while nursing a plum brandy at one of the many local cafés. There is the cozy intimacy of Austro-Hungarian Central Europe enmeshed with the vivid flavor of the Ottoman Near East, all overlooked by mountain fastnesses. The rash of socialist-era concrete does not quite defeat the thrilling sense of a civilizational fault zone. But by the late 1980s, as Yugoslavia entered an economic death spiral and the cosmetic improvements necessitated by the 1984 Winter Olympics here had faded into near oblivion, graffiti began to be ever present in Sarajevo, and the once-intimate town looked mean for a visitor like myself in the late 1980s who had known it in the early 1980s. "What a difference a half decade made!" I thought in 1989. Of course, the wars of the Yugoslav secession a few years later turned this urban jewel into a free-fire zone, with all of the attendant wreckage. It was in the wake of that horror that Gersony first set eyes on the city.

The apartment that Tim Knight had found for Bob and Cindy had no central heating, but it did have a potbelly stove that Knight had had installed for them. The previous occupant had worked for the United Nations and left behind massive stacks of out-of-date U.N. situation reports (sitreps). Bob and Cindy kept warm by feeding the sitreps, one page at a time, into the potbelly stove. Inside the apartment, they never took off their long underwear and gray knee socks. Knight had a similar apartment and situation in Sarajevo: "I slept in my full-sweat outfit," Gersony says. "It was so cold that the first thing I saw in the morning was my own breath. I took spit-baths and subsisted on MREs [military meals-ready-to-eat]. It was absolutely miserable." Cindy adds, "Even indoors we were walking around in our coats much of the time."

That apartment became Bob and Cindy's base for visiting more than seventy towns and villages in Bosnia over an eleven-week period, from Thanksgiving 1995 until early February 1996. Bob drove the Nissan Patrol that Knight had obtained for them. This was one of the few times in Gersony's career when he drove himself, since with all the roadblocks manned by different militias and militaries from different ethnic groups that were still in operation in the immediate aftermath of Dayton, any local driver—even an embassy driver—ran the risk of being abducted. Local people all around Bosnia were generous in the extreme to Bob and Cindy. They gave them rooms to stay in and food to eat. But the rooms usually had no heat and no hot water. Bob and Cindy slept always in sleeping bags. Bob often couldn't sleep because of the Turkish coffee his hosts kept offering, which it was impolite to refuse. Because they were constantly on the move, they had trouble doing laundry. At the beginning of their eleven weeks of journeying the weather was freezing but at least the countryside was dry. Then it began snowing with a vengeance. Bob sweated constantly out of nervousness. He hated driving: he feared the roadblocks, the banditry, the possibility of flat tires and of getting lost in the snow. Yet he was always shivering, too. Alternately sweating and shivering without a change of clothes, he began to smell really bad. Finally he had no choice but to take an occasional bath in cold water. For him, who had always done better in heat than in cold, it was sheer torture. He longed for the warmth of the West Bank, Gaza, Nicaragua, Rwanda, anywhere but Bosnia in winter.

By the time Bob and Cindy finished their work, they had interviewed 400 people give or take a handful, 250 of whom were Bosnians. And of those 250, 150 were displaced persons and the remaining 100 were local Bosnian relief workers. Beyond those 250 Bosnians, Bob and Cindy interviewed 100 expatriates, Europeans and Americans, who worked on the ground in Bosnia for UNHCR and the other NGOs. This was all in addition to the 50 experts they interviewed in Washington, Geneva, and Brussels on their way out to Bosnia.[7] In other words, on the ground throughout Bosnia, they interviewed approximately 350 individuals, each in isolation for an average of two hours: 700 hours' worth of interviewing using 14 different translators.

In each interview, Bob followed every detail of the methodology he had perfected in western Sudan, Mozambique, and elsewhere: noting down the person's village, ethnic group, distinguishing characteristics, and so on, but never their name, all the while assuring the person of anonymity. "Bob wanted to know not just the facts, but what people sincerely believed in their own minds the facts were. Bob was a truth-teller, not a pleaser, so those who disagreed with him and were upset by his truths found him a little hard to take," explains Brunson McKinley, who was with Gersony for a stretch in Bosnia.

In particular, Bob and Cindy would ask:

- What specifically happened to you during the fighting? What did you learn from it?
- What kinds of programs have worked here? What kinds haven't?
- Can you go home? Why or why not? And if not, what's stopping you?
- What do you intend to do next with your lives?

People simply exploded with comments when asked these questions. These people were not African or Central American peasants who in a significant number of cases could literally not count above ten, but Europeans, albeit from a poor and war-torn corner of Europe.

As for the Bosnian fieldworkers and the expatriate NGOs, "they were literally the best and the brightest of the international relief community," Gersony exclaims. "Unlike a place like Rwanda, where the violence had erupted suddenly only a few months before, Bosnia had been at war for nearly four years already by the time we arrived. And thus there had been quite a weeding-out process, so that only the sturdiest and most talented NGO workers had remained. These people were not theorists," he goes on. "They had been setting up emergency centers for the elderly, hiring contractors, doing all the essential work of dealing with displaced persons on an individual basis every day." Truly, they were a ground-level brain trust: basically the RAND Corporation of Bosnia in terms of what they knew. And with the ink not quite dry on Dayton, no one had yet asked them their opinion of it; no one had asked them about things like conditionality and cross-ethnic return in a comprehensive and methodical way.

As necessary and admirable as it was, Dayton was generally a top-down, elite-driven agreement, embodying the hopes and assumptions of its authors, notably Richard Holbrooke (if not of all its signatories),[8] and Gersony was asking the dozens and hundreds of experts living for years on the ground in Bosnia what they thought about this diplomatic coup, in which Holbrooke essentially locked up the leaders of the warring ethnic and religious factions at a military base in the American Midwest until they came to terms.

Of the approximately 250 Bosnians Bob and Cindy interviewed (in addition to the 150 foreigners and expatriates), virtually all of them either did not want the minorities in their villages—whether Muslim or Croat—back, or at least felt it was not viable for them to return, fearing that they would be killed or beaten and their houses burned. The wartime atrocities were still only a few months old at this point. People's minds were still concentrated on what had happened during the war. The most moderate voices told them that "if you push, violence in one place will trigger violence in other places." The Bosnian NGOs said that Dayton's Annex 7 was "a decent goal but unfortunately not possible and dangerous to implement at this time." Bob and Cindy encountered differences in reasoning, but the conclusions were always the same. Reconciliation and cross-ethnic return were unthinkable at the moment.

What did the displaced persons who had been ethnic minorities in their home villages say to Bob and Cindy?

Listen.

"Would you like to return to your original domicile?"
"Absolutely."
"Will you do it now or in the near future?"

"Not a chance. If I go back, who will protect my house from being firebombed? Who is going to protect my children? What school am I going to send them to? [The schools were often controlled by the ethno-nationalists.] My children are going to be bullied and beaten. How am I going to get a job when there is already high unemployment in my home village? Who will protect my family at night?"

Moreover, potential cross-ethnic returnees feared they would have "limited success competing with demobilized combatants and others of the majority ethnic group" for scarce jobs. They feared minority businesses "may continue to be subjected to discriminatory . . . taxes imposed by the majority." An experienced economist for a multilateral organization told Bob and Cindy that he had observed a "natural tendency [by the majorities] to complete ethnic cleansing through nonviolent [economic] means."[9]

The first step, in the opinion of all the interviewees, was to get the majority populations back home: that is, whole Muslim villages had been driven out of their houses by the Serbs, so get them back in place, and only then worry about getting the minority Croats back into those villages. After all, almost everyone was a victim who had lost his or her home, including those of the majority groups. Each group had its own perpetrators and victims. So the vast reconstruction effort should not be held hostage to conditionality and cross-ethnic return. Dayton's Annex 7 was beautiful and necessary as an endgame. But it was premature. At least that's what virtually all the people on the ground in Bosnia, Bosnians and expatriates, had told Bob and Cindy.

As the mayor of Tuzla, Selim Bešlagić, a progressive icon and hero of the international community, who protected minorities in the northeast of the Muslim sector, told them: "Get people home who can go home. Targeting cross-ethnic returns right now heightens resentment and diminishes reconciliation."[10]

A Soros foundation fieldworker told them: "We can't give one more year for the people to suffer while awaiting cross-ethnic returns."

Cindy says, "People didn't want to hear about 'civil society' and 'conflict mitigation.' They wanted houses and stoves and toilets, tangible things."

Armed with these ideas, Gersony was fortunate in identifying a concrete program to test them against. USAID's Office of Transition Initiatives (OTI), whose task it was to move war and disaster zones beyond the emergency phase, was in the midst of completing twenty-five projects in Bosnia designed to leverage conditionality and cross-ethnic return. The head of OTI in Bosnia was Frederick Barton. Tall, gracious, and commanding with a slightly gravelly voice, Rick Barton had first encountered Gersony in Washington during a long briefing that Gersony delivered on Nicaraguan reconstruction. "When I first saw and listened to Bob Gersony, I thought: Columbo meets Indiana Jones," Barton says. It was a powerful, formative experience for Barton, and deeply affected his own methodology.[11] Barton introduced Gersony to Ray Jennings, a PhD with expertise in reconciliation, and Mike Stievater, a practical operations guy. "Their projects had lit a candle in the darkness, and therefore gave me something to focus on," says Gersony.

Ray Jennings gave Gersony a list of what he thought were his ten most successful projects and Gersony looked at seven of them. The projects were not overly ambitious; one could categorize them as mild forms of ethnic reconciliation.

One project was a school where both the Muslim and Croat joint mayors had signed a contract to admit children from both communities. Gersony walked into the school. There was a giant Croatian flag in the entranceway, using the colors and proportions of the World War II–era fascist Croat Ustaše flag. There was not one Muslim child in the school.

Another project in a predominantly Muslim town was a reconstructed health center that the two joint mayors had signed off on. No Croats were allowed inside.

In the town of Vitez in central Bosnia, OTI had appropriated

$30,000 to repair a locker room next to a soccer field. The mayors had signed off on it, and both the Muslim and Croat communities were expected to provide volunteer labor. No volunteers showed up. Contractors were paid to repair it. A Muslim-Croat soccer game was scheduled. It was canceled due to political pressure from Zagreb and Sarajevo. Even when local officials cooperated, national capitals intervened to pursue ethnic agendas. When Bob and Cindy visited the locker room, it had been completely vandalized and destroyed.

In the Croat town of Busovača, surrounded by Bosnian Muslim territory, the mayor's rhetoric was so hateful that Gersony's translator walked out of the meeting.

In the town of Gornji Vakuf in central Bosnia, the Swiss charity CARITAS offered $10 million for cross-ethnic return. The money was refused.

One OTI official admitted: "When you press too much, people get stubborn. Feelings get inflamed. USAID gives the hardliners a platform. They say, 'We're standing up to the Americans, we're not going to let them dictate to us, we'll defend you.'"

The OTI program, in Gersony's mind, was a useful failure. Mike Stievater, who was according to Gersony "the most honest fieldworker" he had ever encountered anywhere, admitted as such, even though he himself had personally tried to implement each OTI project. "We set the simplest criteria we could find and we failed," Rick Barton says unflappably. "My attitude is, if it doesn't work, try something else."

Further buttressing Gersony's findings was a November 1995 diplomatic agreement, a supplement to the Dayton Accords, stipulating that 600 minority families should be allowed to immediately return to four majority-controlled pilot towns. Subsequently, 0 families returned to Stolac; 47 to Travnik; 11 to Jajce; and 2 to Bugojno—for a total of 60 families, one-tenth of the agreed-upon number.[12]

"It was pure fantasy to think that cross-ethnic return would generally work at this moment," recalls Tim Knight.

. . .

Bugojno, in the far western sector of Bosnian Muslim control, near the border with the Croat-controlled sector, was among the pilot towns selected by the architects of Dayton for fast-track reconciliation. A dignified old man, Mesud Durnjak, told Gersony that the mayor, Dževad Mlaćo, wanted to meet with him and invite him to dinner. The old man apologized in advance, telling Gersony that the forty-two-year-old mayor "can be a little direct" in his pronouncements. The mayor was short and stocky, very muscular, with a permanently reddened face.[13] He met Gersony in the small one-room dining hall of the local hotel.

Throughout the meal, the Muslim mayor shouted at Gersony, threatening him often, as if Gersony was the personal embodiment of the international community that he so despised.

"Who do you people think you are? We're not going to trade our interests and our actual experience in the war just for the sake of getting new toilet seats put on our latrines! We can't be bought off so easy! Given what people here have gone through, we would be crazy to do the things you are telling us now to do! Everything you've done is a waste of time."

The mayor's fist kept pounding on the table, his face a few inches from Gersony's. Gersony was more terrified than at any time since he had been screamed at almost two decades earlier by General Lucas Garcia in Guatemala, a man who would go on to commit war crimes.

"We didn't spend the night in Bugojno because I was so scared of what the mayor might do to me. Cindy and I packed our bags and left at nine P.M., right after the dinner. The mayor was a murderer and I wanted to make a statement that this kind of behavior was not on." The dignified old man, accompanying them to the car, kept apologizing for the mayor.

Of course, by the time he got to Bugojno, Gersony had heard the essence of what the mayor told him many dozens of times already in the interviews he had conducted. But he had never heard it in a tone anywhere near as angry, vulgar, and visceral. The mayor's outlook was the crude, very impolite condensation and culmination of many of the interviews Bob and Cindy had conducted.

The last place Bob and Cindy visited was Jajce, in the east-central area of Croat control, another Dayton pilot town. Gersony, now utterly exhausted, was on the brink of another one of his nervous and physical breakdowns. Jajce was nice and charming, and Gersony could use his rudimentary German there. But there was just something about the atmosphere that smelled, he felt. The mayor had told him that there was no chance of a Muslim population return. Bob and Cindy were warned not to leave because of a coming snowstorm. Bob impulsively insisted on leaving anyway. So they headed northwest to Bihać, inside a Muslim enclave. Within an hour of their leaving it began to snow. Six inches must have fallen in no time, golf balls of snow. They had to put chains on the tires. He had never put chains on tires before, but he somehow managed to do it. They were driving maybe five miles an hour. They gave up and entered a local police station at two A.M. "Can we stay here overnight?" they asked. The police replied no, even after Bob and Cindy explained that they had diplomatic papers. They tried to sleep in their sleeping bags inside the car. The car metal only magnified the cold. Every quarter-hour or so, Bob started the car to warm it up. At daybreak they drove on to Bihać, where they found a hotel that had hot water. They took baths, slept, and had their laundry washed.

"I'm done," he told Cindy, still cranky, on the brink of tears. He called the USAID mission in Sarajevo and stupidly said he did not want to return there, but would continue on to the comforts of Zagreb and then to Washington in order to brief Brian Atwood. But his request was rightly refused. He was ordered to drive back to Sarajevo to brief the U.S. ambassador to Bosnia, John Menzies.

John Menzies was the ultimate, solidly grounded, bread-and-butter Foreign Service officer: nothing fancy on his résumé, just supremely smart, with years of experience; a product of non-elite colleges across America's heartland, who would go on to become an educator at start-up universities in the Balkans and the Middle East. He gave Gersony over two hours of his time.

Gersony ran through his methodology, breaking down the categories of interviewees and what they had told him. Then he presented his recommendations:

- Drop or postpone conditionality. It is a gift to the extremists, who consider it demeaning and claim the return of the hated minorities is part of an American and international plot.
- Postpone cross-ethnic return. It is premature.
- Start with fifty of the worst, war-ravaged villages and build or repair fifty houses in each village, raising them to a winterized standard of habitation.
- Fix these 2,500 houses within six months, putting in new roofs and new foundation structures where necessary, and make sure at least two rooms in each house are insulated.
- These 2,500 houses will form anchor communities of fifty families in each village. Because people are too afraid to come back home alone, they will only do so in groups of the same ethnicity. The cost for all of this will be only $30 million.
- If it is done mostly right, international donors will pitch in and build community centers and so forth.
- After all of this is completed, conditionality and cross-ethnic return can kick in.

Menzies considered this a breath of fresh air and "commonsensical."[14] He sent a cable back to Washington, slugged for Atwood.

Bob and Cindy returned to Washington.

Atwood called a Saturday meeting, February 10, 1996, that lasted from nine A.M. to one P.M. Besides the USAID administrator, in the room to listen to Gersony's brief were Carol Lancaster, Doug Stafford, Tom Dine, Barbara Turner, and Mike Mahdesian: every one of them a powerful personality and a high official in the AID bureaucracy. Tom Dine, for example, had run the feared and influential

American Israel Public Affairs Committee (AIPAC) for many years. Dine, one of the sharpest lobbyists in Washington, was "direct, acerbic, self-confident, and effective," according to Atwood, who had brought him onto his team. Barbara Turner, Dine's deputy in USAID/ Europe, was an intimidating career civil servant, who was not at this point intimate or very knowledgeable about Gersony's work in the developing world (although she would later warm up to him). Mike Mahdesian was a major Democratic Party donor from California who had worked on the Clinton campaign.

Gersony, as usual, wore everyone down with details garnered from the field. Actually, it was rare that the USAID administrator would make the time for such a long, mainly factual briefing from anyone; as the man at the top, Atwood generally convened people to ask their opinions.

Deep into the brief, with Gersony emphasizing how necessary concrete things like new housing were to preserve Bosnia's fragile peace, Atwood asked Gersony, playing the devil's advocate:

"What would you say if I told you that housing was not an option?"

"I'd say, pack up and leave."

"That's how important you think housing [for the victims of ethnic cleansing] is?" Atwood asked back.

"That's how unimportant everything else is, compared to housing and what goes with it," Gersony answered.

At the end, Doug Stafford and Mike Mahdesian said, almost in unison, "I'm sold."

Mahdesian felt, after listening to Gersony, that because feelings were still so "raw" in Bosnia, it would be "dicey and dangerous" to insert minorities back into majority areas right at this moment. Thus, what Gersony was proposing constituted "a necessary and doable first step." Atwood himself didn't need much convincing, since he already knew Gersony's work firsthand in Nicaragua and Rwanda. And the USAID administrator was frankly skeptical of "the *kumbaya* approach to the Balkans immediately after such a vicious civil war." Moreover, they had all gotten Ambassador John Menzies's cable from

Bosnia about Gersony's briefing to him. But Dine and Turner at USAID's Europe bureau may have felt that Gersony had invaded their territory with all of his specific conclusions and suggestions. They, according to others at the meeting, were still somewhat doubtful and "less than pleased" regarding Gersony's proposal.

At least according to Gersony's recollection, Dine remarked in an offhand aside, "You and Fred Cuny are the cowboys."

Gersony exploded: "What are you running down Fred for? He is dead [in Chechnya] and can't defend himself."

Gersony knew better than anyone how Cuny could, in fact, behave like a cowboy. But he suddenly felt defensive. He was not about to allow any outsider or Washington operator to make such a charge against one of the greatest and bravest of fieldworkers.

Dine mentioned that the situation in Bosnia might merit another assessment, to see if Gersony's analysis held up. The discussion was descending into nasty bureaucratic politics, in Gersony's view. But Dine had a good point. He may have been a Washington operator, but he was also someone with a Peace Corps background who had traveled several times through the war zone in Bosnia over the previous two years. And he also believed, like everyone else in the room, that new housing was the answer to Bosnia's post-conflict dilemma. He just was inclined at this point to have USAID deal directly with the housing issue, rather than go through Gersony and Tim Knight's disaster assistance response team, as Gersony was proposing: a very reasonable argument.[15]

Brian Atwood kept calm. He realized that Gersony's proposal amounted to practically a U-turn in American policy, just at the time when Richard Holbrooke—the towering, formidable architect of Dayton—was about to leave government in order to write a book about what he had accomplished in Bosnia. *We're on very sensitive ground here,* Atwood realized. But he wasn't worried. Atwood was almost every bit as much the big-time Washington operator and player as Holbrooke. Atwood was a former FSO and assistant secretary of state, a friend of Bill and Hillary Clinton and of Vice President Al Gore, with excellent ties to both the Democratic Party and Capitol

Hill. And everybody knew all these things. In Washington, perception is everything. It had been Atwood who stood down powerful forces that had wanted to fold USAID into the State Department's own bureaucracy: a move Atwood knew would kill USAID.

Atwood sent Gersony around USAID and State to give the same brief to as many officials as he could. Gersony delivered eighteen briefings to groups of four or five people each. The small audiences meant more eye contact and the give-and-take of questions throughout, which Gersony was very good at.

But Bob Gersony never did get to brief—or even argue with—Richard Holbrooke over Bosnia, since Holbrooke left government just as Gersony emerged with his findings.

My own view is that Holbrooke might have screamed at Gersony early in their imaginary meeting, and then listened intently as Gersony wore him down with details just like he did everybody else. At the end, Holbrooke, who was operationally brilliant, would have quietly incorporated at least some of Gersony's recommendations into his plan of action, perhaps without ever giving Gersony credit for them: sort of what had happened to Gersony with Rwanda, when United Nations and State Department officials used his report to pressure Paul Kagame's government in Kigali, while trying to bury the report at the same time. *Admit the truth only to yourselves, not to the outside world: since the essence of many a situation in the developing world (and especially in war zones) is what nobody can state openly and what nobody wants to hear.*

Rick Barton, USAID's head of the OTI, which had overseen all the projects that Gersony judged abject failures, was actually impressed with Gersony's briefing. Barton considered Gersony "more like an anthropologist than a political analyst," and one who had convinced him that "our policy was premature."[16] A very smooth political type in the manner of Atwood himself, Barton told Gersony: "Of course, cross-ethnic return is a straw man. No one really believes it will take place."

Gersony thought this a clever sleight of hand that could ease the bureaucratic deadlock. In this way of thinking, cross-ethnic return was a decent goal, that just by working in its direction—even by beginning with ethnic majority returns as he had recommended— might lead eventually to a better Bosnia: something Holbrooke's team should welcome.

But then Gersony had to brief Gerald Hyman, who worked in USAID promoting democracy abroad. Hyman was a progressive liberal Republican (yes, that type actually once existed) who had dedicated four years of his life to working the humanitarian issue of Bosnia from Washington. He was frankly uncomfortable with Gersony's analysis. His argument was succinct and insightful in its way.

Hyman admits that "much of what he [Gersony] said about the divisions and hatreds in Bosnia are unfortunately well-known . . . It should hardly be surprising after the rapes, eviscerations, expulsions, murders . . . that these are people who hate one another. Nevertheless," he goes on, "rightly or wrongly, the U.S. government has taken the position that we will side with those who do not agree to the ethnic partition. That may be futile, naïve, impossible. But that is our position. Thus, channeling our reconstruction assistance to 'same ethnic returnees,' as Gersony suggests, will result in the reaffirmation, indeed the reconstruction with our assistance, of ethnically pure areas: we become the instruments for solidifying ethnic cleansing and ethnic cantons."[17]

Nevertheless, Gersony did convince Hyman that if cross-ethnic return was ever going to be attempted, "we should at least do it with our eyes open," in Hyman's words.

Hyman clearly saw Gersony's own particular quality as a humanitarian unburdened by naïve optimism, even as he saw the difficulty in agreeing with Gersony completely in this case. Therefore, Hyman is worth listening to for a moment about Bosnia and the intellectual debate it spawned.

Jerry Hyman, a small, thin, voluble dynamo of a man, full of memories and perceptions, was a product of rough Chicago public schools where inner-city Blacks sat alongside poor whites who had migrated from Appalachia—a real petri dish of group interaction— and so he was never naïve himself about racial and ethnic feelings.

Hyman took that experience to the University of Chicago, where he got a PhD in anthropology. He thus understood the Bosnian dilemma in many of its human dimensions, perhaps better than his colleagues.

"While Dayton has been interpreted as a constitutional document, that's not what it really was," Hyman explains. "It was about ending a bloody, intractable war, pure and simple. And Holbrooke made the compromises necessary to do just that. Holbrooke succeeded and is now unfairly criticized for Dayton's imperfections. Holbrooke was a bulldozer by necessity at Dayton," Hyman goes on, "whereas Bob Gersony came at the subject of Dayton with hours of nuance and massive detail. Both approaches were justified by the circumstances. As for ethnic-minority return, you're not going to instantly get people to overcome communal scars and bitterness by giving them rolls of plastic sheeting and other help."

Meanwhile, Gersony was sweating logistics. Plaster didn't dry in winter, he knew. Thus, construction had to start in April in order to be completed by late October, the onset of winter in Bosnia. Villages and beneficiaries had to be selected for majority return. If the bureaucracy did not act soon, it was possible that USAID would be nowhere in Bosnia the following winter, and one year after Dayton.

Also at this time, in late February 1996, Mike Mahdesian—part of Atwood's inner circle—reached out to the NGO community in New York, informing it that USAID was leaning toward opposition to cross-ethnic return. The New York–based NGOs, unlike those Gersony had interviewed in Bosnia, went wild with anger. On February 22, the influential CEO of Mercy Corps, Neal Keny-Guyer, wrote to Brian Atwood with an urgent personal appeal to reject outright Gersony's recommendations.

Gersony and Atwood urged Keny-Guyer to make a trip to Bosnia.

Keny-Guyer came back from Bosnia near the end of March, having himself interviewed refugees and local NGOs there. Gersony was right, he realized.[18] It proved the replicability of Gersony's methodology.

Keny-Guyer explains his turnaround:

"We were originally on the side of being bold and positive with incentives to help people collaborate across ethnic lines. So we were disappointed when USAID retreated from inter-ethnic reconciliation. But after focusing on Bob's analysis he made us rethink it all. You know, he's one of the great human rights characters of the age, who comes at you relentlessly with situational awareness. He made us opt in favor of concrete, tangible things that we could really accomplish on the ground right at that moment—things we might later build upon."

As it turned out, Atwood was able to get unanimous USAID approval for Gersony's plan.

On March 8, 1996, Bob and Cindy flew back to Sarajevo, where Tim Knight had permanently relocated from Zagreb in the aftermath of the Dayton Accords. Knight, an amazing whirlwind of organization, had already sent out Gersony's plan of action for home building to forty NGOs, of which six were selected to do the actual construction work. Bob, Cindy, Tim Knight, and Knight's assistant Lisa Doughten split up to visit thirty villages each in order to prepare the logistics. One NGO was insistent about allowing a small number of cross-ethnic returns in a village, Donji Zezelovo, west of Sarajevo, which it deemed promising for inter-ethnic reconciliation. Gersony and Knight agreed to go along. But the Bosnian Croat authorities in Donji Zezelovo immediately threatened to burn down any of the repaired houses if Muslims were allowed to return. So the idea was dropped. The argument for cross-ethnic return—the return of minorities to majority areas—was dying by the day in Bosnia itself, however fine it was in principle.

The six NGO groups chosen by Knight and Gersony hired 175 contractors who built or repaired 2,548 houses in 48 villages: 80 percent of the houses were for Muslims and 20 percent for Croats, each group constituting the ethnic majority in the respective villages. Knight and Gersony ran roughshod over the NGOs, forcing them to take before-and-after photos for everything they built, arranging for electricity and water projects, and so forth. Knight completed the project on time and under budget.

The prewar local construction industry was reactivated, as roughly four thousand jobs were created. In the process, USAID provided cover and legitimacy for NGOs to start their own building projects in the targeted villages. The sound of guns was replaced by the sound of hammers in Bosnia. The Knight and Gersony building program became the go-to project for congressional delegations and other official visitors to see on their trips to Bosnia. *The Washington Post* called it "one of the best aid projects around." As for the argument that the project was reinforcing the outcome of ethnic cleansing, *The Washington Post* quoted Kevin Mannion, a key NGO official in Bosnia, as saying: "Returns of [minority] refugees to [majority areas] are not going to happen, so why set impossible goals."[19]

Indeed, a year later, the U.S. Congress's General Accounting Office reported on not only the lack of cross-ethnic returns, but of the continued expulsion of ethnic minorities from majority areas, with over three hundred homes destroyed by locals to discourage returnees.[20] In many cases, as discovered by the Rhodes scholar and Oxford PhD Rebecca Brubaker, "most minority returnees sold or rented their properties, after reclaiming them, to members of the majority group."[21]

Alas, two years after Dayton, *New York Times* correspondent Chris Hedges and *Washington Post* correspondent Lee Hockstader were able to report that Croat returnees to Muslim villages and Muslim returnees to Serb villages were being killed with impunity, or having their houses destroyed.[22] After a long study on the possibilities of minority returns in Bosnia, Cambridge University research fellow Marcus Cox concluded:

"Ethnic separatism is not simply a matter of the misbehavior of local nationalist leaders. There are deep-rooted social and political forces which resist integrated governance and living conditions. . . . The path to genuine reconciliation must begin with the normalization of living conditions, easing the insecurity of ordinary people."[23]

In other words, here was a complete vindication of Gersony's analysis of Bosnia.

In fact, Gersony understood that, as one scholar put it, when people are forcibly displaced, "they lose more than their houses. They lose their social and economic networks," their friends and neighbors, "all of which comprise their sense of 'home.'"[24] And you just can't snap your fingers and instantly reverse that process. Rebuilding may have to begin elsewhere.

Of course, by the late 1990s and after, when all these reports and studies appeared, the media spotlight had already shifted away from Bosnia. Thus, in the memory of the elite mainstream media, Dayton was enshrined as a great achievement, pure and simple—when, in fact, like all brave and arduous efforts, Dayton was imperfect. It was all its architects could do just to get some kind of agreement that would stop the bloodshed, and consequently they made compromises along the way.[25] Gersony's work was one useful corrective to Dayton, something that helped save it actually, rather than a repudiation of it.

Yet the harshest critics of Gersony's report charged that he was, in effect, sanctioning ethnic cleansing as a fait accompli, rather than coming up with a plan to create a new order in the Balkans built on minority rights. The whole point, in their view, was not to accept the record of the past as a guide to the future. For that, after all, constituted fatalism. The other way to look at it was to say that Gersony has always been a sort of idealist, but just one without illusions.

Though the former Yugoslavia disappointingly regressed into ethnic cantons in the years and decades since the fighting—something Gersony's recommendations helped facilitate, charge his critics—at least it has remained relatively peaceful, thus far. And so Holbrooke still gets the credit for ending that war. Gersony may not have accomplished much, but at least he helped accomplish something, by working to help stabilize the region in the wake of Dayton. More than that was always a long shot, given the ethnic animosities that are simply impossible to deny, and that certainly did not evaporate the moment that Dayton was signed.

"Dayton," Tim Knight says, "was a very, very fragile peace agreement. And it would not have taken very much to restart the fire." Yet human rights visionaries will always believe that the animosities, so raw in early 1996, could still have been surmounted. It remains an unknowable, but all the minority ethnics that Gersony interviewed told him they had no intention of returning to majority areas in any case. They scoffed at the notion that they could ever be protected by international troops 24/7 indefinitely, which is what it actually might have required in order to keep them safe.[26]

Gersony did not have a philosophically developed worldview per se. At the end of the day, he was a fieldworker. Yet he had read *The Last of the Just* as a young man in Guatemala, and therefore believed in the responsibility-to-protect long before it was popularized as a human rights term. That belief led him to develop a particular methodology, so that his reports of human rights abuses in Africa and elsewhere would be trusted by skeptics in Washington. But that same methodology instilled a practicality in his mind that went along with the responsibility-to-protect: the practicality of allowing the facts of a situation to emanate from the ground up. The result was his exposure of mass murder in Uganda's Luwero Triangle and of ethnic cleansing in eastern Chad and in pro-American Somalia. It was a methodology that led to a solution to the murder and rape of Vietnamese boat people and to a recommendation not to arm the white South African–supported RENAMO guerrillas in Mozambique. And on and on.

Now his methodology, built on hundreds of interviews in the field, made him frankly skeptical about the prospects for the immediate implementation of Dayton's Annex 7. Gersony would have liked to believe the same thing as his critics on Bosnia. But the evidence he had compiled just made it impossible for him to do so. Gersony was a humanitarian throughout, but one who never withdrew into theory, ideology, or social engineering, since to force an impractical principle—no matter how worthy it seemed—on people might only lead to more of them being killed, and more chaos.

As the saying went, *Don't let the perfect be the enemy of the good.* It was such practicality, in addition to his thoroughness and intensity, that was the key to Gersony's influence in Washington.

. . .

In fact, there was little inspiring about Bob Gersony, no great idea that he could propound. Gersony was great-souled without being a moral absolutist. He wasn't burdened by political philosophy not only because he had never studied it, but because he had a surer guide to the world: the experience of having listened to thousands of ordinary people on the ground in the far-flung corners of the earth.

Gersony was a plodding fieldworker without further ambition, with no desire to be an assistant secretary of state or a normal FSO even, who only wanted to interview people and use his background as a commodity trader to understand the economic realities of relief and development. While others in this story—Fred Cuny and Pierre Gassmann, for example—had their youthful rite-of-passage experiences in the humanitarian nightmare of Biafra, Gersony in that rough time frame was in the commodity business, in the army in Vietnam, and starting a language school in Guatemala. His life experience was radically different from others in the humanitarian field. Gersony wore you down with facts and figures—buttressed by individual human accounts—always based on firsthand research, that's all. And thus he always came back to Washington with *news,* as Elliott Abrams had first noticed after Gersony briefed him about atrocities in Uganda in 1984.

Northern Uganda by Way of Nicaragua 1996–1997

"Never Mind the Actual Danger, You Scared Yourself to Death."

I n the mid-1990s, the face of the post Cold War was the former Yugoslavia: a violent conflict inside Europe itself that had been kindled organically from the collapse of the Berlin Wall and the subsequent end of the Cold War security structure, which had kept the Balkans dormant for decades. But the earth is vast, and in most parts of it the end of the Cold War registered only modestly or not at all. Thus, while the media remained sucked into the vortex of the former Yugoslavia, and even as lightheaded proponents of globalization were proclaiming a new era of universal peace, democracy, and prosperity, Gersony headed back to the world as it actually was: namely Nicaragua and northern Uganda. "We ignore these marginal areas at our own peril," he says.

Within the same month that Bob Gersony completed his work in Bosnia, he was called back to Nicaragua. Violeta Chamorro's only term in office was ending and there would soon be a national election. Bob and Cindy flew to Managua to help in monitoring voter registration in the hinterlands.

The pro-American Nicaraguan government had issued *cedulas*, or permanent voter identity cards, valid for ten years, in 119 of the 145 municipalities. But the electoral commission, which was still controlled by the left-wing Sandinistas, had not issued these cards in the 26 municipalities that happened to have been the base areas of the

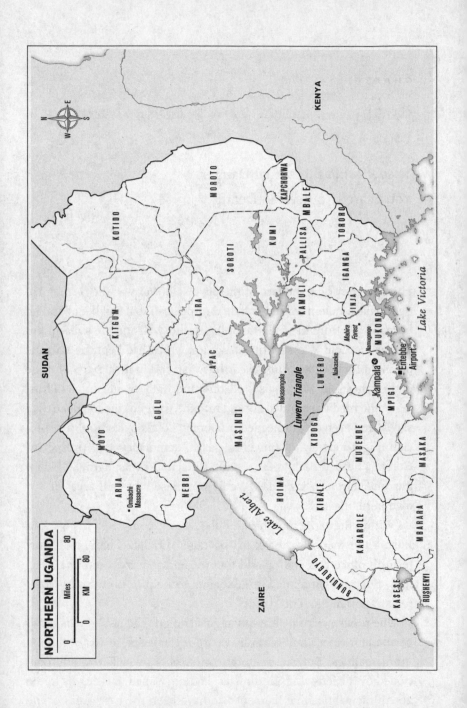

contras during the war. Consequently, Senator Jesse Helms put the entire USAID program for Nicaragua on hold, alleging that anti-Sandinista elements of the population were being denied the right to vote. USAID and Helms, which hated each other and came from opposite ends of the political and philosophical spectrum, both agreed to allow Bob and Cindy to investigate.

The pair divided up the work. Cindy went to the remote region of Jinotega in north-central Nicaragua, traveling all the way down the Coco River along the Honduran border, a lush and yawning landscape reminiscent of central Africa. Bob went south, to the equally remote Rio San Juan region adjacent to Costa Rica. They both set out on May 8, 1996, to observe preparations for the early-June registration campaign. Between the two of them, they interviewed 650 people in addition to 70 officials, all individually or in small groups. They found that people often had to walk as much as ten to fifteen miles in order to register to vote, and many people had lost their documents, or never had them in the first place, so they were not allowed to register. But if you brought witnesses, you would be issued a temporary card, a *libreta cívica*, permitting you to vote. But sometimes there were no registration centers at all. So rather than Sandinista treachery, it was more a matter of confusion over the entire process in somewhat chaotic rural areas that accounted for the problems. Gersony, having returned to Managua, explained all this to Helms's aides visiting the Nicaraguan capital. Consequently, the North Carolina senator set May 31 as the date to lift the hold on USAID's development program in Nicaragua.

In late May, Cindy again traveled down the Coco River to monitor the actual registration, while Bob returned to the remote south of the country to do the same. Cindy was accompanied by former contra commander Gato Negro ("Black Cat," a nom de guerre).[1] The boatman was Andres Pao. She had traveled with both on her earlier trip and trusted them. In fact, this was Cindy's sixth trip down the river. Commander Gato and Pao had already spent a week together on the Coco distributing election flyers and checking on security in advance of Cindy's visit. They had found no problem.

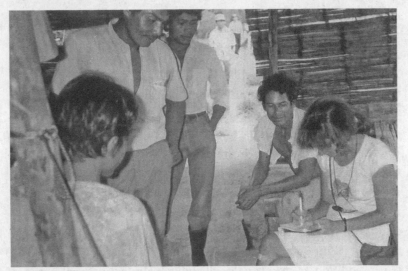

Cindy Gersony, Bob's wife (right), doing research for USAID by the Coco River on the Nicaraguan-Honduran border in 1996.

On May 30, the three proceeded downriver from the frontier town of Wiwili in Pao's *panga* boat with its 65-horsepower engine, arriving at the village of Somotine on the Nicaraguan side of the river several hours later. Somotine was the last Spanish-speaking village on the Coco before one reached the territory of the Miskito Indians. The scenery along the way was bare and sculptural on the hilly Honduran side, where the trees had been cut down for cattle grazing, and deeply forested on the Nicaraguan side. The river traffic consisted of canoes that men steered by long poles. Along the way Cindy saw wooden structures on stilts without electricity, half swallowed by the tall pea-green grass here in the rainy season. It was real jungle, connected to the outside world only by radio communications.

As soon as Cindy's boat arrived at Somotine, a group of young men with uniforms and guns jumped out of the tall grass and surrounded her.

"Why don't we go somewhere to talk?" one of them asked, in a tone that was barely polite, indicating that she had no choice in the matter.

They guided her and Gato to meet the local "peace commission," essentially the community leadership. Now there were thirty-two armed and ragtag former contras, led by a Comandante Pajarillo ("Little Bird"), who subsequently did all the talking.

For several hours he interrogated Cindy about her mission, all the while expressing his political grievances. He was in his midtwenties and had been a soldier most of his life. It was the only life he knew. He said the whole electoral system and power structure were unfair. Cindy tried not to disagree with him.

"We're detaining you, until we are guaranteed the right to vote," Comandante Pajarillo said.

When Cindy, who spoke Spanish, asked why she was being held "hostage," given all that the U.S. government had done for the contras, he objected. "You see that gun against the wall? If you were a hostage, I would point that gun to your head. But you are only being detained."

Cindy was relieved that they weren't bandits, and there was no alcohol in sight. Moreover, Comandante Pajarillo seemed to have control over his men. This was not the worst thing that could happen, she told herself. Nicaragua had never been as murderously violent as Guatemala or El Salvador.

It was dark. Night falls quickly in the tropics. They gave Cindy a cot in the village headman's shack in the midst of the jungle to sleep in. There was no phone, no communication at all with the outside world. She had a flashlight and a mystery novel to read in her backpack.

Very early the next morning the former contras sent Pao upriver in his boat to Wiwili (where there was intermittent radio communication) in order to broadcast their demands to the government. By the end of the day, Cindy's "kidnapping" was on the front page of the Managua newspapers. The word spread, and hours later television crews were camped out on the lawn of Cindy's parents' home in Sarasota, Florida. Ambassador John Maisto was momentarily away and Gersony, in southern Nicaragua, phoned the embassy's deputy chief of mission, Heather Hodges, in Managua, speaking to her as both a concerned husband and a Central America area specialist.

"Tell the Nicaraguans, no heroics, no commando-style raid. We will resolve this problem through negotiations," he told her.

He was less afraid of what the former contras might do to Cindy than the possibility of a raid gone wrong, with bullets flying all over the place. And while Chamorro's government was pro-American, the Sandinista-dominated army would have the political incentive to kill those former contras.

Chamorro's government sent a team from the Organization of American States (OAS) down the Coco River to talk to the former contras. The team was under the direction of Diego Beltrand, a Uruguayan lawyer who was the OAS human rights representative in Managua. Beltrand had been a friend of Bob and Cindy for a few years by now, having gotten to know them during their Atlantic coast development work, so the kidnapping was personal for him.

Beltrand's OAS team traveled down the Coco River, spending the night in Wiwili and continuing at dawn to Somotine. It had a challenge on its hands, not unusual in hostage situations. "It had to make complex political arguments to unsophisticated men isolated in the jungle," as he explains. The team let Pajarillo and his men vent: about access to good land, the need for fair elections, and so forth. The team assured the former contras that the OAS would advocate for their demands with the Nicaraguan government. But first the former contras must produce and then release Cindy, otherwise they would harm their own cause in the outside world, particularly in Washington, which had supported them. Pajarillo and his men talked among themselves for a while. Finally they agreed. Cindy arrived, very calm, after about half an hour.

There was a hand-over ceremony at 11:30 A.M., June 1, 1996, in true Central American style, with speeches and the singing of the national anthem after a guitar had suddenly appeared out of nowhere, all in front of twelve people in Somotine. Afterward, Cindy traveled in Pao's boat to Wiwili, where an AP reporter had come to take her picture, and then by vehicle to Jinotega town, where she was reunited with Bob.

She had spent all of three days and two nights detained in Somo-

Bob reunited with Cindy after Cindy's kidnapping on the Coco River in 1996.

tine, talking to the villagers to pass the hours. She was alternately bored, intellectually stimulated, and full of anxiety the entire time, not knowing if her ordeal would last days or weeks.

The Nicaragua chapter of Gersony's life was finally over. Or at least it seemed so.

Home from Nicaragua for several months in late 1996, the autumn was beautiful on West 72nd Street in Manhattan, with the leaves turning in Central Park, which Bob and Cindy's apartment over-looked. Bob would take walks in the park with his mother and father, who lived nearby, his father in a wheelchair by this time. As lovely as the season was, it was worrisome that the phone in the Gersonys' apartment never rang with a call from Washington. Maybe Bob's luck had run out. Maybe the notoriety of Cindy's kidnapping had a chilling effect on the State Department and USAID bureaucracy. Even if it was not your fault, and even if you were a hero for a brief moment in the media, the bureaucracy had a way of blaming you for anything that draws too much attention to itself.

Then on October 31, 1996, the day of Bob and Cindy's fourth wedding anniversary, Bob's father died at ninety-two. November and December were somber months for Bob, full of reflection and self-doubt.

Finally, after Christmas, the phone rang. It was Joe Williams calling from Kampala, Uganda. His slow Tennessee drawl was unmistakable.

Joe Williams had worked in the USAID mission in Managua when Gersony was managing his Atlantic coast project in eastern Nicaragua. Williams was another devotee of Janet Ballantyne. He was a real Tennessee character, slow and quiet while he was checking you out, then he became a real raconteur, a Fred Thompson kind of guy, charming and engrossing without pretensions, with ideas pulsing out of his brain.

"We have this *situation* in northern Uganda with a group called the Lord's Resistance Army [LRA]. Nobody knows what in the hell is going on there," Williams told Gersony over the phone. "If the army suddenly defeats the LRA, USAID will have to be able to move in quickly with a plan." Joe always knew what he didn't know, Gersony thought. Actually, Joe had been storing in his mind a wealth of stories told by travelers in northern Uganda. "But they were just anecdotal, there was no rigorous analysis to put them together," Joe now recalls.

"I'll be ready to go to Uganda tomorrow," Gersony told Williams.

But first he went to Washington to see his old gang at State for advice: Bob Houdek, the former ambassador and chief of mission in Uganda and Ethiopia, who by now was the State Department's go-to expert on Africa; Margaret McKelvey, the longtime Africa hand in the refugee bureau; Rick Ehrenreich at Intelligence and Research; and USAID veteran Bill Garvelink. They all had lots of questions, but very little information. That was the problem. Regarding the Lord's Resistance Army, everything was just so sketchy.

It was their very questions that essentially gave Gersony his marching orders and expanded his universe of known unknowns:

What were the specific issues that had provoked LRA attacks on villages? Was security in northern Uganda still good enough to support development projects? Was the Ugandan government in a state of denial about the war in the north? Was the national army's ethnic makeup a factor in how it acted? Was the conflict limited to the ethnic-Acholi lands in the north, and if not, could the LRA link up with various tribal groups to expand its influence? What percentage of the Acholis really did support the LRA? Was the feeling of abandonment among the Nilotic northerners (Acholis and others) deep enough to tempt secession from the Bantu-dominated capital of Kampala and the south of the country? Following from that, how severe was the resentment among the Acholis toward the Ugandan leader, Yoweri Museveni, a Banyankole (an ethnic subset of the Bantu speakers)?

Gayle Smith, who would go on to become the administrator of USAID under President Barack Obama, wanted Gersony to find out if the conflict was limited to LRA cattle raids and other criminal acts, or was Acholi society itself actually disintegrating? Since Gersony had last been in Uganda thirteen years before, Museveni had rescued the country from the war-torn hellhole that it was, one that was given to mass murder. But Uganda was still a long way from being at peace in its far-flung regions, which were afflicted still by tribal conflicts.

Remember, these were the late 1990s, the glory days of America's worldwide imperial influence, after the fall of the Berlin Wall and yet before 9/11, when Washington—having taken America's own security for granted—believed it could benevolently deliver democracy and stability literally throughout the planet. And the desire of the USAID bureaucracy to know everything about a place like northern Uganda reflected that. Bob Gersony was the chosen instrument for finding out—though, as usual, he was nervous as could be about the daunting task of answering all these questions. But he knew that it all boiled down to one question, really:

What did the Acholi people themselves think?

In the course of finding out, he would reveal in detail for the first time to the outside world the facts about the Lord's Resistance Army and its exotic, frightening leader, Joseph Kony, who had been leading the LRA since the late 1980s in a bizarre, obscure, and barbaric struggle against the Ugandan regime. Because it was both bizarre and obscure, Gersony himself, even after weeks in the region, wouldn't understand it all until he put his notes together afterward. Like many writers, he didn't really know what he thought until his conclusions emerged through the act of putting them on paper.

Gersony arrived at the Mayfair Hotel in Nairobi on March 6, 1997. He paid a visit to his old friend from his 1993 Liberia assignment, Amos Wako. "I don't understand the LRA myself, and nobody here does," he told Gersony.

Gersony thought: "Wako is the Kenyan president's right-hand man, and even he doesn't know much about the Lord's Resistance Army. I'm really going into the unknown this time."

Gersony settled in at the Shanghai Hotel in Kampala, the kind of two-star establishment to which he was accustomed from his days in Kampala thirteen years before. He was now fifty-two and his career had not witnessed the kind of vertical progression that is the normal definition of success. He had not graduated to better hotels and flying business class. But he still felt entirely fulfilled by what he did.

The U.S. Embassy was no longer the makeshift barracks-style arrangement from 1984. It was now a proper building with a cafeteria even. But the atmosphere wasn't good. The USAID mission director, Don Clark, a former Peace Corps volunteer, and the ambassador, E. Michael Southwick, a generalist who had worked all over the world, were barely on speaking terms. "What fresh hell is this!" Joe Williams, who worked under Clark, exclaimed whenever he went into a meeting, quoting the writer Dorothy Parker. This was not good for Gersony. It meant that whatever he discovered in northern Uganda might get shredded in the grinder of embassy politics. Furthermore, some USAID people in Kampala at first resisted Gersony, believing his presence there was unnecessary—"as if they were going to take the risk of traveling for weeks in northern Uganda, where the LRA was pulling people out of vehicles and disemboweling them at roadsides!" Joe Williams exclaims. But in any case, because of cables sent from Houdek, Brian Atwood, and others in

Washington, at least Ambassador Southwick greeted Gersony as though a conquering hero.

"My first impression of Gersony was of someone clear, purposeful, motivated. When he described to me his research methods, I said to myself, 'He's going to get himself killed in this region of child soldiers and a drunken national army,'" Southwick recalls in his soft, laid-back voice.

The other key character in the U.S. Embassy was George Colvin, the political counselor, one of those area specialists from an earlier age (his specialty was the Acholis of northern Uganda) who brought a genuine love of subject to his job. Colvin was a portly look-alike of Hercule Poirot in the 1974 film *Murder on the Orient Express*, starring Albert Finney. "Colvin was a real eccentric, unusual for the Foreign Service, which prizes conformity," a colleague says. Colvin practically put his arms around Gersony and told him in his typical, memorable way, "The Acholis provide what little yeast there is in a slack-doughed Ugandan parliament." Colvin immediately liked Gersony simply because Gersony was hungry to understand and willing to travel for weeks in the place under question. He wasn't the ninetieth person doing a study on some subject, but the first. And he would be doing it firsthand, like a newspaper reporter. The Ugandan foreign minister, Martin Aliker, an ethnic Acholi, confided to Gersony that the average white person in an embassy in Africa only gets to know three Africans: "his houseboy, his driver, and office messenger."

Joe Williams and George Colvin arranged meetings with everyone in the Ugandan capital relevant to Gersony for his trip north, whether humanitarian aid workers or Ugandan military and security officials. Gersony was told the heroic story of Sister Rachele (Raquel) Fassera of St. Mary's College Catholic boarding school, who, the previous October, had confronted the Lord's Resistance Army after its soldiers had abducted 150 girls (ages eight to sixteen), and got the LRA to release 120 of them. But outside of a spotlight on an event here, or an insight about the Nilotic Acholis there, nobody in Kampala had a comprehensive picture of the state of battle and the human rights situation in the entire north of the country. Once again, despite the illusion of knowledge, there is no substitute for *being there*.

"I was going north alone. I absolutely needed a top-flight person to travel with," Gersony explains.

"Joe, I need a long meeting with the head of the embassy motor pool," Gersony told Williams. It was something that no American FSO usually does. For FSOs, the embassy motor pools represent minimal, transactional business. Most FSOs viewed drivers as servants practically. But Gersony was aware that this would be his most important meeting in Kampala, and he treated the motor pool chief like a high official, a true expert, addressing him very politely and formally. "This is what my work is all about, this type of one-on-one," Gersony observes. After all, the condition of the roads in northern Uganda, the prevalence of land mines—nobody knew.

"Here's what I need in a driver," Gersony began the meeting. "I need an expert mechanic, also someone who inspires confidence at roadblocks, someone who can react instantly, someone who can be my own security officer, preferably with a military background. The actual driving is the least important thing."

Gersony interviewed a number of drivers. He finally settled on Ben Bamulumbye. Ben was tall, with a shaved head. He was on the thin side, but sinewy and very strong, with a deep, authoritative African voice and a military bearing. He had been a driver in the Ugandan army: not the kind of person you wanted to fool around with. He and Gersony would cover three thousand miles together in a silver Mitsubishi Pajero.

"I was curious about him," Ben says of Gersony. "I never met someone from far away who said matter-of-factly that he needed to go to this very dangerous region where even government soldiers were afraid to go. And I never met someone like him again."

Before leaving Kampala, Gersony called his mother from one of those bulky satellite phones in an empty room in the embassy.

"I will never forget you. I love you. I love you. I love you," his mother told him three times.

It was the end of his mother's struggle to remember anything: the last real conversation they ever had together.

The next day Gersony and Ben left for the unknown.

Going north, they first passed through the Luwero Triangle, which Gersony knew in the bad old days of mass murder in 1984, thirteen years before. Now the place was teeming with people bringing produce to market, with bustling fertilizer and hardware shops everywhere. "Everyone was buying and selling. The ghost towns had had a rebirth." There were walls of guinea bananas on tall stalks, which the pair stocked up on. Gersony, with his weak stomach, practically lived on them, along with the rice and potatoes that he and Ben bought locally. "Bob only ate once a day anyway," Ben recalls.

When six hours later they reached Gulu in northwestern Uganda, they stayed at the Acholi Inn, an old-fashioned British establishment with columns, a vast lawn, and shade trees, for $23 per night. In Kitgum, to the east of Gulu, they stayed at Sarah's hotel for $9, and in Moyo, to the west of Gulu, at the B Complex for $4.50. These places, all relatively close to the Sudanese border, were the height of luxury. Elsewhere they slept in huts equipped with a cot or two. In Gulu the paved road had ended, and they realized that no place was safe. The Lord's Resistance Army, the most sadistic of African guerrilla bands, had patrols everywhere. There was no security, no communications. Their single side band (SSB) radio didn't even work. You could be at the wrong place at the wrong time anywhere on this trip.

The payoff was that every word Gersony heard was fresh. These were not people who had spoken to other visitors and NGOs beforehand—there hadn't been any. When you're out on the edge, the encounters are that much more rewarding. "And Bob was such a good listener. He never showed fear. He was always writing in his notebook, and each night he was planning whom he wanted me to find in order to interview the next day," Ben explains.

During six weeks of travel through a sprawling region that the Ugandan government neither controlled nor had specific information about, Gersony interviewed roughly three hundred people in twenty-four towns, half of them in Gulu and Kitgum, and the rest in the villages of West Nile Province, on the other side of the Albert Nile, the far northwest of Uganda where Idi Amin had come from. His main source of help was the Uganda branch of the American relief charity World Vision: a thoroughly efficient, tightly run outfit staffed completely by Ugandans.

"I felt a real explicit trust, a bond, with the people I spoke to," who were mainly all Acholis. "They hated the Ugandan leader, Yoweri Museveni [who was a Bantu southerner]. But they also hated the Acholi-dominated Lord's Resistance Army. They were caught in the middle between an unsympathetic government and crazed mass murderers. That was the anguish of northern Uganda."

But, as Gersony learned, there was a ghost that haunted Acholiland: the atrocities that Acholi soldiers themselves knew they had committed under former Ugandan leader Milton Obote in the Luwero Triangle, which Gersony had documented more than a decade earlier, when over 100,000 civilians were killed.[2] To wit, in a 1987 Easter homily, Msgr. Cipriano Kihangire, the Catholic bishop of Gulu and Kitgum, admonished his own Acholi parishioners:

> Many [of you] joined the army with the hope of getting rich overnight, and were used by unscrupulous political leaders who sent you to carry out "operations," which involved atrocious acts of violence against civilians, including children and women . . .[3]

Collective guilt was tied in with internecine tribal politics. The Acholis had wantonly killed their southern enemies, and nobody in Acholiland could deny it. Yet, as Gersony found out, it was easier to get individual Acholis to talk about the crimes of Museveni or even the Acholi-led Lord's Resistance Army than about their own sins, as though their sullen hatred of Museveni and the LRA were indirect ways to excuse their guilt.

Yet there was a very specific ghost now exacting revenge upon the land: the ghost of a brutally raped and mutilated woman, whose fetus had also been torn out of her. It was a crime that happened by the Karuma Bridge at the Victoria Nile in southeastern Gulu province, perpetrated in 1986 by Acholi soldiers fleeing north from Museveni's newly victorious army. When the woman's relatives found her, according to the story, they sacrificed a black cow or bull at the site, burning it, then deliberately blowing the ashes all around, and vowing revenge.[4]

This specific ghost was the face not just of guilt, but of humiliation. The Acholis constituted a legendary warrior class under the British,[5] and yet they had been defeated in the 1980s by Museveni's Maoist-style army consisting of hordes of child soldiers. Museveni, by delaying his entry into Kampala month after month, had captured the Ugandan capital only when his forces became overwhelming. He had outsmarted the Acholis as well as outfought them, and they knew it.

Then there was economics. Losing control of the army to Museveni meant losing thousands of jobs, so that a third of Acholi families lost the bulk of their cash income. The defeated Acholi soldiery escaped to Sudan seething mad, warning people throughout northern Uganda that Museveni's forces were coming to kill them.

"But the hundreds of people I interviewed in isolation all gave me a different story!" Gersony exclaims while recounting all this history—a history I also knew well as a reporter in Uganda. "I found little evidence that Museveni's army had committed atrocities." Gersony goes on, now delving into the minutiae of Ugandan history and tribal politics. He periodically looks toward the ceiling to make a point, as though in prayer. I have to remind myself that he could also go into such excruciating detail about each of the literally dozens of other countries where he has worked around the world. His knowledge base is both horizontally vast and vertically profound.

Listen to him:

"In all my interviews I could extract only one incident regarding a crime committed by Museveni's army: Namu-okora in northeastern Kitgum. Acholi forces had been sweeping into the area in August 1986. There was a group called FEDEMU [Federal Democratic

Movement of Uganda], a southern Baganda, anti-Obote group temporarily aligned with Museveni—which a few months earlier had
actually been aligned with the Acholis themselves," Gersony explains, pumped with excitement. "Armed FEDEMU troops had captured forty-four civilians and mowed them down when they escaped
off a truck. Museveni then had these soldiers arrested."

He continues:

"'What atrocities has Museveni committed?' I always asked the
people I interviewed. 'Namu-okora,' they always responded. 'What
else?' I asked. They just held their chins and shook their heads. They
couldn't name any. But all these Acholis in the north still hated Museveni, who was a southern Banyankole."

Above every other fear he had in northern Uganda was the fear of
encountering the Lord's Resistance Army, which throughout the area
set the model for mindless cruelty, with a distinct Khmer Rouge element. In Lokung, near the Sudanese border in Kitgum in January
1997, the LRA hacked and clubbed to death over four hundred civilians, purposely leaving a few survivors to tell the story. Bob and Ben
were always within several miles of LRA patrols, especially when
they traveled along the Sudanese and Congolese borders.

Indeed, in all of these six weeks of reporting and traveling in the
LRA-ravaged north of the country, there was the fact of Gersony's
own fear. He remembers how his driver, Ben, once noticing an LRA
patrol in the flat distance, quickly executed a U-turn back to Kitgum
town. "For someone from the outside like me—the only white face in
the region—you never really knew who was who—who you could
trust. People would come with their blankets to sleep each night outside the ramshackle hospitals out of fear of what might happen to
them back in their villages. The tension never ceased. There were a
lot of nights of not sleeping, of hearing what seemed like suspicious
noises. Never mind the actual danger, you scared yourself to death."

Except that, according to Ben, Gersony never once expressed or
emanated fear. He always kept his roiling emotions buried, making
them that much worse.

Gersony recalls Father Carlos Rodriguez, a Spanish priest of the

Comboni missionary movement, who lived alone without security on the outskirts of Kitgum. Gersony spent hours with him, speaking in Spanish about the Acholi past and mindset. "Missionaries often know what is going on. They can be the best people to talk to, and get information from. They have a knowledge base missing in world capitals and even in foreign embassies." Observing the selflessness of the young Father Rodriguez, Gersony felt a momentary pang of guilt: for being a parasite among people who made in a month less than what he made in an hour interviewing them, earning a living on the back of their suffering.

Finally, Gersony returned to Kampala.

In the two-star Shanghai Hotel, he had one of the longest hot showers of his life. He had his laundry done and enjoyed spaghetti Bolognese in the hotel restaurant. Then he went to the U.S. Embassy to see Joe Williams, more as a friend from the outside world than as someone he had to brief. Nevertheless, Gersony had come back after six weeks in the field with a wealth of insights and information. A few years later the Lord's Resistance Army would constitute a cottage industry for a subculture of academics and human rights workers, some of whom would critique Gersony's eventual report at the edges. But he was virtually the first *inside* the region.

Rested up, he went around Kampala trying to get dates, times, and all sorts of other factual backup for the stories he had heard in the field. "Now I had questions to ask that I didn't have before." The next stage was to brief the FSNs, the Foreign Service Nationals, at the U.S. Embassy: these were some of the smartest Ugandans around, and their memories were long-term; they were the most likely to catch his mistakes. Finally, he briefed Ambassador Michael Southwick and political counselor George Colvin for four hours. Colvin, the Hercule Poirot look-alike, though the resident expert on the Acholis, did not feel threatened by Gersony's newly acquired knowledge: he was thrilled, in fact. They both arranged for Gersony to brief the entire diplomatic corps in Kampala. This was not the 1980s, Gersony's first foray in Uganda, when the British High Commission dominated the local diplomatic scene. Now the United States Embassy was *it*.

The local diplomats responded well to the brief, except for the French ambassador, François Descoueyte, who kept challenging Gersony, accusing him of exaggerating the crimes of the Lord's Resistance Army and minimizing Museveni's own bad behavior.[6] The French, keep in mind, as backers of the genocidal Hutu regime in Rwanda up through 1994, were opponents of the Anglophone Tutsi leader Paul Kagame and Kagame's former comrade in arms, Yoweri Museveni in Uganda. Gersony's worldview was different. He saw Museveni as a flawed dictator who nevertheless had to contend with grotesque butchers and mass murderers within his own country, making for a moral distinction that the French didn't see.

Ambassador Southwick thought Gersony's report was "terrific." On Friday evening, June 28, 1997, Gersony, accompanied by Southwick, went to a government lodge outside Kampala to deliver the entire multihour brief to Museveni.

Museveni sat on a slightly raised platform, facing the two chairs arranged for the American visitors. "You are the one who worked on the Luwero Triangle with Mr. Elliott [Abrams]," Museveni said, very pleased, as he greeted Gersony. It had been Gersony's reporting on the Obote regime's atrocities in the Luwero Triangle that played a part in bringing Museveni to power.

Gersony's brief included criticisms of Museveni's own national army in northern Uganda. Museveni interjected, "I have not done a good job of stopping the stealing [by the army], but I have stopped the [army's] killing."

When Gersony followed up, saying that the national army was insufficiently motivated to go after the LRA and related bandit groups, Museveni said, "Must I move up to Gulu full-time [to encourage my forces]?"

Museveni's problem was typical of the developing world, where institutions were either nonexistent or didn't function well, so that the leader in the capital gives orders that are not followed through on. It is the very failure of institutions that encourages strongmen to emerge in the first place, even as such strongmen can inhibit the growth of institutions: a classic dilemma.

When Gersony told Museveni that "people in the north blame you as much as the LRA for the chaos," Museveni responded, "I need peace there. I do not need their votes."

Gersony recommended that South Africa, Switzerland, and Italy form a panel of inquiry to investigate the violence in northern Uganda.[7] Museveni agreed. However, the panel would ultimately never be formed because of bureaucratic slow-rolling in Europe. "Dealing with the Europeans can be like jumping into a pot of glue," Southwick observes. As Gersony recommended, though, Museveni did sponsor an amnesty for all LRA soldiers who willingly gave up their fight for control and power in their region.

In a cable sent to all African and European posts, in addition to U.N. ambassador Bill Richardson and USAID administrator Brian Atwood, Ambassador Southwick wrote that "Gersony has stripped away much of the cant, disinformation, and distortion which has accompanied" discussions of the situation in northern Uganda.[8]

Back in Washington, Gersony briefed everyone at high levels at State, USAID, and the National Security Council.[9] The National Security Council wrote to Southwick on July 25 that Gersony's northern Uganda briefings "have been the stuff of legends."

Finally, Gersony paid a courtesy call on the Washington-based vice president for World Vision, Andrew Natsios, whose humanitarian organization had been so helpful to Gersony in his field research. Natsios already knew and had a high opinion of Gersony from the latter's assessment of a slum neighborhood in Panama in the early months of 1990, in the wake of the U.S. invasion to depose Manuel Noriega. Natsios drank up Gersony's information like few in Gersony's experience had done. He found Gersony methodical in the extreme, analyzing large numbers of interviews in a way that filtered out all ideological and philosophical assumptions, whether good or bad. "Too many contractors tell you what you want to hear, but this guy was someone you could actually trust," Natsios explains, adding

Andrew Natsios, administrator of the U.S. Agency for International Development in the George W. Bush administration, who used Gersony to investigate crises in North Korea, Nepal, and Iraq.

that "in place of the bohemian leftists who often populate NGO ranks," Gersony appealed to his own sensibilities, which were skeptical, somewhat right of center, and internationalist.

Natsios would go on to become the go-to guy on the Lord's Resistance Army in the NGO community. Gersony could not have known it at the time, but after George W. Bush became president in the wake of the Florida recount, he would appoint Andrew Natsios as the new USAID administrator to replace Brian Atwood, a Clinton appointee. Gersony had just set himself up for continued employment in the younger Bush era.

The result of Gersony's efforts was a 107-page study, *The Anguish of Northern Uganda: Results of a Field-Based Assessment of the Civil Conflicts in Northern Uganda,* submitted to the United States Embassy and the USAID Mission in Kampala in August 1997. It was the most comprehensively detailed and richly textured piece of analysis and area expertise that Gersony had written to date in his career. The "Gersony reports" about Mozambique and Rwanda may have been far more famous because of the controversies they stirred up, but it is the lesser-known reports, about Ethiopia and Somalia, and especially about northern Uganda, that were the gems of his particular self-invented genre at this point. They reveal an indefatigable willingness to travel for weeks at a time, covering over three thousand miles, in some of Africa's most dangerous and rugged areas, while producing a dry, dispassionate analysis about the complexity of what was going on there. Journalists can regularly outdo him when it comes to the style and drama of the writing, but no journalist can surpass him when it comes to the clinical objectivity and sheer strength of the research, in which, in this case, he interviewed hundreds in the field.

The Gersony report about northern Uganda begins with detailed maps covering the area's population, topography, and ethnicity, buttressed by tables and historical timelines, all of which he drew and assembled on his own. Then comes an encyclopedic backgrounder on the landscape and history of the Acholi-dominated districts of Gulu and Kitgum, including such things as rainfall and cattle production, which concludes with a description of the fighting in the Luwero Triangle to the south, that Gersony had reported on thirteen years earlier, in 1984; and how the Nilotic Acholis from northern Uganda, who had made up much of Milton Obote's forces, never really got over their defeat at the hands of Yoweri Museveni's National Resistance Army (NRA), made up of Baganda, Banyarwanda, and Banyankole from southern Uganda. For the younger Gersony, the Luwero Triangle had been strictly a human rights issue. Now that he was older and on a different assignment, he explored how the military defeat of Obote's forces in Luwero meant the loss of power, money, and status for the Acholi fighters and their families. Rather than feeling depressed about the fact that he was back in the same country doing the same sort of granular research, still as a freelance contractor for the U.S. government, he exulted in it, happy to be in the field instead of behind a desk. He was like the best foreign correspondents in this regard, the kind who consider coming back to the home office in whatever capacity a demotion.

From an empathetic study of the Acholi predicament, he introduces the exotic character of Alice Auma, the spirit medium or messenger—hence "Lakwena." He describes Alice Lakwena's miraculous conversion during forty days spent in the Nile waters near Murchison Falls, and how she introduced magic into the Acholi cause—using shea oil against bullets, transforming stones into grenades, singing Christian hymns before battle—in a respectful rather than a condescending manner. He writes about how she led her forces south on a long march all the way to the shores of Lake Victoria, close to Kampala.

For Alice in Gersony's telling is merely a symptom of how desperate and demoralized the Acholis had become, especially given the almost total loss of their cattle herds because of raiding from NRA forces and NRA-aligned Karamojong rustlers, which constituted an economic devastation. "For the Acholis," Gersony explains, "the cattle herds were their milk, their meat, the dowry for their daughters, their health and retirement insurance, their *identity*. They talk about the Karamojong raids, with tears in their eyes, in a way that they don't even talk about the machete-inflicted slaughter of children in the course of the chaos in the north."

Here Gersony introduces a cousin of Alice, Joseph Kony, who also claimed to be a spirit medium and who revived her movement when it was close to collapse after she was wounded in a battle and took refuge in Kenya. "It is sometimes reported that Kony is a former Catholic catechist," Gersony writes. "An authoritative source indicates this is inaccurate. Kony's father was a Catholic catechist, his mother an Anglican. His brother is believed to have been a witch doctor; upon his brother's death, Kony believed he inherited his brother's powers."[10] (Gersony remains this nuanced and detailed throughout.)

Kony, who in the late 1980s began fighting and leading the Acholis against the southern-based Ugandan regime of Yoweri Museveni, formed the Lord's Resistance Army (LRA), which came into its own following a breakdown in negotiations with the Museveni regime in 1994. But it was also the end of the Cold War that in an indirect way helped Kony. The collapse of communism and the Soviet Union removed the ballast from Mengistu Haile Mariam's Marxist regime in Ethiopia. This weakened the Mengistu-allied Sudan People's Liberation Army in southern Sudan, a feared enemy of Joseph Kony.[11] Kony's Lord's Resistance Army henceforth began the massive abduction of youngsters, whom it forced to fight in its ranks, all the while using land mines and other weapons to destroy schools and other civilian facilities. This soon became a war of the Acholis against the Acholis, in which Museveni's regime in Kampala, employing brutal realpolitik, was deliberately hesitant to intervene. Kony was, in part, motivated by rage: the rage of being deserted by his own ethnic constituency, which was less militant than he was. Gersony separates the LRA attacks into different categories of horror, and provides exhaustive descriptions of "signal incidents" in its campaign of terror, with large numbers of women and children shot, hacked, and clubbed to death—hundreds, thousands of them. To save themselves, northern Uganda's civilians began sleeping in underground holes and caves, a practice called *alup* in the Luo dialect. Gersony next provides a table of displaced families by region and circumstances for their displacement. He writes that the war is "hopeless," since the Lord's Resistance Army is fighting in isolation and has no possibility of attaining power; nor does it have a political program or ideology.[12] It was an expression of pure anarchy, in other words.

Gersony's report arrived fourteen years before the name of Joseph Kony and the atrocities of the Lord's Resistance Army became infamous in the United States, with social media all of a sudden in 2011 demanding Kony's capture.

But while the war in northern Uganda appeared hopeless in 1997, Gersony was not. He ends his report with page after page of proposals for providing "seeds and tools for agricultural reactivation," for "school reconstruction," for "short-term cash employment," for improving unsurfaced farm-to-market roads, undertaking dam repairs, and so forth.[13] He would never succumb to fatalism.

Gersony's report fundamentally shifted the moral responsibility of the northern Uganda conflict from Museveni to Joseph Kony's Lord's

Resistance Army, where it henceforth stayed.[14] Kony would later deny all charges against him in an interview in 2006 with the German journalist Mareike Schomerus, conducted near the border of Sudan and the Democratic Republic of the Congo.[15] But the interview revealed a figure given to incoherence and gibberish, unable to articulate a specific program for the people he claimed to represent. As Gersony points out, nearly all of the displaced persons ran to Museveni's lines, as much as they distrusted him, while none of the displaced Acholis ran across the Sudan border to the LRA's side. The Acholis truly voted with their feet.

Some academics continued to criticize Gersony for supposedly demonizing the Lord's Resistance Army. Gersony responds:

"Cutting people's ears off and forcing children to kill their parents cannot be justified even indirectly as a political statement. Doing that takes cultural relativism to an extreme. If the Lord's Resistance Army does not constitute barbarism, what does?"

From El Salvador to Ecuador and Colombia, by Way of Africa
1997–2002 and 2008–2009

The Beakless Chickens

Gersony returned to New York from Uganda in September 1997 and his immediate concern was his mother, who could not hold a coherent conversation. Nevertheless, he went for a walk with her every day in Central Park, as well as regularly taking her out to lunch. But he was back home only a few weeks when Bill Garvelink called from USAID with a bread-and-butter assignment for Bob and Cindy.

Africa was exploding with crises, both man-made and climate-related. Bill wanted to decentralize decision-making by setting up a regional office in Africa, quasi-independent from Washington. USAID's Office for Foreign Disaster Assistance simply had to evolve from being a mom-and-pop shop in Washington dealing with plastic jugs and tents for refugee camps to a more efficiently managed bureaucracy pivotally improving countries in varying degrees of chaos: this was the mindset at a time when the United States was still in a position of unchallenged power worldwide, and thus felt a particular responsibility to better the condition of humanity as a whole.

Everyone knew that there was only one place to locate such a regional office: Nairobi, Kenya, because of its level of development and excellent air connections. But this was the U.S. government. Thus, Bob and Cindy still had to justify such a decision for the bureaucracy and figure out what such an office would specifically do and how it would be staffed. They traveled to Geneva, Nairobi, and several other

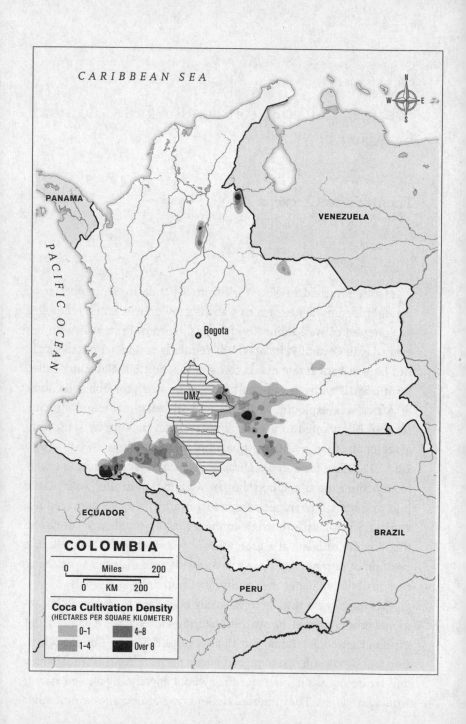

CARIBBEAN SEA

PANAMA

PACIFIC OCEAN

VENEZUELA

Bogota

DMZ

ECUADOR

BRAZIL

PERU

COLOMBIA

0   Miles   200

0   KM   200

Coca Cultivation Density
(HECTARES PER SQUARE KILOMETER)

0–1   4–8

1–4   Over 8

African capitals, interviewing upwards of 150 diplomats and human-itarian field staffers. "It helped pay the bills," Gersony says with a shrug, admitting that this was one of those big-picture assignments where the bureaucracy wastes the public's money. However, Bob and Cindy did eventually recommend the establishment of a cadre of For-eign Service Nationals (FSNs) for the entire continent, locally em-ployed Africans stationed at U.S. embassies who could serve as experts and continuity points for the revolving door of American of-ficials who would be coming and going for years to come.

The Nairobi office was eventually established, but not the FSN corps. Many USAID officials in Washington did not want to cede any central control, and especially balked at giving local Africans any kind of real influence over U.S. assistance policy in Africa. It was a frus-trating, "nothing" assignment.

• • •

By March of the next year Bob and Cindy had completed all the reports related to the Africa assessment. In November, Garvelink
phoned again. Could Bob and Cindy leave immediately for Central
America?

From October 22 through November 9, 1998, Hurricane Mitch
had moved through the region, the second-deadliest Atlantic hurricane on record. The damage from high winds was actually minimal,
but because the storm moved so slowly, it dropped seventy-five inches
of rain—the height of a six-foot-three-inch person—on Nicaragua
and Honduras. There were thousands of fatalities. Once on the
ground, Bob and Cindy split up. She was assigned to Nicaragua and
he to El Salvador, where there was comparatively little damage. Nevertheless, after a week in the field, Gersony reported that thousands
of wells had been contaminated by dead animals floating in the debris. By December he had gotten a project started for under $1 mil-
lion, administered by CARE, to decontaminate wells and build low
walls around them to prevent future storm damage.

Cindy's experience in Nicaragua was more dramatic. She had witnessed multitudes of people with barely any clothes: huddled in
abandoned schools, wet, shivering, with no blankets or any kind of
cover. However, Paul Bell, the head of the USAID disaster assistance
response team based in San José, Costa Rica, believed that the hurricane emergency was nearly over and therefore Nicaragua did not
require more substantial assistance. Bell was all about building up
national capacity in each country, rather than dissipating money on
emergencies, and was actually ahead of his time in this regard. He
had a reputation as an outspoken, somewhat eccentric, quasi-
religious character in humanitarian circles (he was the son of missionaries), and his word mattered. He was known as *Don Pablo* ("Don
Paul") and *El Jefe*, "the boss" in Spanish, "a dense planet around
which many moons circled," in the words of one USAID official. Bell
knew almost every head of state in the greater Central American region and had semi-independent status within USAID, by virtue of
the success of his many training programs. He, Fred Cuny, and Bob

Gersony were "the three iconic figures in relief assistance," according to James Fleming, the USAID division director for disaster response. Yet the Clinton administration, nervous about the Hispanic vote, dispatched First Lady Hillary Clinton to Honduras and El Salvador in mid-November, where she promised $621 million in continuing emergency aid and reconstruction funds for Central America, to include the use of American troops and helicopters. When Paul Bell and others persisted in wanting to scale down the emergency mission despite what the first lady had publicly promised, USAID administrator Brian Atwood—a friend of the Clintons—reportedly stormed into the Office of Foreign Disaster Assistance in the State Department building, demanding acquiescence.

Gersony was back in Washington by this time and learned something important from this bureaucratic food fight:

The various branches of USAID—the Office of Foreign Disaster Assistance, the disaster assistance response team, and so on—made up of liberal humanitarian State Department types, did not always accept guidance from their higher-ups, in this case from the USAID administrator and the White House itself, despite the fact that this philosophically liberal bureaucracy was dealing with a liberal Democratic administration. "Would it probably be worse with a Republican president?" Gersony thought to himself. Moreover, all this came on the heels of USAID's success in Bosnia, where the agency was able to get basic reconstructions started in the immediate aftermath of the Dayton Accords. But that was part of the problem, he realized. The USAID bureaucrats operating in Central America did not share in the success of the Europe division in Bosnia led by Tim Knight, and were doubly jealous because Bosnia had been garnering all of the media attention for years on end by now. This lack of an effective bureaucratic chain of command and teamwork across USAID and the State Department was like a cancer metastasizing in the government, another indirect outcome of the end of the Cold War and the end of the discipline that the Cold War had enforced. As Gersony would learn firsthand a few years later, it was to have devastating consequences for U.S. policy in post-invasion Iraq.

Indeed, the experience of Hurricane Mitch was prologue for what Gersony would find in Baghdad. Hurricane Mitch had identified a lack of discipline within the State Department and USAID that in Iraq would help facilitate the Pentagon's takeover of reconstruction there—to a horrendous result.

But Gersony wasn't in Washington long.

Because half of the disaster relief and reconstruction money that Mrs. Clinton had promised was to be spent in Honduras, Bob and Cindy were ordered back there to do an assessment. In the 1980s, Bob had worked in southern Honduras investigating the Colomoncagua refugee camp and later in eastern Honduras on the contra issue, while Cindy had worked for years on neighboring Nicaragua's Atlantic coast. They now spent more than five weeks driving 4,000 miles, interviewing 460 farmers, cattlemen, and laborers in 90 villages in central Honduras, between December 1998 and April 1999. It was filthy, hot, and humid everywhere, with roads destroyed by landslides and huge chasms where bridges had once stood. At least there were no sensitive political or human rights issues to deal with. It was yet another bread-and-butter assignment, and the results were completely undramatic. They learned that few jobs had been lost in the agro-industry sector because of the hurricane. Seasonal workers for the melon and banana harvests were out of work for up to a year, but were receiving food baskets from their erstwhile employers. Three-quarters of the people in displaced persons centers were still working at their day jobs. The situation was simply not severe enough to warrant the U.S. government spending $50 million on temporary jobs and so on. In a way, it was a disappointment for Bob and Cindy, who would have liked to spend a few years running a long-term reconstruction program in Honduras, much like what they had done on Nicaragua's Atlantic coast. Earlier in his career, Bob had wanted to escape Central America; now, after years in Africa, he didn't mind returning there. But he had to be honest about the fact that he wasn't needed, even though USAID had already been sold on the story of a monumental hurricane catastrophe in Honduras—but yet, once again, on close inspection, things on the ground were not quite what they seemed from afar. The real hurricane destruction was mainly on the farm-to-market roads. So, as Gersony told Brian Atwood in Washington: "Don't send food or create thousands of temporary jobs, just fix roads and bridges and stabilize the hillsides on which the roads are situated by planting indigenous, deep-rooted grasses." He then gave the USAID administrator a long list of all the bridges and roads that needed to be repaired, which would keep people employed for years.[1]

Bob and Cindy would spend the spring of 1999 in Albania dealing with the refugee crisis brought about by the Kosovo War. This was a period when two other of his assignments fell through or were aborted due mainly to bureaucratic foot-dragging: one in Gaza, and another in the desert region of Turkana in northwestern Kenya, where Gersony blew three tires out of his car and worked up a sweat at seven each morning because of the intense heat while interviewing over a hundred people, before the budget ran out at the end of 1999 without him even writing a report on the trip. He also withdrew from a USAID project in Cuba in this general time frame simply out of fear he would be arrested as a spy by the communist regime there. Gersony began to feel that he was washed up. Months of depression followed.

Then in June 2000 he got a cold call from Hilda "Bambi" Arellano, the USAID mission director in Quito, Ecuador. She told him that the United States was about to embark on Plan Colombia, an ambitious nation-building effort to rid Colombia of cocaine-smuggling guerrilla armies. As she explained, there was a fear that the spray-killing of the coca fields in southern Colombia, combined with military operations against the left-wing FARC (Revolutionary Armed Forces of Colombia), would trigger a mass movement of people across the border into northern Ecuador. Because of Colombia's very size and population, the United States organized its approach to the region around Colombia policy, but this also meant that the effects of Plan Colombia would likely be momentous in adjacent Ecuador.

"There is no government presence in the north [of Ecuador by the Colombian border]. We have no idea what is going on there. We need a complete assessment," Bambi told Gersony over the phone, adding: "I've got $8 million to spend for a start, and I want to know exactly how we're going to use it. I'm sick of the old-boy network in USAID. We're not pouring this money out the window just because it's there. I want sound, useful projects that make sense."

"This woman is just like Janet Ballantyne!" Gersony thought. "The drought's over. My life is beginning again."[2]

Cindy was pregnant by this time. Nevertheless, Gersony immediately left for Washington and made the rounds of experts. Tom Cornell, the head of USAID for South America, lamented: "The State Department sees USAID as the development agency that looks down the pike twenty years but can't get anything done in real time." Message: Get something done in northern Ecuador. "What should I get done in northern Ecuador?" Gersony, in turn, asked a USAID environmental adviser, who answered: "I don't see what else can be done, other than to develop natural-resource-based governance of a type that targets the most vulnerable areas." Political science jargon, Gersony thought. But as he knew, you had to talk to people in Washington before your trip, so that they would listen to you when you came back.

QUITO, ECUADOR. The country's capital, an exquisite and rustic overgrown town with amazingly clear, golden air is nestled in the mountains and surrounded by active volcanoes. Residents have to periodically sweep the volcanic ash from their house fronts. Here is a diverse population of indigenous people in a Spanish colonial setting. On the equator at 9,350 feet in elevation, it might be the greenest place on earth at such a high altitude.

He met Bambi, who in person was even more like Janet, full of no-nonsense sparkle. The same with Ambassador Gwen Clare, who told him: "We and the Ecuadorians know absolutely nothing about the north. I'll be fascinated by the results of your work." In other words, this was northern Uganda all over again. Despite the conceits

of the digital age, the world of the early twenty-first century was actually full of empty spaces on the map in terms of what was known
about them in the capital cities. Thus, as in northern Uganda, the
Ethiopian-Somali border, and other places where he had been, he felt
a bit like an explorer, since you couldn't analyze the effect of Plan
Colombia on northern Ecuador without actually going there and
finding out virtually everything about it.

He was heading into a 300-mile-long border area populated with
400,000 people, full of mosquito-ridden rivers that helped feed the
Amazon basin. "It isn't the end of the earth, but you can see it from
there," the U.S. Embassy political counselor, Peter Harding, told him.
This back of beyond was divided into three starkly different provinces, all bordering the Putumayo and San Miguel rivers that formed
the border with Colombia. In the east, as Gersony was to learn vividly
on his own, was Sucumbios: a flat, broiling hot, jungly terrain inhabited by Cofán Indians and ugly new boom-and-bust towns that lived
mainly off oil. In the center was Carchi: cool, high in the mountains,
with picturesque, hundred-year-old villages devoted to cross-border
trade. In the west was Esmeraldas, populated by Afro-Ecuadorians,
the descendants of escaped slaves.

Gersony selected a driver from the embassy car pool: Rodrigo
Viera, a stocky man in his late thirties with a shock of black hair and
a nice countenance, who, in the manner of many Ecuadorians, was
quite formal, always wearing a jacket and tie, and addressing Bob as
Señor Gersony. Gersony addressed him likewise, as Señor Viera.
They would spend six weeks together, covering over 2,500 miles on
unsurfaced roads, interviewing 160 people in 40 towns and villages:
farmers, fishermen, priests, clam diggers, local officials, and so forth.
Like his previous drivers, Señor Viera was Gersony's veritable partner, helping him find people to interview, locating where to sleep out
in the bush, making introductions in some cases, getting him everywhere in an age before GPS existed—and never getting exasperated.

The big questions that diplomats in the capital of Quito wanted
Gersony to answer were: Who were the people of northern Ecuador
loyal to? Did they feel themselves to be Ecuadorians, Colombians, or

what? Or were their identities strictly local? As Gersony discovered, the answer was both simple and complicated. Because so many had migrated to the north from the heart of the country, 100 percent identified themselves to him as Ecuadorians, who spoke with disdain about the "violent" Colombians. Yet thousands of these northern Ecuadorians seasonally migrated across the river to Putumayo in southern Colombia to pick coca leaves for the production of cocaine. And 80 percent of the commerce in Sucumbios, as Gersony learned, consisted of Colombians coming south across the border to buy fertilizer and gasoline, while occupying the hotels and restaurants and visiting the brothels. "Coca tourism," Gersony called it. "Most Colombians treat you okay unless they're drunk," a prostitute named Fanny told him. "But Colombians are very violent. They knife someone in the bar, and you just have to keep dancing like you didn't notice."

Though he would find no overriding theme linking his adventures in northern Ecuador, the economy of this borderland was very precarious. For example, when right-wing paramilitaries battled the FARC in Putumayo, coca production suffered. Almost everyone Gersony interviewed told him they were afraid of a new, self-reproducing bacteria introduced by the Americans to destroy the coca crop. But it would also destroy all kinds of vegetation and could be carried across the border into Ecuador by wind, insects, rain, and people's clothes. There was no such bacteria, but the FARC and local left-wing elements were spreading these rumors. How to stop them? Gersony wondered.

One day in Lago Agrio, the provincial capital, Gersony had Señor Viera drive him up a hill to see the bishop of Sucumbios, Msgr. Gonzalo López Marañon, whose offices were in a grand colonial church building, the most impressive in town. Msgr. López was the leading citizen of the province. He was anti-American and an advocate of Catholic liberation theology, and had also founded a civil society group in order to critique the impact on northern Ecuador of Washington's Plan Colombia. Because there were no phones in town, Gersony just walked in cold to the church offices. Each time he was told the bishop was too busy and that a certain amount of bureaucratic procedure was required to make an appointment. Finally, at 4:30 P.M. one day in early July 2000, Msgr. López agreed to meet Gersony.

As soon as Gersony walked into his office, the bishop had a coughing fit.

"Are you all right?" Gersony asked in his perfect Spanish.

"There is something sticking in my throat. Maybe it is your presence," the bishop responded.

Gersony stayed calm. He wasn't upset. Seeing the bishop was just a box he had to check for his eventual report. Gersony's only goal was to achieve the bishop's "non-opposition" to what he was doing. He engaged the bishop in conversation in Spanish. The bishop warmed up after a bit, and then surprised Gersony with what he said:

"Please do good quality work that's durable. Respect the dignity of the people. Come with goodwill in your heart and you will have support. Give people some hope. Let us remember that Señor Robert Gersony came up here and did a good job for us."

"The bishop's words reminded me of when I put the note into the Western Wall in Jerusalem, asking God to help me get it right in Bosnia," says Gersony. "I really wanted to get this right. I always sweat the details. The bishop inspired me."

Señor Viera drove Gersony in their white USAID vehicle back to his simple hotel in Lago Agrio. Gersony had a quick dinner as the sun went down and the town went black. He returned to his room. Suddenly the hotel phone began ringing by the bed table, competing with the sound of the loud air conditioner. Cindy was on the line. She had just had a sonogram. Her pregnancy was going fine, she told him.

"Oh, there's one other thing," she said before hanging up. "It's triplets."

He was at a complete loss for words. He was delighted, relieved, and absolutely terrified. He was about to turn fifty-six. He had never thought much about kids, having married so late because of all the traveling he did. He realized he didn't even know how to change a diaper.

The next morning he left Señor Viera at the dock and got into a dugout canoe for a journey of several hours eastward down the Aguarico River to where the Cofán Indians lived. The Aguarico was a narrower version of the Coco River on the Nicaraguan-Honduran border, where Cindy had been kidnapped almost four years earlier: the kind of jungle-infested river that one imagines leading to a mysterious destiny of sorts.

He knew that there was an American, Randy Borman, the son of missionaries, who had married a Cofán woman, had kids, and lived among the Indians. Borman's family occupied a thatched wooden structure on stilts above the water without even mosquito nets.

"Come in," Borman said.

In such a place, and without phones, there was obviously no need to make an appointment. Gersony reclined in a hammock and Borman sat in a chair. They talked for hours.

It got dark, and Borman pointed Gersony toward a group of cabins a few hundred yards away. "There are no snakes or scorpions, just a lot of jungle noises," Borman assured him. In one empty cabin there was a bed, a mosquito net, and a little table where Gersony put two candles. He ate from a can of tuna and tried to sleep. A huge cockroach climbed near his bed. As he got up to swat it, he tripped over a large bullfrog. He wasn't at loose ends or depressed here. He always had simple needs, and so didn't mind the lack of food and drink, or the spartan conditions. He thought about how happy Cindy would be to visit this place deep in the Ecuadorian jungle. And he thought now about his mother and father, and the cosmic wonder of the passing of the generations, as the news about the triplets was still just beginning to sink in. Thus, in the jungle dark his mind raced onward about where they would live, how their lives would change, and how he would pay for college for three children. Would he have steady work, given the handful of misfires before this assignment? His mind was thousands of miles away from where he lay in the forest, oppressed by cascading thoughts.

The following morning he continued his talk with Borman. No breakfast was offered, though Gersony rarely ate breakfast anyway. After listening to Borman discuss the failure of one NGO project

after another, Gersony asked, "Is there anything we could do here—
however small—that would actually be useful?"

"You could clear a trail, and put in guard posts and signs, around
a large forest area preserved for the Cofán people, but which is being
encroached upon and cleared by outsiders."

Gersony liked the idea. It was simple and labor-intensive, and
would thus create local jobs. It would allow USAID to work with the
indigenous people, while helping to protect the environment.

Gersony next journeyed back up the river to Lago Agrio to investigate the security situation in Sucumbíos. Señor Viera met him at the
dock in his jacket and tie. Gersony learned from the local authorities
that in the previous eight years, eighteen Americans and Canadians
had been kidnapped and held for ransom here, while four taxi drivers
were knifed to death. The police and army were useless. Often the
FARC—which the Americans were trying to defeat—came across the
border from Colombia and administered justice. An army commander admitted to him:

"Someone stole a taxi around here and killed the driver. The wife
didn't go to the authorities. She went to the FARC. Three days later
the taxi was returned, the thief had been executed, and they charged
her $200 [for the service]. People don't believe in the official justice
system . . . only the guerrillas [from over the border in Colombia] can
solve problems."

Gersony and Señor Viera went on a long trip to Puerto el Carmen
in the northeast of Sucumbíos, several days of driving on bad roads.
They met a farmer who told Gersony that his wife had given birth to
sixteen children, nine of whom had survived. The farmer chopped
down a coconut from a palm tree, quickly carved it out with a knife,
and gave Gersony a straw to slurp up the juice. Gersony can still remember how it felt as the juice coursed through his body in the ham-
mering heat. The farmer told him what everyone else did: the price
of coffee was down 35 percent, there was no work, the NGOs had accomplished nothing, and the only possibility for people was to go
north across the border to Putumayo in Colombia to work as *raspachines,* harvesting the coca crop.

Still, there were rumors everywhere about the evil being contemplated by the Americans with their self-reproducing bacteria.

And in this fetid jungle, just like in the semi-desert of the West Bank, everyone told him they needed *water:* clean water coming through pipes, with storage tanks.

That was Sucumbios.

Gersony and Señor Viera drove west up into the mountains to the province of Carchi. There, they met many traders who hated political stability: it was instability that they liked, which led to fluctuations in the values of the Ecuadorian sucre and the Colombian peso, allowing them to make a profit. The road along the Colombian border was one of the worst Gersony had experienced in all his travels, full of deep, axle-breaking ruts. It hindered commerce, security, and medical help. He next went into the area of the Awa Indians where many of the mammoth pedestrian bridges across the rivers and streams had collapsed, stranding whole communities. He crossed west into the province of Esmeraldas by the Pacific Ocean. Here was a world of generations of Afro-Ecuadorians who had escaped slavery in mines and cotton plantations in adjacent provinces and built redoubts on the hillsides called *palenques,* originally to prevent their recapture. They lived by hunting, fishing, shrimping, and digging for clams in the mangrove swamps.

In recent years the Colombians had crossed the border and introduced the African palm here, whose fruit is processed into palm oil and cooking oil. Small holdings were bought out and big African palm plantations emerged. Unemployment went down and salaries rose dramatically. Then NGO groups began lobbying the Ecuadorian government not to grant licenses for the processing plants because, as they alleged, the new plantations were eliminating the virgin forest. This made the local inhabitants furious with the NGOs.

Again, there was no real theme in northern Ecuador. The vast region's complexities both defeated and made irrelevant every ism: Marxism, realism, neoconservatism, and what-have-you. In that way, it was merely like most of the earth beyond the developed world. The only commonality among the three provinces of northern Ecuador was the hue and cry for clean water.

For Gersony it was back to the capital of Quito and a luxury hotel after many weeks of travel: a shower, laundry, sandwiches, lots of orange juice, then, for good measure, a long hot bath and—a new thing for him—answering emails from the hotel business center.

He told Bambi Arellano that he needed four hours with her.

"No problem," she said.

She had many questions, and didn't want him to skip one detail.

He began with a lengthy disquisition on northern Ecuador's history, economics, and environment, before descending into the minutiae of his journey.

"So what do we do with the $8 million we have to start with?" he asked out loud, rhetorically.

He then provided a list of thirty specific water and sewage projects for the area. He advised USAID to fix the border road in Carchi and repair the pedestrian bridges there. In Sucumbios he wanted the Cofán forest preserve demarcated, and a local commission set up to monitor the environmental impact of Plan Colombia, in order to dispel rumors about the self-reproducing bacteria.

"You can't send Americans to do any of this," he warned, "because they'll be kidnapped by the FARC or the paramilitaries." He recommended that USAID pay aid workers from IOM, the Geneva-based International Organization for Migration, whose South American director was Diego Beltrand, the Uruguayan lawyer who had negotiated Cindy's hostage release in Nicaragua and who knew Bambi well.

Bambi and Bob went to dinner together that night and sealed the deal.

Bambi says this about Gersony:

"Bob was so good at not projecting his experience in other countries onto northern Ecuador. Every place he went in the world was absolutely unique in his mind. He gave you this blank slate without previous assumptions or models about how the world or aid should work. In his mind, not only was northern Ecuador completely different from every place else on earth, but one part of it was completely different from another part of it. All his recommendations worked well and they worked quickly."

As it would later turn out, USAID's inspector general would report that IOM completed 38 water projects and 5 major sewage projects, and built 52 miles of roads, 8 major steel and concrete vehicular bridges, and 13 massive steel pedestrian bridges, as well as hardening 6 irrigation canals and repairing several reservoirs: benefiting 255,000 of the region's roughly 400,000 people—all with maintenance built into the cost.[3]

Back in Washington, Gersony did the usual rounds of briefings at USAID, the State Department, the National Security Council, and this time the CIA, whose own area specialists were curious about northern Ecuador. Everywhere he carried along a Nokia flip phone, awaiting Cindy's call from Columbia Presbyterian hospital in New York City, which had a special unit for multiple births.

In November 2000, Cindy Davis Gersony gave birth to three healthy children: Greg, Lizzy, and Laura. Within a week, Tony Jackson, Pierre Gassmann, and Janet Ballantyne flew across oceans to see the new babies.

Bob didn't work for the next six months.

Getting married is often not the life-changing experience that it is advertised to be, but having children is. And Gersony had three at once, all waking up at different times during the night for the first four months. What's more, Bob and Cindy had to leave their small apartment in Manhattan and close up the apartment of Bob's ninety-six-year-old mother at the same time. New York City had been Bob's base throughout his life into his midfifties. So the departure was final, traumatic. They sold both apartments and moved into a big house in the woods of Great Falls, Virginia, taking Bob's mother with them. "I had always wanted a house with trees, a bit apart from people," Gersony says.

After moving houses and being kept up at night by the kids for months, the phone rang in April 2001, almost five months after the triplets were born: perfect timing, as he really wanted to get back to work. But from now on, Gersony, always emotional, would feel a physical pain in his chest whenever he left the house on an assignment. The experience was overwhelming. For the danger never really ceased. There were relatively few others like him in the diplomatic and aid communities: a middle-aged, self-employed family man going off on his own to places like northern Uganda and northern Ecuador.

When the phone rang in April 2001 it brought very good news. USAID was still in the early phases of launching Plan Colombia, an assistance project with a $1.3 billion down payment—an unheard-of sum at the time—aimed at restoring Colombian government sovereignty over vast swaths of land controlled by drug cartels and left-wing insurgents. With so much money available, USAID wanted Gersony to visit the capitals of all the countries bordering Colombia in order to assess what the multitude of spillover effects might be, as a consequence of such a dramatic political and institutional change for this regional giant. "Finally, a junket for the first time in my life," the fifty-six-year-old Gersony quickly surmised, the best way to ease him into the new reality of traveling throughout the developing world with a family back home. There would be five-star hotels, all in roughly the same time zone as Cindy and the kids. The pay was good. He was forever worrying about the cost of college for the triplets. The ulterior motive of his trip as far as the State Department and USAID were concerned was for him to get all the regional U.S. embassies on board for Plan Colombia.

The dozens of interviews he conducted with diplomats and security officials in each capital revealed a familiar story. Colombia, like so many countries in this world, had remote borders where there was little or no government presence. Drug armies and smaller criminal cartels ran riot, with warehouses in the jungle for storing precursor chemicals for converting coca paste into cocaine. Colombian anarchy had already been regionalized across the country's own borders.

None of the U.S. or other embassies had a clue which group exactly controlled what area. Maps with their neat demarcations lied. It was all a mystery.

He was at home in Great Falls, Virginia, in August 2001, expecting to make another undemanding trip to South America, when he got a call: USAID needed him immediately in southern Colombia itself, near the border with Ecuador. Now things returned to normal: hardship and danger.

The terrorist attacks of September 11, 2001, did not affect his plans. Again, as when the Berlin Wall fell, the so-called new political age did not change the local realities in the plethora of places where he worked. On September 16, he flew to the Colombian capital of Bogotá: a clean, fashionable, and sophisticated city with cool temperatures in the mountains, home to great restaurants and the finest Spanish spoken in Latin America. Colombia was a country of high standards, as I know from my own experience there: it has magnificent cities, good civil administration, and super efficiency—especially in the meticulous planning and cruelty of the murders and kidnappings outside the capital.

The background to what Gersony had to do was simple. The Colombian president who was about to leave office, Andrés Pastrana Arango, had given the FARC (the Revolutionary Armed Forces of Colombia) a *zona de despeje,* a demilitarized zone, in which to live—as a concession in the hopes of arriving at a peace agreement with the group. It backfired. In fact as it turned out, President Pastrana had given the FARC guerrillas their own country larger than Switzerland in south-central Colombia, which the FARC made into the biggest drug-dealing center in the world: a place where it brought in military trainers from the Irish Republican Army (IRA), and which became the headquarters for holding hundreds of hostages.

A desperate Pastrana then conceived Plan Colombia with another president about to leave office, Bill Clinton. The heart of the plan was to provide security in the vast jungly reaches of the country, eradicate coca fields, and provide the farmers and peasants with substitute crops. The most difficult area was Putumayo, located between the *zona de despeje* just to the north and the Ecuadorian border just to the south. Putumayo had 1 percent of Colombia's population and 2 percent of its land area, but 50 percent of its coca production. It was a place of rampant murder and kidnapping. That's where Gersony was headed.

In Washington, Jim Mack, the principal deputy assistant secretary of state in the narcotics bureau—an endearing, yet absolutely direct guy with no tolerance for diplomatic evasions—had told Gersony there were two questions that had to be answered:

- What is the psychology of the area?
- Is there any trust between the people and the government there?

Bill Brownfield, the principal deputy assistant secretary of state for the Western Hemisphere, had told Gersony:

"Nobody goes to Putumayo. We have no idea what's going on there. We're desperate for information." A refrain with which Gersony was long familiar.

Brownfield adds, decades later: "Putumayo, when Gersony went there, was really dangerous. I mean, it was a place where people regularly got whacked."

Gersony made the rounds in Bogotá. A political officer at the U.S. Embassy warned him:

"It's good having information, but it's not worth getting killed for. By the way, the FARC, which is led by psychopaths, is going to take over the crop substitution program. If you can get me the name of a single farmer who signed a voluntary eradication pact—who's going to uproot his coca to plant another kind of crop—I'll eat my hat. The odds of this working are zero."

In late September, traveling alone, Gersony boarded a commercial flight from Bogotá to Puerto Asis, the provincial capital of Putumayo. Heading south, he looked out the window: an absolutely rugged and beautiful landscape, Afghanistan with trees. Colombian chaos was to a significant extent geographically determined. The civilized cities were on the plateaus and mountaintops; the marauders were in the jungly lowlands where the Spanish had killed and enslaved the Indians. Then there were boom-and-bust cycles—centered around quinine, rubber, and coca. No real agriculture had developed and there had been no cultural accumulation of any kind. It was one, dreary history in the lowlands. "Nobody in Bogotá has any idea what is going on down there," Gersony thought to himself in the plane.

Knowing that he was stepping into a kidnapping zone, he decided he would tell everyone that he met the truth: "I work for the mission director of USAID in Bogotá, and he wants to know what you think." *They're going to find out who I am anyway, I might as well get the credit for having balls. By telling them that I work for the U.S. government, I am putting my life in their hands, and by talking to me they are putting their own lives at risk.*

The FARC and the right-wing paramilitaries were everywhere. He never really knew who he was talking to. Whereas the Lord's Resistance Army in northern Uganda were mere anarchic barbarians, southern Colombia was infested with violent organized crime syndicates, with their own armies and intelligence organizations. It was private-sector big business, and bloodcurdling. Gersony's first two drivers quit on him, a bad sign. So he had to get around completely by himself.

His hotel in Puerto Asis had no name and no security, but plenty of bedbugs. It was $20 a night, with no private bathrooms. Puerto Asis was in the southwest of Putumayo, the most intense coca-growing area in the province.

This was no way for a fifty-six-year-old man to earn a living. Every waking hour he was terrified of being kidnapped. He hardly slept. He lived with 0.25 milligram tablets of Xanax, which he popped like M&M's. He ate at burger joints, several steps in quality below American fast food. After dark there was not a soul on the streets. Since he conducted interviews from early morning till sundown, the streets were empty when he walked to dinner. He kept his head lowered, and avoided eye contact. His eyes were in a book while eating. One man shadowed him everywhere. He turned out to be from the right-wing paramilitaries. It could have been worse. At least the man wasn't from the FARC.

He went to markets and all sorts of stores in Puerto Asís and Mocoa to the north, talking to people: shopkeepers, traders, farmers, carpenters, priests, nuns, and so on. To travel outside the towns was too dangerous, and at least here, again, he fell back on his experience as a commodity trader, asking everyone detailed questions about growing coca versus growing cacao, rubber, palm oil, and hearts of palm. He may have been the first foreigner these people had ever talked to. (All the NGO staffers were local hires.) In four weeks he interviewed 160 people (he liked round numbers), 50 of whom were either coca farmers or *raspachines,* the harvesters of coca leaf, who had all come into town from the fields. It wasn't a bad sample given the security situation.

And in the course of all these interviews, Gersony put together the following synthesis of what had happened in Putumayo prior to his arrival:

In late 2000 and early 2001, private contractors working for the U.S. government had sprayed 32,000 out of 60,000 hectares of coca leaf from the air. Because the spray carried an adhesive that stuck to the leaves, the spray was absolutely effective—it was like hitting beehives with a baseball bat. The coca farmers were all in a panic, and quite a few considered moving east, deeper into the Amazon jungle basin, in order to do the backbreaking labor of clearing land to plant coca out of range of the private American contractors. Because of the recent excessive rains and right-wing paramilitary attacks on the FARC, the aerial spraying was the proverbial straw that broke the camel's back for the local coca industry. After the spraying, only 15 percent of the farmers decided to replant. But just as this eradication plan was beginning to work, on February 9, 2001, President Pastrana suddenly suspended the program. Instead, Pastrana instituted a voluntary eradication program, in which each farmer received $900 and a promise from USAID to help provide him with an alternative crop. But because Pastrana had granted the farmers a one-year

grace period, the farmers pocketed the $900 and replanted coca any-
way, this time using a new seed: Tingo Maria, from Peru, which
yields 40 percent more coca. Every farmer Gersony interviewed told
him that they now had no plans to eradicate their coca crop. These
poor farmers had done the rational thing in terms of their own self-
interest. In effect, President Pastrana had used USAID money to le-
gitimize even more coca production. (After all, Pastrana's constituents
in the major Colombian cities were concerned with common crime,
living standards, and so forth, but not specifically with coca production, which was only an American obsession, since it was in the
United States that cocaine was addicting people and undermining
society.) Nobody else but a fluent Spanish speaker with a background
in commodities like Gersony could have teased out this story, which
had further, tragicomic details:

In return for not growing coca, USAID back in 2000 had sent 50
laying hens to each of Putumayo's 1,800 poorest families, along with
a six-week supply of Purina concentrate for the hens to feed on. But
as Gersony learned, after the six weeks were over the farmers could
not afford to buy more concentrate, and had trouble finding substitute foods for these hens, since in the course of shipping the hens
south to Colombia in small cages, their beaks had to be cut off. Thus,
all these beakless hens had trouble eating anything but Purina. By
the time Gersony arrived on the scene, 80 percent of the hens were
dead.

There was more.

Because USAID had failed to take into account the loose, fragile
soils of Putumayo, all its crop substitution plans involving rubber,
cacao, and so forth had failed. *"Elefantes blancos,"* white elephants, is
how the local farmers and traders, literally laughing, kept describing
these plans to Gersony.

"Alternative development is a comedy, a farce," a nun told him.

Said one farmer:

"Cacao? Doesn't work here. Rubber? What do I do for eight years
[while the rubber trees mature]? Hearts of palm? Takes a lot of time

and work. Plantains? Let's say I plant 300 stems—who will buy them? Nobody."

Said another farmer:

"Rubber? I'll be dead before I see my money. Pepper? Nobody knows anything about it. Hearts of palm? Others have tried it, lost money, no market."

A local official summarized:

"Plan Colombia is just another bonanza [boom-and-bust cycle], like quinine, rubber, and coca."

So it went.

As in other places, in southern Colombia there was no mystery to what Gersony did. It was just a matter of going out into the field alone and asking people questions in their own language, and listening to them for hundreds of hours. "He was our secret agent, without needing to work for the intelligence community, always designing low-cost elegant solutions to problems," Mike Walsh, a USAID contracting officer, half jokes about Gersony.

Back in Bogotá, for a few days Gersony did something he had never done before and never would do afterward: he started drinking. Two Brandy Alexanders each evening in the luxury hotel—for him it was a lot. His nerves were shot after living in fear every minute of the day for weeks.

On Wednesday, November 28, 2001, he briefed Ken Ellis, the USAID mission director, and three others for an entire day to get feedback and refine his conclusions. As usual, he started with the history and geography of the area, which determined its psychology and attitude toward the central government. Putumayo was a remote and violent region where USAID was unable to send bureaucrats and its Colombian partners had proved to be incompetent, Gersony said. Nothing could be done there without security. Moreover, there was no political constituency for coca eradication. Local people thought all of USAID's efforts for crop substitution were a joke. The beakless chickens, the $900 payments, and so on were all subject to ridicule.

Colombian president Andrés Pastrana greets U.S. ambassador to Colombia Anne Patterson, who oversaw Gersony's investigative work on cocaine production in the country.

Only African palm, owing to foreign demand, might work, as it did in the case of northern Ecuador. Face it, nothing but coca could grow in the poor soils of Putumayo. USAID should do agricultural projects to the west of Putumayo, in the neighboring provinces of Nariño and Cauca, where the soils were less fragile; which, in turn, would encourage migration and lead to a better life for the farmers of the region.

There was no pushback from Ellis.

The next day Gersony briefed the U.S. Embassy's country team, headed by Ambassador Anne Patterson: a red-haired woman with a crisp manner who was as acute and forceful in intellect as she was slight in stature. Anne Patterson represented the next generation of heavy-hitting ambassadors after Deane Hinton. Born in Arkansas and educated at Wellesley, she would go on to become ambassador in

Pakistan and Egypt. She was always trusted with the big, difficult countries. She wanted granularity, every detail, from Gersony, especially about the history and geography of the region—the smart ones always did, in his experience. She appreciated the contradictions in his presentation and the critiques of the embassy's previous positions. "I'll give you another three hours tomorrow," she told him. It wasn't like she didn't know any of this. It was just that Gersony's briefing allowed her to crystallize her thoughts.

"I had doubts about the spraying beforehand, but the main thing about his briefing was his knowledge of agriculture and how crop substitution was a bust," Ambassador Patterson recalls. "Bob was totally credible. He was not a purist driven by ideology, like others in the aid and humanitarian communities. He was very practical. There's an increasing shortage of people like Bob. Nowadays, inside the bureaucracy there is immense risk-aversion, you would never risk writing a critical report anymore. What's worse is that tours are short, people less and less speak the local language, and people less and less even get out of the embassy building. Bob is from another era."

And even in those days, it was crucial that Gersony was a freelancer, uncompromised by the bureaucratic mindset.

She sent him back to Washington to immediately brief the Latin America and narcotics bureaus in the State Department. When Gersony ended his brief, Bill Brownfield, the force of nature who was the principal deputy assistant secretary of state for the Western Hemisphere, announced: "What Gersony just said, that's what we're going to do!"

Brownfield now explains: "To get disparate parts of the bureaucracy working together, I needed the voice of an independent, outside fact-checker. And rarely in my experience have I encountered such a brave explorer type, who, nevertheless, looks and sounds like an accountant. Gersony wins arguments without stridency, but by piling on data because he has seen more, done more, and collected more information than everyone else in the room combined."

Next Gersony briefed the CIA's National Intelligence Council, which the reader will hear more of in the next chapter.

Finally, Gersony saw Andrew Natsios, the George W. Bush appointee who had replaced Brian Atwood as the new administrator of USAID. A tall, voluble ethnic Greek, Natsios had been chairman of the Massachusetts Republican State Committee and had rescued the Central Artery Project (the "Big Dig") in Boston from cost overruns. He was a cerebral quick study with a fast computerized memory. Though Gersony had first impressed Natsios with his northern Uganda briefing at a time when Natsios had been the vice president of World Vision in Washington, the southern Colombia briefing solidified their relationship, which would lead to much more dramatic assignments in the future for Gersony. "Gersony became my one-man, humanitarian CIA. H-CIA, how's that?" Natsios says.

Postscript:

The moment that the conservative Álvaro Uribe Vélez replaced Andrés Pastrana as Colombian president in the summer of 2002, Gersony's recommendations began to be implemented. Whereas Pastrana had played the role of Neville Chamberlain, naïve to the point of madness when it came to the FARC, only realizing his folly at the end, Uribe, however sordid some of his right-wing paramilitary connections, played the role of Winston Churchill, going after the FARC with everything he had. Though to be fair to Pastrana, had his policy failure not been so obvious, it would have been politically impossible for Uribe to take such dramatic action so quickly.

Seven years later Gersony found himself back in Colombia. It was the fall of 2008 and the United States was soon to have a presidential transition. Bill Brownfield was now the U.S. ambassador in Bogotá, and he knew that whether Barack Obama or John McCain was elected president, new people would be storming into the State Department and USAID brandishing a different approach toward Plan Colombia than that of George W. Bush. Ambassador Brownfield wanted his own reassessment of what had been accomplished and what hadn't in order to have an answer for his new bosses, whoever they might be. Susan Reichle, the USAID mission director in Bogotá, assigned Gersony to Catatumbo in eastern Colombia, along the Venezuelan border. Catatumbo was the new Putumayo, an epicenter of coca production, the FARC guerrillas, and the right-wing death squads.

"I want you to find out why we haven't reduced coca production there, even though we've been spraying," she told Gersony. She was worried that Plan Colombia, which had already cost U.S. taxpayers billions, was still a one-size-fits-all approach, whereas each region of the sprawling country required its own carefully tailored plan.

It was worse than that.

Plan Colombia was a precursor to the fiascoes in Afghanistan and Iraq.

In Catatumbo, for example, 55,000 hectares of coca had been sprayed, even though the CIA said there were only one-third that many hectares to begin with. Something was terribly wrong.

In a world that was being united by technology, where elites believed geography had been conquered—and therefore had theories for everything—nobody in the capital of Bogotá had a shred of knowledge as to what was actually happening in the jungle a few hundred miles away. Gersony shrugged. This was normal for him.

On October 1, 2008, Gersony arrived in Cúcuta, the provincial capital of Catatumbo, located right on the border with Venezuela. At 3:30 P.M.—he will always remember the time—he was riding in a taxi from the airport to his hotel when a man on a motorcycle right in front of him calmly took out a pistol, extended his arm, aimed at another man who had one foot on the curb between two cars, and shot him in the head. Blood pooled in the road. Pedestrians kept walking as if nothing had happened. Gersony's taxi continued on its way. The taxi driver said nothing. Gersony, absolutely terrified, knew enough to stay quiet. The famous line at the end of the eponymous Hollywood film immediately came to him:

"Forget it, Jake, it's Chinatown."

He would spend two weeks in Cúcuta, a bustling commercial town on account of the gasoline, diesel, and fertilizer smuggled across the border from Venezuela, where it was all subsidized. Next, he traveled north along the border to Tibú, hitching rides with cars and on motorcycles. He had no security and no contacts. He was armed only with his fluent Spanish. He would interview 174 people by the end of the project: farmers, shopkeepers, priests, and so forth.

In Tibú he called on the local bishop, Msgr. Camilo Castrellón Pizano, at his palatial residence.

"You know, Roberto," Msgr. Castrellón said to Gersony in a powerful, succinct voice, "I'm going to La Gabarra tomorrow. Would you like to come with me?"

Gersony couldn't believe what he was hearing. La Gabarra, in the north of Catatumbo, was the most dangerous town in the most dangerous province of Colombia. He would never have gone there alone. That's why from Tibú he had planned to return south to Cúcuta.

"Don't worry, Roberto, you will be at my side the whole time in La Gabarra."

Gersony agreed, terrified at his own decision.

It was a time when the FARC was specifically searching for more Americans to capture. Indeed, the previous July, the left-wing guerrilla organization had been humiliated by a Colombian military Entebbe-style operation, in which fifteen hostages, including three American defense contractors, had been rescued in the jungle after five years in captivity.[4]

"I'm going to the heart of darkness, attached to the bishop's rosary," Gersony thought.

Gersony knew of La Gabarra only from an eyewitness *Boston Globe* account of eight years earlier, at the very beginning of Plan Colombia. A correspondent, Richard Chacon, had described how the town's population swelled on weekends from 2,000 to 10,000. Young males, wearing knee-high black leather boots, descended from the coca fields in the surrounding countryside and arrived in the dozens of canoes that transported them along the Catatumbo River. They came here to "*rumbear*," the local slang for partying, which involved heavy beer drinking, games of pool, and spending nights with the many local prostitutes.[5]

The journey in the bishop's four-wheel-drive vehicle from Tibú to

La Gabarra took four hours along an axle-breaking potholed road, which made it difficult for the Colombian security forces to penetrate the area. Gersony was stunned by how dead the town now appeared, so different from the *Boston Globe* account. Soon after they arrived, the bishop was informed that he had to attend a funeral six hours upriver by boat in each direction, and would be away for at least two nights. Gersony was welcome to join him, the bishop said, or he could stay behind in the empty church dormitory with its windows open to the street. It was like that in the developing world, where plans change all of a sudden and people don't possess the obsession with time and scheduling like in industrial and post-industrial societies. Gersony made the agonizing choice to stay behind. But now he was suddenly alone with the bishop's assistant and sullen housekeeper, in a place with no security. For two nights, in the Sudan-like heat made worse by the humidity, Gersony popped Xanax in his dorm bed.

Trapped in the parish, afraid to walk abroad alone in this FARC-controlled town, he coaxed the bishop's assistant to find people to come to the parish for him to interview. So he met farmers, the head of the women's association, the head of the single mothers' association, a beer wholesaler, and so on. All these people had obviously been cleared by the FARC beforehand, he assumed.

He struck gold with the beer wholesaler. Beer is a tropical boom-town commodity, a measure of such a town's disposable wealth. A beer wholesaler in a place like La Gabarra is someone that any good foreign correspondent would want to interview. And Gersony's instincts were those of a journalist, not those of a Beltway consultant or think-tanker.

Well, the wholesaler was out of a job, as he lamented to Gersony. "This is a town closed for business, a ghost town. The hotels and discos are all boarded up," the wholesaler explained. *This was interesting.* The more danger you put yourself in, the more you sweat, the lonelier you feel, the more you learn. The spraying campaign had worked miraculously, at least here. The figures in Bogotá were all wrong. The wholesaler had opened the door to this vital knowledge for Gersony. And Gersony never would have met him had he not come to La Gabarra with the bishop.

At the five-star Hotel Dann back in Bogotá, Gersony drank two Brandy Alexanders each night before bed, while during the day compiling the results of his 174 one-on-one interviews.

Here was his interpretation of Plan Colombia in Catatumbo:

Catatumbo had good soils, unlike Putumayo. The rains came at night, so they did not interfere with the sunshine. There had been cattle, pigs, agriculture, you name it. But coca was much more profitable, and could not be resisted. Coca production was more intense in Catatumbo than in Putumayo even. In Catatumbo there were six coca harvests each year, in Putumayo only four. In Catatumbo, courtesy of Venezuela next door, the processing chemicals for cocaine came at a discount. La Gabarra on the eve of Plan Colombia had been a flat, sea-to-shining-sea of coca fields. It was a real agribusiness. Sources told Gersony of helicopters flying into La Gabarra from Venezuela loaded down with cash and flying back with coca. Of course, there was violence because people were fighting over fortunes.

Meanwhile, the CIA, relying on U.N. data supplied by primitive satellite imagery, still believed the subsequent spraying campaign of Plan Colombia had had little effect. But no one that Gersony interviewed in Cúcuta, Tibú, and La Gabarra agreed with the U.N. statistics. The estimates of the number of hectares of coca production that locals provided Gersony were more than double those of the United Nations and the CIA: 16,000 hectares versus 7,000. And the spraying had destroyed most of it. "You do not have helicopters with cash flying in for only 7,000 hectares!" Gersony exclaims.

But the real evidence of the success of Plan Colombia was the change in the town of La Gabarra itself: something learned by comparing the eyewitness *Boston Globe* report and Gersony's own eyes-on-target report eight years later, which revealed a boomtown that had become a ghost town. For nobody in the course of spending billions of dollars on Plan Colombia had ever even thought of simply walking into the towns of Catatumbo and Putumayo and asking local farmers, "*Hey*, are you still growing coca out in those fields?" Which is exactly what Gersony did. And the answer was no.

Of course, the blind spots of Plan Colombia were part of a larger phenomenon. This is most succinctly explained by Gregory Gottlieb, a longtime senior official in USAID who is now a professor at Tufts University outside Boston. "I had Gersony at Tufts to lecture my students," Gottlieb says. "My students couldn't believe that such a person even exists and could do this stuff during this time in history. Their whole experience, like those of tens of thousands of other students at elite universities and graduate schools throughout the Western world, is to prepare themselves for jobs in elite think tanks and human rights organizations, many of which have strong institutional biases and bureaucratic interests which get in the way of their analyses, and which rarely produce anything original"—whereas Gersony, Gottlieb goes on, refuses to write the executive summaries that are the curse of organizational studies, "but will gladly brief you for eight hours on his findings." In this way, his methodology becomes unassailable—unlike in the world of political science, "where everybody is always attacking everyone else's methodology." Moreover, Gersony has shown a proclivity—most famously demonstrated in Rwanda—to challenge the existing narrative: something organizational culture will rarely do.

One day, before leaving Colombia, Gersony entered the office of the incoming head of the narcotics assistance section, to request that his report on Catatumbo have only a limited circulation for the coming six months in order to protect his sources. The official said that such decisions were none of Gersony's business; after all, Gersony was just a contractor, not a Foreign Service officer. Gersony walked back to his cubicle in the U.S. Embassy and began sobbing uncontrollably: a ridiculous overreaction brought about by the cumulative effect of physical fear and stress over his work.

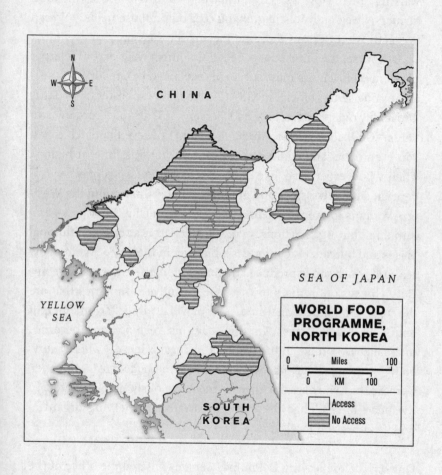

CHINA

SEA OF JAPAN

YELLOW
SEA

**WORLD FOOD
PROGRAMME,
NORTH KOREA**

0   Miles   100

0   KM   100

Access

No Access

SOUTH
KOREA

CHAPTER 16

North Korea

2002

The Last Tofu Meal

ob Gersony's bed was made, so to speak. The regional reassessments from the spillover effect of Plan Colombia never seemed to stop. He was making good pay and was beloved by the Latin America contingent at USAID and the State Department. He had just bought a nonrefundable ticket to Panama in order to travel in the eastern Darien region, an underdeveloped swampland close to the Colombian border. It was not especially safe, but he spoke the language and these trips were all, more or less, in the same time zone as his home, where his three kids were beginning to grow up.

He was at USAID headquarters working up details for his Panama trip when someone told him that USAID administrator Andrew Natsios wanted to see him.

"Maybe we should get you out to the North Korean border area to see what's going on. There may be up to two million dead from the famine there. We have no idea what's happening inside the country," Natsios told Gersony.

Gersony was immediately intimidated. Natsios had just published a book about North Korea, the result of his own days in the NGO community, while Gersony himself knew nothing about the area.[1] Natsios's book contended that there had, in fact, been a widespread famine in North Korea in the 1990s, and he wanted Gersony to find out if it was still going on. "I was obsessed with North Korea, and I knew that Bob wouldn't lie to me," Natsios explains.

"It all sounded dangerous and I had triplets growing up," says Gersony. "I worried about spending ten years as a captive doing hard labor, not getting paid consulting rates." He also sensed a professional danger. Natsios was a handpicked political appointee of President George W. Bush, who was, in turn, in office only because of the Florida recount. Getting too close to Natsios might hurt him later on.

Gersony provided Natsios with a noncommittal answer, agreed to meet again with him on the subject, and continued to prepare for his Panama assignment. His last day in the office he was picking up things on his desk when Fred Schieck, his old buddy from Guatemala a quarter century ago, hurtled in. Schieck was now the deputy USAID administrator, the official number two in the bureaucracy. "Andrew wants you right now!"

Natsios cornered Gersony in a SCIF off his main office: a "Sensitive Compartmented Information Facility," used for classified discussions. There he exclaimed: "Panama! You're not going to Panama! I want you in Chinese Manchuria on the North Korean border!"

Natsios then rattled off questions he wanted Gersony to answer:

"What is the state of the North Korean economy? Is the communist food distribution system still working? Is all the food being donated by the U.N. World Food Programme getting to the people who actually need it? Is there a political angle to the feeding?"

Gersony got the distinctly uneasy feeling that despite all the experts in all the bureaucracies in Washington and elsewhere, the future of food aid to North Korea would be decided by the results of his assessment. After all, the U.N. World Food Programme (WFP) was being funded heavily by the United States, and the United States in this matter would be basing its policy largely on the advice coming out of USAID.

Gersony canceled his plans for Panama and began meeting experts all over Washington. North Korea was the hermit kingdom, and the experts on North Korea inside the Beltway were a bit of a hermit kingdom themselves. They did not welcome outsiders and guarded their information jealously. They were also divided among factions, generally hardliners against accommodationists. Communist North

Korea was one of the last surviving remnants of the Cold War and thus of the Cold War mentality inside Washington. This was an ideological and military struggle.

Gersony also began reading furiously about the subject, beginning with the late *Washington Post* correspondent Don Oberdorfer's classic, *The Two Koreas: A Contemporary History* (1997). It had been almost two decades since he had been to the Far East.

Gersony learned that for 1,300 years, from the middle of the seventh century to the middle of the twentieth, the Korean Peninsula constituted one country, observed warily by China and Japan. At the end of the 1500s, Japan invaded Korea for the first time, as a stepping-stone to challenging China, even as the Chinese employed Korea as a shield against Japan. Meanwhile, from the sixteenth century onward, the Korean people suffered periodic famines, in each of which hundreds of thousands died. This was in addition to epidemics and chaos that led to waves of Korean migration northward across the Yalu and Tumen rivers into China, sometimes instigated by Japanese predations.

The great famine of the 1990s, which formed the background to Andrew Natsios's concerns, occurred in the context of a leadership change in the North Korean capital of Pyongyang, with the death in 1994 of the communist regime's founder and charismatic anti-Japanese guerrilla fighter, Kim Il-sung, and the ascent of his ill-prepared and undistinguished son, Kim Jong-il, to the position of regime strongman. Crucially, around this time, the collapse of the nearby Soviet Union led to North Korea's GDP dropping by a third, even as a quarter of its GDP was going to the military. By 1997, government distribution of food had declined by 85 percent, according to some estimates, with refugees staggering north into Chinese Manchuria. In the midst of the largest international aid effort on the globe at the time, there were suspicions that the food being sent to North Korea under the auspices of the U.N. World Food Programme was being diverted to the North Korean military—something the United Nations strenuously denied.

The fact that North Korea had become a political and human

rights lightning rod was evinced by President George W. Bush's "axis of evil" speech of January 29, 2002, when Bush lumped communist North Korea together with Saddam Hussein's Iraq and the ayatollahs' Iran as constituting the signal threats to America. Just as Gersony was about to travel to the Korean Peninsula, Republican congressman Mark Kirk called the regime-inflicted famine there "the silent massacre," at a May 2, 2002, hearing.

Gersony would spend a combined total of ten weeks in the North Korean border area between May and August 2002, mainly in Chinese territory north of the Tumen River across from the long, northeastern part of North Korea, not far from the Russian frontier. He would conduct eighty-six interviews with refugees and traders in thirteen different locations strung out along the border: not a great number considering his previous assignments, but each interview lasted an average of three hours and was of the highest quality. North Koreans, he found, were not unlike other Asians: whereas Africans were often vague with numbers and details, North Koreans were obsessively precise about everything. Because the Chinese had effectively ceded a ten-mile band of their own territory to North Korean intelligence, Gersony and especially the people he interviewed were in significant danger throughout. Each interview was precious.

Because for his own safety Gersony required a degree of separation from the U.S. government, a Christian organization with an underground network in the border area facilitated his travels, and so far as anyone in the frontier zone knew, he was just another NGO worker. He conducted his interviews in bedrooms, in attics, in the basements of tea houses, in the oddest of places—since he and his subjects were always worried about North Korean intelligence. It was one of the only times in his career when he did not personally select the interviewees: they were selected by local humanitarian organizations, based on criteria he gave them. They had to be people who had arrived from North Korea within the past six months, since he particularly needed to assess current conditions. He wanted people from throughout North Korea, not just from the particularly devastated northeast. His subjects had to be roughly between twenty-five and fifty-five—working-age people, in other words. He insisted on interviewing only one member of each family, again to get as wide a sampling of experiences as possible.

He only accepted findings that were corroborated by at least a dozen people. If he heard particularly interesting or insightful things from one or two interviewees, he would consider the information as *scraps:* to be mentioned to officials in Washington, but with the caveat that he only had a single source.

In the end, he listened for hundreds of hours to factory workers, teachers, doctors, waitresses, students, firewood salesmen, all manner of market traders, policemen, former military and party officials, and so on. Perhaps no outsider at this point had methodically interviewed so many North Koreans. *Los Angeles Times* correspondent Barbara Demick's pathbreaking book, *Nothing to Envy: Ordinary Lives in North Korea,* would not be published until 2009. While Oberdorfer's 1997 book, *The Two Koreas,* as well as other publications, spoke of extreme hardship and semi-starvation, firsthand stories of individual experiences were generally lacking in the literature.

And so, for ten weeks, Gersony entered this grainy, black-and-white prison camp of a country, however vicariously, through his interviews. The stories he gathered humanized the ordeal of the average North Korean.

It became a matter of the microcosm illuminating the macrocosm.

Several fishermen told him how they scoured the waters of the nearby Russian coast for pollock and sea bass. But there were no defections by sea to Russia (or to China for that matter), since if there had been, the North Korean regime might have sent several generations of their families to prison for the rest of their lives. But ultimately, they defected because there was no more fuel to be had for these boats in North Korea. This was after they had restricted themselves to working the North Korean coast close to Russia, which they soon overfished. Whatever they did catch, 60 percent had to go to the government. Despite all this, such fishermen were among the richest people in North Korea at the time.

There was a man who was a laborer in an iron factory in Chongjin with thousands of workers, on the coast in the northeast close to Russia. In 1992, during the final years of Kim Il-sung, the factory maintained 236 trucks; by 2000, 70 percent were out of service. Production had also precipitously dropped, so that the factory closed in 1996. Because the employees were all out of work, food distribution to the factory stopped. The workers cannibalized the ceiling rails, the small motors, everything they could sell. When the government found out, it executed forty of the workers. The other workers and their families began dying of starvation. "No matter the cost, people must see smoke coming out of the smokestacks," Kim Jong-il exhorted the survivors on reactivating the plant in 1997.

The collapse of the Soviet Union made everything worse. (Indeed, here the end of the Cold War had mattered for Gersony's work, just as it had in Bosnia.) For their walls, the copper, lead, and iron mines were all dependent on timber from the Russian far east, which stopped coming in the early 1990s. Mining, fishing, steel production, and other parts of the economy were gradually lost. Among the surviving factories were those for making guns and ammunition and extracting gold. The NGO and intelligence organizations in Washington and elsewhere were aware of little or none of all this prior to Gersony's report. Gersony heard of a uranium mine not far from the demilitarized zone (DMZ) between North and South Korea, where political prisoners worked twelve-hour shifts with little food until they died. It was like a concentration camp. But as Gersony told U.S. intelligence officials later, he had only a single source for this particular information.

Gersony discovered from multiple sources that the only places where civilians regularly received food handouts from the U.N. World Food Programme were in the capital, Pyongyang; in the region of Hyangsan, where the ruling Kim family had its mountain retreat; in the army gold mines; and in some other locations. In most of the rest of the country, WFP food would arrive only on official holidays, such as the birthdays of Kim Il-sung and Kim Jong-il.

The efficacy of the U.N. kindergarten feeding program, a flagship World Food Programme operation, was a sensitive issue that Gersony bore down on in his research. Half of the eighty-six people he conducted extensive interviews with—parents, teachers, former party officials—had direct knowledge of what was going on. They reported that the overwhelming majority of the kindergartens were, in fact, closed in the course of the 1990s famine since feeding had stopped, with the WFP food going instead to members of the army and internal security organizations, and their families.

U.N. officials conducted periodic inspections of their own at the kindergartens that did remain open. Twelve people who Gersony interviewed explained how these officials were deceived. As it turns out, the U.N. inspections had to be scheduled a week in advance and the United Nations was not allowed to bring its own Korean translators. North Korean security officials arrived two days in advance, provided food for the children, and coached them about what to say—not that it mattered much, since the United Nations depended on regime translators. Not one person Gersony interviewed had ever witnessed a U.N. feeding at a kindergarten, elementary school, or high school. Twenty-one interviewees reported seeing U.N. medicines on sale in local markets. Deceiving the "big noses," as North Koreans called the white foreigners of the United Nations, was a standard operating procedure of the regime.

In Hampyong, in the northernmost part of North Korea, there was one hospital that had no medicines, but that did display empty boxes of United Nations–donated medicines on a top shelf of the hospital pharmacy: U.N. inspectors never bothered to reach up with their hands to check the contents of the boxes, which had already been emptied by the military.

Gersony, after dozens of interviews, came to the conclusion that the U.N. World Food Programme in North Korea at the end of the twentieth century justified the suspicions of the international body's worst right-wing ideological critics, who were always disparaging the so-called fecklessness of the world body, even as he knew from his own experience elsewhere in the world how much good the United Nations had accomplished.

So where did all the food and medicine that the United Nations was donating to North Korea end up?

Thirty-eight of Gersony's interviewees reported their own specific eyewitness sightings of food deliveries to army and intelligence units, to workers in essential war industries, and for the rebuilding of military reserves. At the country's ports, army and security vehicles were disguised as civilian trucks with their license plates "muddied" and altered in order to collect the U.N. food deliveries. Gersony's sources were port traders, local residents, and an artist who had repainted army license plates. There is little public vehicular traffic in North Korea and military trucks are very distinctive, so noticing the deception was not difficult. "This food distribution is life and death for us. Every old lady knows which truck is which," said one interviewee. Another reported that "the U.N. foreigner who lived in the Chanma-san Hotel [in Chongjin] came to watch the unloading: he just drove in and out of the port, without following where the trucks were going."

Gersony estimated that as much as 80 percent of U.N. food aid went to the military and other security services. Given the scale of the diversions, you had to look at U.N. food aid as an indirect budget support for the North Korean military, he says. The figure was even higher for bilateral aid donated by individual European countries, such as German beef, which was all diverted to the North Korean army.

Almost all of Gersony's interviewees proved useful on the question of food deliveries because food was in such short supply during this period in North Korea, and therefore food deliveries were a big event everywhere.

The food and agricultural situation proved to be even worse than foreign intelligence assets were reporting. For example, satellites from space took pictures of what looked like normal cornfields. But as Gersony learned from his one-on-one interviews, because of the mass starvation people had already gone into these fields and stolen the ears of corn before they had a chance to mature.

There was cannibalism and suicide, often by ingesting rat poison, on a significant scale.

One vignette in Gersony's voluminous notes was titled "The Last Tofu Meal," told to him by an elderly lady:[2]

Before this woman left for China in April 2001, she rented a room in her home to a family—a man, a woman, and two children aged 11 and 14. They came from Unsan, North Phyongan near the Chagang Province border. One day, January 18, 2001 (she will never forget the date), they asked for some tofu, and she gave them some. At 3 A.M., the family would usually go outside to collect grass and roots. But that day she heard nothing stirring, so she went to look after them. She found the four completely still, seated in a circle, hugging each other, dead. They had mixed rat poison with the tofu and taken it together. The elderly woman had already lost three of her own children, and she just hadn't enough food to help the family more than she had, she said with regret.

Because he now had three children of his own, this story affected him even more than that of the woman in Mozambique who had let go of her daughter in the river.

There was also the story he heard about the women's section of a prison in Chongjin.

"We were always filthy and insects would suck our blood. Talking was prohibited. You sat all day in the same position. There was a video camera and guards: if you moved, it was a big disaster. If you stretched your legs, the guards made you do sit-ups. Sometimes people passed out. We received some spoonfuls of corn skins with a few beans, and a little cabbage. The cooks stomped on the food with their feet. Of 150 prisoners, 35 died in a single month from starvation and an epidemic. The prisoners were mainly political: those who had tried to escape to South Korea and China, and those who had contact with foreigners—like you," the woman said, looking hard at Gersony.

Gersony gulped.

Then there was the laborer on a farm of 18,000 *chambas* (6,000 hectares).

"How many *chambas* were cultivated?" Gersony asked.

"Ten thousand were for rice, and five hundred for corn."

"Why so little corn?"

"People steal the immature ears."

"What about the remaining 7,500 *chambas*?" Gersony continued to probe.

"That's the uncultivated part."

"You mean virgin forest?"

"No, I mean it was the uncultivated part," the tractor mechanic insisted.

"What? Uncultivated? You mean there is crop rotation?" Gersony persisted.

"No! It's the opium."

A lot of the best material came by accident, by journalistic-style questioning.

The mechanic explained to Gersony that at the end of May, "outsiders" would come to harvest the "uncultivated" areas.

"Outsiders?" Gersony asked.

"The clean people."

Who?

"Trusted party members."

"They had a language all their own," Gersony explains. "'Big noses,' 'uncultivated,' 'outsiders,' 'clean people.' It really was like *1984*."

Gersony furiously typed up a thick stack of such stories in his hotel room in Yanji, which served as his base for roaming the border area. As one interviewee after another told him about "muddied" license plates and how the "big noses" were forever being deceived, he realized that he had never worked in a place where the recollections were so specific and meticulous. In the course of these conversations he uncovered one- and two-source *scraps* about revolts and mass executions with hundreds killed at a time, mainly by firing squads: 10 percent of the officers of the Sixth Corps in Chongjin were dispatched this way. This was all before the World Food Programme had come on the scene to feed the army.

He continued interviewing even though he already knew he had a gold mine. As usual, he ate one meal a day: spaghetti Bolognese with a glass of orange juice, one of the only non-Korean dishes on the hotel menu. (He was not one for exotic food.) He continued to worry about the many North Korean agents in the border zone where his hotel and meetings were located.

Then, near the end of ten weeks of interviewing refugees and traders in the ten-mile border zone—part of Chinese Manchuria but patrolled by North Korean agents—Gersony began to get a bad feeling. He had just interviewed two weepy old women who told him about how they had to harvest wild edible plants in order to survive. They hadn't added much to his knowledge base, and the next day he saw one of them talking to two men wearing suits and ties at the drive-in entrance to the hotel. Next, a bizarre man insisted on talking to him about the contraband trade. A day after that, he received a letter from one of the women that provided a phone number for him to call and warning him of a negative portrayal of North Korea. He handed the letter to one of his NGO translators in a basement tearoom. The translator shrugged it off, telling Gersony that the woman was merely trying to get money out of him. Finally, he was informed by the hotel desk clerk that a man from the Chinese internal security bureau was looking for him.

It was all a bit shady and perhaps coincidental, yet he worried that he was being set up. It was hard not to think that there wasn't a thread running through it all, even though he was consciously aware of his tendency toward paranoia, especially in such lonely circumstances. He couldn't help but think about Daniel Pearl, the *Wall Street Journal* correspondent in Karachi, Pakistan, who only a few months earlier,

in February 2002, had been set up through a series of seemingly
fishy yet innocuous little occurrences, resulting in his kidnapping
and beheading by al-Qaeda. The comparison was certainly a far
stretch, yet Gersony was in a panic. He was getting old, with three
kids. His nerves, never good, weren't what they used to be.

He had a contingency plan with Cindy for just such a situation.
He called her with a local SIM card. "Thick glasses" meant that he
was being watched. "Hiccup" meant that he was worried about a dis-
ruption in his plans. "Eyes red and inflamed" was the most serious
signal: it meant she should call USAID and the State Department
immediately, and alert the embassy and consulate to a potentially
serious security problem. Over the phone, he told her that his "eyes
were red and inflamed" from all the pollution. Cindy did manage to
get in touch with a middle-level bureaucrat, who decided inexplicably
not to do anything. So Gersony called his most senior Christian NGO
contact, who asked him, "Would you be willing to leave China now?"

He left all his clothes and laundry littered about the room, packed
his toiletries and his heavy stack of typed notes in his red Kipling
shoulder bag, and walked out of the lobby near midnight—there
wasn't even a clerk at the desk—and headed in the blackness to the
far corner of a parking lot. Waiting there was a car and driver, who
took him to another parking lot not far away, where he slipped into
the freezing back of a truck and wrapped himself in a carpet that happened to be inside. The truck rode through the mountains and plains
all night while he read by flashlight *The Catcher in the Rye* by J. D.
Salinger. He was let off at a regional airport, where he flew to Beijing
and then out of China.

After kissing the floor of his home and hugging his wife and three
children, Gersony holed up for several days in September 2002 sort-
ing out and writing up his notes (he never wrote a formal report on
North Korea). He delivered an eight-hour brief, divided over two days,
to Andrew Natsios and Natsios's powerful policy adviser Patrick Cronin. Cronin, a modest, intensely serious guy with a light sense of
humor always at the ready, was the one who had months before

opened all the doors for Gersony to the hermit kingdom of North Korea experts around Washington. Natsios and Cronin now wanted to squeeze every detail out of Gersony. "They wouldn't let me alone with questions," Gersony says.

Cronin remembers the briefing well:

"It was utterly enthralling. Every sentence was an impactful gut punch as Gersony described the misery of daily life in North Korea. It was like a vivid documentary of a whole subject unknown to the world, since nobody in the intelligence community collected human intelligence the way that Gersony did. He gave voice to the voiceless."

"I want it all reduced to two pages, and I want it by tomorrow!" Natsios sternly ordered Gersony.

Gersony meekly complied, breaking his rule to never write executive summaries.

Natsios gave Gersony's two pages to his oldest friend and Republican buddy from the Massachusetts legislature, Andy Card, President George W. Bush's chief of staff. Card promptly gave it to Bush. Natsios had just jumped the whole bureaucratic system of cabinet secretaries, undersecretaries, and assistant secretaries: he went "out of channels," in Washington terminology. But nobody was pissed off. As soon as everyone heard that the president had read the two-page summary of Gersony's briefing, they all wanted the same brief.

So Gersony made the usual rounds, armed with maps and doughnuts to hand out. He had learned by this time that people wouldn't sit for hours without maps to look at and something to munch on. But he had a rule: never use PowerPoint, which was a visual crutch in place of an authentic narrative.

"You've done it again, another Gersony report with a major impact on foreign policy," Elliott Abrams, now the humanitarian point man on the National Security Council, announced to Gersony.

After briefing Abrams, Gersony next briefed Carl Ford, the assistant secretary of state for intelligence and research; Mike Green, a director for Asian affairs on the National Security Council; Jim Kelly, the assistant secretary of state for East Asian and Pacific affairs; and Kelly's sidekick, David Asher, who was crucial on this issue. Asher, co-chair of the State Department and National Security Council work-ing group on North Korea, was a brilliant, mile-a-minute talker and goal-oriented bomb thrower, who ran over some mealy-mouthed desk officers who represented the passive State Department bureau-cracy at its worst. Asher, as they said, was "off the reservation." In small doses, mind you, someone like him was absolutely crucial to making the system work. When Gersony asked him a week after briefing him and Kelly about the effect of his report, Asher said with an ecstatic look on his face, "There's flames going up everywhere!" It was through Gersony that USAID came to dominate the interagency process on humanitarian issues regarding North Korea.

At a September deputies' meeting, where the number two and number three persons at each major Washington bureaucracy meet to plan the nuts-and-bolts of foreign policy, the issue of the North Korea report came up. Ambassador Marc Grossman, undersecretary of state for political affairs and the number three person at Colin Powell's State Department, said: "I know the gentleman who did the study. I've worked with him for years. If that is what the researcher says is going on, it's happening. There's no doubt in our minds on its validity."

Grossman's vouching for Gersony was over a decade in the mak-ing. Gersony had first briefed him on Mozambique in 1988,[3] and over the years, as the situation in each place turned out as Gersony had said it would, Grossman gradually became impressed.

Next Gersony saw Paul Wolfowitz, the deputy secretary of defense. Gersony hadn't seen Wolfowitz for eighteen years, when he had briefed him on South China Sea piracy in 1984. Wolfowitz was visi-bly older now, and more self-confident, no longer accompanied by overbearing Foreign Service officers proffering advice as he had been back then.

In October 2002, Wolfowitz assembled a dozen officials in addi-tion to military staff aides at a long table in the Pentagon. "Okay, let's hear it," he ordered Gersony.

There were no interruptions throughout the brief. But early on Gersony was disconcerted by loud snoring. Peter Rodman, the late assistant secretary of defense for international security affairs, had fallen into a deep sleep, and would not wake up until the end of the brief. Wolfowitz leaned over and said to Gersony, "I apologize. He was up all night planning for Iraq."

Finally, Gersony briefed two dozen people of the CIA's National Intelligence Council (NIC). It would be about the sixth time he had done so in the course of his career, brought in often by David Gordon, the national intelligence officer for transnational issues and later the NIC's vice chairman. The people at the CIA listened in awed silence to Gersony. Some in the room thought he was a regional expert on North Korea because of how deeply and obsessively he had gone into the subject. The intelligence officers also liked the fact that Gersony always revealed the status of the information he was providing: sourced by several individuals, or a *scrap* based on one source. Above all, as Gordon explains, "with Gersony it was always clear that he was in the humanitarian community, but not exactly of it, and therefore was able to smartly extract ideas and information from the humanitarian world and incorporate them into his overall analysis. Gersony rarely thought in good guy/bad guy terms," Gordon goes on. "He didn't start from any general set of assumptions, but was completely empirical, going wherever the evidence might lead him. It was because he obviously had no agenda that he was so effective in influencing government."

It was Thanksgiving before Gersony finished delivering all of his briefs on North Korea to the upper levels of the Washington bureaucracy. As a consequence, the United States announced that it was suspending its share of food aid to North Korea through the U.N. World Food Programme for six months. Natsios told a congressional committee, "We are going to insist on the same standards for monitoring and distribution [of food] that we use everywhere else in the world. . . . We're drawing the line now with the North Koreans."[4]

World Food Programme and other NGO officials complained, saying there was "no hard evidence" that aid was being diverted to the North Korean military.[5] Some NGO officials claimed that, in any case, the North Korean military preferred local rice over the WFP rations. But this was sort of a non-denial denial, since the whole North Korean economy had seized up at this time, and thus there was very little local rice to begin with. Others claimed that providing a week's advance notice before inspections was necessary to prevent attacks against U.N. personnel at the inspection sites.

Finally, high politics intervened. As a conciliatory gesture toward the new South Korean president, Roh Moo-hyun, who desired better relations with North Korea, Secretary of State Colin Powell told a press conference that U.S. aid through the U.N. World Food Programme "would resume" at "35 to 75 percent" of the previous year's totals.[6] The 35 percent figure was meant to satisfy the Washington hardliners on North Korea and the 75 percent figure to satisfy the accommodationists. It was a cynical diplomatic sleight of hand. (Later on, the United States would agree to provide North Korea with several hundred thousand tons of food a year, provided the North Korean regime sign ten provisions for distributing the food, all designed to make sure the aid got to those most in need. The North Koreans agreed to the provisions, then violated them, so that the aid was stopped.)[7]

"I had no dog in this fight," Gersony says. "But I believed that whatever we did, we should do it with our eyes wide open."

The intelligence reports and newspaper accounts kept coming in. They never wavered, with world-renowned area specialists such as Nicholas Eberstadt and Andrei Lankov providing support for Gersony's documentation about North Korea in the 1990s.[8] More independent reports kept backing up Gersony's claims about the diversion of food aid, opium production, and other North Korean iniquities as told to him firsthand by the refugees themselves who had experienced it all.[9]

Nepal
2003

A Room with a View

In January 2003, while Washington was consumed with the buildup to the invasion of Iraq, Joe Williams sent Bob Gersony an email from Kathmandu, Nepal. It was the northern Uganda assignment all over again. But this time, instead of the Lord's Resistance Army that Joe—always thinking ahead—wanted investigated, it was the Nepalese Maoists. The Maoists openly identified with the Cambodian Khmer Rouge, with Mao Zedong's Great Leap Forward, with the Indian Naxalites, and with the Peruvian Shining Path. Western analysts were terrified of a group modeling itself after so many mass murderers. Yet they knew next to nothing firsthand about these Maoists. Gersony would have to construct a narrative history from scratch.

Andrew Natsios got wind of Joe Williams's request to Gersony and was enthusiastic. "Are we headed for another Khmer Rouge scenario?" Natsios asked Gersony. "Let's put this to rest, or let me know the degree of likelihood. If the answer is yes, the administration's got a big problem, and we should deal with this early, while there's still time."

Gersony said that he would like to do the assignment in cooperation with Mercy Corps, a Portland, Oregon–based relief charity whose work he respected and whose directors he knew. This would allow him to escape the bureaucratic clutches of the regional security officer at the U.S. Embassy in Kathmandu, who could deny him permission to travel in the Nepalese countryside.

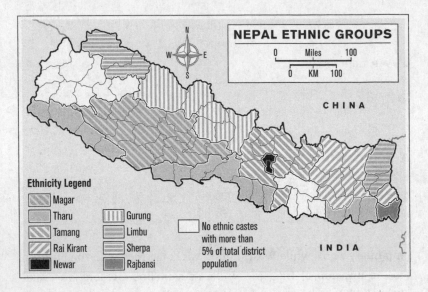

In this new assignment, Gersony would not expose a human rights problem nor propose a strategy for development. Rather, he would try to answer a big question, one that pertained to both human rights and development and that had perplexed senior policymakers: Were or were not the Nepalese Maoists like the Cambodian Khmer Rouge? He would do it by amassing a meticulously detailed report that, even more than the one he had written about northern Uganda, would turn a traditional country study into a form of literature all its own.

Immediately, he realized that his assignment involved nothing abstract. For the only way to find out if the Maoists were indeed the next Khmer Rouge was to travel around the affected area itself and methodically ask lots of people questions. Of course, this was the modus vivendi of all his assignments. But rather than collect facts as in the past, this assignment involved making a judgment call about a future likelihood, whether or not it led to U.S. action. It was an intimidating mandate because of the possibility of a colossal mistake. It was a binary call. He neurotically believed that his whole reputation could go down the drain if he got this one wrong.

First he went to the CIA, to see two people he deeply respected at the National Intelligence Council, David Gordon and Paul Pillar. They prepared him with a list of questions to answer about the Nepalese Maoists, which helped organize his research. Unlike other members of the humanitarian community, Gersony did not consider the CIA an enemy. "You'd be defeating the humanitarian purpose if you did not consult with the CIA," Gersony explains. "Since whenever I'd come back from the field—from Mozambique, from the North Korean border, from wherever—the White House would always cross-check everything I reported with the CIA before acting on my recommendations."

Gersony arrived in the Nepalese capital of Kathmandu February 19, 2003, on his fifty-eighth birthday.

The U.S. ambassador to Nepal, Mike Malinowski, a real meat-and-potatoes South Asia hand and Foreign Service lifer, had a list of questions similar to the CIA's. Joe Williams, who had done prodigious work on the Maoists, nevertheless summed it up at an embassy meeting: "We need a CAT scan of the Maoists. Few go into their area of influence and few come out. We have no real information, even though Kathmandu is inundated with Western PhD folks specializing in conflict resolution and mitigation."

"What have you learned from them?" Gersony asked Williams.

In his mild Tennessee accent, Williams replied: "I can't make sense out of a bunch of horseshit."

KATHMANDU, NEPAL. A ragged, jungly, hilly confection of moldering walls set amidst stage-prop bluish mountains, with occasional clouds that have the look and texture of dirty sponges. As crowded and polluted with motorbikes, automobiles, and rickshaws as it is, Kathmandu never quite gives up the atmosphere of a small town that has simply grown too big. Durbar Square, notwithstanding its rambling clutter of Hindu and Buddhist temples, appears small and intimate for a turn-of-the-twenty-first-century visitor: unmanageable in its number of gods but quite manageable in its absence of yawning space.

• • •

On the one hand, given the fear of what the Maoists might do and yet how little was known about them in the outside world, you had *Time* magazine warning about the "Year Zero" in Nepal, with the Maoists instituting a "purification campaign to reduce their territory to chaos and rubble."[1] On the other hand, you had a Boston University professor whom Gersony had consulted, David Scott Palmer, pouring cold water on the whole thesis, saying that the Maoists were just a bunch of high-caste Brahmins who had originated within the Nepalese political system and were limited in their violent intent. Finally, in the middle, was the Washington bureaucratic fishbowl, in which the National Security Council was poised to blame USAID for something that hadn't even happened yet: the Khmer Rouge–like takeover of Nepal.

To find the answer, Gersony spent the better part of 2003 traveling in and studying about Nepal's midwestern region, including the districts of Rolpa and Rukum—considered the Maoist insurgency's heartland. His fieldwork also included four adjacent districts, sometimes called the Rapti River Valley. He covered 2,200 miles of the world's most rugged and mountainous terrain, conducting lengthy interviews with over 150 inhabitants from 66 different villages, in addition to speaking with dozens of specialists in the Nepalese capital of Kathmandu and abroad. He left Kathmandu for the field soon after the U.S. government put the Maoists on a terrorist watch list, causing the Maoists to start an all-Americans-out-of-Nepal campaign. Out of fear of being killed or captured, he avoided hardcore Maoist base areas, but stayed in villages immediately adjacent to those areas, interviewing people who went in and out of them to visit local markets.

It was another hard, lonely trip.

In the large village of Liwang, in Rolpa district, he was surrounded by sheer, towering hills the spectacular yellow-green of the inside of an avocado. These were the foothills to the snowy granite fastnesses of the Himalayas. He stayed in a barracks-style, dry-wood firetrap of a hotel, on the lip of an amphitheater that culminated at the bottom in a large flat space used as a soccer field. The room was small, filthy, smelly, and he shared a bathroom with everyone else on the same floor. He slept in the same room with his Nepalese translator. There was no telephone, no radio signal, and of course no electricity or Internet connection. He spent a week in that room, never leaving it. His one meal a day was brought to him by the translator. He had no choice but to keep the lowest possible profile. It was that dangerous, he felt. The hotel proprietor lent him a small table and two chairs. The translator would randomly select people in the nearby market for him to interview inside the room. He typed his notes by candlelight.

The room had a small smudgy window. One morning he looked out of it and saw men bringing palm fronds into the soccer field. He thought nothing of it. The next morning he saw them hauling in lumber. He was now curious. On the third day they started building a stage, which they decorated with the palm fronds.

"What's going on?" he asked his translator.

His translator went out for a while and when he returned said, "Bob, there's going to be a big meeting: a Maoist convention."

"I had a brave, exuberant, Fred Cuny moment," Gersony recalls. "I thought to myself, 'Why don't I just sit here and be a spectator at the convention, and have my translator tell me what is going on?' But then I thought it over some more and decided, 'Let's get the hell out of here!'"

"Okay, Bob, okay," the translator said.

The two quickly packed up and jumped on one of those gaily painted jitney buses that were packed with people and chickens. The bus careened around mountainous curves, stopping often and suddenly to discharge and take on passengers, dust flying. Gersony feared the roadblocks, manned by Nepalese police in some sections and Maoist guerrillas in others. The journey ended when the bus came down out of the mountains and into the flat plain, called the Terai, where Nepal abuts India and where all the good paved roads in the country were. Truly, where the bad roads begin, so too begins the Maoist insurgency. He thought: If only USAID had continued its decades-long road-building project in Nepal, then perhaps there might never have been a Maoist insurgency of such magnitude.

Heading back on the paved road to Kathmandu, he worried that he had been a coward by not staying to observe the Maoist convention. Maybe he was and maybe he wasn't a coward. The difference between catastrophe and no danger at all can often be slight. The fact is, his innate caution, based in large part on his own paranoia, probably played no small role in a lifetime spent alone in conflict zones without a disastrous incident.

The scores and scores of interviews he had conducted, however imperfect the knowledge of the interviewees, constituted real detective work, in the manner of his reporting on the utterly confusing situation on the Ethiopia-Somalia border and in other places. One person tells you to speak to another person, whom the translator then locates, and who then provides half of a puzzle piece of information. For in reality, many oral traditions are extremely fragmented and leave much unclear. And it wasn't as if there were a local historian to talk to, or even books to read about what he specifically needed to find out here. There were no local elites. The closest he came to finding anyone who had a coherent sense of the recent past in this Nepalese rural back of beyond were some elderly men. Up to a point, he was assembling a people's recent history.

The result was a 101-page report supplemented by twenty maps, entitled *Sowing the Wind: History and Dynamics of the Maoist Revolt in Nepal's Rapti Hills*. The maps, which he personally selected and in some cases designed himself (and were digitally produced by a Nepalese expert), cover in rich, suggestive detail Nepal's topography, population density, and ethnic and caste diversity, district by district. As usual, he did all the work alone, without research assistants, interns, and secretaries—the staple of consultants and think tanks. Like his other projects, the Nepal report was the product of an obsession. Otherwise, why do it? Topography and the linguistic and ethnic breakdowns were the key to his study, as they always were. This was vital because culture remains the dominant factor that Washington is increasingly unwilling to talk about, because it can't be quantified and is thus subjective—even as culture is the sum total of a people's experience in a given geography over hundreds and thousands of years.

Interviewees were broken down according to their caste and ethnic origin: 17 percent Brahmin, 24 percent Chhetri, 16 percent Magar, and so on. He knew that ethnic identity was tangible to common people to a degree that abstract ideas like democracy and freedom were not. And if you couldn't remote-sense the life of the common people and their daily, moment-by-moment concerns, you knew nothing about them. While nineteenth-century British explorers (with all of their prejudices) thought like this, increasingly few people in Washington did.

Gersony's laboratory was what he labeled "the Red Zone," the heartland of the Maoist insurgency. It is, as he writes, a heavily forested, mountainous area that achieves a maximum altitude of over 22,000 feet, nearly the roof of the world, where sheepherding overshadows farming, and where the population is more animist than Hindu. "Not a single motorable road serves the Red Zone," whose population is overwhelmingly of the Magar ethnic group, who live in a particularly fractured and isolated terrain, among the harshest in Nepal.[2] Gersony then offers disquisitions about the decline of sheepherding and iron mining, and about the area's tradition of supplying the British imperial forces with fierce Gurkha fighters.

But, as Gersony tells the reader, beginning in the 1930s and continuing for four decades, the Red Zone became the principal producer of Nepalese marijuana and hashish, even as the Magar people consumed little of the stuff themselves. But just as prosperity came to the area on account of the hashish, the government in Kathmandu, which heretofore had no presence at all in the Red Zone (and had done nothing for it), enforced a strict prohibition on the production and sale of hashish. Nascent prosperity gave way once again to grinding poverty. "The hashish ban, while more than two decades old, has not been forgotten and remains a source of bitterness" among the local people, Gersony reports. He then weaves an intricate story about how geographic isolation, discrimination against an untouchable caste, the bonded labor of the Tharu ethnic group, the rise of Christianity, the continued general indifference of local authorities, the lack of roads and economic development, election fraud, and the failure of the authorities to complete the building of a hospital all bred an attitude of resistance to the Nepalese government. He even goes into excruciating detail about how young Tharu girls were "reportedly obliged to have sexual relations with their landlords," and elderly men were humiliated when their wives, because of extreme poverty, were forced to sell their traditional jewelry.[3]

To state that the Red Zone was among the poorest regions of Nepal was really to say something. Indeed, Nepal was a country where illiteracy was 50 percent and infant mortality 60 percent; a place where 200,000 people, mainly children as Gersony reports, died each year from malaria. As he observes, however uncomfortably, the very lack of colonization by European powers—with the measure of development it brought—combined with an attitude of self-imposed isolation, only made Nepal further removed from modernity.[4]

In all of this, as Gersony learned from his interviews, the hashish ban was the beginning of the thread that led to the Red Zone's radicalization. In the four years after the ban was enforced, allegiance to the Communist Party rose from 10 percent to 60 percent. "By the 1980s, what would become the Red Zone was solidly anti-government and many were convinced that only violent opposition would lead to solutions. . . ." It was in February 1996 that the Maoists launched their People's War with attacks against police outposts: a reaction to a government-instituted campaign described by human rights activists as "state terror," even though, as Gersony records through his interviews, the number of incidents and the extent of the overall government campaign may well have been exaggerated. The Maoists, for their part, engaged periodically in abductions, beatings, and burning and mutilation atrocities that are too horrible to quote from Gersony's study.[5]

"Nonetheless," as Gersony concludes, "up to now Maoist conduct, in comparison with the Khmer Rouge in the two years before it came to power, is significantly different: the frequency of violence has been much lower [generally], and the Maoists have implemented none of the radical social and economic policies which the Khmer Rouge applied throughout areas under their control. A fundamental difference is that outside their heartland [the Red Zone], the Maoists have not found a national issue with which to mobilize a larger movement."

In sum, according to Gersony, the Maoists showed little proclivity for social reorganization and engineering. The Maoists simply lacked the systemization and regimentation to inflict their will over large masses of people. They hadn't succeeded at redistributing land or affecting routine commerce. Even their periodic attempts to ban alcohol and regulate moneylenders had failed. There was simply no *totality* to their rule. Villages weren't burned; children weren't indoctrinated.

Comparison, as any good analyst knows, is the beginning of all serious scholarship. And Gersony, while not flinching from descriptions of the worst of the Maoist atrocities and the awful social conditions that gave rise to them, nevertheless coolly states that in comparison to the Cambodian Khmer Rouge, the Nepalese Maoists represented much less of a threat.

History has proven him right.

A few years after he left Nepal, the Maoists came to power: through an election and negotiations. There were no atrocities or land redistributions. Rather, they were co-opted by the democratic system. On September 6, 2012, the State Department removed the Maoists from its list of terrorist organizations, citing their "credible commitment to pursuing the peace and reconciliation process in Nepal."

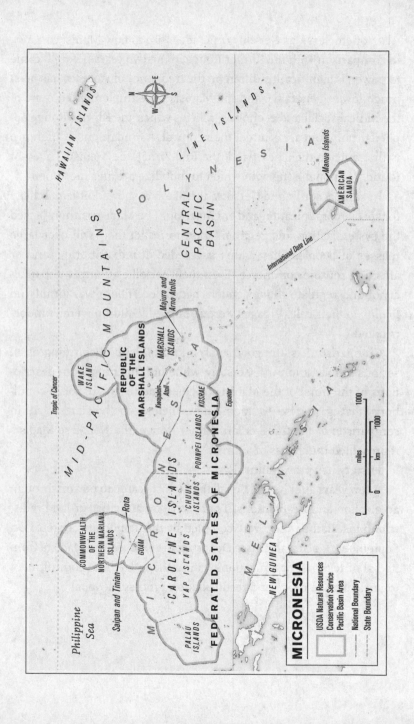

MICRONESIA

USDA Natural Resources
Conservation Service
Pacific Basin Area
———— National Boundary
------- State Boundary

CHAPTER 18

Micronesia by Way of Iraq
2003–2008

The Ghastly Waste and the Looming Threat

In late 2003, Andrew Natsios rushed Gersony to finish his Nepal assessment. He needed Gersony to investigate something that had gone seriously wrong with USAID's disaster assistance response team in Iraq.

The problems with the USAID bureaucracy that Gersony had had hints of starting years ago in Central America were about to hit him in the face.

Up to this point, the disaster assistance response team, or DART as it was known, had performed magnificently in northern Iraq in 1991 and in Bosnia in 1996. Northern Iraq in 1991 was Fred Cuny's finest hour, when Cuny's bulldozing force of personality, in cooperation with Army Lieutenant General Jay Garner and U.S. ambassador to Turkey Mort Abramowitz, had created a security umbrella for Iraqi Kurds in the wake of the First Gulf War and the predations of Saddam Hussein.[1] In 1996 in Bosnia, Tim Knight, leveraging Gersony's concept of ethnic-majority returns, got 2,500 houses built and restored for returning Muslims, helping to avert a possible slide back into civil war. "Fred and Tim both understood that it was only through the unity of political and humanitarian ends that you could really get things done," Gersony observes, "because humanitarianism doesn't operate in a vacuum. There are always other considerations," tied to national interest and what is practical at the moment.

But then came Hurricane Mitch in 1998, when the late Paul Bell, the head of the DART in Central America, wanted to move on to disaster preparedness training, even as people were still shivering without blankets after their homes had been destroyed and even as the Clinton White House declared the emergency still ongoing. That crisis exposed sharply divergent views born partially of a weak chain of command inside USAID and the U.S. government that bore fruit in Iraq following the March 2003 invasion, when the DART's humanitarian projects simply failed to materialize, despite cooperation from the U.S. military.

So in December 2003 Gersony flew into Baghdad from Amman, Jordan, in a darkened plane that landed in a virtual vertical spiral in order to avoid ground fire, sending his stomach into his mouth. Then, along with everyone else on the plane, he was marched to a grim and massive hooch where cots were stacked together. After only a few hours of sleep, at around three A.M., an armored bus escorted by armored personnel carriers transported him and the others into the Green Zone, where U.S. Embassy personnel slept in ugly trailer and bungalow parks amid a maze of tunnel-like concrete Alaska and Jersey barriers. This dirt-filled urban landscape, with its Stalinist-cum-Babylonian architecture—the legacy of Saddam's megalomania—was bleak, soulless, and sterile. Gersony might as well have been a prisoner of war, surrounded by American soldiers and grizzled contractors. The whole experience somehow reminded him of his days in Vietnam. There was just something so wrong about it all, he thought.

The entire time in Iraq, except for short trips to Basra in the Shi'ite south and Erbil in the Kurdish north, Gersony never left the Green Zone. The lesser reason was that you generally couldn't leave except in an armed convoy. The greater reason was that USAID's disaster assistance response team hadn't done a single project worth seeing. It was a disgrace, since USAID and its personnel on the ground constituted America's interface with the Iraqi people and thus with world opinion. Indeed, history remembers how a great power performs in a humanitarian emergency. Can you provide people with comfort in their hour of epic distress?

It took Gersony 137 lengthy interviews conducted with USAID personnel during January and February 2004 in the Green Zone, as well as back in the United States, to find out why nothing had been built, why nobody's distress had been relieved.

The chronological mosaic he pieced together revealed a completely dysfunctional interagency process, where the head of the DART was not cooperating with the USAID administrator, nor with the U.S. military and U.S. civilian occupation authorities. The civilians from USAID were suspicious of the military and therefore slow-walked cooperation. Indeed, among USAID personnel there was a deep-seated resentment on philosophical grounds to the invasion itself, and this had a corrosive ripple effect throughout the bureaucracy. They were accustomed, as in the Balkans, for example, to working on a mission that was primarily humanitarian. They therefore could not get used to the fact that humanitarianism, whatever the rhetoric of the Bush administration, was only an adjunct to the military occupation. Tim Knight himself offered to step in and help, applying his lessons from Bosnia, but was told "no thanks" by the powers that be in Washington. The issue had gone up all the way to President George W. Bush in two meetings, but even he couldn't resolve it; nor could Secretary of State Colin Powell and Secretary of Defense Donald Rumsfeld. The failure had much to do with one particularly problematic personality whom I will leave unnamed—someone who had influenced the workings of the DART and the Office of Foreign Disaster Assistance in Iraq—and who was symptomatic of how not only the Bush administration but Washington and the American system itself were simply not ready for prime time in terms of occupying a complicated Muslim country of 26 million people. In the end, the saga that Gersony unraveled was tedious and unoriginal, given all the books and investigative reporting about the failure in Iraq of the Coalition Provisional Authority (CPA), the bureaucratic mechanism for American imperial rule in the country in which USAID was integrated. It adds nothing particularly substantial to the larger picture. So I will not burden the reader with it, except to say that having completed telling me the tale, Gersony throws up his hands, and says what he once said about Vietnam:

"Iraq was not just beyond America's capability, it was beyond doing, period," adding, "but different approaches to the occupation could have resulted in a far less disastrous outcome."

Andrew Natsios adds this:

"We never should have stood up a Coalition Provisional Authority in Iraq in the first place. We should have worked with what we were bureaucratically comfortable with for decades: simply a very large U.S. Embassy staff and USAID, coordinating with the military."

Even though Gersony's damning report on USAID's disaster assistance response team reflected poorly on Natsios's own leadership of USAID, Natsios—after he had fired several people connected with the affair—wanted everyone in Washington to know just what had happened, and thus he sent Gersony around town to brief his findings.

When Gersony finished making the rounds, Natsios sent Gersony back out to Baghdad at the beginning of 2005. He now wanted Gersony to do an assessment of the entire civilian aspect of the occupation itself. The USAID administrator, having been burned already in Iraq, was no longer confident that he knew exactly what was happening on the ground there. And he wasn't sure that Washington as a whole knew either.

Gersony was overwhelmed. Iraq was the biggest American nation-building project since postwar Germany and Japan, even as it bore a closer resemblance to the American occupation of the Philippines at the turn of the twentieth century. This assignment meant investigating massive infrastructure rehabilitation, the recovery of an entire national power grid and sewage system, fiscal and central bank policy, industrial and agricultural regeneration, and the holding of elections: things he knew little or nothing about.

He would interview 230 people who worked for the occupation authorities, each for several hours, some of whom were just finishing their tours. In the process, the situation became clear to him.

Gersony first observed that Ambassador John Negroponte, who had replaced Ambassador L. Paul (Jerry) Bremer in July 2004 as the head of the Coalition Provisional Authority, had finally brought in the "pros": capable and senior diplomats who took over from the ideological "clowns" on the Bremer team, many of whom had gotten their jobs through the political machinations of the Bush White House. Bremer had been a career diplomat and a success in the private sector, but he had relatively little experience running large organizations and was chosen to run the CPA, partly because he was the only figure that Powell and Rumsfeld could agree on. He was hampered by decisions that came from Rumsfeld and Vice President Dick Cheney, and harbored what appeared as arrogance in dealing with Iraqis: Iraq began to fall apart under his watch.

But with the DART disbanded and Bremer gone, USAID was working with "incredible competence," according to Gersony's report, thanks in large part to Ambassador Wendy Chamberlin, the very able assistant administrator for USAID's Asia and Near East Bureau who was part of Negroponte's new order. There were many other examples Gersony documented, where things were done right and fast: from changing the currency to releasing funds for agricultural development, to improving the functioning of municipalities, to setting up Internet cafés in Iraqi towns and stocking local libraries with Arabic-language textbooks, to restoring electric power in many areas, to killing Bremer's white elephant ventures, and on and on.

But the problem was ultimately with the Department of Defense. And this made all the difference. Bremer may have been gone, but Rumsfeld was still the defense secretary. "DoD," Gersony reported, "had no plan, no coordination, no connection with the grassroots, and was obsessed with projects that common Iraqis could not experience the value of." For example, rather than fix the sewage pipes in Sadr City so that people wouldn't smell human waste every morning when they woke up, the Department of Defense was renovating faraway plants that the Soviets had built decades before and which had never worked properly to begin with. This is why U.S. Army brass were constantly complaining that there weren't enough projects to help them build rapport with the population. "Where there was raw sewage in the streets and no electricity, there were also frequent armed attacks against American forces," Gersony reported.

Natsios chimes in: "In Iraq we were too focused on construction projects rather than on building civilian institutions—exactly what had worked for us around the developing world throughout the Cold War. But DoD was obsessed with rapid, demonstrable, and visible results whereas institution-building is long-term and operates behind the scenes. We knew DoD and Rumsfeld were wrong," Natsios goes on, "since we in USAID had decades of expeditionary experience in the Third World to rely on." Indeed, because USAID was established during the early Cold War, its roots in development work were venerable.

"For too long, DoD had no bottom-up connective strategy in Iraq," says Gersony. He adds, "You needed a bossy, big-city-mayor type—a Mayor Daley of Chicago—who knew from the first day of occupation that it was all about creating jobs for young men: temporary jobs, permanent jobs, jobs in the army, whatever. Just employ young men and do it fast!" Instead, Bremer famously disbanded the Iraqi army.

None of this was original thinking. Gersony was neither the first nor the last to discover what was amiss. Nevertheless, working alone, listening for hundreds of hours to different people, utilizing the same methodology as he always had, he came up with a hard, uncomfortable truth that couldn't be denied, and that backed up other people's assessments.

At the end of 2005 and the beginning of 2006, Gersony again made the rounds back in Washington: briefing the National Security Council, the CIA, and the Defense Department about what he had discovered on his second assignment in Iraq. "We knew things were bad, but not this bad," said one of the high officials Gersony had briefed. Gersony's findings constituted one small element in the eventual removal of Defense Secretary Donald Rumsfeld in November 2006, after the younger Bush administration had suffered a disastrous midterm election defeat. Rumsfeld had as early as autumn

2004 and spring 2005 repeatedly submitted his resignation. But President Bush kept him on, partly to resist pressure from the media and a collection of former generals who were publicly calling for Rumsfeld's head. Had Rumsfeld been ousted after Bush was re-elected in November 2004, rather than two years later as he was, the Iraq War might have turned out measurably different.

Knowing all that I know now about Iraq, Gersony's description of the occupation makes it impossible for me not to think of Graham Greene's novel about Vietnam, *The Quiet American,* published in 1955. As cruel a caricature as it was of American motives and sensibilities in the Third World, the subsequent debacle in Vietnam and the invasion and occupation of Iraq have proved the book incredibly clairvoyant. As it concerns the book's protagonist, the American diplomatic and intelligence operative Alden Pyle, Greene's narrator says, "I never knew a man who had better motives for all the trouble he caused." Pyle saw Vietnam only through the abstract mental concepts about democracy that he had heard in the "lecture-hall." He had no feel whatsoever for the vivid complexity of the country itself—"the gold of the rice-fields under a flat late sun: the fishers' fragile cranes hovering over the fields like mosquitoes: the cups of tea on an old abbot's platform . . . the mollusc hats of the girls repairing the road where a mine had burst," and so forth. People in Vietnam (or, for that matter, Iraq) did not want democracy or any ism, Greene concludes. "They want enough rice . . . they don't want to be shot at. They want one day to be much the same as another. They don't want our white skins around telling them what they want."[2]

Bob Gersony intuitively grasped this. He was immersed in the local complexities of every situation he came across around the globe, even if he had no eye for the local landscape. He was intense and committed, but at least not in the way that Greene decried. He hated grand schemes and formulas, as Tim Knight had learned about him in northern Peru and Bosnia, and as Bambi Arellano had learned about him in Ecuador. He understood the tragedy and irony of good intentions. Graham Greene certainly would have approved.

. . .

In the early spring of 2006, just after Gersony had finished his second Iraq project, Andrew Natsios, thoroughly exhausted after five years as USAID administrator during both the Iraq and Afghanistan wars, submitted his resignation. Natsios's replacement was Randall Tobias, a big Republican donor and the former CEO of the pharmaceutical company Eli Lilly, which he had, in fact, rescued. The result: Gersony was again in the wilderness with no onward assignment. Tobias, according to observers, was primarily interested in the organizational aspects of USAID rather than in the bread-and-butter work of the agency in the field. Tobias cared about position and authority, and was determined to be a deputy secretary of state, so that the actual projects of USAID on the ground concerned him relatively little. He simply had no interest in a Bob Gersony.

And there was something else about Randall Tobias. He wanted to downsize USAID and fold it into the State Department: make the agency disappear, in other words. Whenever USAID's invaluable foreign area specialists gradually retired, he didn't replace them. He was following a classic corporate strategy of hollowing out an organization by attrition. And everybody in USAID knew what he was up to.

Gersony went a year without the phone ringing. Nobody in the USAID hierarchy seemed to be able to find work for him. But in April 2007, Joe Williams was at his desk when he suddenly heard a commotion all around him. "It was like being at a soccer stadium when someone scores a goal," he remembers. "People were practically dancing and celebrating around their cubicles." The news had just broken that Randall Tobias had been forced to resign—after he was caught making phone calls to an escort service linked with prostitution. The effort to fold USAID into the State Department was stopped in its tracks. Not long after Tobias was gone, Joe Williams, who was as wry and laid-back in manner as Gersony was perpetually earnest, called Gersony. Williams needed help with a problem that had recently been thrown into his lap: a typhoon planning assessment required for the Federated States of Micronesia in the Pacific.

Micronesia, along with the Marshall Islands, spans an arc of

2,000 miles of ocean, with a population of only 180,000 people spread over 2,000 islands. The Micronesian and Marshall EEZ, or exclusive economic zone, is around twice that of the Mediterranean. This vast stretch of sea came under U.S. jurisdiction as a result of the Spanish-American War of 1898 (when the U.S. conquered the nearby Philippines) and World War II. It was a storied American legacy, in other words. Thus, when these islands became independent, they opted for "compacts of association" with the United States. Under these compacts, Washington had both the right and the obligation to provide entirely for their defense.

Yet something had recently changed. Congress in its wisdom had decided that no longer would Micronesia and the Marshalls, in the event of natural disasters, be helped by FEMA, the Federal Emergency Management Agency, but instead would come under the jurisdiction of USAID. This constituted a weakening in the link between the United States and Oceania, since FEMA dealt with the fifty states and USAID with foreign countries. The islanders were rightly worried that henceforth they wouldn't be getting the same level of assistance.

To investigate the islanders' concerns, Joe Williams dispatched Gersony to Oceania to do a blueprint for USAID typhoon planning. Gersony, sixty-two, in the professional wilderness for a year without an assignment, had no problem with a winter in the South Seas, where there were no dangers, no health risks, and no political controversies.

It would be in Micronesia where the full reality of America's misadventure in Iraq hit Gersony squarely in the face; by way of the contrast. Iraq constituted the bleak, ghastly, bloodstained imperialistic waste of U.S. foreign policy: the ultimate fatal distraction. Micronesia would constitute the soft, caressing crystalline seascape of Oceania, where the more crucial and intensifying challenge of China loomed just over the horizon. Iraq was the past; Micronesia, the future. In Micronesia, for a pittance compared to what a few days of the Iraq occupation was costing America, authoritarian China's geopolitical rise might have been diluted and delayed. I say this as someone who had been an early supporter of the Iraq War—which Gersony obviously was not.

Micronesia, as the twenty-first century wore on, would become a litmus test for the U.S.-China competition. The United States military was trying to manage the Chinese threat in hub-and-spoke Bismarckian fashion: that is, from a geographic point of comparative isolation—the Hawaiian Islands—with spokes reaching out to major allies such as Japan, South Korea, the Philippines, Thailand, and India. These countries, in turn, formed secondary hubs to help the U.S. manage the Micronesian, Melanesian, and Polynesian archipelagoes, as well as the Indian Ocean. China, for its part, had its sights set on dominating the South China Sea, which would enable Beijing to soften up Taiwan, as well as gain naval access to the Indian Ocean and the wider Pacific: this would mean effective Chinese control over the Micronesian and Melanesian archipelagoes.

Put another way, China's strategic goal was to control the First Pacific Island Chain, meaning the large landmasses off the mainland of Asia stretching from Japan south to the Philippines. Once that was accomplished, China would be able to project power outward to the Second Pacific Island Chain, encompassing Guam and the Northern Marianas Islands, the gateway to Micronesia. China was already flooding Micronesia with investments and aid packages. Truly, in this emerging naval century, where power means the ability to oversee the sea lines of communication that enable container shipping—the very foundation of globalization—Oceania was indeed at the heart of geopolitics.[3]

"We need to do a good job on these disaster services or the Chinese will use our inaction and mistakes as a wedge," one highly respected expatriate in Micronesia told Gersony soon after he arrived. "The Chinese are already quite active here—we can't leave a vacuum," warned one U.S. ambassador.

Gersony was instantly overwhelmed by the seascape of Micronesia. It offered a true demonstration of infinity, the next best thing to space travel. The water was an interminable panel of vast blue and pearly welts interspersed with reptilian green islands, which might as well have been small planets, volcanic and coral both, with the coral islands shaped like narrow flat daggers that were easily overrun by tidal waves. Indeed, the typhoons never really stopped here. In terms of Mother Nature, local populations lived on the edge. "People here needed reassurance that we were not nickel-and-diming them by switching from FEMA to USAID, and by removing the local U.S. post office. Such a petty thing to do," Gersony complains.

Indeed, the historical markers on these islands were a stern reminder of a U.S. legacy and sustaining commitment: the deaths of thousands of U.S. Marines who had stormed these beaches, fighting inch by inch to take a pillbox. The European theater in World War II produced one D-Day; the Pacific theater produced one after another: Tarawa, Guam, Saipan, Enewetak, Kwajalein, Truk . . . Micronesia and the nearby island groups also represent significant fish stocks, as well as votes at the United Nations. Yet, as Gersony immediately saw, it was now China that was building hotels, sports stadiums, and other infrastructure on these islands, as well as sending its most able diplomats here. China had spent $5 million on just one sports stadium in Majuro, the capital of the Marshall Islands, as well as $80 million on other projects. Taiwan had built a convention center in Micronesia, and Japan had spent tens of millions of dollars on school and health-care systems throughout the far-flung archipelago. But it was China that had been using America's distraction in the Middle East to slowly, methodically, and quietly expand its influence throughout all of the Indo-Pacific. The mega-concerns of Afghanistan and Iraq in Washington were working to obscure the very fact of these islands, as well as so much else. The U.S. military, particularly the Navy, would not be able to fully respond to the danger until around 2017.[4] (Indeed, as I write, the U.S.-China competition is assuming the characteristics of a bipolar, Cold War–style conflict, but one with an important asterisk: the lesser threat of Russia.)

Because Gersony had spent time getting briefed in both Washington and Honolulu before arriving in Micronesia, he quickly became aware of a cultural challenge, in terms of how the U.S. government's different bureaucracies viewed the South Seas.

Gersony was aware that he had spent his life at the intersection of politics and humanitarianism, and it was often at this intersection where it was easiest to get things done, since Washington was usually more likely to appropriate money for humanitarian concerns if it saw a geopolitical interest in a place. But here in Micronesia and the Marshalls, both USAID and the State Department lived far away from that intersection. The Pentagon's Pacific Command, however, headquartered in the Hawaiian capital of Honolulu, lived right at the heart of it. That's why Gersony found the uniformed officers at Pacific Command more enthusiastic about humanitarian assistance in Micronesia and the Marshalls than were the bureaucrats at USAID and State. Because the Pentagon's Pacific-based bureaucracy knew the value of these islands, it wanted to help any way it could, even if it was diverted in the Middle East and thus had its hands somewhat tied.

Gersony sensed a "minimalism" about Micronesia at the State Department and USAID, the kind of lack of urgency that he had also sensed during Hurricane Mitch and the first days in Iraq when the DART leaders had failed. In his mind, what was needed was a proactive approach best epitomized by Fred Cuny in Kurdistan in 1991. It would be hard to generate interest, though, mainly because of the tyranny of distance: each of these islands was just so far from the others, and all of them were so far from Honolulu, and Honolulu so far from Washington. Who said geography no longer mattered?

Gersony traveled from island to island for several months on two separate trips, interviewing 266 people in fifteen locations, including Guam and the Philippine capital of Manila. His conclusion was stark. The Federated States of Micronesia and the Marshall Islands constituted, much like Puerto Rico, a U.S. dependency, entailing a special obligation. Yet USAID had no one permanently stationed here on the ground, and despite the regular typhoons, there were almost no emergency supplies. "When disaster struck, these places were completely on their own for a week, since in the context of a typhoon, we would be unable to get there for quite a few days," he explains. About the suffering, he says: "Storms cause mudslides. You can't imagine how painful the wounds of a mudslide are, because of the stones, sticks, and other debris that hit people with such a powerful force!" One boy he interviewed had to have part of a stick removed from his stomach without anesthesia.

Thus emerged his recommendations, all of which were obvious: Position in advance, on the islands, anesthetics and other emergency trauma supplies. Pre-position generators and desalinization units. Despite the willingness of the U.S. military to help, use regional NGOs in any emergency since they were less bureaucratic than the Department of Defense. Bundle projects together to attract outside contractors, with all the projects coming under the direction of a "master NGO implementer," who would coordinate the work of the various non-governmental organizations. Employ private-sector companies in Guam and Honolulu to avoid the far less efficient U.S. Army Corps of Engineers. Bury high-voltage electric lines so they wouldn't be toppled in a storm. Create water-collection units on rooftops to capture clean drinking water from the rains. Replenish mangrove swamps as natural barriers against sea and wind damage.

Eventually, everything he recommended was implemented. "Gersony's work in Micronesia was a tour de force," says Peter Morris, an unassuming USAID official who had also worked with Gersony in Albania. "Gersony practically negotiated the details of the changeover from FEMA to USAID on these islands. Others had methodologies like Gersony's. But he had this special genius arising from an ability to conduct a dialogue with ordinary people, take voluminous notes, and then brief it down to the last detail."

Still, Gersony was discouraged. After a dreary and drawn-out bureaucratic battle, he ultimately failed to get a USAID officer permanently stationed in Pohnpei, the Micronesian capital—the officer went instead to the Marshall Islands capital of Majuro, a bit further removed. Small bureaucratic potatoes, but it mattered to him.

He was clearly troubled. Maybe it was his age and the fact that he was now working exclusively with lower-level people, not with the USAID administrator himself, or with assistant secretaries of state, but Gersony detected a new and growing weak-kneed avoidance of controversy and taking hard decisions in the bureaucracy. Every decision was more of a struggle now. Alas, USAID had never fully recovered from the short, disastrous tenure of Randall Tobias. Although new civil servants and Foreign Service officers began being hired after Tobias left, because of the downsizing during his reign, these new people lacked a sufficient number of mentors and the tradition that the old subject-matter experts embodied. The Iraq War also played its part. Humanitarian development workers were supposed to always be "neutral," but in Iraq you couldn't be, since you were part of an occupation.

Gersony perceived that the military takeover of foreign policy of recent years may have been not only the result of faulty analysis, romantic delusions about exporting democracy, and misbegotten wars, but also an organic osmosis that had been years in the making, ever since the end of the Cold War undermined disciplined thought. The military was simply the force of nature that had filled a vacuum: the vacuum of a slowly declining USAID and State Department bureaucracy, of which Hurricane Mitch in 1998 had provided Gersony with his first inkling. He felt that he was headed downhill, with fewer consequential assignments, and the State Department and USAID were headed in the same direction.

Says one longtime USAID official about the situation today:

"The Bob Gersonys, Fred Cunys, and Paul Bells of this world are gone. We're outsourcing our assessments to consulting groups now. We assume because of Twitter that we know what's happening on the ground in distant places, even if we don't."

CHAPTER 19

Northern Mexico by Way of Central America

2010–2013

Sleeping with His Notebook Between His Legs

Indeed, Bob Gersony looked around and did not like what he saw. One by one, all his senior mentors had retired or left: Fred Schieck, Gene Dewey, Jim Purcell, Jonathan Moore, Janet Ballantyne, Brian Atwood, Andrew Natsios. He was now working with people with insufficient bureaucratic clout to enforce decisions, and who generated far less of a sense of mission. Instead of two long and substantive assignments per year, he was now averaging one that was less substantive, more routine, and less prominent on account of how Iraq and Afghanistan had swallowed up all bureaucratic energies. The stage lights were dimming for him. In his midsixties, he was doing curtain calls.

But these curtain calls were dangerous and consequential and shed a light on the current mayhem on America's southern border.

They constituted three long trips: first it was back to Nicaragua's Atlantic coast, then to northern Mexico, and finally to the remote northeastern region of Mosquitia in Honduras. But all these assignments had to do with just one thing: the scourge of narcotics.

On May 11, 2012, a passenger boat was slowly moving along a river in Mosquitia when it was fired upon by a Honduran military helicopter. The nighttime action killed four civilians. Because the helicopter was actually being operated by the State Department's International Nar-

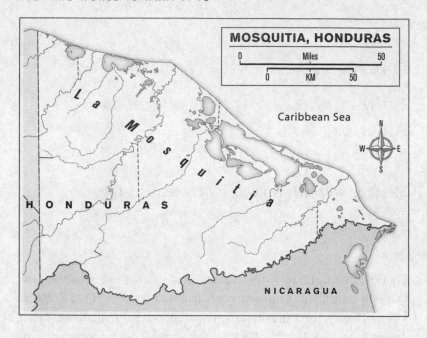

cotics and Law Enforcement bureau (INL), with an adviser from the U.S. Drug Enforcement Administration on board, a small controversy erupted in Washington.

In particular, Vermont Democratic senator Patrick Leahy was concerned. Over the decades, Leahy had carved out an important niche as a liberal Democrat absolutely committed to the rule of law, to human rights, and to pushing back at the increasing militarization of U.S. foreign policy. Right behind Leahy stood Tim Rieser, Leahy's powerful aide, who actually articulated the senator's foreign policy instincts on a day-to-day and issue-by-issue basis. Rieser may arguably have been the most formidable staff aide in Congress when it came to matters of human rights intersecting with strategic interests. He was one of those people who are famous and influential in Washington and unknown just about everywhere else. Whereas Leahy had been a county prosecutor, Rieser had been a public defender, so both men's commitment to justice at all costs was baked into their professional life experiences. And both internalized a par-

Vermont Democratic senator Patrick Leahy (seated) with his top foreign policy staffer, Tim Rieser. Rieser supported Gersony's work in Central America.

ticular clear-eyed form of idealism and fair play, arguably unrealistic at times, yet characteristic of rural Vermont, the same state that had produced Bernie Sanders.

In the wake of the helicopter incident, Tim Rieser had a conversation with Mark Wells, the director of INL's Latin American and Caribbean division. Rieser and Wells agreed that INL did not have an acceptable strategy for dealing with the Honduran Mosquitia. The two men also agreed that it was Bob Gersony who should travel through the region in order to design a strategy for fighting narcotics that did not infringe upon human rights. As Rieser recounts:

"The area was very remote, very dangerous, where it was hard to distinguish fact from fiction. So Bob Gersony was a good choice. There is only one Bob Gersony in this world."

As a State Department official told me, "Tim Rieser was a formidable policy intellect and he was therefore hard to argue with, but Bob Gersony could move the needle on him."

Between Nicaragua's Atlantic coast, where he had recently been, and the adjacent Honduran Mosquitia, Gersony would end up visiting 75 towns and villages where he would interview 357 people, 75 percent of whom were Miskitos and Creoles, and the rest Spanish-speaking. He would cover 750 miles of lakes and rivers, and 625 miles of road, through pine savannas, tropical forests, swamps, and steep mountains, interviewing every kind of person from jellyfish harvesters, disabled lobster divers,[1] fishermen and farmers, and small cattle owners, in addition to the usual drumroll of teachers, clerks, local officials, and so on. He will always remember the big turtles sunning themselves on logs as he sped along the vast rivers.

Gersony discovered that because Mosquitia had relatively few roads, no governance, and complete isolation, it had one asset: it could easily be taken over by narcotics traffickers, which is exactly what had happened. In particular, the traffickers had essentially made their own sovereign little country out of the northeastern corner of Mosquitia, located on the Atlantic coast, hard up against the Nicaraguan border. An army of thugs maintained this territory and had turned it into a principal trafficking point for Colombian cocaine on its way to the United States.

Gersony dared not enter this sovereign narcotics terrain, but he did interview dozens who lived right on the edge of it. As per his modus operandi, he traveled alone. But now for the first time in his life he grew a beard, in order to look like an aging hippie or butterfly collector, so as to attract a bit less suspicion. He slept with his notebook high up between his legs, "because my notebook was a death sentence for those I had interviewed, who had told me about what the narco-traffickers were up to."

The story he composed, based on his interviews, had many themes and avenues of entry. Here is one:

The narco-traffickers often transported the cocaine from Colombia northwest to the United States on boats, hugging the Atlantic seaboard of Central America, storing the cocaine in tightly sealed, waterproof bundles. The smugglers would be regularly attacked by Nicaraguan and Honduran naval vessels, forcing the smugglers to ditch some of the bundles in the water. The floating bundles later

washed ashore and were discovered by the local Miskitos and Creoles, who referred to the bundles as *langostas blancas,* or "white lob-
sters." Because of the sheer amount of cocaine that washed ashore,
many in Mosquitia and Nicaragua's Atlantic coast became addicted:
15 percent of the men aged 12 to 40 on Nicaragua's Atlantic coast and
40 percent in the Honduran Mosquitia, according to Gersony's calcu-
lations, based on his interviews. Moreover, this cheap bulk cocaine
became the organizing principle and unofficial currency of this remote region. Gasoline for boats was paid for in cocaine. Political and
cultural organizations came under the influence of those tied to the
local cocaine traffic.

Crime surged. Gersony ticks off:

"You couldn't leave your house unguarded. You couldn't leave
your pigs and chickens without somebody watching them. You
couldn't leave your propane cylinder outside, or your yucca field un-
attended at night. . . ."

In Puerto Lempira, the capital of Mosquitia located on a swelter-
ing long lagoon parallel to the Atlantic coast, Gersony watched as
"13- to 14-year-old girls were sold as prostitutes." The cocaine that had
not managed to make it through the Nicaraguan and Honduran security gauntlet to the United States was enough to corrupt an entire
population.

States in the developing world fail or are weakened for a plethora
of simple and complex reasons: environmental deterioration, demo-
graphic explosions, bad governance, ethnic and tribal divisions, and
so on. In Central America it was simple: the key ingredient to state
failure—which was in turn driving migrants to the U.S. border—was
America's own appetite for cocaine and other drugs, and the profit
motive that subsequently kicked in, undermining people's values and
state institutions.

Meanwhile, various NGO projects, mainly European, had failed in
Mosquitia. Electrification, mechanized rice milling, gravity-fed water
systems, and other ideas never succeeded not because of lack of
money, but because, at least in Gersony's opinion, of bad designs
caused by NGO workers not listening sufficiently to the advice of the

local inhabitants about what would work for them. This only intensified cynicism in the area.

Gersony's suggestions at the end of his journey were "modest" in
the extreme. "People here liked the United States," he advised. "It
wasn't like in the Spanish-speaking heart of Central America where
they distrusted us. So the relationship that the U.S. government builds
with Mosquitia and the Atlantic coast should not be transactional"—
that is, it should not be reduced to cynical deal-making.

He recommended the establishment of interagency working
groups in the U.S. embassies in Managua and Tegucigalpa, and the
continual cratering of runways in the region, using small explosives,
in order to reduce the number of planes landing to drop off cargoes
of cocaine, refuel, and return to Venezuela or Colombia. Yes, the runways would be repaired, but it would slow down the trafficking nonetheless and help demoralize the traffickers. Moreover, he wanted to
bring the number of State Department INL helicopters used against
cocaine traffickers down from six to two, in order to satisfy Senator
Leahy's office. Also, he suggested that the United States begin ac-
tively supporting non-narcotics, civil society elements throughout
Mosquitia and the Atlantic coast, and do the usual road and bridge
repairs in order to announce a benign presence.

Very small stuff. Completely unoriginal. Rolling the rock back up
the hill considering all the work he had done for years in the 1990s
on Nicaragua's Atlantic coast.

The embassies were delighted. But as obvious and minimalistic
as Gersony's recommendations were, not one thing was implemented. The Obama administration, in addition to its obligations
in Iraq and Afghanistan, had its priorities set more on sub-Saharan
Africa now; so that America's troubled near abroad in Central
America—the consequence of America's own appetite for drugs—
got shortchanged once again, even though Tim Rieser believed Gersony's recommendations were generally spot-on.

There was also an honest and legitimate disagreement in Washington bureaucratic circles, based on genuine philosophical differences, regarding what to do in yet another deeply troubled state of

Central America run by corrupt elites. Some wanted to work with those elites, however corrupt, since there was no other choice; others wanted to do the minimum in order to be completely true to America's values. Nevertheless, it might also be argued that, little by little, a spirit of distraction and contentiousness—the fruit of too much ideological confrontation—had been gradually taking over Washington, as facts on the ground in this overwhelmingly complex world of ours, best revealed by gumshoe reporting, became less relevant to decision-makers. The Internet had theoretically united the world, but the world remained more a mystery than ever. Nobody cared about a crisis if the media wasn't talking about it.

It was now 2013. Mosquitia would turn out to be Gersony's last assignment, yet there was no gold watch.

But let me go back in time to describe an earlier trip, which in a thematic sense concluded Gersony's career.

On Monday, October 17, 2011, Bob Gersony took a trolley south from San Diego and walked across the international border to Tijuana, Mexico. It was the first time that he had ever walked to an assignment. He was about to travel clean across northern Mexico, parallel to the U.S. border, from the Gulf of California in the west to the Gulf of Mexico in the east, a region where 90 percent of the cocaine and much of the marijuana and methamphetamines were coming into the United States.

The specific background to this assignment had started half a decade back in December 2006, when Felipe Calderón assumed the presidency of Mexico. At that time, northern Mexico was settled down. The small number of major drug cartels were all established and up and running. Each cartel had its own retail operation. The drug lords were dominant in the country, but, at least in cynical terms, it was a nice quiet business. However, Calderón was dead set on defeating the cartels and establishing the rule of law in Mexico. Rewarding his enthusiasm for such a risky venture in late 2007, the administration of President George W. Bush made a pact with Calderón known as the Mérida Initiative, named after a resort town in

Mexico where the two leaders met. Henceforth, the United States poured $1.4 billion into training Mexican counter-narcotics squads. But because the two leaders decided to decapitate the cartels, going after their leaders, the very success of the initiative led to an explosion underneath. After all, the cartels were really federations with component units and individual gangs, which, without the big leaders at the top, began fighting for turf and killing each other in the process.

Bush and Calderón had no idea what they had set in motion. All order was destroyed, as a significant part of northern Mexico was plunged into an abyss. It was vaguely like what had happened when the United States toppled Saddam Hussein, only more anarchic. In Iraq it was wholesale murder of Sunnis versus Shi'ites. In northern Mexico there was block-by-block retail murder of one gang against another. By the time Gersony crossed into Tijuana, four years after the signing of the Mérida Initiative, 47,000 people had been killed. In part, the Mérida Initiative was an outcome of insufficient knowledge, not only in Washington but also in the capital of Mexico City, about the lawless north of the country—Mexico being one of the most sprawling and mountainous countries on earth, breeding incredible diversity and historically weak central control.[2]

Thus, in 2011, as a result of all the violent chaos, Mexico and the Obama administration initialed Beyond Mérida, a development program to help communities that had been destroyed on account of the original Mérida Initiative. But before money could be spent, a situational analysis on the ground was needed. This is where Bob Gersony comes in.

He began his research in the three most drug-affected neighborhoods of each of the three most drug-affected cities: Tijuana, Ciudad Juárez, and Monterey. It was no world shaker of an assignment. Sort of like his assignment in Gaza, he merely had to identify activities for high-risk youth that would have a quick impact. And like in Bosnia, he was under pressure to do it quickly. Still, he had 340 meetings with 320 people (20 of whom he interviewed twice). Of course, he saw mayors, other local officials, and NGO workers. But 40 percent of his interviewees were ordinary people. He wandered the streets of these violent, high-crime neighborhoods alone, without a bodyguard but armed with his Spanish, buttonholing people, with sometimes a driver a discreet distance away in some of the neighborhoods. And he never went out after dark.

The people he met complained to him about burglaries, even as violence had actually come down because the cartels had recently been working their way back to agreements on territory. Nevertheless, the local economies were depressed because many shops had closed, unable to pay the rate of extortion demanded by the newly conceived, post-Mérida narcotics regimes. The local economies had also been hurt by the effect of the Great Recession in the United States.[3]

Gersony's starkest realization was just how out of touch officialdom in Mexico City was. Educated at the finest European and American schools, burdened by too many political science theories, this oligarchic Mexican elite talked to him only in abstractions about the situation in northern Mexico, which might as well have been another country to them: Mex-America, Greater Texas, what have you. "I was like a dentist probing for cavities, searching high and low to identify these new, experimental ideas that officials in Mexico City kept telling me about, but I uncovered nothing. Conversations in Mexico City were like drawing blood from a rock," Gersony exclaims, in a tone of special pleading, his bush hat touching the top of his glasses. "But while Mexico City was full of pretentiousness and theoretical talk, all the people I found up north, as poor and crime-ravaged as they were, were thoroughly grounded."

In particular, Ciudad Juárez set him on fire with the high quality of its local NGO workers and volunteers. Ciudad Juárez was reputed to be the murder capital of Mexico. In this city of 1.2 million at the time, 700 people were murdered in the early months of 2010 alone, and 2,600 had been killed the year before; while 200,000 or more had fled.[4]

But Gersony discovered, under the leadership of one Enrique Suárez y Toriello, feet-on-the-ground, nuts-and-bolts, locally driven efforts with little buy-in from Mexico City. For example, there was an "extended hours" program in the most drug-infested neighborhoods. Here troubled youth received help with their homework, had access to recreational activities, music and dance, and ethics training, while their parents were working all day and commuting back and forth for two hours to *maquiladoras,* factories where products were assembled for export to the United States.

"Ciudad Juárez is the thing that sings," Gersony told his USAID superiors when he had finished his assignment. "Build out from it. Don't do everything. Just replicate one or two things everywhere based on that model." The boys' and girls' after-school model served a similar, fundamental purpose as the capturing of potable rainwater in the West Bank had. There were also remedial learning programs for academically challenged kids who wanted to leave school after the sixth grade, as well as micro-credit schemes. After beginning with a storm of unknowns, with Mexico City elites leading him down rabbit holes about doing something "new" and "experimental," he had arrived at the mundane obvious. So often it was not about being creative, but merely about being practical. With the lights of El Paso, Texas, in the distance just over the border as evening descended, Gersony found poor and violent Ciudad Juárez to be one of the most inspiring places he had ever been in the developing world. He had come home, almost.

Gersony's long career was over now. From Guatemala in the 1970s to northern Mexico of the 2010s, it charted the history of humanitarianism since the Vietnam War. After all, the State Department's refugee bureau, for which Gersony worked, had its beginnings under President Jimmy Carter, when communist takeovers in Vietnam and Cambodia led to a humanitarian cataclysm as millions streamed out of those countries into Thailand and elsewhere. Gersony was still dealing with it while engaged in solving the problem of piracy against Vietnamese boat people in the mid-1980s. The Indochina refugee crisis was also where the NGO industry as we know it today really came into prominence. President Ronald Reagan picked up the torch as his secretary of state, George Shultz, seamlessly combined hard-headed realism with humanitarianism in Africa, exemplified by Gersony's work in Uganda, Sudan, and Mozambique, where war and famine led to millions of refugees and displaced persons. Indeed, when I began to read about how human rights had only come to the forefront in the 1990s upon the conclusion of the Cold War, it was news to me, since I was one of hundreds of journalists covering the humanitarian catastrophe of the mid-1980s in the war-and-famine-plagued Horn of Africa and Sudan: a catastrophe that the United States played a major role in alleviating and which was front-page news at the time, as was the earlier Indochina refugee crisis. In fact, my first book, *Surrender or Starve* (1988), was about the humanitarian catastrophe of Marxist Ethiopia during the Cold War, which I was researching when I first met Bob Gersony.

Of course, those claiming that the end of the Cold War allowed at first for a greater focus on human rights did have an important point. Finally free of the geopolitical nightmare of competing with a world-wide bloc of Soviet-aligned states, the United States and the West in general no longer had the excuse of turning a blind eye to human rights abuses simply because the perpetrators in question were anti-communist. And now because survival was assured with nuclear Armageddon avoided, our higher values could assume their rightful place. Though, at the same time, the very fact that we had been in a worldwide geopolitical competition with the Soviet Union did give us a naked self-interest in engagement with virtually every country in the developing world. USAID's highwater mark was during the Cold War, when it had intensive foreign aid programs in many dozens of countries. Realism, in the person of George Shultz, a thoroughly decent man and an extraordinary leader of organizations, easily encompassed a concern for human rights during this latter period of the Cold War, when moral action was grounded in strategic needs.

Alas, realists have lately had a tendency to drift into neo-isolationism. As they would put it, with the Cold War over for many years now, the United States has no need to be as concerned with defending its values abroad as vigorously as in the past, and should therefore concentrate on perfecting its own society at home.

So was the Cold War—especially the latter part of the Cold War when Bob Gersony was in his prime—an aberration: a unique moment when realism and human rights could be reconciled? No, I don't think so. Technology is making the world a smaller and smaller place, even as this world becomes ever more crowded, where a crisis anywhere can affect politics everywhere: where, thanks to jet travel, a disease outbreak in sub-Saharan Africa or China can have national security implications for the United States. This is to say nothing about northern Mexico and Central America, whose crises still have an obvious bearing on both our domestic and our foreign policy, a decade after Gersony last worked there.

We cannot hide from the world. Thus, realism and idealism may be destined to get along somehow, even in a new era of great power competition with China that has similarities with the Cold War. Realism never dies because it is about limits, constraints, and hard choices. But idealism never dies because, ever since the morally urgent messages of the Hebrew prophet Isaiah and the Greek playwright Euripides, it has appealed to the human spirit. The path forward requires mingling the sensibilities of both. That is the ultimate lesson of Bob Gersony's life.

Antigua, Guatemala
May 2019

The 12,336-foot-high stratovolcano looms over a late-seventeenth-century arch and one-story gridwork of cobblestone streets like Vesuvius over Pompeii.[1] There is a stark, monolithic, camera-like sharpness to these houses naked to the sky, with their blotched, conical clay roof tiles and pastel facades effecting the drama of an archaeological site. In every direction you turn, your jaw drops from the breathless intensity of the view. I can see how living here for seven years in his impressionable twenties, almost straight from the grueling horror of Vietnam, obscured in Bob Gersony's memory all the other landscapes he was to see over the next four decades.

Gersony is now standing with me down the street from the arch with the volcano just behind it, his hand on the curvaceous grillwork of a window open to the street. "Here in this window is where Max the Wonder Dog would crouch for hours looking at people passing by. This house is where I first lived in Antigua in the very early 1970s.

"I remember it was a midafternoon," Gersony says out of the blue. "I was standing outside the front door on this very spot with Terry Kaufman. I'll never forget his earring and ponytail. He was wearing a pink Mayan *traje* from Lake Atitlán that day. I had asked him, 'If we could find native Mayan speakers with at least six years of education and put them together with professional linguists in one-on-three settings, do you think they could learn descriptive linguistics? That way, instead of all these foreigners, it could be the Mayans themselves who would be the linguists for their own language.'

" 'I think it's possible,' Kaufman answered.

" 'Would you be willing to help us?'

" 'Yeah, I could come down every summer. And I won't charge you anything.' "

Gersony smiles at the long-ago memory. Admiring the view, I ask myself, How could Terrence Kaufman have refused such an offer given this setting, where spread out here and there among the one-story houses and loud flowers bursting through all the grillwork are the ruins of baroque cathedrals from hundreds of years ago, their stone and brick formations scarred and dissected and chewed away by earthquakes, volcanic eruptions, and time itself? Way back then Antigua was an empty stage set for Gersony and his companions, faded and shabbier, yet even more evocative, without the crowds and tourist police of today.

We wander over to the house built around a courtyard where Gersony, Jo Froman, and Tony Jackson used to live. It is now a boutique hotel bursting with fantasy vegetation and fountains. "Bob Gersony changed Antigua," Elizabeth Bell, a historian and preservationist who has lived here since 1969, tells me. "The boutique hotels, the perfectly landscaped baroque sites, the small-scale culturally sensitive tourism, it all began with Bob's network of language schools with its focused, one-on-one approach."

A little later, I am sitting with Bob Gersony on a bench in the cathedral square, exactly the same spot where he was getting his shoes shined when he met Luis Monzon, the garage worker who agreed to be his friend and teach him Spanish for a dollar a day. It was one of the early turning points in Gersony's life. That was a half century ago. Gersony is now bald, with a clipped white beard and glasses. He is demonstrably spiritual with his stoic, faraway look and owl eyes, even as his insights remain relentlessly practical.

Indeed, Gersony spans that yawning gap in sensibilities between idealism and realism, between human rights and national interest. For he was one humanitarian who internalized the interests of state—a reason why he was able to be so effective with officials in making U.S. foreign policy a bit smarter and a bit more humane.

In the course of over four decades of work, he estimates that he
interviewed on the order of 8,200
people around the world in 54 assignments, quite a few of which I
have described. It was grueling
labor. As Thomas Mann writes,
quoting the Letter to the Hebrews,
"He who seeketh hard things shall
have it hard."[2]

"For the most part," Gersony
begins, "I interviewed very busy
people. They were people busy
collecting firewood in order to sur-

Bob Gersony in 2020.

vive. They were people on line for water. They were people selling
corn and beans for basic sustenance. They were people waiting patiently in a local mayor's office where everyone was sweating profusely because there was no air conditioner. They were nurses in the
middle of a cholera epidemic, getting only a few hours of sleep a
night. They were all gracious enough to talk to me. All these people
were experts about what they knew. We depend on them to learn
about the world.

"The issue is," he continues, "how can we turn talking with ordinary people into useful facts rather than a mere collection of anec-
dotes? One simple way is by constructing a system: interview a large
number of people randomly selected, from a variety of towns and
villages, and try as hard as you can to eliminate your own passions
and biases. For what we can learn from ordinary people is much
more than the human rights situation, as absolutely critical as that is,
but the political and military situation, too, as it exists in conflict
zones. What you learn from refugees and displaced persons you
often cannot learn from satellite photos and wire intercepts—you
learn the very nuances and texture of situations. And what you learn
in the field should be integral to policy formulation."

Indeed, everyone who mentored and helped Gersony, from Jonathan Moore and Tim Rieser on the left of center, to Gene Dewey and Andrew Natsios on the right of center, with Brian Atwood, Janet Ballantyne, and Chester Crocker and the mass of the diplomatic cadre in the middle, was united on the primary importance of facts on the ground, and letting the facts on the ground influence policy. The views of all of them, and of Gersony especially, were evidence-based. We have less and less of that nowadays, as mere opinion, often unseasoned, seeps into the media more and more, influencing government decisions, and drowning out old-fashioned reporting in the back of beyonds away from capital cities.

While not officially a reporter, Gersony was one in a spiritual sense. There is an overwhelming, quiet exactitude about him. Of the nearly one hundred people, including former ambassadors and aid workers, that I interviewed, none contradicted Gersony's version of events in any substantial way. As much as I tried to find mistakes in Gersony's memory, I tripped him up only on minor matters. A long-ago colleague from middle Tennessee was really, as I found out, from western Tennessee. A principal deputy assistant secretary of state was really an acting principal deputy assistant secretary of state; a Wednesday years back was really a Monday. He wasn't infallible, but he was close to being so, since he was always worried about getting things wrong.

"People imagined Bob as some strapping, Cary Grant figure in a field jacket. But when they met him they found someone touchingly vulnerable and earnest, always shy and nervous before each assignment," say both Carol Chan and James Fleming of USAID.

For people in USAID, the State Department, and the other agencies and branches of the U.S. government, getting a briefing from Bob Gersony was almost a kind of respite, since as urgent as his reporting was, all passion was extruded from it. All day long these people had passion thrown at them, and passion can put you on the defensive. Keeping passion out of his briefings was a hard-fought task, because of all the anger that would build up inside him, on account of all the atrocities and bureaucratic stupidities he confronted. It was in talking to me for hundreds of hours that Gersony has finally released his passion, which had been gathering force for nearly forty-five years since the Guatemalan earthquake.

Gersony's adult life and work stretches from the Vietnam War to the second decade of the twenty-first century—the Cold War and its aftermath, when the United States was at the center of the world. It was a time of American triumphs and American follies, much of which were secondary to Gersony's immediate concerns, even as his labors, practiced in the obscurity of remote places, quietly dignified the idealism of the American brand (in all its self-conceived purity). Indeed, the aim of his fieldwork—investigating human suffering and how to alleviate it—punctuated what American foreign policy was supposed to be ultimately about, and what our national interest was supposed to be a road to. In the best sense of the word, Gersony's own story has been that of America in the wider world.

Gersony, who hid from the media and eschewed publicity, because that would have made him less effective than he was, was ambitious mainly as it concerned his search for the truth in a given crisis or situation on a variety of continents. Otherwise, he always felt more secure being virtually unknown and unpromoted. Throughout his life he has avoided dinner parties and diplomatic receptions. I learned about him only by accident, by being introduced to him through a relief worker in the stifling dining hall of the Acropole Hotel in Khartoum in the spring of 1985. I have tracked him ever since, finding myself in many a place around the globe just before or just after he had been there. He was so much more interesting than many of the big shots I have met over the years. The only demand that he ever made of me as a writer was to not betray the people who had helped him in certain countries, where despite the passage of time, their lives (he believes) might still be in danger. To call Gersony great is to diminish him, since greatness usually involves an unusual degree of ambition, concealed or unconcealed. Gersony achieved his ambition, over and over again, by recording people's stories in his notebooks while under a tree or inside a tent somewhere, with the dulling heat, buzzing flies, and wafting dust intensifying the silence. That was his glory.

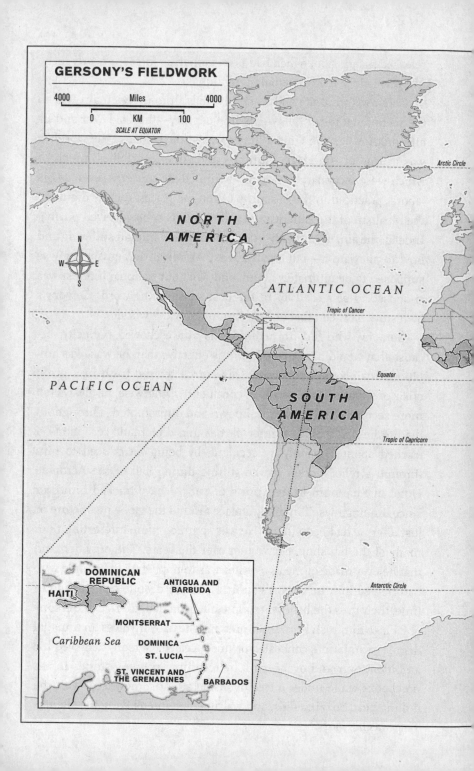

GERSONY'S FIELDWORK

4000   Miles   4000

0   KM   100

SCALE AT EQUATOR

Arctic Circle

NORTH AMERICA

N
W   E
S

ATLANTIC OCEAN

Tropic of Cancer

PACIFIC OCEAN

Equator

SOUTH AMERICA

Tropic of Capricorn

Antarctic Circle

DOMINICAN REPUBLIC

ANTIGUA AND BARBUDA

HAITI

MONTSERRAT

Caribbean Sea

DOMINICA

ST. LUCIA

ST. VINCENT AND THE GRENADINES

BARBADOS

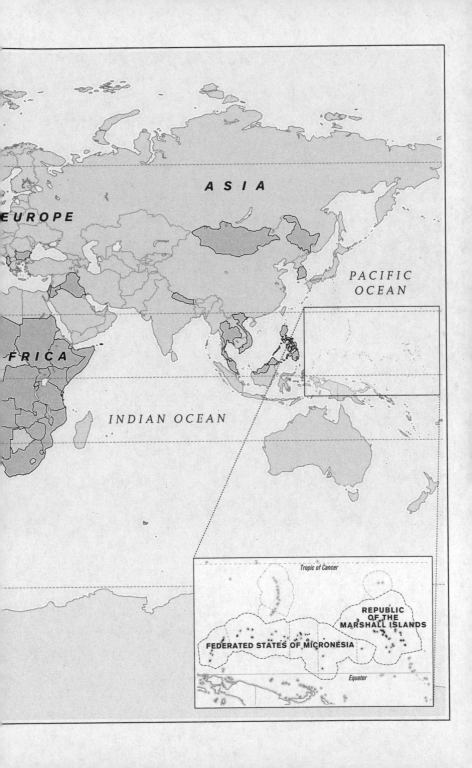

ASIA

EUROPE

PACIFIC
OCEAN

AFRICA

INDIAN OCEAN

Tropic of Cancer

**REPUBLIC
OF THE
MARSHALL ISLANDS**

FEDERATED STATES OF MICRONESIA

Equator

Acknowledgments

In 2017 and 2018, during the early phase of my work on this book, I received financial and logistical support from the Center for a New American Security (CNAS) in Washington, for which I thank CEO Richard Fontaine and Director of Operations Ellen McHugh: friends both. At CNAS, close friendship and advice also came from Elbridge Colby, Adam Klein, David Romley, and Matt Seeley.

I conducted many of the interviews at the Cosmos Club in Washington, whose warm and ornate rooms provided a perfect setting to quietly engage with people over their diplomatic and Foreign Service memories.

Former *New York Times* foreign correspondent James Brooke and former CBS News foreign correspondent Allen Pizzey both helped in specific aspects of my research, owing to their matchless knowledge of the developing world at ground level. Help also came from my colleague Erik Fish at Eurasia Group.

Rebecca Cox, director of the office of public liaison in the Reagan White House, was generous with her time regarding research requests. Jennifer Newby, archivist at the Reagan Presidential Library in Simi Valley, California; Cody McMillian, archives technician at the George H. W. Bush Presidential Library in College Station, Texas; and Dana Simmons, supervisory archivist at the Clinton Presidential Library in Little Rock, Arkansas, all provided assistance for which I am grateful.

Charles Hill, diplomat-in-residence at Yale and executive assistant to George Shultz during his years as secretary of state, read the manuscript, commented on it, and made a number of corrections. I am deeply thankful for his help.

Henry Thayer at Brandt & Hochman Literary Agents was a calm and subtle magician in the way that he analyzed this book and helped move its publication date forward, ahead of another book that I had already completed. Working with him in flipping the order of publication was my editor at Random House, Molly Turpin, who labored tirelessly to mold an unwieldy manuscript into a finished product. Anna Pitoniak was the acquiring editor before Molly came on the scene, and was a promoter of this book at the beginning. I am also grateful to Kate Medina and Tom Perry at Random House for their enduring support of my work over the years. My literary agents, Gail Hochman and Marianne Merola, continue to be there for me.

Carol Poticny helped enormously with the maps and photographs, as she did for an earlier book of mine, *In Europe's Shadow*. Finally, I thank my trusted assistant of many years, Elizabeth M. Lockyer, for ordering my professional life in a way that allows me the time to write and research in solitude. Diane and Marc Rathbun have also helped me with the logistics of life. Then there is my beloved wife of thirty-seven years, Maria Cabral, without whom none of this would have been possible.

Glossary

CIO—Zimbabwe's Central Intelligence Organization

CODELS—Congressional delegation tours

CPA—Coalition Provisional Authority (Iraq)

DART—Disaster assistance response team

DAS—Deputy assistant secretary of state

DCM—Deputy chief of mission—the number two person at a U.S. embassy

DEA—Drug Enforcement Administration

DIA—Defense Intelligence Agency

DMZ—Demilitarized zone

ECOMOG—Economic Community of West African States Monitoring Group

EEZ—Exclusive economic zone

FARC—Revolutionary Armed Forces of Colombia, an insurgency supported by drug trafficking

FEDEMU—Federal Democratic Movement of Uganda, an anti-government insurgency

FEMA—Federal Emergency Management Agency

FMLN—Farabundo Martí National Liberation Front, Salvadoran left-wing guerrillas sponsored by the Sandinistas in Nicaragua and facilitated by the Cubans

FRELIMO—Front for the Liberation of Mozambique, an anti-Portuguese guerrilla group, with some support from Cuba and the Soviet Union

FSN—Foreign Service National

FSO—Foreign Service officer

ICRC—International Committee of the Red Cross

INL—International Narcotics and Law Enforcement Bureau of the U.S. Government

IOM—Geneva-based International Organization for Migration

IRA—Irish Republican Army

LRA—Lord's Resistance Army of northern Uganda

MILGROUP—Military group within the U.S. Embassy in El Salvador, at the heart of U.S. military assistance to the Salvadoran government

NGO—Non-governmental organization, usually within the humanitarian aid category

NIC—National Intelligence Council, for middle-term and long-term thinking within the U.S. intelligence community

NPFL—National Patriotic Front of Liberia, a rebel group

NRA—Uganda's National Resistance Army

OAS—Organization of American States

OFDA—Office of Foreign Disaster Assistance within the U.S. Agency for International Development (USAID)

OTI—Office of Transition Initiatives within the U.S. Agency for International Development (USAID)

Oxfam—Oxford Committee for Famine Relief, founded in Britain in 1942

PLO—Palestine Liberation Organization

RENAMO—Resistência Nacional Moçambicana, an indigenous African anti-communist insurgency supported by apartheid South Africa

REST—Relief Society of Tigre (Ethiopia)

RPF—Tutsi-dominated Rwandan Patriotic Front

RSO—Regional security officer in a U.S. embassy

SCIF—Sensitive Compartmented Information Facility for classified discussions and material

SNM—Somali National Movement, a rebel group

TPLF—Tigre People's Liberation Front (Ethiopia)

UNAMIR—United Nations Assistance Mission for Rwanda

UNDP—United Nations Development Program

UNHCR—United Nations High Commissioner for Refugees

UNRWA—United Nations Relief and Works Agency

USAID—United States Agency for International Development

WFP—United Nations World Food Programme

Notes

MANY SMALL BEGINNINGS

Chapter 1. Vietnam, 1966–1969

1 W. H. Auden, "Brussels in Winter," December 1938. In Auden's *Collected Poems* (New York: Vintage International, 1991), p. 178.
2 Bernard Fall, *Street Without Joy: The French Debacle in Indochina* (Mechanicsburg, PA: Stackpole Books, 1961), p. 209.
3 Ibid., pp. 144, 184, and 188.

Chapter 2. Guatemala, 1970–1977

1 See Stephen Kinzer's *The Brothers: John Foster Dulles, Allen Dulles, and Their Secret World War* (New York: Henry Holt, 2013).
2 Just as the CIA overthrow of Mosaddegh was a formative event in the life of Ayatollah Ruhollah Khomeini, the overthrow of Árbenz was likewise for Ernesto "Che" Guevara. See Jim Newton's *Eisenhower: The White House Years* (New York: Doubleday, 2011), pp. 162–69.
3 Odd Arne Westad, *The Global Cold War* (Cambridge: Cambridge University Press, 2005), pp. 4–5.
4 Robert J. McMahon, *The Cold War in the Third World* (New York: Oxford University Press, 2013), p. 3. I am paraphrasing Columbia University's Robert Jervis.
5 John Darwin, *After Tamerlane: The Rise and Fall of Global Empires, 1400–2000* (New York: Bloomsbury Press, 2008), p. 469.
6 Jeffrey James Byrne's essay in McMahon's *The Cold War in the Third World*, pp. 111–12.
7 Odd Arne Westad, *The Cold War: A World History* (New York: Basic Books, 2017), p. 261. McMahon, *The Cold War in the Third World*, p. 1.
8 Westad, *The Cold War*, p. 56.
9 Westad, *The Global Cold War*, p. 4.
10 McMahon, *The Cold War in the Third World*, p. 3.
11 Westad, *The Global Cold War*, p. 399.
12 Ralph Lee Woodward, Jr., *A Short History of Guatemala* (Antigua, Guatemala: Editorial Laura Lee, 2005).

13 Mark Bosco, introduction to Graham Greene's *The Honorary Consul* (New York: Penguin Books, 2008).

14 The Guatemalan Congress would eventually adopt the alphabet developed by Gersony's organization over that of the Protestant Summer Institute of Linguistics for the official Mayan script, with one change in a single character.

15 Brigittine M. French, *Maya Ethnolinguistic Identity: Violence, Cultural Rights, and Modernity in Highland Guatemala* (Tucson: University of Arizona Press, 2010), p. 54.

16 André Schwarz-Bart, *The Last of the Just* (1959; New York: MJF Books, 1960), pp. 4–5.

17 An independent British auditor working for a Dallas-based consulting company wrote: "Both the assumptions on which the program's hypothesis was founded and the style of management adopted by AID represented an unusual, sensitive and innovative approach to intervention in a post-disaster situation. . . . [It] was assumed that the inputs made by AID would result in maximum satisfaction for the beneficiaries, provided that they themselves made the decisions and managed the deployment of materials as they saw fit. . . . This approach is in sharp contrast to that pursued by most relief and reconstruction agencies which act in response to what *they* think are important needs. . . . The result was a program with very considerable benefits to the rural poor . . . almost all of the rural people benefited to some degree. . . ." Alan J. Taylor, *USAID Guatemala: Lamina and Housing Materials Distribution Program; Ex-Post Evaluation Report* (Dallas, TX: Intertect, June 1977).

Chapter 3. Dominica, El Salvador, and South America, 1979–1983

1 The United States would eventually give Charles's government millions of dollars in aid, in addition to a supplement from the CIA. Bob Woodward, *Veil: The Secret Wars of the CIA, 1981–1987* (New York: Simon & Schuster, 1987), pp. 278–79.

2 Otto Reich, "The Day the Evil Empire Retreated," *Wall Street Journal*, October 25, 2018.

3 Robert Reinhold, "U.S. Agency Disavows Forecast of Quakes," *New York Times*, January 30, 1981.

4 Joan Didion, *Salvador* (1983; New York: Vintage International, 1994), pp. 13–15, 22, 34, 37–38, and 72–73. Mark Danner, "The Truth of El Mozote," *The New Yorker*, December 6, 1993.

5 Elisabeth Malkin, "Honor Comes Late to Oscar Romero, a Martyr for the Poor," *New York Times*, May 22, 2015.

6 Larry Rohter, "4 Salvadorans Say They Killed U.S. Nuns on Orders of Military," *New York Times*, April 3, 1998.

7 Anthony Lewis, "Paying for Murder," *New York Times*, April 24, 1990.

8 Robert D. Kaplan, *Imperial Grunts: The American Military on the Ground* (New York: Random House, 2005), pp. 45–46.

9 Didion, *Salvador*, pp. 87–88.

10 Deane Roesch Hinton, *Economics and Diplomacy: A Life in the Foreign Service of the United States* (Washington, DC: Association for Diplomatic Studies and Training; New Academia Publishing/VELLUM Books, 2015), pp. 337 and 343.

11 Ibid., p. 334.

12 As it happened, Álvaro Magaña was chosen as president for two years, and

would be succeeded by Napoléon Duarte. Hinton, *Economics and Diplomacy*, pp. 348–49. Tom Buckley, *Violent Neighbors: El Salvador, Central America, and the United States* (New York: Crown, 1984), p. 28. Didion, *Salvador*, p. 31.

13 Edward Schumacher, "Floods and Droughts Sweep Across South America," *New York Times*, June 12, 1983.

BIG PLAYS

Chapter 4. Uganda, Luwero Triangle, 1984

1 Over the years, cables have gone from being sent by telex and finally by computer. But they have always been put in code and then decoded on arrival, and they are still referred to as cables.

2 Paul Kenyon, *Dictatorland: The Men Who Stole Africa* (London: Head of Zeus, 2018), pp. 284–87.

3 Robert D. Kaplan, "Uganda: Starting Over," *The Atlantic*, April 1987.

4 Ibid. I have relied mainly on my *Atlantic* essay for historical background.

5 David Lamb, *The Africans* (1983; London: Methuen, 1985), p. 78.

6 Ibid., p. 88.

7 Bob Gersony, letter to Ann Siegel, March 18, 1984.

8 In mid-October 2003, the ICRC mission in Baghdad, run by Gassmann, was attacked by a truck bomb, killing two guards.

9 Kaplan, "Uganda: Starting Over."

10 Ibid.

11 Years later, in 1989, Oliver Furley, head of the politics and history department at Convent Polytechnic School in Nigeria, wrote the story of these events in an article, "Britain from Uganda to Museveni: Blind Eye Diplomacy." It was included in the volume *Conflict Resolution in Uganda*, ed. Kumar Rupesinghe (Oslo: Peace Research Institute, 1989; Athens, Ohio: Ohio University Press, 1989; London: James Curry Ltd., 1989). Furley writes that following Elliott Abrams's public denunciation of the Luwero Triangle atrocities, "the British government was ready to switch its view of the matter. Malcolm Rifkind, Minister of State at the Foreign Office, said . . . 'our view of conditions in Uganda does not differ significantly from that of the Americans.' This was quite a switch, and he was responding to strong criticism [by] Amnesty International, which had accused the Foreign Office of being 'craven' and 'pussy-footing' in its response to Abrams' claims." Furley quotes a May 5, 1985, London *Times* article by Richard Dowden, reporting that in the Luwero Triangle, "there is no one left for the army to kill."

12 Don Gregg and Bill Eckert, "Memorandum for the Vice President: Archbishop of Uganda; Set-up for June 27, 10 a.m. meeting." Washington, June 19, 1984.

13 Years later, the Swiss authorities would settle on a figure of 300,000 killed.

14 Allen C. Davis, oral history, interviewed by Peter Moffat (Washington, DC: Association for Diplomatic Studies and Training, June 26, 1998). An oral history is exactly what the name implies: a recently retired diplomat sits down with a researcher operating a tape recorder and speaks for many hours, recounting the story of his life and of his career in the U.S. Foreign Service.

15 Graham Greene, *The Quiet American* (1955; New York: Penguin Books, 2004), p. 20.

16 Caryle Murphy, "New Ugandan Crackdown Said to Kill Thousands." *Washington Post,* August 5, 1984.

17 "What Uganda's Flag Is Hiding," *New York Times,* August 11, 1984.

18 Clifford May, "Amid the Agony of Uganda: The Puzzle of Obote," *New York Times,* September 21, 1984.

19 In particular, the September 1984 issue of *South* magazine (published in London) carried a long report by correspondent William Pike, "Behind the Guerrilla Lines," about Pike's 100-mile journey on foot across the Luwero Triangle, in which he wrote about seeing large mounds of bodies on both sides of the road, and the widespread scattering of bones (pp. 29–30).

20 Helen Epstein, "The Mass Murder We Don't Talk About," *New York Review of Books,* June 7, 2018.

Chapter 5. South China Sea, 1984–1985

1 Ambassador Chas W. Freeman, Jr., oral history, interviewed by Charles Stuart Kennedy (Washington: Association for Diplomatic Studies and Training, April 14, 1995).

2 Nick Williams, Jr., " 'Boat People' Now Safer: Thailand Cracks Down on Pirates Raiding Refugees," *Los Angeles Times,* March 28, 1987.

Chapter 6. Sudan and Chad, 1985

1 This section is drawn from my 1993 book, *The Arabists: The Romance of an American Elite* (New York: The Free Press), chapters 10 and 11.

2 This completes the summary of Operation Moses extracted from *The Arabists,* which has a much more detailed account of how Weaver carried out the Falasha rescue plan.

3 Edward Girardet, "From Khartoum to Capetown/An African Journey: Meet the Pagoulatoses and Their Hotel, the Place to Stay in Khartoum," *Christian Science Monitor,* July 8, 1985.

4 Robert D. Kaplan, *Surrender or Starve: The Wars Behind the Famine* (Boulder, CO: Westview Press, 1988), p. 166.

5 Robert D. Kaplan, "Sudan: A Microcosm of Africa's Ills," *The Atlantic,* April 1986. Robert D. Kaplan, "Uganda: Starting Over," *The Atlantic,* April 1987.

6 Hendrie would later receive an OBE (Order of the British Empire) from Prince Charles for her humanitarian work.

7 Scott Anderson, *The Man Who Tried to Save the World: The Dangerous Life and Mysterious Disappearance of Fred Cuny* (1999; New York: Anchor Books, 2000), pp. 4 and 160.

8 Ibid., p. 236.

Chapter 7. Honduras, 1985–1986

1 Corr had sparred with Gersony in Bolivia a few years earlier over the latter's fieldwork there. But a third of a century later, Corr graciously downplays his disputes with Gersony in both Bolivia and Central America, saying: "I believe that we in the embassy understood there were bound to be some differences. My memory is there were concerns, but our view was that his work was professional."

2 Médecins Sans Frontières, "Salvadoran Refugee Camps in Honduras 1988," *MSF Speaks Out*, 2004 and 2013.

Chapter 8. Mozambique, 1987–1988

1 Ian Martin, eulogy for Jonathan Moore, June 3, 2017.

2 Freeman, oral history, April 14, 1995.

3 Ken Flower, *Serving Secretly: An Intelligence Chief on Record, Rhodesia into Zimbabwe, 1964 to 1981* (London: John Murray, 1987), pp. 300–302.

4 For a complex, blow-by-blow description of the entire war, see Stephen A. Emerson's *The Battle for Mozambique: The Frelimo-Renamo Struggle, 1977–1992* (Warwick, UK: Helion & Company, 2014).

5 Malyn Newitt, *A Short History of Mozambique* (New York: Oxford University Press, 2017), pp. 12, 19, 161, and 164.

6 Gersony left Zambia out of his proposed itinerary because its border was the most marginal to the conflict zone, and it had the fewest Mozambican refugees.

7 The Polana plays a crucial role in Graham Greene's emotionally deft, late-career thriller *The Human Factor* (1978).

8 Cape Town is the legislative capital and Bloemfontein the judicial one.

9 Actually, there were different factions within the South African clandestine services and not all of them were enthusiastic about helping RENAMO. In truth, South African support for RENAMO was not always as clear-cut and wholehearted as it seemed. Paul Moorcraft, *Total Onslaught: War and Revolution in Southern Africa Since 1945* (Philadelphia: Pen & Sword Books, 2018), pp. 256–96.

10 According to the Reagan Library's records.

11 www.youtube.com/watch?v=jnhpjP4teqQ. Others at the meeting included Gary Bauer, Rebecca Gernhardt Cox (née Range), T. Kenneth Crib, Frank Donatelli, William Pascoe, Paul Stevens, and Paul Weyrich. Frank Carlucci, a fluent Portuguese speaker and experienced Africanist, had been suspicious of RENAMO for some time already, and Gersony's report confirmed his suspicions. Carlucci was an important Crocker ally in denying RENAMO Reagan Doctrine support.

12 David Ottaway and Lou Cannon, "Conservatives Oppose Afghan Peace Accords," *Washington Post*, April 13, 1988.

13 Quote supplied by sources close to the White House. For further background, see Gus Constantine, "Report by State Discredits Rebels in Mozambique," *Washington Times*, April 21, 1988.

14 Notre Dame anthropologist Carolyn Nordstrom observed a village shortly after a RENAMO attack: "Every structure had been carefully burned to the ground. Acres upon acres of charred circles extended in all directions, the only testimonial to the fact that a village . . . had recently stood on the site." Nordstrom, *A Different Kind of War Story* (Philadelphia: University of Pennsylvania Press, 1997), p. 98.

15 Karl Maier with Ben Penglase, *Conspicuous Destruction: War, Famine and the Reform Process in Mozambique* (New York: Human Rights Watch, 1992), p. 104.

16 William Mintner, *Apartheid's Contras: An Inquiry into the Roots of War in Angola and Mozambique* (1994; North Charleston, SC: BookSurge Publishing, 2008), p. 3.

17 The CIA's directorate of operations was separate from its directorate of analysis, which supported Gersony's findings.
18 This view is also maintained in Emerson's *The Battle for Mozambique*, which pins part of the blame for civilian atrocities on FRELIMO, pp. 153–82 especially. See also Moorcraft's *Total Onslaught*, pp. 256–96.
19 "Mr. Crocker's Propaganda Blitz," *Washington Times*, April 29, 1988.
20 Peter J. Boyer, "Frat House for Jesus," *The New Yorker*, September 13, 2010.
21 Letter on State Department stationery to George Gersony, dated February 10, 1988.
22 Some right-wingers were even calling Savimbi the "black George Washington."
23 While the conservative *Washington Times* was blasting Gersony's report, the liberal establishment media had rushed to his defense. A lead editorial in *The New York Times*, entitled "The Killing Fields of Mozambique," a reference to the Khmer Rouge, stated:

> "Rarely does a State Department document evoke a nightmarish Conrad novel. . . . Civilians have been shot, knifed, axed, bayoneted, burnt, starved, beaten, drowned, and throttled. . . . So writes Robert Gersony, who spent three months interviewing hundreds of refugees. . . . Incredibly, the rebels of RENAMO are depicted as 'freedom fighters' by Senator Jesse Helms and a vociferous lobby that now includes Senator Bob Dole. The Reagan Administration has shown greater honor and sense, not least by detailing the truth in the State Department report. . . ." ("The Killing Fields of Mozambique," *New York Times*, April 23, 1988)

A few days later, on April 28, a *Washington Post* editorial chimed in:

> "One of the troubles in a place like Mozambique, which is going through hell, is that it lies just outside the perimeter of international attention . . . This condition of obscurity has now been banished by a thoroughly documented report by an experienced refugee consultant, Robert Gersony. He makes it next to impossible for anyone to ignore further the atrocities committed by RENAMO, a guerrilla organization sponsored by the apartheid regime in South Africa. . . ." ("Pretoria's Victims in Mozambique," *Washington Post*, April 28, 1988)

There was still a rear guard of conservatives supporting RENAMO, led by Republican congressman Dan Burton of Indiana, who even in late May told *The New York Times* that RENAMO guerrillas were the only "freedom fighters" in the world that the Reagan administration was still not supporting. Robert Pear with James Brooke, "Rightists in U.S. Aid Mozambique Rebels," *New York Times*, May 22, 1988. Yet the South African government itself changed its policy two weeks after Gersony's report was issued. Pretoria announced that it was shifting alliances, and would begin to train and equip Mozambican government troops against RENAMO. (By late July, right-winger Paul Weyrich was still trying to convince vice president and Republican presidential candidate George H. W. Bush to publicly back RENAMO. But Bush, aware of the Gersony report, wrote to his aide, Don Gregg, that "I am not in accord" with Weyrich's "suggestions on Mozambique. Please be sure that whoever is representing me at the Platform Committee does not go overboard on Mozambique." Memo: the Vice President to Don Gregg and Dennis Ross, Washington, July 26, 1988.)

24 At the end of it all, Secretary of State George Shultz wrote to Gersony: "On behalf of the Department of State, I would like to express my profound thanks for
your exhaustive work . . . under difficult and often hazardous conditions. . . . I
was particularly struck by your meticulous methodology and the clarity of the
briefings you gave me and other senior government officials." Private letter
dated July 26, 1988. Shultz repeated some of this in his diplomatic memoir:
George P. Shultz, *Turmoil and Triumph: My Years as Secretary of State* (New
York: Charles Scribner's Sons, 1993), p. 1111. Furthermore, in a May 2, 2019,
letter to key members of Congress considering budget cuts to the State Department's Bureau of Population, Refugees, and Migration, the ninety-eight-year-
old Shultz wrote, "The refugee bureau . . . digs into root causes and resolves
problems before they become disasters at our doorstep. It stopped mass murder in Uganda; used intelligence assets to stop piracy against Vietnamese boat
people; and played a crucial role in stopping the war in Mozambique, avoiding
tens of thousands of deaths, short-stopping the flight of millions more refugees. . . ." In every one of these cases, Gersony had played a leading role.
25 Chas Freeman, "A Rusting Tool of American Statecraft," February 7, 2018.
Based on lectures at Harvard, the Massachusetts Institute of Technology
(MIT), and American University, unpublished.
26 Chester A. Crocker, *High Noon in Southern Africa: Making Peace in a Rough
Neighborhood* (New York: W. W. Norton, 1992), p. 250.

Chapter 9. Ethiopia and Somalia, 1989

1 Robert D. Kaplan, *Surrender or Starve: Travels in Ethiopia, Sudan, Somalia, and
Eritrea* (1988; New York: Vintage, 2003), p. 137.
2 Ibid., pp. 15, 20–25, 27, and 169–71. See all of chapter 3, "The African Killing
Fields."
3 Evelyn Waugh, *Remote People* (1931; New York: Penguin Books, 1985), pp. 89–91.
4 Robert D. Kaplan, "No Dilemma in a U.S. Blast at Somali Ruler," *Wall Street
Journal*, October 23, 1989.
5 Sidney Waldron and Naima A. Hasci, *State of the Art Literature Review for Somali Refugees in the Horn of Africa* (Oxford: Oxford University Refugee Studies
Programme, 1995).

Chapter 10. Liberia by Way of Nicaragua, 1990–1993

1 Lyman would go on to become ambassador to South Africa and be involved in
the negotiations that led to the collapse of the apartheid regime, thus representing the United States at the highest level in sub-Saharan Africa's two most
important nations.
2 See James N. Purcell, Jr.'s *We're in Danger! Who Will Help Us? Refugees and
Migrants: A Test of Civilization* (Bloomington, IN: Archway Publishing, 2019).
3 Shirley Christian, *Nicaragua: Revolution in the Family* (1985; New York: Vintage, 1986), pp. 4, 35, and 188.
4 Ibid., pp. 158 and 169.
5 Timothy C. Brown, *The Real Contra War: Highland Peasant Resistance in Nicaragua* (Norman: University of Oklahoma Press, 2001), pp. xv–xvii, 3–4, 11,
and 199.
6 Christian, *Nicaragua*, p. 368.

7 One example of news coverage of the project appeared in *The New York Times*, written by Shirley Christian: "Back Home, Miskitos Can Sing Again, but Face Daunting Job of Rebuilding," April 3, 1992.

8 V. S. Naipaul, *A Bend in the River* (London: Penguin, 1979), p. 63.

9 See the El Salvador section of chapter 3.

10 Reuters, "Liberia Troops Accused of Massacre in Church," *New York Times*, July 31, 1990.

11 "Executive Summary: The Carter Camp Massacre; Results of an Investigation by the Panel of Inquiry, Appointed by the Secretary General into the Massacre Near Harbel, Liberia on the Night of June 5/6, 1993." Panel Members: The Honorable S. Amos Wako, chairman; Robert Gersony, member; Ambassador Mahmoud Kassem, member. Secretariat: Gianni Magazzeni. September 10, 1993.

12 William Powers, *Blue Clay People: Seasons on Africa's Fragile Edge* (New York: Bloomsbury, 2005), pp. 15–16.

13 "Executive Summary: The Carter Camp Massacre."

14 Ibid.

15 Ibid.

16 "Full Report: Liberia; Panel of Inquiry Appointed by U.N. Secretary-General Boutros Boutros-Ghali. The Carter Camp Massacre," pp. 57–58.

17 Associated Press, "UN Blames Liberian Army Troops for Massacre," *New York Times*, September 20, 1993. "Liberian Massacre Blamed on Army," *Washington Post*, September 18, 1993.

Chapter 11. Rwanda, 1994

1 Gérard Prunier, *The Rwanda Crisis: History of a Genocide* (New York: Columbia University Press, 1995 and 1997), pp. xi–xii and 2–3.

2 Ibid., pp. 9, 35, 39, 46, and 61. Moreover, Philip Gourevitch writes that in the precolonial era, "The regime was essentially feudal: Tutsis were aristocrats; Hutus were vassals." Later on, in the colonial period, "Tutsi elites were given nearly unlimited power to exploit Hutus' labor and levy taxes against them." *We Wish to Inform You That Tomorrow We Will Be Killed with Our Families: Stories from Rwanda* (New York: Picador, 1998), pp. 49 and 56.

3 Gourevitch, *We Wish to Inform You That Tomorrow We Will Be Killed with Our Families*, pp. 64–65.

4 Prunier, *The Rwanda Crisis*, pp. 111–12, 140, and 226–27.

5 Pentagon Document Number I94/16545, May 5, 1994.

6 Prunier, *The Rwanda Crisis*, pp. 237–38, 265, and 312–13.

7 Blaine Harden, "At 81, Japan's Outspoken Force for the World's Poor," *Washington Post*, September 30, 2008.

8 Sadako Ogata, *The Turbulent Decade: Confronting the Refugee Crises of the 1990s* (New York: W. W. Norton, 2005), p. 190.

9 Ambassador Robert and Kathleen Tobin Krueger, *From Bloodshed to Hope in Burundi: Our Embassy Years During Genocide* (Austin: University of Texas Press, 2007), p. 109.

10 Ogata, *The Turbulent Decade*, pp. 190–91.

11 They were Augustin Mahiga, Leonardo Franco, and Sanda Kimbimbi.

12 See Ogata, *The Turbulent Decade*, pp. 190–95, for a brief description of the high commissioner's account of Gersony's work, which she said "forced a necessary policy review for UNHCR."

13 James Traub, "Kofi Annan's Tragic Idealism," *New York Times*, August 20, 2018.

14 Stephen Kinzer, *A Thousand Hills: Rwanda's Rebirth and the Man Who Dreamed It* (Hoboken, NJ: John Wiley & Sons, 2008), p. 270.

15 The others were Iqbal Riza, Ismat Kittani, and Hans Correll.

16 Cable from Marrack Goulding to Boutros Boutros-Ghali, September 16, 1994. Goulding later wrote that "practical peacemaking depends on establishing" facts, and not ignoring them. Kevin M. Cahill, ed., *Observation, Triage, and Initial Therapy: Fact-finding Missions and Other Techniques* (New York: Basic Books, 1996), p. 213.

17 The others present were Doug Stafford, Arlene Render, Margaret McKelvey, Doug Bennet, and John Hicks—the same John Hicks who had been so helpful to Gersony in Malawi six years earlier.

18 The RPA, or Rwandan Patriotic Army, was officially the military wing of the RPF, the two being mainly synonymous. Arlene Render, September 20, 1994, cable number 254232. There was also a second cable, 200310Z, describing Gersony's whole trip and indicating that both the United Nations and the State Department would take the matter up with the Kagame regime.

19 About this time, U.N. Emergency Office head Charles Petrie and a USAID disaster relief specialist visited the Byumba region in northeastern Rwanda, one area not visited by Gersony's team. But this new investigation also found that information collected by interviews with local inhabitants "strongly suggests that [the] RPA has carried out systematic reprisals against Hutu populations . . . the team heard similar stories as those recounted to the [Gersony] UNHCR team by refugees who came from the northeast. . . ."

20 Holding this job between Maurice Baril and Guy Tousignant was Roméo Dallaire, who, having been witness to the genocide of the Tutsis, and having gotten no help in the outside world to stop it, went home disillusioned and suicidal. See Roméo Dallaire, *Shake Hands with the Devil: The Failure of Humanity in Rwanda* (Toronto: Random House Canada, 2003).

21 Luc Reydams, *International Prosecutors* (New York: Oxford University Press, 2012), p. 34.

22 According to a September 22, 1994, cable (number 001588) from the U.S. Embassy in Kigali to Washington, Tousignant admitted "he did not know what was happening in the southeast region and other areas where UNAMIR was not present."

23 Twagiramungu would years later admit that the Gersony team report was "congruent with lists he had compiled of thousands of Hutu civilians killed by Tutsi forces." Howard W. French and Jeffrey Gettleman, "Dispute Over U.N. Report Evokes Rwandan Deja Vu," *New York Times*, September 30, 2010.

24 Frederick Ehrenreich, August 5, 1994, State 214379 101516Z.

25 American Embassy, Bujumbura, August 11, 1994, 02708 111704Z.

26 Rawson later told *Atlantic* writer Samantha Power that he was "looking away from the dark signs. . . . We were naive policy optimists. . . ." Though this was in reference to his actions before the original genocide, it may be indicative of his troubled state of mind through Gersony's visit. Samantha Power, "Bystanders to Genocide," *The Atlantic*, September 2001.

27 "Human Rights Watch and the FIDH Condemn Assassination of Seth Sendashonga," Human Rights Watch, May 18, 1998.

28 Alison Des Forges, *Leave None to Tell the Story* (New York: Human Rights Watch, 1999), p. 146.

29 One factor weakening Assistant Secretary of State for Africa George Moose
was that Secretary of State Warren Christopher, focusing on Arab-Israeli peace
negotiations and other matters, had relatively little interest in Africa.

30 Embassy Kigali to Secretary of State, September 23, 1994, 01606 23132222.

31 As it happened, the joint team, which included Ambassador Shahryar Khan,
left Kigali late the next day, traveled for two hours, and found no evidence except a mass grave dating back several months. The Gersony team had spent
more than a month visiting close to a hundred sites and interviewing 300 witnesses. Luc Reydams, *Let's Be Friends: The United States, Post-Genocide Rwanda,
and Victor's Justice in Arusha* (Antwerp, Belgium, and South Bend, IN: University of Antwerp and Notre Dame University, 2013), p. 27.

32 Meanwhile, back in New York, Annan pinned back Shahryar Khan's ears in a
September 29 cable, voicing "dismay" at public statements made by U.N. officials in Kigali "impugning" UNHCR and the Gersony report. Source: U.N.
Cable Number 3172. Kofi Annan died just as I was engaging his staff for an
interview with him.

33 Des Forges, *Leave None to Tell the Story*, p. 137.

34 Letter from François Fouinat, chief of staff for Sadako Ogata, to B. Molina-
Abram, secretary to the commission of experts on Rwanda, Geneva, October 11, 1994.

35 UNHCR Document Number R0002907.

36 To be sure, the report was suppressed, even if the details of Gersony's findings
became known. According to a Wikileaks cable released many years later,
Boutros-Ghali and George Moose told the Rwandan government "that if the
killing of Hutus stopped, then a detailed report [the Gersony report] about
the Tutsi massacre of approximately 30,000 Hutus would be swept under
the rug." Source: Embassy/Madrid confidential cable number 00000201.
Wikileaks: February 22, 2008.

37 Gersony had warned that if the United Nations and the Clinton administration
did not take firm action against the RPF, "in a few months they will be murdering people right in front of your eyes." To wit, on April 22, 1995, in the largely
Hutu refugee camp of Kibeho in the southwestern corner of Rwanda, RPF
soldiers fired into crowds of people, killing about 4,000 and wounding 650,
according to the Australian blue-helmeted peacekeepers in the vicinity who
used clickers to count the bodies. Source: Terry Pickard, *Combat Medic: An
Austrian's Eyewitness Account of the Kibeho Massacre* (Wavell Heights, Australia:
Big Sky Publishing, 2008), pp. 80–81. Stephen Buckley, "At Least 2,000 Refu-
gees Die in Rwandan Violence," *Washington Post,* April 24, 1995. David Rieff,
A Bed for the Night: Humanitarianism in Crisis (2002; New York: Simon &
Schuster, 2003), p. 188.

38 Prunier, *The Rwanda Crisis*, pp. 323–24.

39 On October 18, 1994, in an op-ed in *The Washington Post,* Democratic congressman Tony Hall, the head of the Congressional Hunger Center, defended
Gersony, writing that senior officials "who are familiar with the author's track
record, would stake their lives on the [Gersony] report's veracity and his methodology." Two days later, an Amnesty International report was issued, detailing
significant numbers of "deliberate and arbitrary" RPF killings of Hutus. And
two days after that, on October 22, both the London *Independent* and *The New
York Times* wrote of "systematic revenge killing" by the RPF throughout
Rwanda. In 1999, in her definitive 789-page book on Rwanda, *Leave None to*

Tell the Story, the Yale-educated expert on East Africa, Alison Des Forges, would write that Gersony's team, "although few in number . . . covered more RPF territory and spoke to a wider number and variety of witnesses than any other foreigners working in Rwanda during this period." Sources: Tony Hall, "Cycle of Revenge in Rwanda," *Washington Post,* October 18, 1994. "Rwanda: Reports of Killings and Abductions by the Rwandese Patriotic Army, April–August 1994," Amnesty International, October 20, 1994. Richard Broadbent, "UN Urged to Halt Rwandan Violence," *The Independent,* October 22, 1994. Editorial, "Again, Killing in Rwanda," *New York Times,* October 22, 1994. Des Forges, *Leave None to Tell the Story,* p. 127. See, too: Howard W. French and Jeffrey Gettleman, "Dispute Over U.N. Report Evokes Rwandan Déjà Vu," *New York Times,* September 30, 2010, and Howard W. French, "How Rwanda's Paul Kagame Exploits U.S. Guilt," *Wall Street Journal,* April 19, 2014.

40 Years later, Hank Cohen, who replaced Chet Crocker as assistant secretary of state for Africa in the elder Bush administration, would write that Gersony had "shamed the U.S. Government" and others into acknowledging the hard-to-admit, complicated truth about Rwanda. Email sent by Cohen, June 11, 2014.

41 Prunier, *The Rwanda Crisis,* p. 360.

42 Gérard Prunier, *Africa's World War: Congo, the Rwandan Genocide, and the Making of a Continental Catastrophe* (New York: Oxford University Press, 2009), p. 355.

THE WORLD IS WHAT IT IS

Chapter 12. Gaza and the West Bank, 1995

1 Chris Hedges, "A Gaza Diary," *Harper's,* October 2001.

2 Saddam would increase the payments to $25,000 per family after 9/11. "Iraqi Ties to Terrorism," Council on Foreign Relations, February 3, 2005.

3 "Arafat's Costly Gulf War Choice," *Al Jazeera,* August 22, 2009.

4 Ami Ayalon, *The Middle East Contemporary Survey (1990),* vol. 14 (Boulder, CO: Westview Press, 1992), pp. 226 and 265.

5 An Israeli commando unit assassinated Abu Jihad on April 16, 1988, at Sidi Bou Said, north of the Tunisian capital of Tunis.

Chapter 13. Bosnia, 1995–1996

1 Robert D. Kaplan, "Europe's Third World," *The Atlantic,* July 1989.

2 Robert D. Kaplan, "Balkans' Fault Line: Yugoslavia Starts to Feel the Tremors," *Wall Street Journal/Europe,* November 30, 1989. Though my reporting depressed an American president regarding the possibilities of military action, I supported military action from the beginning. In the March 1993 issue of *Reader's Digest,* the same month that *Balkan Ghosts* was published, I wrote: "Unless we can break the cycle of hatred and revenge—by standing forcefully for self-determination and minority rights—the gains from the end of the Cold War will be lost. All aid, all diplomatic efforts, all force if force is used, must be linked to the simple idea that all the people of Yugoslavia deserve freedom from violence." Soon after I appeared on television (CNN, C-SPAN) to urge intervention. I unambiguously urged military intervention on the front page of

The Washington Post Outlook section more than a year before we intervened ("Into the Bloody New World: A Moral Pragmatism for America in an Age of Mini-Holocausts," April 17, 1994). There is no contradiction between my early support for military action and the dire record of religious and ethnic conflict I described in *Balkan Ghosts,* since it is only the grimmest human landscapes where intervention is required in the first place.

3 The twin categories of "refugees" and "displaced persons" could appear somewhat confusing in the Yugoslav context, since if you accepted the continuation in some form of the Yugoslav state, then an overwhelming majority of people were displaced persons rather than refugees who had crossed an international border. But if you accepted the facts on the ground—the emergence of new and formal geographically based entities—then there were obviously many more refugees.

4 Knight's cable went out under the name of the ambassador, Peter Galbraith. Daniel Williams, "Grim Balkans Outlook Affected U.S. Position," *Washington Post,* August 19, 1993.

5 Galbraith had been an influential staffer on the Senate Foreign Relations Committee. He was a world-renowned expert on the Kurds, as well as on the brutality of Saddam Hussein's Iraqi regime. He also spoke several languages.

6 Galbraith would later use Knight's cable about Sarajevo as an example of how an individual action had the power to change events.

7 Thirty-three interviews were conducted in Washington, fourteen in Geneva, and three in Brussels.

8 Daniela Heimerl, "The Return of Refugees and Internally Displaced Persons," *International Peacekeeping* 12, no. 3 (2005).

9 Robert and Cindy Gersony, "Summary of Findings and Recommendations: Bosnia Reconstruction Assessment," U.S. Agency for International Development, Bureau for Humanitarian Response, Washington, DC, April 1996.

10 Bill Egbert, "A Noble Act of Harmony in the Balkans: Maverick Mayor Who Protects Minorities Won Reelection in Bosnia Last Month," *Christian Science Monitor,* October 9, 1997.

11 Barton would go on to praise Bob and Cindy as "the premier conflict researchers of the era." Rick Barton, *Peace Works: America's Unifying Role in a Turbulent World* (New York: Rowman & Littlefield, 2018), p. 104.

12 The scholars Gerald Toal and Carl T. Dahlman have somewhat different figures. They also report that Stolac took no families, but say that 44 families instead of 11 returned to Jajce. However, they report that around six months after Dayton, the Muslim houses in outlying villages that had not yet been destroyed were firebombed. In 1997, two years after Dayton, Jajce police ordered those Muslims who had returned to leave. In sum, the pilot town project was a failure. *Bosnia Remade: Ethnic Cleansing and Its Reversal* (New York: Oxford University Press, 2011), pp. 196–97.

13 Mayor Dževad Mlaćo, a former math teacher, would be implicated in covering up the disappearance of twenty-one Bosnian Croat men from Bugojno in 1993. Letter from Carlos Westendorp and Norbert Klingler, Office of the High Representative for Bosnia and Herzegovina, February 12, 1999. "Unsuccessful Reconciliation of Federal Partners," AIM, Sarajevo, January 30, 1997.

14 "Menzies loved" Gersony's report. "He was very supportive as the report represented progress and movement forward," Tim Knight confirms.

15 Dine, in an email, said he has no memory of ever meeting Gersony, and none of working to delay the implementation of his plan. This is in contrast to the memories of Atwood, Mahdesian, and Gersony himself. Carol Lancaster and Doug Stafford are deceased.

16 Barton, *Peace Works*, pp. 61–62.

17 Jerry Hyman, internal USAID email, February 14, 1996.

18 Neal Keny-Guyer, letter to Brian Atwood, March 25, 1996.

19 John Pomfret, "Rivalries Stall Reconstruction of Bosnia," *Washington Post*, October 13, 1996.

20 General Accounting Office, *Progress Toward Achieving the Dayton Agreement's Goals*, Washington, DC, May 1997. See as well Vesna Bojicic-Dzelilovic, "The Politics, Practice and Paradox of 'Ethnic Security' in Bosnia-Herzegovina," *Stability: International Journal of Security and Development* 4, no. 1 (2015): 1–18.

21 Rebecca Brubaker, *From the Unmixing to the Remixing of Peoples: UNHCR and Minority Returns in Bosnia* (Geneva: UNHCR Policy and Evaluation Service, 2013), p. 4.

22 Chris Hedges, "At Home and Under Duress with Bosnian Croats," *New York Times*, November 16, 1997. Lee Hockstader, "Bosnia Not Sold on Multiethnic State," *Washington Post*, December 7, 1997. Moreover, the International Crisis Group, reversing its optimistic stance of the year before on the possibility of minority returns, reported that such returns were rarely occurring and were limited to elderly people. *Bosnia: Minority Return or Mass Relocation?* Brussels: May 14, 1998. A later BBC report echoed the same observation: "Bosnia Refugee Policy Failure," BBC, December 13, 1998.

23 Marcus Cox, *Strategic Approaches to International Intervention in Bosnia and Herzegovina*, War-Torn Societies Project, Center for Applied Studies, Sarajevo, October 1998.

24 Brubaker, *From the Unmixing to the Remixing of Peoples*, p. 5.

25 These compromises, such as rewarding the perpetrators of ethnic cleansing by creating a Serbian republic within Bosnia, led quite a number of academics and intellectuals to criticize Dayton, and blame it for all the problems in the former Yugoslavia ever since.

26 The visionary view was most elaborately presented by John Fawcett and Victor Tanner, two prominent members of the NGO community, in a 242-page report. Early on in this report, they honestly lay out what they see as a stark philosophical difference between people like themselves who believed that the Bosnian war was a matter of specific actions taken by political leaders and those like Gersony who apparently believed that it was the result of long-standing communal divides and passions. Of course, the complex truth of it all can easily encompass both beliefs. Fawcett and Tanner did not request or receive the full multihour oral brief that Gersony delivered to 80 officials in 18 separate sittings; they relied instead on Gersony's more condensed written report, which was clearly marked as a "summary." Whereas Gersony interviewed 250-odd Bosnians on the ground in wintry, wartime conditions, Fawcett and Tanner interviewed 54 in easier circumstances. Whereas 70 percent of all the people Gersony interviewed and consulted for his findings were Bosnians, 40 percent of the people Fawcett and Tanner spoke with were Bosnians (the rest were international aid officials and experts). Gersony had several months to conduct all of his interviews, to prepare and deliver his many oral briefings,

and to write a condensed report; Fawcett and Tanner had several years to work on their more extensive written project. Fawcett and Tanner complain that Gersony's Bosnia work lacks the detail and rigor of his other work, such as on Somalia and northern Uganda. Yet Somalia and northern Uganda were long-term assessments with only soft deadlines, whereas Bosnia was an emergency action report. John Fawcett and Victor Tanner, *The Political Repercussions of Emergency Programs: A Review of USAID's Office of Foreign Disaster Assistance in the Former Yugoslavia (1991–1996)* (Washington, DC: Checchi Consulting, April 2000).

Chapter 14. Northern Uganda by Way of Nicaragua, 1996–1997

1 His real name was Antonio Blandon.
2 Some, including the International Committee of the Red Cross, reported over 300,000 people killed in the Luwero region. Thomas Ofcansky, *Uganda: Tarnished Pearl of Africa* (1996; Boulder, CO: Westview Press, 1999), p. 54.
3 Robert Gersony, *The Anguish of Northern Uganda: Results of a Field-Based Assessment of the Civil Conflicts in Northern Uganda* (Kampala, Uganda: USAID, 1997), p. 9.
4 Kevin Ward, "'The Armies of the Lord': Christianity, Rebels and the State in Northern Uganda, 1986–1999," *Journal of Religion in Africa* 31, no 2 (May 2001).
5 Richard J. Reid, *The History of Modern Uganda* (New York: Cambridge University Press, 2017), p. 67.
6 *The Economist* would later contradict the French ambassador, reporting that Gersony did in fact criticize Museveni's army, "which has not demonstrated the capacity and commitment" required to end the war, leading to a rebuke of Gersony from Museveni's media adviser, John Nagenda. "Uganda: A Dirty War That Can't Be Won," *The Economist*, October 4, 1997.
7 Gersony chose post-apartheid South Africa for its moral authority, Switzerland for its well-respected leadership in the humanitarian field, and Italy because of the presence of the Comboni missionaries in the region.
8 Embassy Kampala, cable 1741, July 7, 1997.
9 One of the people Gersony briefed in State's Africa bureau was April Glaspie, who he remembers was "straight-forward," "supportive," and "friendly enough" throughout. Glaspie is known to the outside world only through her ill-fated meeting with Iraqi dictator Saddam Hussein prior to his invasion of Kuwait in 1990. But she had a long career before that meeting and a significant career afterward.
10 Gersony, *The Anguish of Northern Uganda*, p. 30.
11 Prunier, *Africa's World War*, pp. 81–82.
12 Gersony, *The Anguish of Northern Uganda*, pp. 38, 48, and 59.
13 Ibid., pp. 97–100.
14 Michael Harris, retired director of Oxfam and the Anti-Slavery Society, wrote in his 1997 Christmas letter, "I have never seen an official document that ensures such an understanding to its readers."
15 Tim Allen and Koen Vlassenroot, eds., *The Lord's Resistance Army* (London: Zed Books, 2010), pp. 113–31. Lawrence E. Kline, *The Lord's Resistance Army* (Santa Barbara, CA: Praeger, 2013), p. 17.

Chapter 15. From El Salvador to Ecuador and Colombia, by Way of Africa, 1997–2002 and 2008–2009

1 The project that Gersony designed would be completed in December 2001, with over 2,000 kilometers of roads and 2 kilometers of cement and steel bridges rebuilt or repaired. A U.S. government audit would reveal that there was no corruption involved, even though Honduras at the time was rated as one of the most corrupt countries on earth.

2 "Bambi" Arellano, like other Gersony admirers in USAID, such as Janet Ballantyne and Chris Crowley, would rise to the top ranks of the organization. She would run the missions in Egypt and war-torn Iraq before becoming counselor to the administrator, the third-highest position in USAID.

3 Regional Inspector General's Office, *Audit of USAID/Ecuador's Northern Border Development Program,* Number 1–518–04–010-P, San Salvador, September 3, 2004.

4 Coincidentally, I was at the Colombian military base of Larandia near Putumayo, researching a book, on February 13, 2003, when the three contractors were captured by the FARC close by.

5 Richard Chacon, "Target Coca: Officials Try to Break Drugs' Deadly Grip on Colombia," *Boston Globe,* February 20, 2000.

Chapter 16. North Korea, 2002

1 Andrew S. Natsios, *The Great North Korean Famine: Famine, Politics, and Foreign Policy* (Washington, DC: United States Institute of Peace Press, 2001). For his research, Natsios drew partially on Fred Cuny's own posthumous book, *Famine, Conflict, and Response: A Basic Guide* (West Hartford, CT: Kumarian Press, 1999).

2 Not every interviewee was between the ages of 25 and 55. Some, like this woman, turned out to be older.

3 Grossman was an aide to Deputy Secretary of State John Whitehead at the time.

4 Doug Struck, "Aid Used as Lever with Pyongyang," *Washington Post,* December 4, 2002.

5 Steven Weisman, "Threats and Responses: U.S. in No Rush over North Korea's Food Aid," *New York Times,* January 6, 2003.

6 James Dao, "U.S. to Resume Food Aid to North Korea at a Reduced Level," *New York Times,* February 26, 2003.

7 Choe Sang-Hun, Gi-Wook Shin, and David Straub, *Troubled Transition: North Korea's Politics, Economy, and External Relations* (Palo Alto, CA: Shorenstein Asia-Pacific Research Center, 2013), pp. 136–37.

8 Nicholas Eberstadt, "The Most Dangerous Country," *The National Interest,* September 1, 1999. Andrei Lankov, discussion at the Cato Institute in Washington, October 2017.

9 In 2008, though, CNN's Mike Chinoy wrote in a book, quoting a few unnamed sources, that Gersony's North Korea report was flawed. It alleged that Gersony interviewed only "dozens" of refugees, when in fact he had interviewed 86 for several hours each. It claimed Gersony said that the Pyongyang regime "could be close to collapse," even though Gersony had said no such thing, and even

said the opposite in his report; indeed, a major theme of his briefings was that the diversion of food aid succeeded in helping to keep the regime out of danger. Chinoy appears to obscure the fact that Gersony's interviews in 2002 documented individual accounts of what had happened in North Korea since the mid- and late 1990s, almost a decade and a half before Chinoy published his book. Mike Chinoy, *Meltdown: The Inside Story of the North Korean Nuclear Crisis* (New York: St. Martin's Press, 2008), pp. 139–40.

Chapter 17. Nepal, 2003

1 Alex Perry, "Return to Year Zero," *Time*, Asia edition, May 8, 2002.
2 Robert Gersony, *Sowing the Wind: History and Dynamics of the Maoist Revolt in Nepal's Rapti Hills* (Portland, OR: Mercy Corps International, 2003), pp. 7–8.
3 Ibid., pp. 14 and 53.
4 The British never outright colonized Nepal, even though they recruited soldiers from there.
5 Gersony, *Sowing the Wind*, pp. 25, 28, 38–39, and 71.

Chapter 18. Micronesia by Way of Iraq, 2003–2008

1 Cuny's blinding, seminal insight was that if the hundreds of thousands of Kurds did not return to their homes, protected by U.S. airpower, they would linger in refugee camps along the Turkish border and become a long-term international humanitarian problem like the Palestinians.
2 Greene, *The Quiet American*, pp. 17, 23, 29, 52, 85, and 86.
3 Robert D. Kaplan, "The Coming Era of U.S. Security Policy Will Be Dominated by the Navy," *Washington Post*, March 13, 2019.
4 Ben Kesling, "U.S. Refocuses on Pacific to Check China Ambitions," *Wall Street Journal*, April 4, 2019.

Chapter 19. Northern Mexico by Way of Central America, 2010–2013

1 These were men who had developed pulmonary and other medical conditions from constantly diving in deep waters for lobster.
2 Robert D. Kaplan, *The Revenge of Geography: What the Map Tells Us About Coming Conflicts and the Battle Against Fate* (New York: Random House, 2012), pp. 335–36 and 340.
3 Monterey was an exception, though, with a still-vibrant economy.
4 Kaplan, *The Revenge of Geography*, pp. 335–36.

Epilogue: Antigua, Guatemala, May 2019

1 See John Byron Kuhner's inspired essay on Antigua, Guatemala, and the Latin poet Rafael Landivar: "In Search of the American Virgil," *The New Criterion*, February 2019.
2 Thomas Mann, *Doctor Faustus: The Life of the German Composer Adrian Leverkuhn as Told by a Friend*, trans. from the German by John E. Woods (1947; New York: Vintage, 1999), p. 232.

Illustration Credits

Page 7: Courtesy Teddy Strauss.

Page 13 (top): Courtesy Bob Gersony.

Page 13 (bottom): Bernard B. Fall Collection.

Page 20: Courtesy Jo Froman.

Page 29: Courtesy Bob Gersony.

Page 31: Courtesy Jo Froman.

Page 34: Courtesy Jo Froman.

Page 42: Courtesy Bob Gersony.

Page 52: Courtesy Bob Gersony.

Page 65: Collection of Arthur Eugene Dewey from the Palace of the
    King of Bhutan.

Page 88: Courtesy Bob Gersony.

Page 118: U.S. Department of State.

Page 147: Courtesy Tony Jackson.

Page 169: Courtesy State Department attorney Catherine Brown.

Page 170: Diana Walker/The LIFE Images Collection via Getty
    Images.

Page 241: Courtesy Bob Gersony.

Page 247: The Courtauld Gallery, London/Peter Barritt/Alamy Stock Photo.

Page 249: Courtesy Bob Gersony.

Page 270: Pierre Virot/Reuters.

Page 326: © Shepard Sherbell/CORBIS SABA/Corbis via Getty Images.

Page 333: Collection of Timothy R. Knight.

Page 358: Courtesy Gersony family.

Page 361: Courtesy Bob Gersony.

Page 374: Mike Theiler/Getty Images.

Page 402: PRESIDENCIA/AFP via Getty Images.

Page 453: Courtesy of the Office of Senator Patrick Leahy.

Page 465: Elizabeth Gersony.

Index

(Page references in *italics* refer to illustrations.)

INDEX 513

ROBERT D. KAPLAN is the bestselling author of nineteen books on foreign affairs and travel translated into many languages, including *The Good American, The Revenge of Geography, Asia's Cauldron, Monsoon, The Coming Anarchy,* and *Balkan Ghosts.* He holds the Robert Strausz-Hupé Chair in Geopolitics at the Foreign Policy Research Institute. For three decades he reported on foreign affairs for *The Atlantic.* He was a member of the Pentagon's Defense Policy Board and the Chief of Naval Operations Executive Panel. *Foreign Policy* magazine twice named him one of the world's Top 100 Global Thinkers.

robertdkaplan.com